Letters from AE

G. W. Russell (AE), 1885-6
*from the bust moulded in plaster by John Hughes
at the Metropolitan School of Art, Dublin
Coloured by* AE

Letters from AE. Selected and edited by Alan Denson. With a foreword by Dr Monk Gibbon

Abelard-Schuman *London New York Toronto*

LONDON Abelard-Schuman Limited 8 King Street
NEW YORK Abelard-Schuman Limited 6 West 57 Street
TORONTO Abelard-Schuman Canada Limited 57 John Street
© *Diarmuid Russell 1961*
© *This Edition Alan Denson 1961*
Library of Congress Catalogue Card Number 60: 13700

PRINTED IN GREAT BRITAIN AT THE UNIVERSITY PRESS, ABERDEEN

To Sir Thomas Beecham, BT, CH
and to H.N., my true friend

Commemorating
Ivy Maud Denson [1896-1958]

We must pass like smoke or live within the spirit's fire:
For we can no more than smoke unto the flame return
If our thought has changed to dream, our will unto desire,
    As smoke we vanish though the fire may burn.

Lights of infinite pity star the grey dusk of our days:
Surely here is soul: with it we have eternal breath:
In the fire of love we live, or pass by many ways,
    By unnumbered ways of dream to death.

                [Collected Poems by AE: p. 49]

Foreword

ICONTRADICT myself? Well, then, I contradict myself. I contain multitudes. Walt Whitman's words, which AE was fond of quoting, should be the motto to any edition of his correspondence. Not only are his interests multiple but the tone of each letter adopts itself to its particular recipient. He is not afraid to be inconsistent, since opposites can each have a measure of truth. He writes to James Cousins in England: "The land of the Gael is in an awful state just now. . . . You are well out of it, and I have no doubt you will like all Irishmen do well outside Ireland and write better poetry about it than in it." And a few weeks later, if Mr Denson's conjectured dates are right[1], he writes to James Stephens in France, "Ireland is just as good as any of them. . . . Why the blazes are you in Paris? Your own soul couldn't find an excuse which would not be as shallow as the German excuse for invading Belgium. . . . May the Lord have you in his keeping and bring you out of that city of exile home to your own people."

Both propositions were true. It was good for a poet to be out of Ireland. It was good for a poet to return home. As a writer in the Greek Anthology says, "All the ways of life are good—" The warm-hearted but irascible Sean O'Casey thought it absurd that AE, "the glittering guy", should preach Japanese austerity in the matter of wall pictures, and then, shortly afterwards, under a different pseudonym, suggest a room papered with nineteenth-century book illustrations. He drew an amusing picture of Y.O. hanging the pictures up and AE taking them down. But, again, the answer is that there can be divergent virtues in quite separate paths.

It was all a part of the ambivalence of an ardently-questing mind. What interested him were aspects of truth rather than certainties. We are not here, he would have said, to pass cast-iron judgments, but rather to detect directions. Man's best moments "are blind and dense with revelation and his intuitions are beyond his intellect." On all the essentials, the tide of his conviction set firmly in a particular direction. Goodness and magnanimity and kindness were not terminological playthings. Light and

---

[1] I absolutely agree with the attribution.

darkness were not interchangeable. Men must be prepared to pay their spiritual debts to the uttermost farthing. But apart from these basic intuitions, he allowed speculation to roam freely. "That myriad-minded man", as Archbishop Gregg, Primate of Ireland, once said to me, pointing to a copy of *The Living Torch* on one of his study bookshelves.

As a letter-writer AE can be absorbing, although he has few of those qualities which give the most famous letter-writers and autobiographies their fascination for us. He is not an egoist, and he is lamentably sparing in any reference to the trivial, day-to-day detail of life. The immediate is of much less importance to him than its cosmic origins. One might imagine him a man almost without relatives or any connections other than talkative friends. Even when he becomes a father his mode of commenting upon the event to Yeats is: "I think experience is good. Now like a Brahmin after having begotten a son I retire again into a life of ascetic meditation." A little later he strikes a more human note, but in the briefest phrase: "The 'boy' is growing in beauty and impudence."

Occasionally he mentions his environment. ". . . here in a little cottage on a hill farm I can see seven seas as I look round through gaps in the hills and rocks, there is a lake in the valley below me, beyond are Breaghy dells and bay. . . ." Or he can describe a drive on an outside car in the wilds of Mayo and, having outlined its severities, can add, "A fat little country girl kept me warm part of the way and quoted local poetry to me and also fairy yarns and such like. But the rest of the way was a chill desolation." He can harvest a folk phrase like "God builds the nest of the blind bird", or "Ah, sure your shadow is only a light at the door"; or he can give a thumb-nail impression of a friend, "I spoke sternly to Hone who listened with that air of listless agreement which distinguishes him from all other Irishmen". But for the most part of his letters—when they are not polemical, championing some cause in the columns of a newspaper[1]—are letters of ideas, the ideas of a thinker plunged into an active philanthropic life, or the ideas of a man of letters, immersed in the job of editing a weekly journal.

In those given us here he passes few literary verdicts. He knows his critical limitations. "About some things I can write and about other things my mind remains lethargic. I could not if you offered me a thousand pounds write about let us say Tom Jones." There is a rare reference to an English poet of his time when he mentions, "Ralph Hodgson, the best of

[1] Both the London *Times* and the *Irish Times* gave him carte blanche on these occasions.

the younger poets". But he is allergic to the trends of the early 'thirties. "The poets like Eliot and Spender have no light in their minds. They are the dead end and when Eliot writes a volume of criticism of poetry the effect is to make me never want to read poetry any more in the world. I think there is a revolt beginning against his influence. But what will the revolters do if they cannot intoxicate us with exuberant imaginations themselves? It will be like ghosts electing new leaders who are ghosts themselves."

Irish poets were a different matter. He cannot do enough for them. He scents them out, fosters their talent, tries to protect them against themselves. He will lend five pounds to a young poet "on a promise to return it next day", and when the borrower vanishes his comment is quite gentle, "I would share my possessions with a fellow poet cheerfully, but I object to their telling me a little tale, always, about their ship coming in next day, when they might have had what they wanted without straining an imagination better employed upon their art."

James Joyce was one of his beneficiaries. But the three who meant most to him were Colum, Stephens and Starkey (Seumas O'Sullivan). "I have discovered a new Irish genius—Columb: only just twenty, born an agricultural labourer's son. . . . When he has three or four more years at his back he will be a force and I believe a name." Three years later— "Colum's poems rude as they are reveal a talent which I think one day Europe will recognise." And, thirty years later, writing to Colum himself, "You are always kind. You are as good as you were when you were young, which is saying a great deal about anybody." Almost another thirty years have passed since that was said, but to those of us who know Colum today the words are as true as ever.

With Synge AE never seems to have been intimate. There is a note to him possibly as early as 1897. But after his death AE wrote to John Quinn in New York, "I did not know him very well, though I liked him much from the little I knew him." The same letter gives complete support to the theory that the famous Playboy row was exaggerated in the first instance, and fomented later, in the interests of publicity, and by the indiscretions of one of the play's defenders. AE writes to Quinn: "The row at the Abbey was really a newspaper row which got its ferocity to a great extent from certain defences made by unpopular people like 'Pat' the journalist, who would have it that the Playboy was a most accurate representation of Irish life. . . . On the first night of the performance at which I was present there was a great deal of applause and only just at the last a little hissing and booing over one or two of the phrases, and I am convinced that it would never have been much worse than that only for the defenders, who almost went to the point of stating that any Irish family would welcome a parricide."

AE, like Colum, gives the credit for the founding of Ireland's national theatre to the Fays. Speaking of Lady Gregory's book, *Our Irish Theatre*, he says, ". . . the two Fays are entitled entirely to the credit of starting an Irish school of acting. Without them it could not have been done. They trained the actors, they established the tradition, and they worked for years at it without aid from Yeats or Lady Gregory. . . . I knew all about their work before Yeats or Lady Gregory came on the scene at all and I always felt the Fays never got the credit they were entitled to get. It was at their suggestion, not Yeats's or Lady Gregory's that the National Theatre was formed."

Of all those who figured in the letters given here the sidelights upon Yeats and Moore are probably the most interesting. AE's attitude to the latter was a little equivocal and to some extent the same could be said of Moore's to him. In *Hail and Farwell* AE is drawn in heroic proportions, a most noble and lovable figure. It was only when Moore got the idea that his friend had connived in Susan Mitchell's impertinent volume on him that his loyalty wavered and that AE became for a time "the Donegal Dauber". Moore had quickly become prominent in the literary life of Dublin. In 1902 we hear, "George Moore is giving an open-air performance in his front garden to all Gaelic-speaking Dublin. No English speakers allowed". Later that same year, Joyce is told, "I have written Miss Gonne and Lady Gregory and will let you know anything further I may hear from them. George Moore is useless. I saw him today and he was in one of his bad moods, irritable about everything, and as I expected before I went he said his friends in Paris would wonder why the devil he sent anybody to see them who was not in their craft."

In April 1909 Moore announces, "Russell, I have written two thousand words about you." "I nervously enquired whether I might see them." "No, you will see them later on." AE's only consolation was the thought that they were friends and that Moore was probably keeping most of his satire for the church and W.B.Y. By the time the book appeared its author had already flitted from Dublin. "George Moore has gone! Alas, he has carried out his promise or threat and is going to settle down in Chelsea. I miss him very much. For the last two Saturdays I have wandered about trying to find a way of spending my Saturday night, which for seven years I spent with Moore. I think George Moore ought to be a generic title, like Pharaoh, King of Egypt, and when one goes another qualified person ought to take his place and fulfil his functions. Moore was so much alive all the time, and the Irish people who write whom I meet here are anaemic, they have prejudices and no ideas."

Two years later he writes, "I suppose you saw Moore's *Salve*. His vision gets blurred as he recedes from his subject. I don't know why he wanted to leave Ireland. He is lonely and out of it now in London, I think." Another year passes and we find him telling Quin in America, "Moore's *Vale* is out, the most scandalous of all his books. I escaped with a halo, but halos fixed on one's brows by the wicked don't add to one's glory. I can't help liking Moore in spite of his bad taste. He is no hypocrite and is never afraid to say what he thinks. . . ." Moore must often have shocked him, and a passage in *The Avatars* reveals deep, latent resentment on AE's part, although the actual words are put into the mouth of a girl. There is an acid touch too about his remark in a letter to the American book-reviewer Huntly Carter, "I do not think George Moore has serious views about anything except his own writing". But, faced in 1933 with furnishing a valedictory upon his friend, he rose to the occasion brilliantly and set out to placate the angry patriots, whom Moore had so much enraged as well as the devout, to whom his views were anathema. "He loved the land even if he did not love the nation. Yet his enmities even made his nation to be as much admired or loved as the praise of its patriots. . . ." And then "It is possible the artist's love of earth, rock, water and sky is an act of worship. It is possible that faithfulness to art is acceptable service. That worship, that service were his. If any would condemn him for creed of theirs he had assailed let them first be certain that they laboured for their ideals as faithfully as he did."

Perhaps the most striking of his letters to Yeats, is the one in which he prophesies the coming of an avatar to Ireland, a theme which he used in an oil painting, once owned by Katherine Tynan, and which now hangs on my walls. Even in the early days, when Yeats was to a large extent his hero, he can poke gentle fun at him. When the poet goes to London in 1887 AE wrote to Carrie Rea, ". . . it will not make much difference about my not seeing Willie Yeats as I intend opening communication with him through the medium of the astral light—that is—try thought transference between Grosvenor Square and Eardley Terrace. No doubt he will have imagination enough to think he is receiving messages from me and whenever I write to him about these airy conversations I will use expressions which will suit his conversation at any time, 'Your poem is splendid'. 'Your paradoxes are getting more startling every day.' 'You should not say harsh things about your friends.' These remarks will convince him more than ever of my occult powers and he will tell everyone that I can hear his smallest whisper over a thousand miles away and exalt me generally about M. Blavatsky."

There was a nine years' gap in their correspondence and the note from the office of the *Irish Homestead* in 1913 in which AE praises Yeats's espousal of the cause of the strikers was almost certainly the olive branch which marked the end of this coolness.

Two years later, in a letter to Moore he gives a most remarkable analysis of Yeats's character: "He began about the time of *The Wind in the Reeds* to do two things consciously, one to create a 'style' in literature the second to create or rather to recreate W. B. Yeats in a style which would harmonise with the literary style. People call this posing. It is really putting on a mask, like his actors, Greek or Japanese, a mask over life. . . . The present W. B. Y. is the result. The error in his psychology is, that life creates the form, but he seems to think the form creates life. If you have a style, he argued once with me, you will have something to say. He seems also to have thought though he never said so, that if you make a picturesque or majestic personality of yourself in appearance, you will become as wonderful inside as outside. He has created the mask and he finds himself obliged to speak in harmony with the fixed expression of the mask. . . . He bores me terribly now and he was once so interesting."

Yeats's doctrine ran counter to AE's firm conviction that it was the inside of the platter which counted. Even art had no intrinsic holiness. Its holiness arose out of the fact that it was a revelation. He wrote to Clifford Bax, "I have no interest in people who find in literature anything but an avenue to life. Every thought or mood is the opening or closing of a door to the divine world and who is there we would not laugh at who went to a door and only admire or looked at it forgetting its uses. Art for art's sake is considering the door as a decoration and not for its uses in the house of life." It was the same conviction which made him write to Weekes "a man's success or failure is always with his own soul. You would like to see me well known, writing wise and beautiful books, hailed by the applause of the best critics. I might be all this and a failure in my own eyes, and wretched and unhappy."

On painting he has surprisingly little to say in these letters either on his own or on the other men's pictures. When he is in London in 1913 he goes to see an exhibition of post-impressionists but is not favourably impressed. "I think it is the second childhood of art with Noah's ark, trees, houses and animal only rather more badly drawn than the Noah's Ark trees and houses of first childhood. Gaugin and one or two others of the pioneers of this movement had a kind of hopeless drivel of line and colour and ideas which makes one feel unhappy as if one were in the society of lunatics." Ten years later he writes to Quinn, who has been collecting the moderns, "I remember mention of Picasso and the cubists in your case and I see you have Seurat. I do not deny he is an artist. I only say he, Gaugin and Van Gogh are spiced art for jaded palates, and so are many others . . . if one expects eternal excitement from art, it leads to the futurists, post-impressionists, cubists and all those in whom a delirium of the fancy or imagination leads to abnormalities of colour or design. I get modified pleasure myself from the abnormal in art, because the sane academic mind is tiresome in its products. The real thing which excites in art or literature is imagination and we don't tire of it. The fault with the academicians and the faultless painters is that they too often have no inspiration but only a science. . . ."

Many of the letters in this selection are the outcome of one of AE's periodic plunges into the economic or political affairs of his nation. When he took to polemics, he always surprised his friends. The gentle, bearded, shaggy individual whom they used to see puffing at his pipe and speaking slowly and with a strong Armagh burr when he removed it from his mouth, suddenly became an angry knight, mounted upon a steed of almost rhetorical eloquence, charging down, with lance levelled, upon the enemy. Such letters, especially when they come from the columns of newspapers, need to be taken in their historical context. But, with the aid of the copious notes and miniature biographies provided here, a reader should be able to furnish that context. AE had not come into the world a controversialist. He tells Quinn, "It seems odd that a person like myself, originally shy, should get caught into labour or economic movements". It amazed him too to find in the office of the *Irish Homestead* that his colleagues generally "leave all arrangements to me as the practical person of the group. I am sorry I lost my old reputation as a dreamy unpractical man."

Nevertheless he was a shrewd tactician, as his suggestion that T. W. Russell, who was being very unhelpful to the Irish co-operative movement, should be counter-attacked through the English liberal papers, shows. He expounds a situation to Balfour at great length; he praises the Anglo-Irish for what many of them have done for their country, but sees no future for them; prophesies coming bureaucracy, if the 1914 war against Germany is won, thanks to that exchange of characteristics which leads us to become like what we hate and concentrate upon; and has a plan for hierarchical elections which has a touch of Plato about it. When he did descend into the market place he brought with him the thunderbolts of Jove. He could be-rate the Dublin employers and tell them, "If you had between you collectively a portion of human soul as large as a threepenny bit, you would have sat night and day with the representatives of labour trying this or that solution of the trouble, mindful of the women and children, who at least were innocent of wrong against you." He could write to a newspaper: "You and readers of your paper have told me how impossible it is to love or even forgive our enemies. I, on the contrary, assert that it has always been possible, and is not only possible but natural, for us to do so. Human nature is found in the depths and not on the surfaces, and is revealed in moments of exaltation and not otherwise." Utterance like this was natural to him, although he only resorted to it, and only invaded the columns of a daily paper, when the occasion seemed to him one of grave importance.

For the real man was the mystic, out of the depths of whose nature all the other multiple activities drew their strength. The mystic is he who believes in being for its own sake. AE can say to Weekes, "I will go back to the stars without any flourish of trumpets but I won't weep as I go back or whine about circumstances. Don't expect anything from me. I am not going anywhere I can be seen."

Early in life he had nursed, he once told me, a hope that he might give to the world brief, religious aphorisms in the manner, say, of a Lao Tse. The hope had come to nothing, but the aspiration, which prompted it, helped to give nobility and insight to all he wrote and the measure of the man can be found again and again in chance phrases in these letters. There is nothing in the least inconsistent about his spirituality. It glows throughout.

He saw a world which was striving hard to find cultural substitutes for religions which it considered outworn. Though it was part of his doctrine that childhood is decisive in matters of the soul he does not seem to have realised how much the other-world, evangelical Christianity of his parents may have influenced his own character. He urges Carrie Rea, "Remember for all your doubts 'We live and move and have our being' in the Great Life and the sun and the stars, wind, tides, people, are only shadows moving through it and moved by it for its own ends." Illumination, in his case, had come to him from India. "Any way all these things are verifiable only by an entrance into the inner life—into the Christ-soul of the universe which is at once 'the Way, the Truth and the Life' and because I find the mystical literature of the East fuller of words like those quoted, which insist upon the exercise of a spiritual faculty for their comprehension, I think it is so far superior to that of the West." And—nearly thirty years later—"I have watched with interest so far as I could the economic and spiritual movements in India, a country which I regard as a kind of spiritual fatherland and whose influence on the thought of the world must I think, grow greater because in no literature is there such a reservoir of divine truth as in the Indian."

Both AE and Yeats thought at one time that Madame Blavatsky and her movement might be the forerunners of a new age of spiritual efflorescence in contrast to the crude materialism of the post-Darwinian epoch. Madame herself, however, prophesied spiritual darkness until at least two-thirds of the twentieth century were completed. The theosophic movement itself split into factions and, as early as 1888, we find AE writing in a long letter which Mr Denson has cleverly unearthed from *Lucifer*, "I am not a proclaimed Theosophist. I do not belong to the Society. For some reasons I am sorry; for many reasons I am glad. And one of the most cogent of the latter is the almost certain degeneracy of any Society or Sect formed by mortal hands." This was perceptive for a young man of twenty-one. And, although he later became a member, the Society was to lose him in 1898, when its internal dissensions became acute.

Nevertheless the key to AE's life is the fact that he had elected to be a student of esoteric wisdom, and that his interest in literature, in poetry, in painting and in practical affairs were all to a large extent rooted in this original impulse. At the age of twenty-seven he writes to Professor Dowden, "I am glad you have regarded me rather as a mystical poet than as a poetical mystic. To the title of mystic I have really no claim. I am not capable of leading the pure ascetic life in thought and act which alone could develop any spiritual insight worth acquiring." This was just about the time he was leaving the community of theosophists in Ely Place, having found—he admitted to me—that the path of initiation was beginning to tell on his health.

But, despite this self-verdict, written to Dowden, AE's most characteristic utterances invariably reveal him as the natural mystic which he was. He looks always beneath surfaces and towards a Primary Cause, and at the same time he relates his intuitions to the immediate event. L. A. G.

Strong quotes his dictum, "Seek on earth what you have found in heaven". And he can say in a letter to the *Irish Times*, "Ideals descend on us from a timeless world, but they must be related to time; for this world has its own good, and, if we do not render to it its lawful rights, neither will it receive our message, and Heaven and Earth are divorced and both are wronged."

In old age and in a moment of passing depression AE once hinted to me that he felt his life had been spent too much in bondage to economic necessity. As a young man he had felt happy and free on a salary of fifty pounds a year; and as a married man with two children he had no complaints to make on the score of the modest salary which he drew as an organiser in the co-operative movement. Actually he had much which must have seemed to him more precious than wealth; life at a moment of great historical interest in a small country where national hopes ran high; a circle of intimate literary friends which a much larger capital than Dublin might well have envied; and talk as good as any in the whole world. And though he might have become a celebrated painter if he had devoted his whole life to it, nevertheless it would be wrong to think that it was the necessity to earn his livelihood which had made him choose a different path. He told Yeats that he was giving up the Art School because it weakened his will. He had chosen the path of enlightenment. And who that reads his many reflections in the pages which follow will say that he was wrong?

MONK GIBBON

Contents

ERRATUM

"Scenes from *Deirdre* by A.E."
[between pages 36 and 37]
The cast should read: "Naisi *played by AE*: . . . ."

Illustrations

George William Russell (AE) *frontispiece*
From the plaster bust by John Hughes, RHA
(*The Dublin Corporation and the Director of the Municipal Gallery, Dublin*)

Thomas Elias Russell and his wife, Marianne Russell *between pages* 36–37
From a photograph

Scenes from *Deirdre* by AE
(*The late Dr Richard Best*)

Specimen page from letter to C. C. Rea (? June 1886)
(*The County Museum, Armagh*)

Violet Russell (AE's wife) with Sara Allgood and others, 1911
(*Lady Glenavy*)   *between pages* 196–197

Specimen page from letter to T. B. Mosher, October 26, 1901
(*The Houghton Library Harvard University*)

G. W. Russell, 1935
From a photograph
(*The United States Department of Agriculture*)

Preface

THIS selection from the letters written by George William Russell (AE) is issued with the approval of the literary executor, his son Mr Diarmuid Russell. All the transcriptions have been made by the editor from the holograph, or from photographic copies, if they have been available. Other sources are cited in footnotes.

The original selection from the vast accumulation of letters and notes comprised more than 700 letters, and approximately 450,000 words. Through the exemplary patience and generosity of Mr Lew Schwartz, the publisher, the editor was given leisure to reduce his selection still further, to present Russell's *Letters* in comprehensive scope but quintessential form.

Many valuable letters remain interred in the original typescript.[1] A typed copy of the original selection has been given under seal to the National Library of Ireland, by the editor. Other omissions from this book include letters which AE reprinted in *Imaginations and Reveries* (1915, 1921, 1925).

Much ancillary bibliographical and biographical information concerning AE and his *milieu* has been arranged in *Printed Writings by G. W. Russell, a Bibliography with some notes on his paintings etc.*, compiled by this editor: referred to in this book as *Bibliography*.[2]

Among AE's correspondents some failed to preserve his letters. Others have survived in copies. Some letters to Bernard Shaw are in the British Museum Library: copies of others are in private hands. George Moore destroyed his correspondence. Daniel Dunlop is presumed by all his

[1] This editor's typescript of the complete selection, together with his own annotated final draft of his AE *Bibliography*, and thirty unique photographic negatives and prints portraying AE's friends, were despatched to the National Library of Ireland on February 9 and 10, 1960, in two parcels. The parcel containing pp 1–500 of the *Letters*, and the *Bibliography* and photographs was reported not delivered to the Library (letter to the editor, March 15, 1960). The British and Irish postal authorities failed to locate the parcel which was evidently either lost or stolen *in transit* from London.

[2] Published at Evanston, Illinois, by the Northwestern University Press: 1961.

children to have destroyed all his correspondence. Letters written to W. B. Yeats before 1896 have not been located. Charles Weekes destroyed all the letters which he received prior to his marriage. Letters to James M. Pryse were dispersed by sale after his death. Letters to F. S. Oliver have not been found: those to W. Q. Judge may yet be found, although the Theosophical Library (Pasadena, Calif.), lately indexed, did not expose them. The late Dr J. S. Starkey ("Seumas O'Sullivan") assured the editor he had received letters from AE which were either too personal for publication, or inconsequential. Mr C. P. Curran wished to preserve the full text of AE's letters for use in his own *Memoirs*, but with inimitable courtesy copied from them extracts which would, he believed, have special value for this selection. The letters which AE wrote to C. C. Rea (Mrs R. E. Coates in later life) were not preserved among the letters which she gave to the County Museum, Armagh; nor were they among the papers inherited by her heirs. Hugh and Charlotte Law received few letters from AE: none could be found in 1950. Simone Téry lost virtually all her possessions, in Paris, during the Second World War: among them many long letters from AE. Mr Diarmuid Russell believes any correspondence between his parents will have been destroyed by them. AE was a copious correspondent and this list of omissions could be extended for several pages; suffice rather in the assurance that this compiler's search has been protracted over many years, widespread, and supported by helpers whose names would seem endless if listed entire.

The letters to John Quinn were transcribed by the late Lennox Robinson. He generously permitted the editor to copy that script. A typescript of that correspondence is in the H. W. and A. A. Berg Collection, the New York Public Library. The letters to C. M. Grieve are in the Lockwood Memorial Library, University of Buffalo.

Mr James A. Healy of New York City presented an extensive collection of autograph AE letters and manuscript, with a collection of AE's printed work, to the Library, Colby College, Waterville, Maine. Dr Carlin T. Kindilien's list of that collection was published in the *Colby Library Quarterly*, Series 4, No. 2 (May 1955). Despite Mr Diarmuid Russell's request, this editor was denied permission to order photographic copies of any AE letters in the Colby College Library. Access to them is reserved for the scrutiny of "Colby scholars". Mr Diarmuid Russell presented to Colby College Library some letters and copies of others; but he could not remember which, nor had he preserved any record of their extent. To date Colby College has not published a list of those letters.

The County Museum, Armagh, contains AE's early letters to C. C. Rea (Mrs Coates) and to C. A. Weekes, presented by the recipients. The National Library of Ireland has received many AE letters: to R. I. Best, Alice Stopford Green, Stephen Gwynn, Edward MacLysaght, Maurice Moore, Joseph O'Neill, Sarah Purser and others. Other letters are preserved in the Yale University Library; Indiana University Library (Bloomington); the Houghton and Widener Libraries at Harvard University; University of Kansas, Lawrence, Kansas; and elsewhere in the United States. The Co-operative Reference Library in the Horace Plunkett Foundation, London, contains some letters to Horace Plunkett; the Balfour letters are in the British Museum Library.

Specific acknowledgement for considerate attention to persistent enquiries is due to many distinguished people. The late Dr W. K. Magee ("John Eglinton") had answered many questions: his book *A Memoir of G. W. Russell (AE)* remains indispensable for any study of AE's life and work, despite inaccuracies. Mr C. P. Curran, Mr Padraic Colum, Sir Patrick Hannon, Professor Richard Ellman, Dr Edward MacLysaght, Dr Henry Kennedy, the late Dr R. I. Best, the late Joseph Hone, the late Senator James G. Douglas, the late James H. Cousins, the late George Roberts, the late Osborn Bergin, the late Joseph O'Neill, Mr St John Ervine, Dr Heinz Hoepf'l (and to Mrs Hoepf'l for their warm hospitality), Mr Dudley W. Barr, Mr Boris de Zirkoff, Mr Clifford Bax, Professor David H. Greene (of New York University). All these have cheerfully encouraged the editor by constant interest in his work, and by constructive criticism. Dr R. J. Hayes, Dr Patrick Henchy, Mr Alf' MacLochlainn and Mr Tom O'Neill in the hospitable National Library of Ireland, have given assistance ungrudgingly. Mr N. F. Sharp and his staff in the British Museum Library; Miss M. Digby, OBE (Secretary) and the Librarian in the Horace Plunkett Foundation; the staff of the I.A.O.S., at the Plunkett House, Dublin; the Secretary and Librarian of the Theosophical Society in England; the Theosophical Society (Pasadena, Calif.) and many individual Theosophists throughout the world, have all rendered assistance in varying extent.

Dr Gerald Heard (Sir Horace Plunkett's literary executor) graciously permitted scrutiny of Plunkett's private diaries and miscellaneous papers. The *Irish Statesman* correspondence file in the Plunkett Foundation, should be used by future biographers of AE.

Mr George Paterson wrote his invaluable *Notes on Lurgan, Armagh and District in the late Nineteenth Century* at the editor's request. Thanks are also due to Dr Monk Gibbon for his *Foreword*, written at the request of his friend Mr Diarmuid Russell.

Mrs W. B. Yeats, the late Mrs James Stephens, Mr Herbert E. Palmer, Miss Ruth Pitter, Mrs Constance Sitwell, the late C. C. Riddall, the late Miss Beatrice Skipworth, kindly permitted transcription of their letters from AE. Mrs Charles Weekes counselled the editor wisely for many years, and she read with approval part of the original typescript before her death.

Miss Joanna Fortune and Miss Pamela Hinkson have been most kind, answering all questions clearly, and allowing the editor access to all AE's letters. Professor Herbert Howarth, with buoyant enthusiasm and penetrating critical comment has proved a steady helper and friend.

Professor Bonamy Dobrée, the late Dr Thomas Bodkin and Dr M. J. Bonn have patiently guided the editor with good advice. Their unerring judgment has exposed to him flaws in his knowledge, and his blunders in not having recognised some crucial features in historical perspective, and good taste. These words seem inadequate to express the sense of intellectual indebtedness incurred by the editor towards those wise and generous and genial men. The late Mrs Thérèse Bonn supplemented her husband's interest with the practical stimulus of her lively encouragement.

Professor Y. J. Padmarajiah (of the Maharajah's College, Mysore) and Dr Soli Hakim, erudite scholars in oriental and occidental systems of thought, kindly discussed with the editor the apparent impact on AE's thought of Indian religious systems and doctrine. Dr Hakim, equally erudite in Theosophical literature, kindly checked transcriptions of those letters in which AE had used terms peculiar to Indian psychology; and kindly illumined them with his comments.

Collating copies of the complete typed manuscript, and drafting several indexes, a discouraging prospect, shook the editor's nerves. His brilliantly accomplished friend Dr S. P. Choong generously volunteered to share those tasks. His joyful industry and unerring accuracy, dancing through that mass of paper, was a refreshing stimulus which eliminated the editor's fatigue and revived his interest in concluding the work.

The letters have been arranged in chronological order of composition, so far as that could be accurately ascertained. AE often avoided dating his letters. Conjectural dates have been enclosed in square brackets. The addressee's name has been placed on the left, and address and date to the right, heading each letter. Any sequence of letters from one address to one addressee has rendered practical omission of the address from all but the first letter. To conserve space the closing phrase and signature have been run into the last paragraph. To prevent confusion the conjectural dates have been stylised to read month, day and year: other presentation follows AE's own dating. After the first use of an address abbreviations have been used. Thus, *The Plunkett House, 84 Merrion Square, Dublin* has been reduced to *The Plunkett House*. AE variously wrote from home or office address.

The text reproduces what AE wrote, even his erratic punctuation has been generally preserved. In speech he was copious, and slow in delivery. But in his letters the rapid movement of his brain is evident, despite occasional repetitions. In this book repetitions have been expunged from the text. Such omissions are indicated by a sequence of dots [...]. Certain words proved indecipherable. The illustration between pages 196-7 gives a fair indication of the textual conditions which the editor has been privileged to meet, and decipher. AE practised writing his letters on both surfaces of news-print paper: his ink stained through the paper. Insoluble riddles in transcription are recorded as [*illegible*].

The editor will be glad to receive precise details of any AE letters, mss., paintings, sketches or portraits. Such information should be addressed to him in care of his publisher's London office.

His publisher, Mr Lew Schwartz, most gallantly sponsored this book in 1956; at which date AE's life and work had been long eclipsed. Mr Schwartz's staff in London and New York have all proved most helpful. In London Mr John Buchanan-Brown has been particularly kind, considerate, discreet and practical.

Miss E. M. Glanville, Mrs G. L. Marsh, Miss M. E. Frazer and Miss N. Stone patiently persevered without complaint, typing the letters from the editor's transcripts. They thereby eased his labours and won his gratitude.

Quietly efficient, Mr J. M. M. Mair, M.A., as a generous and characteristic token of pure friendship, collaborated with the irascible editor in proof-checking.

The editor's long and arduous task searching for, transcribing and editing AE's letters has been conditioned by his love for the Irish countryside and for the beautiful characteristics of the Irish nation. He has survived the task with increased respect for AE's life and work, and fresh absorption in AE's writings.

The editor is alone responsible for editorial blemishes.

ALAN DENSON

1960

Acknowledgments and Thanks

THE editor, a green novice in the quest for letters, may be almost romantically ardent. But he is a negative quantity to whom the owners of letters re-act. Elemental romance proscribes the wooer with the prize. In his long and tricky task he has enjoyed unqualified kind assistance from most of those, but not from all, to whom he has applied for information.

He can imagine two charges being laid against his editing. First, that there are *lacunae* in the notes. Where detail is inadequate to suggest a composite characterisation or chronology (e.g. of A. W. Dwyer, Edmund King or Susan Varian), the impulse to adverse criticism should be tempered by his assurance that all the facts presented were won by unremitting enquiry, after a search for more answers than could be found. Any supplemental accurate information concerning AE's family, the Rea family, and others of his early friends, will be welcomed for inclusion in revisions of this book. A contrasted viewpoint may bring about complaint at the extent and mass of annotation. Anglo-Irish literature and politics being seldom familiar to any except a minority of the Irish nation, the editor is unwilling to apologise for loading his pages with proof of his own initial ignorance. If copious factual notes should cause offence he recommends exclusive concentration on the text.

Besides those deep obligations acknowledged in the Preface there remains a host of correspondents whom, as yet, the editor has missed the pleasure of meeting. They have supplied, so far as they could, information for which they were asked. The list below registers those correspondents who have given their time and effort on several occasions. Will others who have helped the editor pardon him for making this general acknowledgment of his profound gratitude to them, without names?

All the addressees or owners of letters included in this book. Professor C. C. Abbott, American Irish Historical Society, Rt Hon. J. Amery, MP, Sir Norman Angell, *Aryan Path*, R. B. Arbib, University of Aberdeen, Mrs K. Aumann, Univ. of Arizona, Mr R. L. Atkinson (Historical MSS Commission), Mr H. F. Armstrong, Mrs E. A. Ansell, Mr VanWyck

Brooks, R. G. Allen, Lady Bantock, R. O. Ballou, Dr D. A. Binchy, Mrs M. Boyd, Dr Francis S. Bourke, Belfast Public Library, Boston College Library, Lord Bridges, British Electrical and Allied Manufacturers' Association, Brotherton Library, Brown University, Miss M. Barker, Miss A. Barnard, Dr M. Benkowitz, University of Buffalo, the British Museum Library, and Department of MSS, Mr E. Blundell, Mr E. Blunden, J. D. Bolton, Sir A. Bax, C. Bax, the late Jocelyn Brook, Mrs C. Bewglass, Universities of California, Southern California, Chicago, Columbia, Cornell, Mrs M. A. Childers, Miss H. Cohen, CBE, D. Coffey, the late Professor G. D. H. Cole, Co-operative Reference Library, Rev. E. J. Coyne, SJ, Mrs V. Crichton, Mesdames J. and N. Cunningham, H. Cairns, A. Clarke, Miss H. K. Challoner, Library of Congress, the late W. J. de la Mare, R. O. Dunlop, RA, Mrs E. Dunlop-Young, Mrs Dunlop-Sicré, Professor Myles Dillon, Professor E. R. Dodds, Miss W. R. Dunn, the late Lord Dunsany, Mr T. S. Eliot, OM, Dr W. Y. Evans-Wentz, Mr L. and Mr C. Elton, FRS, Professor W. Y. Elliott, Mrs V. D. Franklin, Mrs C. Gill, G. P. Gooch, CH., C. M. Grieve, Mrs P. Greacen, Professor J. M. Gaus, Mr C. R. Groves, Mr H. Glanville, Mr D. Gould, Mrs E. Garbary, Miss M. E. Griffiths, the late O. St J. Gogarty, Robert Graves, Professor W. Cabell Greet, Francis Hackett, P. Haley-Dunne, T. E. Hanley, Lady Harty, R. Hart-Davis, Sir P. J. Hannon, Miss I. Haugh, Mr Henchy, Controller of H.M. Stationery Office, J. J. Horgan, Mr R. Hodgson, Mr J. Hewitt, Mr L. A. G. Strong, Mr J. A. Healy, Mr G. Hetherington, Harvard University, and the Huntington Library, I.A.O.S. (Dublin), Indiana and Illinois Universities, Mr John Irvine, University of Kansas, Miss M. L. Johnston, A. Kamal, P. Kavanagh, W. R. A. Keller, J. Larkin, Mrs C. Law, Col. F. Law, Miss E. M. Leech, the late Mrs N. V. Lindsay, J. London, Miss N. E. Myers, Mr S. MacBride, the late Madame M. Gonne MacBride, Dr C. A. McDonnell, Senator Dr R. McHugh, B. Morley, the Rt Hon. M. H. Macmillan, PC, Mr D. Macmillan, Mr T. Mark, Messrs Macmillan and Company, for their kind permission to quote freely from AE's books published by them, Mr A. Marsh, Miss S. Mitchell, Mr T. McGreevy, Mr D. Morrah, Mr J. H. Masui, Mr C. D. Medley, Mr H. M. Magee, Mrs D. B. Melville, Mr M. K. Mazundar, Mrs H. K. Massingham, Universities of Minnesota, Michigan, Missouri, Notre Dame, New York, Ohio; National Library of Ireland, Newberry Library, Mrs R. Nivison, Dr W. S. Noble, New York Public Library (Berg Collection), Dr. B. O'Brien, Mr William O'Brien, Mr F. O'Connor, Mr S. O'Faolain, Dr George O'Brien, Dr D. O'Sullivan, Séan O'Sullivan,

RHA, Mr Séan O'Casey, Pierpont Morgan Library, Miss E. Philpotts, Mr P. L. Pielou, Professor A. C. Pigou, Mrs A. Kingsley Porter, Dr Macdonald, Lord Pethick-Lawrence, Miss M. Patten, Miss R. Pitter, Mr H. E. Palmer, Mr Vance Palmer, Mrs L. M. Purser, Public Record Offices in Belfast, Dublin and London, Philadelphia Museum of Art, Mr Justice K. Reddin, Mr D. C. Russell, Mr Bryan Hartley-Russell, Sir Bruce L. Richmond, the late Mr J. D. Riley, Mr J. Roche, Sir J. Rothenstein, Professor R. L. Ramsay, Miss B. Skipworth, Lady M. Sackville, Dr H. Shearman, Dr B. A. H. Solomons, Mr R. Speaight, Sir J. A. Shane Leslie, Bt, the late G. B. Shaw, Sir J. C. Squire, Senator O. Sheehy-Skeffington, P. B. Saint-Hilaire, the late Miss M. Stewart, Sir L. Smith-Gordon, Mrs C. Sitwell, Mr A. J. Scull, Stanford University, Mr W. Sullivan (T.C.D.), Theosophical Society, Pasadena, Theosophical Reference Library, London, Mrs L. Tottenham, Mr G. O. Thomas, United States Department of Agriculture, John Vetterlein, Victoria and Albert Museum, Vassar College, the late Allan Wade, the late R. H. White, Miss I. White, Mr G. Watkins, Mrs M. Wells, Miss A. Wolfe, Mr W. M. Whitehill, Mr V. Waddington, Mrs B. Werthan, Mr M. L. Wilson, Miss H. Waddell, State Historical Society of Wisconsin, Universities of Washington, Wisconsin, Yale, Princeton; K. Williamson, the late Miss Ella Young, the late Jack B. Yeats.

His special thanks are extended to Messrs Macmillan & Co. Ltd. London, and to their American branch, the St Martin's Press, Inc., 103 Park Avenue, New York, publishers of AE's *Selected Poems*, from which poems are quoted in the *Letters*; and for the kindness with which, in London, he has been assisted with answers to every enquiry. His thanks are also tendered to the Macmillan Company, New York, for their kindness in responding to enquiries. Also to Messrs Faber and Faber, and the Talbot Press, Dublin.

Chronological table
of principal events in AE's life

1867 April 10	George William Russell born to Thomas Elias Russell (book-keeper) of William Street, Lurgan, County Armagh, by his wife Marianne Russell (*formerly* Armstrong). Mrs Russell's name was wrongly registered on the birth certificate as Mary Anne Russell.
1871 February	G. W. Russell enrolled as a day pupil at the Model School, Lurgan.
1878	T. E. Russell was invited to join his friend Robert Gardner's business, chartered accountants, Dame Street, Dublin. The family left Lurgan to reside at 33 Emorville Avenue, Dublin. G. W. Russell generally passed part of his school holidays with an aunt resident in Armagh.
1880 [early]	G. W. Russell enrolled at the Art School, Kildare Street, Dublin as a day pupil.
1882 [early]	G. W. Russell enrolled at Dr C. W. Benson's Rathmines School (*School Roll No. 1272*).
1883 October	Attended evening session art classes at the [Metropolitan] School of Art, Kildare Street, Dublin. Continued attendance until July 1885. There he probably first met John Hughes, W. B. Yeats, Oliver Sheppard and Charles Johnston.
1884 October 13	Mary Elizabeth Russell, G. W. R.'s only sister died, aged 18, in Dublin.
December	G. W. R. left Rathmines School. Studied privately?
1885	The family moved to 67 Grosvenor Square, Dublin.
1885–7	G. W. R. attended evening sessions at the School affiliated to the Royal Hibernian Academy. Employed?
1887 December 11	W. B. Yeats introduced G. W. R. to Katharine Tynan.
1888 [early]	Attended meetings of the Dublin lodge of the Theosophical Society. Perhaps joined the T.S. late 1888, or 1889?
1890 August 1	Appointed a clerk with Messrs Pim Bros, drapers, Dublin. Salary £40 p.a. Resigned November 1897 (£60 p.a.).
December 9	G. W. R. was admitted to probationer membership of the Esoteric section of the Theosophical Society, "having signed the

pledge". The small certificate of enrolment was signed by H. P. Blavatsky. Russell's counterfoil numbered 939.

1891 April   Mr and Mrs Frederick J. Dick, tenants of 3 Upper Ely Place, Dublin, established a small residential community of theosophists: with D. N. Dunlop, H. M. Magee, Edmund J. King and G. W. Russell. Magee left in 1894: the room he had shared with Russell was taken over by A. W. Dwyer. Dunlop left probably in December 1892 to marry Eleanor FitzPatrick. This small community moved to 13 Eustace Street, in December 1896 or January 1897.

May 8   H. P. Blavatsky died in London.

October 6   Charles Stewart Parnell died aged 45.

1892 May-June   T. E. Russell and family moved from Rathmines to 5 Seapoint Terrace, Monkstown.

1895   G. W. R. joined the Irish Literary Society, Dublin. From 1901-4 he was a member of their Publications Committee.

February (?)   Miss Violet North (from Bow, London) and James M. Pryse moved to Dublin; perhaps taking rooms in 3 Upper Ely Place.

1896 March 21   William Quan Judge died in New York, aged 45. James M. Pryse left Dublin, returning to New York.

1897 October 9   Marianne Russell died aged 61 at 5 Seapoint Terrace.

November 3   G. W. R. resigned his employment with Messrs Pim Bros.

November 11   G. W. R. had been mentioned to Horace Plunkett by P. J. [*later* Sir Patrick] Hannon. Plunkett had met Russell at Pim's store and interviewed him November 11. He appointed Russell to his staff on the Irish Agricultural Organisation Society, as a Banks' Organiser (under the co-operative credit system devised by F. W. Raiffeisen [1818-1888]) in the Congested Districts of western Ireland, Donegal, Mayo, Galway, parts of Sligo and Kerry.

1898 March   Russell seceded from the T.S., disappointed by the new head of the organisation, Mrs Katherine Tingley.

June 9   G. W. R. was married to Miss Violet North (daughter of the late Archibald North) in the Dublin Registry: both resident at 10 Grove Terrace, Rathmines (from March?). Marriage ceremony witnessed by John Hughes and A. W. Dwyer. Russells moved residence to 6 Castlewood Avenue?

[mid-]   T. E. Russell moved from Seapoint Terrace to "Hillsborough", Blackrock.

[late-]   G. W. R. appointed assistant secretary of the I.A.O.S. jointly with P. J. Hannon.

November 2   Russells moved residence to 28 Upper Mount Pleasant Avenue, Rathmines.

1899 February? Perhaps the Russells' first son was born; named Brian? [The official search made for this compiler revealed no such registration of birth or death. The child died in early infancy.]

1900 Their first surviving child, Brian Hartley Russell, was probably born. The official search did not reveal the registration.
April 23 Russells moved residence to 25 Coulson Avenue, Rathgar.
October 31 T. E. Russell died aged 78, at "Hillsborough", Blackrock.

1902 The Irish National Theatre Society formed. President, W. B. Yeats; Vice-Presidents, Douglas Hyde, Maud Gonne and G. W. Russell.
April 2, 3, 4 *Deirdre* by Russell, and *Kathleen ni Houlihan* by W. B. Yeats, first performed by W. G. Fay's Irish National Dramatic Company at St Teresa's Hall, Clarendon Street, Dublin.
November 17 The Russells' younger son born, Diarmuid Conor Russell.

1903 July 14 Plunkett, T. P. Gill, Professor J. R. Campbell and Russell appointed by the I.A.O.S. Committee to devise means for adjusting relations between the I.A.O.S. and the Department of Agriculture and Technical Instruction (Ireland).
Introduced to Sir Frederick Macmillan by S. L. Gwynn. Russell offered Macmillan & Co. *The Divine Vision*, and the option to publish all his later poems.

1904 July (?) Russell resigned Vice-Presidency of the Irish National Theatre Society.
August 23 to Russell publicly exhibited some of his pictures in Dublin, with
September 3 other artists [see compiler's *Bibliography*].
October 20 Colonel H. S. Olcott (1832-1907), President of the T.S. (Adyar) issued a charter establishing a "second Dublin Lodge": members, Mr and Mrs G. W. Russell, Mr and Mrs Powis Hoult, W. G. Fay, J. S. Starkey, Mrs Greene, Mrs Charles Kelly, John Quigley: secretary, H. F. Norman. They met weekly in 34 Wicklow Street until March 25, 1909. This group seceded from the T.S. (Adyar) in 1909 when Mrs A. Besant succeeded to the Presidency. As an independent group the Dublin "Hermetic Society" persisted until Russell left Dublin in 1933: he had been its president. P. G. Bowen succeeded him.

1905 August Russell was appointed editor of the *Irish Homestead* (Dublin), in succession to H. F. Norman. Russell continued for several years to supervise the organisation of co-operative banks. H. F. Norman worked as a banks' organiser.

1906 [early] Russell family moved residence to 17 Rathgar Avenue, Rathgar, Dublin.

1907 March 16 John O'Leary died.

1908 November 11	The Plunkett House, 84 Merrion Square, Dublin, opened as I.A.O.S. headquarters.
1909 March 24	J. M. Synge died, aged 38.
1911 March	George Moore retired from exactly ten years' residence in Dublin, to London.
1912 April 11	Third Home Rule Bill for Ireland introduced in the House of Commons. This inflamed resentment in Ulster, which issued in the formation of the Ulster Volunteers' Force. James Connolly began forming the Irish Labour Party.
1913 May	All rights in AE's poetry transferred from John Lane (The Bodley Head) Ltd., and T. B. Mosher, to Messrs Macmillan & Co. Ltd.
June	Russell at Breaghy, Ballymore, county Donegal, arranging the sequence for his poems in *Collected Poems*.
July	Returned corrected proofs of *Collected Poems* to Macmillan & Co. [Published September 23].
August 26	Dublin Tramways' workers' strike began, and was continued throughout Horse-show week: organised by the Irish Transport and General Workers' Union, led by James Larkin.
30	A meeting of Union members was interrupted by the police. They arrested Larkin and Connolly, and killed two other people.
September 12	Connolly released from prison. Larkin discharged from prison. William Martin Murphy successfully arranged a federation of 400 employers, to counter the strike by locking-out their 24,000 employees: depriving them of all honest means to earn subsistence. An Industrial Peace Committee was formed by people unattached to the Unions; among them AE. The committee was later re-formed as the Civic League.
October 5	Public rally in the Phoenix Park, Dublin. Larkin proposed the formation of an Irish Citizens' Army to be led by Captain Jack R. White.
27	Larkin's trial for sedition: seven months imprisonment, his sentence.
November 1	In the Royal Albert Hall, London, a mass meeting to sponsor support for the Dublin strikers. Addressed by Bernard Shaw, F. W. (*later* Lord) Pethick-Lawrence, Ben Tillett, James Connolly, Mrs Montefiore, Miss Sylvia Pankhurst, Mrs Despard, Miss Delia Larkin (James' sister), AE and two other speakers: chairman, George Lansbury. Russell and Shaw were attacked by the press: S. L. Gwynn, MP, dissociated himself from those attacks (*Freeman's Journal*, November 5).
14	Larkin discharged from prison. He moved to England to address trades' unions.

25	The Irish Volunteer Force launched at a rally in the Rotunda, Dublin.
1914 [early]	The T. & G. W. Union strike collapsed in Dublin. But the Irish Volunteer Force did not collapse.
April 24	Guns and ammunition for the Ulster Volunteers landed at Larne.
June 23	Bill to amend the proposals for Irish Home Rule, by stipulating the exclusion of Ulster (commercially the most prosperous area). Its introduction in the House of Lords was instigated by Sir Edward Carson and Andrew Bonar Law.
July 26	Guns and ammunition for the Irish Volunteers landed at Howth.
August 4	British declaration of war against Germany.
1916 April 20	[Thursday] AE left Dublin to spend the Easter week-end as a guest of Edward MacLysaght at Raheen, Tuamgraney, county Clare. Nationalist revolt in Dublin over the week-end.
26	Left Tuamgraney, probably arrived in Dublin April 27.
May 8-12	Leaders of the revolt were executed.
1917	Defence of the Realm Act enforced in Ireland. 450 people arrested without right of trial.
July 25	Inaugural session of the Irish Home Rule Convention, in the Regent House, Trinity College, Dublin. 95 members representing the varied secular and religious interests of the Irish community: representatives of Sinn Fein abstained from attendance. Fifteen of the delegates were British government nominees, among them AE. Plunkett was unanimously elected Chairman. Meetings adjourned until August 8.
September 25	Russell co-opted to membership of the Grand Committee (reformed) to settle procedural method.
October 11	Russell one of the Committee of Nine, which sat in private, attempting to find a basis for general agreement. Under D.O.R.A. 1,651 people imprisoned without trial.
1918 February 1	Russell resigned from the Convention believing its constitution precluded honest discussion and settlement of the Anglo-Irish dispute.
November 11	The First World War ended.
25	Parliamentary general election. 73 Sinn Fein candidates elected to Irish constituencies, and 26 Unionists, 6 Parliamentarians.
1919 January 20	Michael Collins summoned a meeting of the Irish M.P.s.
21	Session at the Mansion House, Dublin at which the proceedings were conducted in Irish. A Declaration drawn up, arguing the present existence of an Irish republic.
March	All Irish political prisoners were released.
April 1	Mr Eamonn de Valera was elected President of Ireland by the executive members of the Irish Republican Brotherhood, and its supporters, as Dáil Eireann.

2 Mr de Valera nominated a cabinet of seven (including Collins and Griffith). By assuming directive authority this executive sought to undermine the local governmental boards; and the judiciary by adjudicating in disputes. A curfew imposed by the British administration.

September 10 Dáil Eireann suppressed: led by Collins as a guerilla force.

The Royal Irish Constabulary was stiffened in resistance by two supplementary units from England: non-commissioned ex-soldiers, dressed in black and tan coloured uniforms, and ex-officers styled Auxiliary Cadets. Under D.O.R.A. 15,818 people were imprisoned without trial during 1919, in Ireland.

1920 February 25 The fourth Home Rule Bill was introduced to the House of Commons by Lloyd George's coalition government. It prescribed Antrim, Armagh, Down, Fermanagh, Londonderry and Tyrone to be excluded from an Irish republic.

December 23 The Bill received the Royal assent.

Cork, Kerry, Limerick and Tipperary subject to martial law.

1921 January Clare, Wexford, Waterford and Kilkenny subjected to martial law.

May 19 General elections in southern Ireland: Sinn Fein majority.

24 General elections in Ulster: Unionist majority returned.

June 24 Mr Lloyd George invited Mr de Valera to consultations in London with Sir James Craig (the Ulster leader). After protracted negotiations a treaty was drafted.

July 11 The British and Irish armies negotiated a truce.

[later] The draft Treaty was revised by Dáil Eireann. That assembly then charged five plenipotentiaries (Robert Barton, Arthur Griffith, Michael Collins, G. Gavan Duffy and Eamonn Duggan) with responsibility to negotiate its settlement with the British government, in London.

December 6 After some hesitation the Treaty was signed by all parties.

16 Treaty ratified by the British Parliament.

1922 January 7 Dáil ratified the Treaty by 64 votes to 57. Because the Treaty did not yield full Republican status to Ireland Mr de Valera disapproved it, and resigned the Presidency. In his stead Griffith was elected: he nominated a pro-Treaty cabinet.

January–March Anti-Treaty members of the Irish Volunteers repudiated their allegiance to the Dáil and to Mr de Valera. Led by Rory [Roderick] O'Connor this group was commonly called "the irregulars": they proclaimed a military dictatorship.

March 15 Mr de Valera adapted himself to fresh activity, forming a new Republican party under his Presidency.

June 16 General election in Ireland (proportional representation) 58 pro-Treaty members elected, 35 other members incidentally pro-Treaty, and 35 members anti-Treaty. The anti-Treaty faction incited their followers to begin a civil war.

August 12	Griffith died. Collins president.
22	Collins killed in an ambush. Mr William T. Cosgrave succeeded as president.
December 29	Russell's "Open Letter to Irish Republicans" was printed in the *Irish Times*.
1923 January 8	Claude Falls Wright (one of AE's early theosophical friends) drowned in Lake Nicaragua, near Bluefields: aged 56.
April	The anti-Treaty supporters abandoned the conflict: excepting only Mr de Valera and his personal followers. They maintained a type of opposition "underground". Mr de Valera, with a show of exemplary stoicism, refused nomination to the Dáil until 1927.
September 15	First issue of the [second] *Irish Statesman* (Dublin) edited by Russell, with J. W. Good and Susan L. Mitchell as assistants, The *Irish Homestead* was merged with it: issued weekly.
1926 March 4	Susan L. Mitchell died in Dublin, aged 60. Russell's younger son, Diarmuid, succeeded her as editorial assistant (£100 p.a.) until April 1929. From May 1929 until the *Irish Statesman* ceased publication his junior editorial assistant was Miss Irene Haugh, BA.
September 14	Russell arrived in Paris for his sole continental holiday, spent with Mr and Mrs C. P. Curran. Mme Simone Téry and James Stephens were also frequently AE's hosts there.
1927 May 25	Frederick J. Dick died at Point Loma, California, aged 71.
July 10	Kevin O'Higgins murdered, aged 35.
15	Constance Markiewicz (*née* Gore-Booth) died aged 59.
1928 January 14	AE sailed for America: arrived in New York, January 25 and began lecturing there, to raise funds to maintain production of the *Irish Statesman*, which had been launched with funds guaranteed by a group of Horace Plunkett's friends. AE returned to Ireland at the end of March.
June 18	Russell arrived in New York (by boat).
20	Yale University conferred on Russell an honorary DLITT.
October 29 to November 13	Séamas Clandillon and his wife charged Dónal O'Sullivan and the editor of the *Irish Statesman* and its publishing Company with responsibility for a libel which they had read into a review of their book *Londubh an Chairn* [a song-book] which they had edited for the Oxford University Press. Review printed in the *Irish Statesman* November 19, 1927. Mr Clandillon was Director of the Dublin broadcasting station, which may explain why Russell was never invited to broadcast in Ireland. Dr O'Sullivan was Clerk to the Irish Senate. The High Court jury failed to agree to a decision, after seven and a half hours deliberation. The judge (Mr Justice Hannah) refused the plaintiffs' request for judgment. Their subsequent appeal was

	dismissed. The defendants' costs were £2,500. A public appeal was immediately launched to defray those costs.
1929 May	Russell's younger son emigrated to America. His elder son Brian Hartley Russell had emigrated to India about 1922, returning to England and Ireland about 1931.
July 2	Trinity College Dublin conferred on Russell their honorary D LITT.
[later]	*Irish Statesman's* American guarantors withdrew their support, probably affected by their own financial shortage occasioned by the Wall Street stock crash.
1930 April 12	Last issue of the *Irish Statesman*.
May 2	Death of James Winder Good, aged 53.
[summer]	Lyon Phillimore, Oliver St John Gogarty and J. M. Hone, with some other friends appealed by private circular letter for money to present to Russell as a token of public esteem for his character and his work in Ireland.
September 3	The Governor General of the Irish Free State, Mr James McNeill (1869-1938), presented a cheque for £800 to Russell at a meeting in the Plunkett House: the proceeds from the appeal.
23	AE arrived in New York on the *Cedric* to lecture throughout the United States, mainly on "rural reconstruction". The object was chiefly to earn money to afford for his wife the best medical attention.
1931 mid-May	Returned from U.S.A., first to London. He visited George Moore for the last time. Thence to Dublin.
[summer]	Russell wrote one article for publication in the year following the final issue of the *Irish Statesman*. Humbert Wolfe importuned him to review one of his books. (*Observer*, July 12, 1931).
1932 February 3	AE's wife, Violet, died aged 64, at their house, 17 Rathgar Avenue, Dublin. After the funeral he went to England to be solitary for a week, in the Euston Hotel, London.
March 26	Sir Horace Plunkett died aged 77.
April 3	W. B. Yeats proposed formation of the Irish Academy of Letters. He invited AE to draft *Rules*, and to perform the various secretarial functions for which he believed himself inept. The *Rules* were registered in Dublin on September 12, 1932.
18	Thomas Matthew Russell [insurance inspector] [AE's brother?] died at Raven Lodge, Summerhill, aged 63.
May 22	Lady Gregory died aged 80.
1933 January 21	George Moore died in London, aged 80. Colonel Maurice Moore invited AE to compose and speak a tribute at the funeral. AE wrote a tribute which R. I. Best spoke over Moore's ashes. [First printed in full in this edition of AE's *Letters*.]
July [early]	Russell sold his home, 17 Rathgar Avenue, and gave away most of his possessions. "Frank O'Connor" has recorded that Yeats

told him this procedure "wrung Russell's heart". AE contemplated taking a world tour, but did not do so.

July 8   Russell went to spend a holiday with his friends Arthur and Lucy Kingsley Porter. He arrived at the Donegal *rendezvous* to meet Mrs Porter alone. Her husband had been accidentally drowned that day.

August 2   He arrived in London. At his request Charles Weekes had arranged accommodation for Russell at 41 Sussex Gardens. Weekes and his wife had asked Russell to live with them, but he preferred to be unattached.

September 28   G. R. S. Mead died aged 70.

1934 March 8   Stephen MacKenna died aged 62.

April   Russell left London to reside in Donegal for May, June and July.

July 31   Arrived in Dublin.

August 9   Returned from Dublin to London. His former lodgings occupied, Russell moved to 1 Brunswick Square, W.C.1. [Premises demolished by bombs in the Second World War.]

November 5-6   A. R. Orage died, aged 61.

AE was invited to America, to be the guest of the Roosevelt administration's Adviser to the National Emergency Council, Mrs Mary Harriman Rumsey.

December 13   Russell sailed for America from Southampton, on the *Aurania*.

18   Mrs Rumsey died, aged 53.

27   Russell arrived in New York. The Hon. M. L. Wilson, the Hon. H. A. Wallace (Secretary for Agriculture) and Judge Richard Campbell were mainly responsible for arranging Russell's heavy schedule of lectures throughout the country, on "rural policies".

1935 February   Ailing, Russell sought curtailment of his trip.

March 1   Russell sailed for England on the *Aurania*.

16   Arrived in London. Moved his residence to 14 Tavistock Place, W.C.1.

May 30   Daniel N. Dunlop died, aged 67.

June 14   Russell signed his last Will: witnessed by Mrs Sophie Jacobs and Miss Kathleen Goodfellow. He bequeathed all his real and personal property to his younger son.

21   To a small nursing home run by Miss Phoebe Myers at "Havenhurst", Canford Cliffs, Bournemouth. Charles Weekes took Russell there by train from London.

July 10   A surgical operation on his abdomen, in the Stagsden Nursing Home, Bournemouth.

16   Mr C. P. Curran arrived at the nursing home and visited Russell. He was conscious and freely discussed his affairs, receiving gratefully messages of affectionate concern from his Dublin friends, H. F. Norman, Joseph O'Neill, Osborn Bergin, T. G. Keller, F. R. Higgins and others.

The Irish Academy of Letters awarded AE their Gregory Medal for distinction as a writer.

17   Oliver Gogarty flew from Ireland to be with AE. W. B. Yeats telegraphed an affectionate message to Russell (solicited by C. P. Curran and Pamela Travers): his silence had clouded AE's cheerfulness a little.

Soon after 11 p.m. AE died, whilst sleeping, surrounded by his friends C. P. Curran, Weekes, Gogarty and W. K. Magee. A. R. Orage's widow arrived and visited the body soon afterwards.

18   Simone Téry, his gay young French friend (also a friend of Mrs Russell) arrived in Bournemouth from France. She had felt grave forebodings about AE, and came uninvited. Mr Curran had the thankless task of greeting her.

19   Russell's body was taken by rail to Holyhead *via* London: James Stephens, Helen Waddell and other friends escorted the coffin: thence by sea to Dun Laoghaire, with aeroplane escort on arrival. AE's death was certified caused by carcinoma of the rectum, by James Alexander Walker [1901–December 22, 1953. Sometime honorary surgeon and resident obstetrician, St Mary's Hospital, Paddington, etc].

20   The modified Church of Ireland service was conducted by the Rev. C. C. Duggan. Principal among the congregated mourners was AE's elder son Brian Hartley Russell. Others in attendance included President de Valera, W. B. Yeats, R. A. Anderson, "Seumas O'Sullivan", Joseph O'Neill, F. R. Higgins, Mr W. T. Cosgrave, Oliver Gogarty and James Stephens. "Frank O'Connor" (representing the Irish Academy of Letters) delivered the *oraison funèbre* over the grave. The body was interred in Mount Jerome cemetery.

July 22   Diarmuid Russell arrived in London, by aeroplane from America. Whilst settling his father's business affairs he was guest of Mr and Mrs Charles Weekes.

August 27   Probate of AE's Will was granted to the Westminster Bank Ltd. Effects £2,298 1s. 7d. : re-sworn, £2,449 1s. 7d.

November   A four-page leaflet *Memorial to George Russell (AE)* was circulated by C. P. Curran and H. F. Norman, the honorary secretaries of the AE Memorial Fund Committee. W. B. Yeats was President; Senator James G. Douglas was Chairman; James Montgomery and "Seumas O'Sullivan" honorary treasurers.

1939 October 4   *Indenture* between the AE Memorial Committee Members and the Governor and Company of the Bank of Ireland. The funds subscribed by the public (less out of pocket expenses) were £898 0s. 4d. Accrued interest from the investments to which that sum was applied should occasionally be awarded as a cash prize to native Irish writers under 35 years old, for meritorious creative or scholarly work, published or in manuscript.

Chronological table
of AE's main publications

1894 *To the Fellows of the Theosophical Society* (letter dated
March 26, 1894)
Homeward Songs by the Way (published in June)

1897 *The Future of Ireland and the Awakening of the Fires* (? March)
Ideals in Ireland: Priest or Hero? (? May)
The Earth Breath and Other Poems (September)

1898 *Co-operative Credit* (? December)

1901 *An Artist of Gaelic Ireland* (? October)

1903 *The Nuts of Knowledge* (? December)
Deirdre : a Drama in Three Acts

1904 *The Divine Vision and other Poems* (January 14)
[edited] *New Songs* (March)
Controversy in Ireland (September)

1905 *The Mask of Apollo* (January 6)

1906 *Some Irish Essays* (January 22)
By Still Waters (December 14)

1909 *The Hero in Man* (May)

1910 *The Building up of a Rural Civilisation* (? January)

1911 *The Renewal of Youth* (? May)

1912 *Co-operation and Nationality* (February)

1913 *The Rural Community* (? Summer)
Collected Poems (September 23)
To the Masters of Dublin (October)
The Tragedy of Labour in Dublin (November)
The Dublin Strike (November)

1914 *Oxford University and the Co-operative Movement* (June)

B*

The Letters, 1886-1935

67 Grosvenor Square, Rathmines
                                          [? June, 1886]

My dear Miss Carrie,

Before commencing to talk of my own affairs I will go a little into yours. I told Yeates[2] of your idea of the tale with the odd characters, the poetical princess and the restless fairy, and he thinks it is very good indeed as I expected he would. Lipman[3] is not yet back from Bray or I would have asked his opinion also. I think you [may *cancelled*] should commence to write.

I am going to put my great theory, which I have almost completed, into the form of a short story of about six or seven pages. You have heard part of it already, but I will give you a short description of it all, again, that you may judge of the effect. I commence by saying that there are men, who, by the continual contemplation of spiritual things have half with-drawn their souls from the earth into the hereafter, that sometimes these men in the course of their strange studies, chance on what seem to their fellowmen to be the highest truths, but more often they form theories which are so much at variance with accepted opinions, that they are looked upon as mad; that it was an autumn evening when I first met this strange spirit, a white mist rose a few feet from the earth like the restless phantom of a snow that fell long ago, striving to reach its original heaven. I had wandered down a little valley wherein was a lake when I beheld a rapid figure clad in grey walking up and down, his manner alternated between a state of constrained quiet and wild unrest, he seemed to me like a man who had thought out all the thoughts of his time and time past and who was now trying to grasp at some of the secrets which lay hid in the illimitable

---

[1] Caroline Clements Rea (1865 ?-1954) is "Arkon" in these letters; Russell is "Zorak". Mr Herbert Rea declared that she insisted on being called Caroline; nonetheless two of their sisters inveterately described her as Carrie to the editor's friend George Paterson, who knew them well. (*See also* Biographical Notes.)

[2] The poet William Butler Yeats (1865-1939). They were friends from 1883 or 1884.

[3] Friedrich Lippman, a Russian. He died by his own hand, in America, probably in 1890. (*See also* Biographical Notes.)

future. I approach him and we enter into a conversation which is brought on by an accident. In this conversation the theory you know is brought out. This man could not believe that a deity had existed for ever, he thought that there were the elements of life, but no actual life, in Chaos, but that perhaps Nature as a whole had felt a great drowsy feeling as of a God who is for ever about to awake but who awakes not; that once, in the jarring and the shifting of the atoms, these elements came together and flamed into life, a feeble being chanced into existence, what became God was created. But this being was miserable, he had no past to reflect on, there was no joy in the never ending space out of which he came, but he determined to make for himself a great future he found that all things can be conquered by will, so he gathered unto himself life, and the innumerable worlds he formed out of matter. In these worlds he placed animate and inanimate beings, he gave them physical and spiritual life, and in all his inanimate creation, from the cedar in the forest to the tufted grass on the hilltop; in the starry worlds, and in all animate life in them, in the birds who float over them in the men and beasts who walk on them, in the huge subterranean monsters who labour in the centre of them, in all insects, in everything, he placed part of his own eternal being, and he enjoys all creation through them, all feeling is to him joy, our pain is but to him another kind of pleasure; He lies for ever in some great valley drawing from the united feelings of many universes a vast low exquisite pleasure, passionless and without distinction.

Now this man had the idea that the deity possessed power over him absolutely when he was in a body created by the deity, and over his spirit when it was passive and without knowledge of its power, but if his spirit being of the same essence as God defied him he could have no power over it, and he thought that if he could escape from the earth he might enter into chaos, create worlds and become a God.

At the close of the conversation the man became violently moved and when he had concluded he parted from me abruptly and climbed the side of the hill like a great mist rising from the valley. The next evening I go forth, eager to reenter into conversation with him, and I find him lying by the side of the tarn with a look of strange triumph on death-pale features,—he had committed suicide. This is the skeleton of the story, the idea which holds it up, on which I will enlarge considerably. I want to have your opinion of it.

I have got another idea for a story which I will tell you again. The little decorative heading shows the spirits,—that is the wind, tearing the leaves of the trees in autumn. The man on the scull[1] is one of our small descendants, myriads of years hence, observing, from a relic of our gigantic bodies, the moon rising with a dulled and deadened lustre beyond the little hills. Tell Leonard that I will allow him to answer my letter as I suppose The Isle of Man is only a distant speck on the horizon of his life now [*watercol. sketch of brown man, holding a spear, sleeping?*] but give him a hint that I have twenty-three folio volumes dealing with this subject. Have you any new theories about spirits at present I am full of them. Yeates will have a beautiful little ballad in the next number of the *Irish Monthly*.[2] His great drama "The Equator of Olives" is finished. The episode of the Sculptor's Garden is in it. It will appear shortly after his first volume is published. I was wrong when I told you that Blake admired Swedenborg. What he said was, that it was partly true, but that any man with mediocre ability might construct books just as valuable. He says in one of his books that the fact of having imagined a thing makes it so. I am glad that he says so as I have been trying to argue it with a coldly scientific friend [of mine *cancelled*]. This drawing is called "Night Birds". [*water colour; heading next sheet.*] What it means I have not the slightest idea, but of course that does not make any difference. I am doing a little drawing now called "The time of the Dying of Roses" I do not think I have anything more to say except that I hope you will commence to write. By the by I met your ugly little veiled woman seeking for beauty, in one of my nightly mooning expeditions [*pen and ink sketch of her with opened umbrella*]. Will you kindly tell me which of us looks the biggest oddity. I would like to hear your latest fancies. Adieu! Yours sincerely, Zorak

TO CARRIE REA   67 Grosvenor Sq
                                                        [? autumn 1886]
My dear Arkon,

I see I must make another effort to induce you to forgive my long silence. Was there anything particularly disagreeable in the tone of my last letter? I think I must have talked too much about myself and my

---

[1] One of several water colour illustrations beside the text of this letter. It was a subject frequently portrayed by Russell. There is another among W. B. Yeats's papers.

[2] Perhaps "Remembrance", published in *The Irish Monthly*, July 1886; or "Meditation of an Old Fisherman" (October), or "The Stolen Child" (December). See *A Bibliography of the Writings of W. B. Yeats*, by Allan Wade (London, 1951: Hart-Davis), pp. 286-287. "Equator of Olives" was not published. "Sculptor's Garden": *see* "The Island of Statues".

theories. I was just then bubbling over with the theory that our intellects
and bodies are not our real personalities our real personality being the
spirit within us, and if we could rise to this high level of consciousness
there being but one spirit through all, we could not distinguish between
ourselves and anyone else. As I looked upon my lower Ego merely as a
means of bursting my ideas upon my friends, my conversation and letters
must have had a peculiarly conceited tone. Pray forgive me. It is very
hard to keep from talking about one's self St. Paul even could not do it.
How is your story getting on, is it finished? If you have two copies you
might let me read one, I would like to do so very much. My dear friend
Lipman has absconded from Dublin with the proceeds of two forged bills,
several odd sums of money which he had borrowed, the books and ideas
of his friends. I am a slight sufferer. I am really very sorry about his
conduct. I liked him very much, he was a very clever writer and a very
clever rogue as I found later on. He had got excellent moral ideas which
he did not put into practice. He has done more good and more harm than
any fellow of my acquaintance. He ransacked the brains of all his friends for
ideas which he put into his novels under the plea of drawing from life and
produced a very good effect with them. He levied toll from Yeats,
Johnston, Miss Rose Kavanagh,[1] John O'Leary[2] and several others. I am
looking out in the publishers' lists for a new book of his *The Diary of a
Lunatic* in which I believe I figure as the hero. How are Leonard and all
my other friends at the Courthouse. Remember me to them. Try and
train yourself to see colours when you hear music (mentally of course). I
have set some of my friends to do so. At present I am engaged on two
experiments, one is original the other I have heard of. The original idea
is to find out the primeval language by the same means as the early races
found it or the same means as I think they found it out by. My proposition
is, that speech was originally scientifically constructed on the principle
that every sound had in it something which would render it a suitable
expression for a corresponding idea or form, and if we could get at the
meaning of the forty or fifty primary sounds we would be enabled to
understand much better than at present the early languages of the world
such as Coptic Sanskrit and Hebrew which being near to this primeval

---

[1] Rose Kavanagh, the poet, born 1861, died March 1891. W. B. Yeats wrote an
obituary tribute for the *Boston Pilot;* his article dated March 17 was printed in the issue
dated April 11. Reprinted by Horace Reynolds in *Letters from the New Island* (Cambridge,
Mass., 1934: Harvard University Press), pp. 118-123.

[2] John O'Leary (the Fenian). (*See* Biographical Notes.)

language would contain most of the important words, such as the expression for the "Deity", for "life", for "light", for the "sun" and "moon" and many others. . . .

. . . Did you read the *Idyll of the White Lotus* yet. If you have not you have missed a great deal, it will bear reading hundreds of times, and each time you will find something new in it. It is the story of one of the early seers of Old Egypt which he communicated in his astral body to the lady who wrote it down. You should try and remember some of your previous existences. I remember slight fragments of my last. I was an [old *cancelled*] Assyrian, I think I lived among the roses of life and passed my days in mystical reveries without any action either good or evil, except in so far as action was beautiful or good and evil seemed lovely to me. So I weakened the will which I have now to strengthen and made the life I now live distasteful to myself – O you must become a Theosophist! I will commence a series of letters to you if you will permit me on the doctrines of this primeval religion. I do not mind even if you limit the ground from which we will both draw our supplies of arguments to the *New Testament*. It is all there and has been misapprehended by those who professed it. [Our *cancelled*] The God which the Christians have imagined for themselves is the result of the sentimentality into which they have coddled themselves, he is merely a gigantic and rather good-natured baby who now and then gets into a tremendous passion and kills a few hundred thousands in his rage – This kind of a God was never preached by Paul or Christ – Do write soon my dear Arkon to Yours fraternally – Zorak

TO KATHARINE TYNAN[1]   67 Grosvenor Square
                                    [Late December 1887]

My dear Miss Tynan,

    I am sorry that I was unable to come to Mr. O'Learys last evening. But it will not make much difference about my not seeing Willie Yeats as I intend opening communication with him through the medium of the astral light – that is – try thought transference between Grosvenor Square and Eardley Terrace.[2] No doubt he will have imagination enough to think he is receiving messages from me and whenever I write to him about these

[1] Katharine Tynan, the poet daughter of Andrew Tynan. (*See* Biographical Notes.)

[2] Yeats left Dublin after December 13, 1887, returning to 58 Eardley Crescent, London. The Yeats' family moved to 3 Blenheim Road, in March 1888. Yeats had arrived for his Irish holiday probably Thursday, August 11, 1887.

airy conversations I will use expressions which will suit his conversation at any time. "Your poem is splendid" "Your paradoxes are getting more startling every day" and "You should not say such hard things of your friends." These remarks will convince him more than ever of my occult powers and he will tell everyone that I can hear his smallest whisper over a thousand miles away and exalt me generally above M. Blavatsky. It was very kind of you [to] write to me. Cutting the panel[1] down will not harm it in the slightest. But I will take care to measure the next more accurately. Yours sincerely, Geo. W. Russell

TO KATHARINE TYNAN   67 Grosvenor Square
                                                            [? February 1888]
My dear Miss Tynan,

I hope you will excuse me for not appearing yesterday. It was snowing so heavily all the morning that had I started I would have been a most miserable draggled specimen of a Theosophist at the time of my reaching you.

The panel which I had promised you was so tame that I became disgusted with it and commenced another subject which I think is more respectable. It will be finished in two or three Sundays more when I will avail myself of your kind invitation and bring it out to you. Yours sincerely, Geo. W. Russell

TO H. P. BLAVATSKY[2]   6th November 1888

[*Possibly written by George W. Russell, although no address is printed and the initials are its sole signature*][3]

Nothing that has yet appeared in your magazine has been so much in concord with my own humble views as your Editorial[4] in the October Number on "Lodges of Magic".

I am not a proclaimed Theosophist. I do not belong to the Society. For some reasons I am sorry; for many reasons I am glad. And one of the

---

[1] Small wooden panels. Miss Pamela Hinkson kindly showed the editor two paintings given to her mother by AE. One is the panel referred to here, on which figures aureoled as if with white head dresses are apparently in procession. Similar paintings by Russell were reproduced in *The Irish Theosophist*.

[2] Helena Petrovna Hahn (1831-1891). (*See* Biographical Notes.)

[3] Text from *Lucifer* (London), vol. 3, no. 16, pp. 339-341 (December 15, 1888).

[4] *Lucifer*, vol. 3, no. 14, pp. 89-93 (October 15, 1888): unsigned.

[6]

most cogent of the latter is the almost certain degeneracy of any Society or Sect formed by mortal hands. I mean no disrespect to the founders of the T.S. They were animated by the purest motives; inspired by the noblest resolves.

But, being human, they cannot control the admission of members. They cannot read the heart, not [*sic*] know the mind. And, consequently, the T.S. is not representative of Theosophy, but only of itself – a gathering of many earnest seekers after truth, many powerful intellects, many saints, and many sinners and lovers of curiosity.

If I have learned aright the lesson you have endeavoured to teach, it is this. That development must be harmonious, and must be unconscious.

The danger which attends the desire to know is that the knowledge to be gained too often becomes the goal of our endeavours, instead of being the means whereby to become perfect. And by "perfect" I mean Union with the Absolute. A young man, whose intellect is of the keenest, and with great power of assimilating and applying knowledge, is devoured by a desired [*sic*] to attain a lofty ideal. He feels there may be something beyond the facts of material science, beyond the anthropomorphic religions of the day. Drifting into that mysterious current which is now flowing through the century, he becomes attracted by Theosophy. For a while he studies it with avidity, strives to live "the life", to permeate himself with its teaching.

His intellect is satisfied for the time.

But, alas! he commits the fatal fault of forgetting that he has a soul. He does not, indeed, forget that he is immortal, but he neglects to feed his soul on spiritual things.

His science becomes wider, he grasps the idea of universality – and generally becomes a rank pessimist.

But, through the above mentioned fault, Mystic Union with the Higher Self becomes more and more phantasmal, he recognises its necessity, but postpones the ordeal.

"First let me prove the lower realms of Nature" he cries, and plunges into the phenomena of spiritualism, table rapping, and the evocation of spooks. He declares that Knowledge is Power, and carries his assertion to no further issue. He is remonstrated with. He replies that it is necessary to test all experience, and construes that axiom into a law that Karma is to be moulded and shaped by the conscious Ego. Carried to a logical conclusion, his rendering of the axiom would lead him into the lowest depths of vice to the hurt of his higher nature. He would seek in this transient incarnation to gratify every lust, passion and ideal of his personality. Whereas, surely the true meaning of the Law is that the Ego must of necessity taste of every experience in its progression up the Scale; must pass through every grade, ascend every step of the ladder.

It does not mean that when we know the good we must follow evil, nor that our higher must sometimes be actively degraded to the level of our lower self.

And so, step by step, it seems to me our neophyte wanders toward the broad path that leadeth to destruction. Confident that he is able to use the little knowledge he has gained, assured of his own powers, and disdainful of the terrors that lie in lurk for him, he goes on his way. His weapon is self-confidence and his armour Ignorance.

There is no turning back when once the path is trod, and the only hope is in his being vanquished in the first trial. Should he conquer his earliest foe, he will only meet a direr fate.[1]

Now, is this Theosophy? If so, I will have none of it. I own I should like to see phenomena, to "call spirits from the vasty deep" with success.[2] But I do not flatter myself that this longing is of a pure nature. If I did not sometimes wish to take a short cut to knowledge, I should not be a man as we know him. But I believe this desire after manifestation to be of the earth, earthy. With faith we can do all things, yet we should not desire to do all things, but simply to have the faith.

I recognise the essentiality of establishing the scientific basis of Theosophy, of studying it from all sides. I do not wish to be merely a metaphysical mystic. I am sadly afraid, however, that most of us followers of Theosophy are but just out of our swaddling clothes. We must have our toys and picture books.

My ideal is to worship the One God in spirit and in truth. Is that the aim of the T.S.? . . .[3]

I have expressed myself to you, not with any wish to see my feeble endeavour in print, nor from any presumptuous thought that I have written anything new or authoritative, much less have I written in any carping or judging spirit. I have no right or desire to criticise people better than myself, but I feel it on me to ask for an assurance that the T.S. as a whole is doing the work it is meant to do—not merely expanding

[1] See AE's Foreword to *Island Blood* by F. R. Higgins (1925).

[2] Madame Blavatsky's editorial footnote: "It is not in the Theosophical Society that our correspondent can ever hope to evoke spooks or see any physical phenomena."

[3] Editorial footnote: "There is no religion higher than truth is the motto of our Society."

the Intellect of the World, but also drawing the Soul of Humanity towards its Higher Self[1]. AE

TO H. P. BLAVATSKY[2]   [December 1888]

Madam,

I have only two remarks on your notes to my letter published in the December number of *Lucifer*. (1) I do not "hope" to see spooks by the help of the Theosophical Society. My baser part sometimes desires manifestation, but I recognise such desire to be impure. I earnestly trust no Member of the Society will ever indulge in the evocation of phenomena, whether for curiosity, or for the gratification of the intellect.

(2) I asked if the worship of the One God in spirit and in truth was the aim of the Society. You reply with the motto of the Society. But your real answer appears to be in the opening article of the Magazine on Denunciation.[3]

I candidly think the formation of the Society was a mistake. Not a mistake in motive, but a mistake in generalship. The speed of the slowest ship marks the rate of progress of a fleet. The weak ones of the Society mark its position in the world. But if the Society has only helped one brother to right living, then it has done much to justify its existence, and I have naught to say.

My real reason in again addressing you is to call attention to a Novel written by A. de Grasse Stevens.[4] At page 141 is a reference to yourself as a Russian spy who was ejected from India by Lord Dufferin.

I have never before seen this curious slander in print, and, although you may consider it beneath contempt, I think it a pity to allow it altogether to escape notice.

The reprehensible conduct of the Publishers in allowing an Author to libel a living person, and that person a woman, is such that I do not care to express my opinion on paper more fully than in this letter. I am, your most faithful servant, AE

[1] Editorial footnote indicating the true nature of esoteric philosophy, to train in the "occult hygiene of mind and body".

[2] Text from *Lucifer* (London), vol. 3, no. 17, pp. 437-438 (January 15, 1889).

[3] The unsigned first article in vol. 3, no. 16, pp. 265-273, "Is Denunciation a Duty".

[4] H. P. Blavatsky's signed "Reply" following AE's letter notes: "As to the authoress of this would-be politico-social novel, a rather green than young American, it is said her exceptional claim to distinction from other trans-Atlantic writers of her sex, would seem to be an intimate acquaintance with the lobby and the back stairs of politics." Madame Blavatsky answered the alleged libel in the *Pall Mall Gazette*, January 3, 1889. *Miss Hildreth a novel* by A. De Grasse Stevens, 3 vols. (London, 1888).

TO CARRIE REA

3 Up Ely Place, Dublin

[? July 1892]

Dear Carrie,

I am returning your book to you. I have not read it through as I consider it to be a heap of unutterable trash. The writer knows nothing at all about magic "that lofty and divine science" which Iamblichus wrote of and Plato commended; . . .

TO SARAH PURSER[1]

5 Seapoint Terrace, Monkstown

9.7.94

Dear Miss Purser,

Book is called *Homeward*, *Songs by the Way* Publisher, Whaley, 46 Dawson Chambers, Dawson Street, Dublin, where McGee can obtain it during the hours 11 to 2. I hope you will like it, though full of that mysticism which you have so often smiled at. I would like to know what you think of it. Sincerely yours, Geo. W. Russell

TO EDWARD DOWDEN[2]

5 Seapoint Terrace

6 Aug. 94

Dear Sir,

I have read your kindly and appreciative review of my *Homeward Songs* for which I thank you, and which coming from you must give the verses a publicity which a review from few other authors could give. It may seem ungracious after all this to demur to anything you have said,

---

[1] Sarah Henrietta Purser (1848-1943). The portrait painter. (*See* Biographical Notes.)
[2] Born 1843, died April 4, 1913. In scholarship, a prodigy. Professor of English Literature at Trinity College, Dublin, 1867-1913. He wrote a *Life* of Shelley (superseded by Newman Ivey White), and edited Shakespeare. His review of *Homeward* was printed in the *Illustrated London News*, vol. 105, no. 2885, p. 142 (August 4, 1894). He is just and appreciative, discerning in the poems an impulse through strong personal experience towards objective understanding. Whilst he indicates AE's lack of practical shrewdness in feelings, he compares him to Emerson. He briefly winds up with censure of AE's use of the word "Brahma", evidently disliking transliteration from non-European sources. He expresses his own hope that AE will not become addicted to the least sincere Theosophists. He wished the Preface had been omitted. See *Edward Dowden's Letters* (London, 1914: Dent), pp. 273-274 for his opinion of AE's *The Earth Breath*, in a letter to W. K. Magee (November 4, 1897). See also *Edward Dowden: an Address* by Professor Herbert O. White (Dublin, 1943: T.C.D.).

and if what I objected to had reference merely to my own faculty or the quality of my verse I of course could only keep silence. But in just one remark it seemed to me that perhaps you went rather beyond the province of the artist in literature. Surely, to mention "Brahma" and to use the sacred feeling with which long generations of Hindus have chanted the spirit as "Om", is not to come near losing oneself in the cheap Theosophy of the East. When the artist in literary things meets any statement of such matters, his function I think is simply to decide whether it is beautiful as literature, as in the "Paradiso" or the "Ancient Mariner" all are agreed about the stateliness or beauty, and are unconcerned whether the author has introduced impossible conditions. A thousand beliefs have occupied the minds of men and probably as many more will follow, and in all of these the protean soul takes on strange graces which it is the business of the artist to record. The question of the truth can only be approximately decided by the psychologist, and definitely by each individual as in his spiritual development he comes nearer to God. I might also demur-though this is by the way-to the word "cheap" as applied to Eastern mysticism. Surely this could not be said of some Upanishads or of the *Bhagavad-gita*, in which the unutterable longing of myriads of mystics to draw nigh to "the Lord, the Comforter, the resting-place and the friend" finds expression. I could perfectly well understand the word as applied to much western mysticism, as that of Swedenborg, with his astral shepherdesses and etc. After all, it was not to say all this, but mainly to thank you, that I write. Perhaps I am something of a fanatic, and feel unduly touched when anything is said lightly about ideas which have helped me to live properly and to touch the sweetest core of life. I am glad you have regarded me rather as a mystical poet than as poetical mystic. To the title of mystic I have really no claim. I am not capable of leading the pure ascetic life in thought and act which alone could develop any spiritual insight worth acquiring.

Meanwhile I try only to put into intelligible form such beauties as I can feel. Yours very sincerely and gratefully, George W. Russell

TO SARAH PURSER 5 Seapoint Terrace
7.8.94

Dear Miss Purser,

Many thanks for your notes. I had almost thought, save for your note and another, that I had missed the gift of transmission. My reviewers and correspondents have credited me with intentions I never had, and it is a real pleasure to get a letter from some one who really seems to like the book and not to look upon it as so much doctrine chopped into rhyme. Yours sincerely, Geo. W. Russell

TO EDWARD DOWDEN 5 Seapoint Tce
Sunday [*Postmark:* Dublin, August 13, 1894]

Dear Professor Dowden,

I find all you say wise, but still I am unable to make use of it. The choice of symbolism and a method of thinking is a matter of temperament. I can only work within a little space at present; while I see with you quite clearly that the truest mystical spirit will and must finally unite itself with exact observation of fact and mastery of details: still I think that facts and details with many of us hardly subserve the purposes of soul. We are for the most part overpowered by material forms; whereas we ought to be free and to be able to oppose as vivid and rich a consciousness welling up within ourselves to that which day and sunlight give projected on us from without. Until we can do that we only heap up riches of fact and detail in vain: we cannot use them with understanding. To get free; to be able to rise from the region of dependent things into the self existent spiritual life is the first need of the mystic. He is most aided to do this by pondering over statements which for the time draw the mind away from nature and need a kind of self illumination for their proper significance to be grasped. Such are:

The Knowledge of It is a divine silence and the rest of all the senses.
Hermes

And

The soul is its own witness and its own refuge. *Upanishad*

And

Iswara is a spirit untouched by troubles, works, fruits of works or desires. *Yoga Aphorisms*

Or

Night and day are undistinguished on the Path. Whether one would set out to the bloom of the East or come to the chambers of the West

[12]

without moving is the travelling on this road. In this Path to whatever place one would go that place ones own self becomes. *Dnya-
neshvair*

All these statements are a chaos to the reason; only the imagination
kindled at the inner shrine can realize their truth. It draws little or no
aid from experience or memory. Age is no nearer than childhood to the
grasp of the Sceptre. Perhaps indeed childhood and innocence come
nearer. Anyway all these things are verifiable only by an entrance into the
inner life into the Christ-soul of the universe which is at once "the Way,
the Truth and the Life" and because I find the mystical literature of the
East fuller of words like those quoted, which insist upon the exercise of a
spiritual faculty for their comprehension, I think it is so far superior to
that of the West. Another reason I may give why I think it is inadvisable
to pass from a symbolism which we understand and love; and "then
laugh at it", passing on to another, is that the very words we use as symbols of spiritual ideas become potent – become sacred. As the enchanter is
said to call up heroic forms of the past by his spells, so such words as
Om, Brahma, Christ, invoke in us and cause to reappear moods long ago
felt of spiritual sincerity and aspiration. Our past is still living within us
or we could never recall it. We can draw from that spiritual past its living
energy and pour it into a dark today. Such words by a strange affinity call
forth the power. But to what Brahmin will Christ be the word of power
though it signify the same as Krishna? or to what Christian will Brahma
be potent? I was pagan in my childhood and have grown naturally into
Indian methods of thought and so I must continue until I can see the True
without a veil. To depart from it would be to act like a man who has cut
steps for himself half way up a steep hill and then half way he stops,
descends, and cuts other steps elsewhere. Again, from a merely literary
point of view it is advisable not hastily to change from symbol to symbol,
for then our words do not bear the burden of dreams and the tradition of
long endeavour which every line should bear if it is to affect people at all.
Of course all this is defence purely from the point of personal fitness.
There is nothing I would like better than to be able to think and will from
my own centre independent of all aids. However I suppose all this must
be only commonplace to you who have spent your life in mastering the best
thought of the world and I feel an absurd stiffness about nearly every
prose sentence I write. If it is any compensation for a long lecture on
mysticism I append verses in which I feel more at home and which you
may like better. Yours sincerely, Geo. W. Russell

IN THE WOMB[1]

Still rests the heavy share on the dark soil;
Upon the black mould thick the dew-damp lies;
The horse waits patient; from his lowly toil
The ploughboy to the morning lifts his eyes.

The unbudding hedgerows dark against day's fires
Glitter with gold-lit crystals; on the rim
Over the unregarding city's spires
The lonely Beauty shines alone for him.

And day by day the dawn or dark enfolds
With dreams of beauty eyes that cannot see
How in her womb the Mighty Mother moulds
The infant spirit for eternity.

TO CARRIE REA   5 Seapoint Tce
                                                              6.9.94

Dear Carrie,

I have sent you today Yeats' second volume *The Countess Kathleen*[2] also a book which I hope you will like *Letters that have helped me*. They are written by a man whom I consider the wisest and sweetest of any I have ever met W. Q. Judge[3] (Z.L.Z.). I have more reverence for him than for any other human being I know of. I hope they will mean as much to you

[1] In *Collected Poems*, p. 127. This poem, revised, was first printed in *The Irish Theosophist*, January 15, 1895. It was reprinted in Mosher's first American edition of *Homeward* (1895) and in Britain, in *The Earth Breath* (1897).

[2] Published, September 1892.

[3] William Quan Judge, born in Ireland April 13, 1851; taken to America in childhood and was employed for several years in an attorney's office in New York. There he fell under the influence of H. P. Blavatsky, and joined the Theosophical Society. After Madame Blavatsky's death (1891), Judge and Annie Besant conducted a public wrangle concerning the validity of certain written "messages" which, Judge declared, were authentic communications from a disembodied "master" on the astral plane. Mrs Besant swore they were forgeries written by the spirit in Judge's body, which she evidently disliked. The rather sordid vilification in which supporters of both leaders indulged, effected an irreconcilable split among the sheep in the T.S. The Dublin Lodge remained loyal to Judge. He died in New York, March 21, 1896. In *The Irish Theosophist*, vol. 4, p. 121 (April 15, 1896) an unsigned poem by AE eulogised Judge. In the same issue, pp. 122-123 Russell, in a prose "tribute" wrote he had "first glimpsed Judge's real greatness" in London at the T.S. Convention, 1894. Mrs Katherine Tingley led the T.S. in America, after Judge: but the Dublin lodge soon seceded from all association with her policies. See W. B. Yeats's *Autobiographies* (1955), pp. 239-250.

as to many of us. They are not badly written; but do not think of fine or beautiful phrases when reading them, but only of the things it is good to live with and ever to keep in mind. I think he says only things he *knows*.

I am glad you have met Yeats. He is really a poet, exuberant, with a royal imagination the like or which has not been heard in England since the time of Keats and Shelley. Do not forget in analysing yourself to correlate your various moods and the state of growth to ideals with the various people you have met. Every person you meet is an affinity of temper or thought. You were brought near to that person by the Great Law to attain self-consciousness. I am angry. I am brought by the law of attraction to meet angry people. Our moods clash, and then we destroy ourselves or learn a lesson. I am mystic, aspiring. I meet mystics continually. I develop a strange desire for the quiet life in woods whereon to worship the over soul. A fortnight after I meet my counterpart. The more swiftly you live, the more intensely you will, the more the great magician makes the forms of life come and go in accordance with your thought. Yeats reflects some mood, I another, your brothers again other phases of your consciousness. This is a law of life. Remember for all your doubts "We live and move and have our being" in the Great Life and the sun and stars, wind, tides, people, are only shadows moving through it and moved by it for its own ends. This again is not fatalism, for we may say of it "I am that" as the Brahmans old say, adding "the ancient heroes and poets knew it, they became it, and are immortal". Just as your will joins your two hands together for one purpose so the one conciousness which pierces up and down through every plane of being brings you and another together. It is well to know the meaning of the mystic hours as they pass. If I can help you in any way or clear up anything do not fail to write. I am always glad to hear from you so no more nonsense about "troubling" etc. Yours fraternally, Geo. W. Russell

Love to Bertie.[1]

TO KATHARINE TYNAN HINKSON
5 Seapoint Terrace
[November 1, 1895]

Dear Mrs Hinkson,

I hope next Sunday afternoon to walk to Clondalkin, if the Storm Gods permit. I will write to Weekes[2] to meet me in town if he can come. I am

---

[1] Carrie's younger brother Herbert Rea.
[2] Charles Alexandre Weekes (the friend and adviser of Russell). (*See* Biographical Notes.)

glad of the prospect of seeing you again after so many years. Sincerely yours, Geo. W. Russell

TO W. B. YEATS   5 Seapoint Terrace
                                                [? November 1895]
Dear Willie,

Herewith is a copy of *I.T.*, and first chapter of astral records concerning Cuchullain.[1] This is mine. Pryse[2] will do the rest. I saw a splendid notice of your book[3] in *Daily Chronicle*. I suppose Lionel Johnson's?[4] I think you should clear out of Arthur Symon's[5] vicinity, and come over here. It will be much better for you morally, and as a place to get inspiration. Charlie Johnston[6] is here, and is going to make a long stay. Weekes[7] is going shortly to publish translations of three Upanishads, and perhaps later on another book of his own. I do not know whether he wishes this last to remain a secret or not, but it would be best not to mention it until he does himself. I would like to know how your book will be received. Weekes thinks revision of *Usheen* and *Countess Kathleen* improves them much. Yours in a hurry, Geo. W. Russell

TO SARAH PURSER   5 Seapoint Tce
                                                      [April 1896]
My dear Miss Purser,

The editor[8] of our magazine has just gone to America for a month leaving me as editor during his absence, but not leaving me any copy. He

---

[1] *The Enchantment of Cuchullain* by AE and Aretas; a story published serially in *The Irish Theosophist* beginning in vol. 4, pp. 32-35 (November 15, 1895). "Aretas" was James M. Pryse. (He joined the Ely Place Lodge, probably at the same date as Miss Violet North, January 1895.) (Resident members?) Miss North supervised the printing of *The Internationalist* (October 1897-March 1898).

[2] James M. Pryse, the American Theosophist (1859-1942). (*See* Biographical Notes.)

[3] *Poems* (London: Fisher Unwin), published October 1895.

[4] Lionel P. Johnson (1867-October 4, 1902), the English Catholic poet.

[5] Arthur Symons (1865-January 22, 1945).

[6] Charles Johnston (1867-1931). (*See* Biographical Notes.)

[7] Whaley (Weekes's firm), published Charles Johnston's *From the Upanishads*, in January 1896. It is prefaced by a long dedicatory letter to AE. Weekes did not publish any book written by himself.

[8] D. N. Dunlop, the editor of *The Irish Theosophist*. A report of the Theosophical Convention was printed in *The Irish Theosophist*, May 15, 1896. (*See also* Biographical Notes.)

told me kindly something would surely turn up. It is turning up, in me, because I am forcing it out day by day for a hungry compositor. I am not exceedingly melancholy but have a chastened spirit when I reflect on the number of pages I have to fill. I am really so busy hunting ideas which vanish catlike into the recess of my mind leaving only elusive tails whereby to draw them back again, that I will not be able to see you until after the middle of next week. I won't forget sure, and I will come round just as soon as this nightmare of "copy" leaves me free. Also another reason for re-membering is that I owe you sixpence having unconsciously swindled you out of that sum over some old magazines. I put it in my pocket, a pocket all to itself for some time, then I applied it to personal purposes, I think tobacco, but doubtless I will get another before I face you.

I always intended to make my conscience ache to the extent of sending it, but I have kept it clearly if lazily in my mind, as you may see – Yours sincerely, Geo. W. Russell

TO W. B. YEATS   3 Up Ely Place
                                                              2.6.96
Dear W. B. Y –

I am not going to bother you about any derned thing this time but simply to tell you some things about the Ireland behind the veil. You remember my writing to you about the awakening of the ancient fires which I knew about. Well, it has been confirmed from other sources and we are likely to publish it. The gods have returned to Erin and have centred themselves in the sacred mountains and blow the fires through the country. They have been seen by several in vision, they will awaken the magical instinct everywhere, and the universal heart of the people will turn to the old druidic beliefs. I note through the country the increased faith in faery things. The bells are heard from the mounds and sounding in the hollows of the mountains. A purple sheen in the inner air, per-ceptible at times in the light of day, spreads itself over the mountains. All this I can add my own testimony to. Furthermore, we were told that though now few we would soon be many, and that a branch of the school for the revival of the ancient mysteries to teach real things would be formed here soon. Out of Ireland will arise a light to transform many ages and peoples. There is a hurrying of forces and swift things going out and I believe profoundly that a new Avatar is about to appear and in all spheres the forerunners go before him to prepare. It will be one of the kingly Avatars, who is at once ruler of men and magic sage. I had a vision of him some months ago and will know him if he appears. America is on fire with mysticism just now and the new races are breaking the mould of European thought and psychics abound. Their light reflects itself in Ireland, and the path of connection has been seen. Now I wish you could come over to this county Sligo or wherever you like and absorb this new force. To me enchantment and fairyland are real and no longer dreams. . . .[1]

By the way I want to spend a week or ten days in the neighbourhood of Sligo this year to hunt up some old currents. Can you tell me some moderate priced hotel to put up at. I wish you could be there. I will start I think about the 4th or 5th of August. My holidays beginning then. Would there be any chance of your roaming about there for a while with me and talking over magic, the Celt, and the old country amid the ancient sites of the mysteries? Tell Weekes[2] if you see him that he owes me a letter, also ask him for God's sake to write his address clear. W. K. Magee[3] and myself have spent maddened hours trying to distinguish between his 2's and his 7's. C. W. makes no difference. May the Opal Fire Kings have you in their keeping. Yours ever, Geo. W. Russell

TO W. B. YEATS   5 Seapoint Terrace
                                                  3rd April 1897

Dear Willie,

I came home last night big with radiant ideas and full of wrath over the priests. Ah wicked wizard, it will take me weeks to get together the "Will to do" you have dissolved in dream. There I have been trying to disentangle myself from the Enchanted World, and nerving myself for deeds, and you send up a spray of lovely colours to draw me away again into the byways where these shadowy beauties create only endless desire and there is nothing for the will to do. I must forgive you for many reasons, mainly for the stories of the Red One. Many things which I used to think were due in your work to a perverted fancy for the grotesque I see now in another way.

---

[1] One sentence omitted, introducing what AE describes as his "first definitely Irish poem". The poem is also omitted here. It was first printed in *The Irish Theosophist*, vol. 4, p. 190 (July 15, 1896). Reprinted in *The Earth Breath*, p. 30, and in *Collected Poems*, p. 108; first line, "The children awoke in their dreaming".

[2] *See* Note 1, page 229.

[3] William Kirkpatrick Magee (1868-May, 9, 1961), Essayist. (*See also* Biographical Notes.)

Your visionary faculty has an insight more tender than the moralist knows of. Just in the same way as O'Grady[1] always seems to detect under the rude act the spirit of defiant and heroic manhood, so you unveil beneath excess and passion a love for spiritual beauty expressing itself pathetically in the life of this wayward outcast. That insight is indeed an ennobling thing to impart, and I suppose just because the highest things are the most dangerous you will find a number of people, who have not got your mental balance, using your visionary revelation of a hidden spirit seeking for beauty as justification and defence of passions which have no justification, except that they are the radiations of a spirit which can find no higher outlet. The *Rosa Alchemica* is a most wonderful piece of prose. Everything in it thought and word are so rich that they seem the gathering in the temple of the mind of thousands of pilgrim rays returning and leaving there their many experiences.

A book sustained at that level throughout would be one of the greatest things in literature. I notice a change in your lyrics. They are much simpler, more classic, and with a better feeling for the form of the idea, nothing of unnecessary beauty in them. You used to be carried away by every lovely fancy into side images which marred a little the directness and effect of the central plan. The little song in the *Rose in Shadow* is simply perfect. Long ago you would have said some beautiful thing, say about the sea or stars in this, which we would have forgiven for its beauty, but which would have destroyed the passionate intensity of the poem as a whole. Your art gets more perfect in these things. I suppose it is a necessity of your life that you must write these dreams in prose, but never forget that poetry is their proper language. They are there uncontested. When you put them into prose you invite opposition and argument, from which may the gods save us. I wish I could congratulate myself upon such a steady movement to mastery over my art as you. I write fitfully. Then one of your "moods" comes and afflicts me and tells me it is only working in shadows I am, and it is all worth[less] and so I lose heart in it all and get no further. I have vague ideas of trying a long poem but I am afraid I must wait for happier days. My new book *The Earth Breath* will I suppose be out sometime this spring as it has been set up in America. I think sadly of it though I don't think there is anything really bad in it. It is too melancholy. This is a cursed disease Pryse left me as a legacy when he went to America. It did not make me unhappy long ago to remember

---

[1] Standish James O'Grady (1846-1928) an Irish barrister who turned to provincial journalism and literature. (*See also* Biographical Notes.)

greater things but now it puts me in hell. I am afraid it would be a futile task to try consciously for the Celtic traditional feeling. A certain spirit of it I have but I am not Celt inside, not for many lives. I remember vividly old America and Chaldea, and sometimes as a mountain beyond lesser heights I get glimpses of the Dedanaan days but they lie behind tradition and history; all we know of them come strained through the Bardic mind of fourteen hundred years ago and it is very inferior to the truth. It is no use writing of these things for a vision of great mystical beauty is not necessarily an inspiration to write beautifully about it. This I know well. Indeed as my perceptions widen I find my inspirations, my genuine ones, narrow to a few emotions of earth. Interpret this for me. When I knew comparatively little of the invisible and my blood was hot I wrote most spiritually. Now as I perceive more and feel less I feel more drawn to write of the ordinary human emotions. Here is a song of the later kind.

> *On me to rest, my bird, my bird!*
> *The swaying branches of my heart*
> *Are blown by every wind toward*
> *The homes where to their wings depart.*
>
> *Build not your nest on me, on me:*
> *I know no peace but ever sway:*
> *O lovely bird, be free, be free,*
> *On the wild music of the day.*
>
> *But sometimes when your wings would rest*
> *And winds are laid in quiet eves,*
> *Come, I will bear you breast to breast*
> *And wrap you close with loving leaves.*[1]

There is a certain songfullness about it, but whether it has any value I am in the dark. Here is another in which I want counsel.

> *Could you not in silence borrow*
> *Strength to grow from us ungrieving?*
> *All these hours of loving sorrow*
> *Only make more bitter leaving.*

[1] Printed in the "Celtic Christmas" issue of the *Irish Homestead*, December 8, 1900, p. 16. Reprinted in *The Nuts of Knowledge* (1903), p. 10 and in *Collected Poems*, p. 28.

You will go forth lonely, thinking
Of the pain you leave behind you:
From the golden sunlight shrinking
For the earthly tears will blind you.

Better, ah, if now we parted
For the little while remaining;
You would seek when broken hearted,
For the mighty heart's sustaining.

You would go then gladly turning
From our place of wounds and weeping,
With your soul for comfort burning
To the mother bosom creeping[1]

I think I would break any woman's heart whoever happened to love me. She would find me as elusive as the spirit itself. Perhaps it may be I am half a woman inside. My reviewers could never make out whether AE was he or she. Perhaps I am making ready for another life as in one of my verses a lover supposes a change of condition and sex.

Your flight shall be in the height above,
My wings droop low on the lea:
For the eagle must grow a dove, my love,
And the dove an eagle be.

The best of all these recent verses is a poem on Blindness which Magee thinks is the best of all.

Our true hearts are for ever lonely:
A wistfulness is in our thought:
Our lights are like the dawn's which only
Seem bright to us and yet are not.

Something you see in me I wis not
Another heart in you I guess:
A stranger's lips, but thine I kiss not,
Erring in all my tenderness.

I sometimes think a mighty lover
Takes every burning kiss we give:
His lights are those which round us hover;
For him alone our lives we live.

---

[1] Printed in *The Earth Breath* (October 1897), p. 82. Reprinted, *Collected Poems*, p. 188.

> *Ah, sigh for us whose hearts unseeing*
> *Point all their passionate love in vain,*
> *And blinded in the joy of being*
> *Meet only when pain touches pain.*[1]

The fact is I have I believe inwardly passed out of love and cannot write any true love poems. I would like to get a little book of verses which would infect with this weariness in the midst of delight which is the beginning of the divine love. The sudden upstarting of the spirit from its bed of roses, the vanishing of desire as the loved eyes and lips yield themselves, all these things want expression. I think the best use to make of the weariness of life is to impart it to our too lusty generation, so cheap in its affections, so proud like Le Gallienne of informing people in verse that they know pretty girls and often kiss them. I would make them sadder if they read me

> *We are desert leagues apart:*
> *Time is misty ages now*
> *Since the warmth of heart to heart*
> *Chased the shadows from my brow.*
>
> *Oh, I am so old, meseems*
> *I am next of kin to time:*
> *The historian of her dreams*
> *From the long forgotten prime.*
>
> *You have come a path of flowers:*
> *What a way was mine to roam.—*
> *Many a fallen empire's towers,*
> *Many a ruined heart my home.*
>
> *No, there is no comfort none:*
> *All the dewy tender breath*
> *Idly falls when life is done*
> *On the marble brow of death.*[2]

There I will cut this one short for you. It is too damnably melancholy. It would turn you grey inside to read. But I wish the Le Gallienne's and the lusty poets of love, would not fall so readily into the bait of wide open arms. I think they never found a girl to love them until this life and they are still in the boyhood of the passion. You know now the kind of poems you

[1] Printed in *The Earth Breath*, p. 47. Reprinted, *Collected Poems*, p. 170.
[2] Printed in *The Nuts of Knowledge*, p. 24. Reprinted, *Collected Poems*, p. 130.

will have to review if it falls your way. My poems have come out of a sad heart, Willie, and a desperate endeavour to shake myself from it must be the excuse for the longer ones you do not care for. Adios, dear Brother. May the Rose flourish. AE

TO J. M. SYNGE[1] Erris Hotel, Belmullet, Co Mayo
[Christmas 1897]

Dear Mr Synge,

Your letter has followed me from one place to another until it has reached me here. I am sorry to miss seeing you again but I hope when you are next in Ireland I will be settled in Dublin. I do not know anything of Yeats, his London address is 18 Woburn Rd., off Euston Rd., London, and a letter will be forwarded to him.

This wild country here has imposed such a melancholy into my blood that I have not had the heart to write to him or anybody else if I could help it. I had nothing to say except accounts of the distress here which is a disgrace to humanity and that is not cheerful subject matter for a letter. Yours sincerely, George Russell

TO W. K. MAGEE Erris Hotel
Christmas [1897]

Dear W. K. M.,

I'll call on you when I get back which I guess will be about the middle of January. I am mewed up here in this desolate bogland with priests as my advisers and an ardent young Parnellite to balance. Still I am not bored. One of the young priests is a jewel. I will have heaps of meetings next week,–one at Belmullet, one at Grisella, one at Aughoose. Yes I will be very very glad to get your article,[2] you know I will. The more derisive the better pleased I will be. Apostolic succession may work very well in Rome but in Belmullet its not worth a damn as I learn from my young Parnellite who has told me many tales of his battles. I must say I admire his pluck. I am too busy otherwise and too full of dreadful anticipations

---

[1] *See* Note 2, page 229.
[2] Magee's essay "Apostolic Succession" was printed in *The Internationalist* (Dublin), January 15, 1898. (*The Internationalist*, October 1897-March 1898, was edited by Russell in Dublin, and by H. A. W. Coryn in London.)

of public speaking to find another Ballykeele but I catch the gleam of sentences below the still waters of my mind. They no doubt will come to the surface sometime with a rush. The drive from Ballina to Belmullet 40 miles on a frosty day from 2 p.m. to 10 o'clock was a terrible experience. I was only saved from a frosty death by my dread of going into a bog. I heard the car went into one the night before and drenched its wretched load of passengers. "The horses shie sometimes," I was calmly told as if it were nothing. A fat little country girl kept me warm part of the way and quoted local poetry to me and also faery yarns and such like. But the rest of the way was a chill desolation. I arranged the contents of next *Internationalist* before coming down and I do not know how far it is set up. So if you like to hold your article over for another week or two it will do month after. I would like to have it anyhow down here to read as I have no literature except the weekly *Irish Times*. I brood much and dont feel inclined to read anything. Write like a good fellow and tell me any news you have got. Gregan[1] will have a still finer poem in next number. He is improving wonderfully and sometimes will be a rather weighty addition to the dignity of the Celtic renaissance. My head is stupid just now, no ideas. I sat up until three at a party here, comprising the Priest, the doctor, the Clerk of Works, a shopkeeper, his wife, his two girls, his son (the young Parnellite) and two fellows from Cambridge. They all but myself drank whisky and sang songs and played various musical instruments and I the only child of light and the light in me turned to darkness.[2] Pity me. Geo. W. Russell

TO W. B. YEATS   Flynns Hotel, Ballina
                                                          1.2.98

My dear Willie,

I thank you for your very kind letter. I have made my path inevitable and I have only to go on. I believe from the material side I have not done so badly. I have doubled the number of banks in a month. I have started one at Kilcommon, one at Kilmore Erris and another at Ballyglass. That is my record so far, and I believe the I.A.O.S. are satisfied. It may be as you say that I will gradually absorb and harmonise these things and something new will grow out of them. I hope so. But at present no vision, no inspiration visit me. I hope I shall see you when you come over. I may

---

[1] Paul Gregan (1876–May 7, 1945), a Banks' Organiser for the I.A.O.S. (*See also* Biographical Notes.)   [2] *See* Note 3, page 229.

be in Dublin then but cannot say. You could live in some hotels for 35/- a week I did so at Belmullet. But all the places I have been at with the exception of Aughoose Kilcommon are not beautiful. Ballyglass is a haunted place. I heard lots of faery tales, while there, much like the tales, you gathered at Gort, one curious belief I never heard before. They will not weep at a death, but sit grim and silent, and if grief overpower they go far away and sob in some lonely place for they believe that to weep over the dead would attract the phantom Hounds to chase the soul newly gone from the body, so until it has passed unto the other world they maintain their silent sorrow. You might work a story out of this weird belief. I saw there the great grand child of a fairy queen but I regret her royal descent was not evident. At Ballyglass I met Major Maurice Moore[1] the brother of the novelist, an interesting man. Do you know O'Grady has gone to Kilkenny. He has taken over the *Kilkenny Moderator*, and is going to make it the organ of "All Ireland". How are the mighty hurled from their seats. You mixed up with "98". O'Grady edits a local bi-weekly paper. I explain to starved looking peasants how advantageously they could buy pigs under the benign influences of a rural bank! I remember once as I lay on the mountains seeing in dream a figure moving into the heart of the dawn, sadly, slowly alone it went into the golden fire and I knew that it saw nothing and the dawn was invisible and the golden fire only a chillness around it, and the dawn light may be glittering everywhere for all I know. I tried running a Mayo legend into verse later, but it was no good as you can see.[2] It is the story of one Caden More.

> *It's a lonely road through bogland to the lake at Carrowmore:*
> *And a sleeper there lies drowsy where the water laps the shore:*
> *Tho' the moth wings of the twilight in their purple are unfurled,*
> *Yet his sleep is filled with gold light by the masters of the world.*
>
> *Far more tender than your colleen is the heart we'll bring you near.*
> *What's the starlight in her glances when the stars are shining here?*
> *And who would kiss the shadow when the flower face glows above?*
> *Tis the Beauty of all beauty that is calling for your love.*
>
> *And the mountain-gates of dreamland close behind his spirit's feet,*
> *And a heart enraptured meets him, and a music far and sweet,*
> *And a cry exultant ringing over cabin bog and shore,*
> *Say a spirit's leaped to dreamland from the lake at Carrowmore.*

[1] *See* footnote 2, p. 33, to letter May 8, 1899 to Horace Plunkett.
[2] *Collected Poems*, p. 106.

Letters from AE

I groan when I write like that. "Beauty and loveliness have passed away."
I began again this morning.[1]

> *What call may draw thee back again?,*
> *Lost dove, what art, what voice may please?*
> *The tender touch, the kiss are vain:*
> *For thou wert lured away by these.*
>
> *Oh, must we use the iron hand*
> *And veil with hate the Holy Breath;*
> *Through alien lips give love's command,*
> *As they through love the call of death.*

The first is undigested new matter, the second the phantom apparition of
old inspirations. But I am glad you like *The Earth Breath* better. I think
in many things in it there is a more passionate human sincerity than in
the Old Songs. I think Blindness, and Janus are good. I can honestly say
that there is not a single insincere line in the book. I have not heard how
it is liked. Do you hear any remarks from [Lionel] Johnson or [Arthur]
Symons? Johnson might like it. Letters sent here will find me until
Sunday, after that better send them to 13 Eustace Street to be forwarded.
I will try to get to Dublin while you are there. Maybe my spirit will come
back. Yours ever, George Russell

TO W. B. YEATS

[13 Eustace Street]
Cousins Hotel, Crossmolina
[February 10, 1898]

Dear Willie,

I have found that around Mt. Nephin the atmosphere is so thick with
faerys that you draw them in with every breath. I spoke to a farmer
named Caden More living two miles or so from Crossmolina. He when a
young man of twenty-three spent a whole night with the fairies in a
great palace below Nephin. He remembers it all most distinctly and gave
me a vivid account of his reception his feelings and his behaviour. He is
now a most beautiful tall old man if he was as handsome as a young man
I do not wonder at the fearys' invitation. He told me also that the people
living on Nephin always see a death in the *air* there a month before it
takes place. It comes lower and lower and when the death touches the

[1] *Collected Poems*, p. 148.

[26]

ground the mortal goes. That is very extraordinary. My landlord, Mr Cousins, a well-to-do tradesman and farmer, after a while confessed his belief, and once committed, he told me all sorts of beliefs and experiences. He was getting in his cattle one evening with his man who is a noted seer, and this man suddenly stopped and pointing to the air above a rath near said "Whist, whist! there they go, there they are!" and again and again he pointed here and there to the invisibles flying in a dance. A man near Ballina pulled up a "lonam" an isolated thorn tree, and got his arm paralysed. Caden More had to shift his pigstye. It was "in the way". The barmaid at my hotel in Ballina who comes from near Partry, told me that a neighbour's sister was taken and she used to come back and crouch by the fire and complain that the faeries did not treat her kindly. My authority for the people not weeping for dread of the phantom hounds is old Mrs Fitzgerald Kenny of Clogher Ho. Ballyglass, Co. Mayo. Of course you cannot publish her name. She is the owner of a very large estate here, something like Lady Gregory's but encumbered. She is a wonderful old character, could tell fairy yarns by the hour and believes in them all. She has heard the banshee. Is a type of the good natured intolerant old aristocrat. "I do not believe in all this education," she said. "We are the upper classes born so; they are born to serve us and ought to remain where they are born." The fall of a poker is a dire portent to her "Indeed Helena", to her daughter a very pretty girl, "You ought not to laugh. It fell the night before your father's death." She is amazingly dignified and as kindly as all the West of Ireland people are. I hope Lady Gregory[1] won't write to Mr Plunkett.[2] I do not want to take any holidays until the Summer. It is very kind, but I do not think I ought to ask after being only a couple of months on the organising. I may have to go to Arran Isles in a week or so. I have written to the P.P. there offering to organise a bank. It is curious that Symons should like *The Earth Breath*. I am forced to the conclusion that he has a soul or has only lately lost it, or else on an application of the principle "that the devils also believe and tremble" his inverted spiritual nature finds some application of the divine laws. "The devil can quote scripture." Anyhow he is not a bad devil and if he was confined in a hermitage on the top of Mount Nephin with no women near he might get purified after a twelvemonth. I am going to try to get up to Dublin for

[1] Russell first visited Lady Gregory at her home, Coole Park, Gort, County Galway, on July 26, 1897.
[2] Horace Curzon Plunkett, the Irish politician (1854-1932). (*See* Biographical notes.)

a day or two the end of this week. If you are there and inquire at 13 Eustace Street Miss North will let you know if I am in town, or drop a note to me there. It is really a wonderful country. I saw a most pathetic parting of boys. One going to America and his old father and five or six boys seeing him off on the car. The boys all flung their arms round him and kissed him. I watched them there looking after him with the tears rolling down their cheeks on the lonely road. It was the wild bogland near Erris. And such beautiful turns of language. "Ah sure your shadow is only a light at the door," said one to Miss Kenny. Yours ever, George W. Russell

TO W. B. YEATS   13 Eustace St., Dublin
                                                    P.O. Letterkenny
                                              Easter Sunday [April 10, 1898]

Dear Willie,

Your review[1] received. I think it is the best I have yet received. The other reviews you said you sent I have not found enclosed. I suppose you mislaid them. . . . The horrible word "sense" you suggested, I remember,

> *Glory and shadow grow one in*
> *The hazel brake*
> *Laughter and peace in the stillness*
> *Awake and awake.*[2]

Well I could not get over the incorrectness of peace "awaking", and I could not find anything better, so I had to let it go for the present. I will hunt for another word though. I have written nothing for a long time, and have given up the *Internationalist* editorship as I had no inspiration to aid it with. I feel all my old yearning to tramp through America come on me, and if I get a chance, I think I will go. I seem to myself to be doing no good anyhow, and Agriculture Banks could be organised by anyone with a clear head and a capacity for smiling when he is bored. Look what you have drawn me into. I dine with P.Ps. every week. Today I dine with a Bishop.[3] I gave evidence before a money-lending Commission; I am asked to enquire the price of pigs; I have been forced to learn the different properties of manures; I have lived in country hotels, and been a thing

---

[1] "AE's Poems"; Yeats reviewed *The Earth Breath* in *The Sketch*, April 19.

[2] In *Collected Poems*, p. 212. First printed in *The Irish Theosophist*, vol. 4, p. 107 (March 15, 1896).

[3] His Eminence Cardinal Patrick O'Donnell (1856–October 22, 1927). Bishop of Raphoe, 1888–1922: Cardinal, 1925: Archbishop of Armagh from 1925.

apart from the "wholesome cheerful life of men", because I won't get drunk. I have been infernally bored with the faery and folktales, and you tell me to excite the compassion of such a wretched being as I am "that you have sat up late, and have paid a bill," whereas you ought to be glad there is anything sufficiently interesting in your life to make you sit up late, and that you have money enough to pay your bills. I have hopes, though, that the Bishop will talk theology, and that I may fence with him through the evening in a polite way. That is a streak of light in my immediate future. Then there is a row in the T.S. and I cannot take part, hampered as I am, and I longing to go for everybody, and charged up with suppressed malignity. I feel cross, but I hope to be in better humour after dining with the Bishop. I feel a worthy foeman in Dr. O'Donnell. I remember sending him *Priest or Hero*, and have a pleasant feeling that he knows I am the author. I get cheerful as I think of it. This in a hurry for post. George W. Russell

TO W. B. YEATS   I.A.O.S., 22 Lincoln Place, Dublin
30 August, 1898

My dear Yeats,

All right, I wont attack O'Grady's book.[1] I never intended to—only to separate ideal from method, but as you say it is best to leave him alone. I do not feel any inclination to write at present for any cause, person, or paper. I am resolving many things about Ireland in a voiceless meditation and do not feel justified in writing until I have made my own sight clear. Gill[2] has asked me many times to write but what have I got to say. The shadow of a vanished mystical period; the raw materials for a concrete philosophy; and only incoherent flashes of an altogether new line of thought and action. I am not the man for Gill indeed, I do not know what good I am for anything, feeling no cause, among the many [which] people about me take up so enthusiastically. By the way that amazing little German Dr Moritz Bonn[3] is going to Arran in a couple of weeks and you may meet him. He is a man of genius (German genius). If you listen to him you will get many ideas about the state of Ireland. He is tracing the

[1] Standish James O'Grady's *All Ireland* (Dublin and London, April 1898: Sealy, Bryers & Walker; T. Fisher Unwin).

[2] T. P. Gill (*see* Biographical Notes.)

[3] Moritz Julius Bonn, the eminent economist and author. (*See* Biographical Notes.)

growth of individualism in Ireland at the present time. He thinks Ireland is three hundred years behind Europe[1] and our day is coming. The ideas which have become tradition and culture in Europe are beginning to be living powers here. I think he is going with P. J. Hannon one of our organisers who lives at Loughrea.[2]

Plunkett thinks this little German quite the cleverest man he has met. Do not forget your own literary work for "98" or even for Celtic Mysteries. "98" was well in its day and the mysteries are here for five years (or ten more likely) in the future. Your verse universally intelligible will help you more powerfully later on than a secret propaganda now. *Religio Poeticae*[3] a wonderful book. His opinions on women absurd. Geo. W. Russell

TO W. B. YEATS   28 Upper Mount Pleasant Avenue
Rathmines
[March, 1899]

My dear Willie,

Many thanks for your letter. I think experience is good. Now like a Brahmin after having begotten a son I retire again into a life of ascetic meditation. I am glad Moore likes my landscape sketches but he must have formed his judgement on a very limited survey as neither you or Lady Gregory have really good sketches. I always thought my landscape faculty was greater than my power of drawing figures. Our loan exhibition which will begin in April will be good I think. We have nearly six hundred pounds guaranteed.

I will look out for your Saturday article.[4] I promised in a weak moment to speak on Monday next at the lecture Castletown will deliver on our Celtic Inheritance, and have been regretting it ever since. I hate speaking but thought I would like to go for Atkinson. If it is any use I will follow up your article with another. But perhaps it is not well that we should "hunt in couples" too often. I have done one or two new poems–Irish– which I think good, and would like to do more but the I.A.O.S. shapes the convolution of one's brain to a different kind of work.

---

[1] Expounded in *Die Englische Kolonisation in Irland* (Stuttgart and Berlin, 1906: Cotta. 2 vols.); dedicated to his friend Horace Plunkett.
[2] Patrick Joseph Hannon (born in Ireland, 1874). A member of I.A.O.S. staff. (*See also* Biographical Notes.)
[3] By Coventry Patmore (London, May 1898: Bell).
[4] "The Academic Class and the Agrarian Revolution", in the (Dublin) *Daily Express*, March 11, 1899.

When is your new book coming out? Will it herald the next publishing season also? As you will be over soon there is no use writing a long letter. By the way, I asked Pollexfen to cast a horoscope for my boy. He promised but never wrote. Does it take long? He has had a month now. Geo. W. Russell

P.S. I hope all is well with yourself and M. G.[1] I do not think Paris with its associations of a different kind would foster the growth of the relation between you. Ireland is better.

TO W. B. YEATS   28 Upper Mount Pleasant Avenue
[April 1899]

My dear Yeats,

Many thanks for the *Wind Among the Reeds*.[2] I know all already but the effect is much heightened by their being brought together and read as a whole. I like all the verses except the "Elemental Powers" which I think the weakest poem you have yet published. The notes here and there unsatisfactory as they do not elucidate the more abstruse symbols. You ought not to give your readers too much trouble in this matter, or should have referred them to authorities here and there. Your proof-reading is abominable. You are the worst culprit I know in this respect. I am bad, but you! You have left out one whole line in "Far off most secret and inviolate Rose". Look it up. I think it ought to run "By a grey shore where the wind never blew".

Having eased myself of these matters, which are more irritating because your verses are so perfect I confess that many of my old objections to verses, which I have mentioned to you, have melted away. There are more perfect poems in it than any previous book of lyrics of yours. I could pick out of the first book the "Kanva", and out of the second the "Lake Isle" or "Who dreams that beauty passes like a dream" easily as being best, but in this half a dozen at least make it difficult for me to say. Your detestable symbols too get a reflected light from the general twilight luminousness and beauty which does not belong to them by right, just as moonlight makes an ugly scene beautiful. I suppose you calculated on this.

[1] Maud Gonne. (*See* Biographical Notes.)
[2] Published by Elkin Mathews, London, April 1899.

I asked Gill to let me review it for the *Express* on Sunday but this morning Fiona Macleod[1] wrote asking also so I gave way as it would I think be better from her. But I will, if anything in her review gives me an opening, write later on calling attention to the importance of your book as the most extreme reaction from the old popular poetry with semi-political aims, which Davis, Mangan and the '48 men made popular, and as the most complete escape from the tyranny of the ephemeral passions of the hour into the world of pure art, idealism and beauty. You have written so often about my own work that I am doubtful of the wisdom of my reviewing your verse except through some side issue, which might be raised such as I have mentioned. Gill says our pamphlet will be out this week and wonders could you get anyone in London to call attention to it. Lionel Johnson, Moore or any other body who is interested in Irish things.

I heard you called with Miss Gonne on Plunkett. I am doing all I can to get a good provisional Committee together to take the question of the tenants up. I have at least half a dozen very good men interested, and will give their names. One man offers an estate to divide. I will get together a preliminary meeting during the Ballsbridge Show when some others will be up in Dublin whom I hope to get to join. There was some talk of sending me down to investigate the evicted estates, and to furnish a report. I may be sent but am not sure yet.

I will speak more fully about the poems when you come over as I have not had time to form any definite judgement; that they have beauty of form, colour invention equal to anything you have done goes without saying. But I have to make up my mind about the wisdom of your notes. I thought you intended them to be a defiant statement of your position as a symbolist, but you are too apologetic (that is hardly the right word but I cannot get another to say what I mean). I wish you had said something more full of the pride of your art such as:

I made it out of a mouthful of air
Their childrens' children shall say they have lied.

[1] William Sharp (1856-December 14, 1905) a poet born and bred in the Scottish western highlands, afterwards sent to Australia to re-coup his delicate health. Sharp settled in London in 1879 and aesthetically was deeply influenced by D. G. Rossetti. He wrote Rossetti's biography (1882). From 1893 he cultivated a second literary style, innately feminine, publishing books under the pseudonym "Fiona MacLeod". His more masculine and flexible writings he signed with his own name. Certain contemporary lady journalists may well resemble the psychological condition exemplified by Sharp's strange yet energetic duality. Elizabeth A. Sharp wrote a sympathetic *Memoir* of her husband (London, 1910: Heinemann).

I see you triumphed and had the gold on the cover. I hope it won't reduce the royalties. Good luck. Geo. W. Russell

TO THE RT HON HORACE PLUNKETT, MP   22 Lincoln Place
Prince's Hotel, Hove, Brighton   8th May 1899

Dear Mr Plunkett,

Yours of the 7th to hand. I am sending to the Viscountess Castlerosse to Pall Mall and Killarney, copies of the *Homestead* as requested and am also sending the two copies to you. We are trying to raise a discussion and have written to a number of people asking them to take the matter up and try and create some interest on the subject through the medium of the *Homestead*.

The first performance of the *Countess Cathleen* comes off this evening. I am very much in doubt about it after having seen the rehearsal, not on account of the play but lest some of the unfortunate things which always happen at half amateur performances may injure its success. A very serious matter is that the daily *Nation* has made a most venomous attack on it on the score of religion and anti-nationalist feeling. [I don't know how *deleted*.]

They buttress up their case by quoting the sentiments of the demons and lost souls without saying how they occur in the play. A pamphlet by Frank Hugh O'Donnell,[1] of the most scurrilous character, has been circulated extensively by the author. But still I think on the whole it will be a success to those who really care for beautiful and delicate performances.

If I see Moore over here, I will try and pump the true national spirit into him and instruct him in what is necessary for the good of Ireland. I only hope he won't go for information to his brother, Major Moore,[2] in Mayo. Just now we are in the latter gentleman's black books.

---

[1] The author of *Stage Irishman of Pseudo-Celtic Drama* (London, June 1904: Long) and other corny tracts. F. H. MacDonald O'Donnell (1848-November 5, 1916).

[2] Maurice George Moore (August 10, 1854-September 8, 1939), brother of the novelist and art-critic George A. Moore. A regular army officer who served in South Africa. Retired as Colonel. See J. M. Hone's *The Moores of Moore Hall* (London, 1939: Cape). Col. Moore wrote, *An Irish Gentleman: George Henry Moore* (London, 1913: T. Werner Laurie); *Rise of the Irish Volunteers: 1914-1917* (serially only, in the *Irish Press*, 1938), and *Financial Relations, Ireland and Britain*. Col. Moore was a foundation member of the Irish Free State Senate. See letters of April 10, 1917 and following.

I am delighted that you are going down to the sea and I hope that your visitors will not be so exhausting as in London. The sea air ought to pull you up. I cannot imagine anybody getting well of anything in London, which I think is a hell upon earth and has a kind of vampirising effect on one's health and good spirits. Yours sincerely, Geo. W. Russell

P.S. I enclose a reprint of Gregan's about Clare Island, which may interest you.[1] We sent a copy to the C.D.Bd.[2] Please return when you have looked through it. G. R.

TO W. B. YEATS   28 Upper Mount Pleasant Avenue
19th January 1900

My dear Yeats,

I have been so busy for the last ten days that I have not been able to do anything for you. Anderson[3] of the I.A.O.S. has been laid up and I have been flooded with economic "currents" to the complete exclusion of anything else. I do not see any chance of getting less busy for another week. I am sorry as I would liked to have written for *Beltaine*. I will keep a look out for your letter in the Dublin papers, of which you say you enclose a copy which I did not get. I am going to the country on Friday morning and may miss some of the papers but will try to get them all if possible in county Tyrone. I have brought all the influence I could to bear on Redmond about Hughes[4] but I am afraid it is practically decided that it is to go to St. Gaudens[3] who is an Irish American and who certainly will do a fine thing. Gill has made them promise that if Hughes sends in a design it will be considered but I think it must have been settled in U.S.A. to give it to St. Gaudens as nearly all the money subscribed is Americans. I was making fair headway with my long poem when Anderson grew ill. Now I could not write any decent sentence in prose or verse so much am I obsessed by activities not of the spirit. I get tired like a diver too long under seas when I cannot get time to retire within myself.

I was up early in the morning in the hills a fortnight ago and I saw a harper of the de Danaans and heard him playing. The sounds were

---

[1] Perhaps from the article in the *Irish Homestead*, vol. 5, p. 31 (January 14, 1899), "Clare Island", which was unsigned. Plunkett had visited Clare Island during January.
[2] Congested Districts' Board.
[3] Robert Andrew Anderson (Secretary of the I.A.O.S.). (*See* Biographical Notes.)
[4] John Hughes, the sculptor, born in Dublin 1864. (*See* Biographical Notes.)
[5] A. St Gaudens (1848-1907), the celebrated American sculptor.

wonderfully clear and I was able to repeat them to myself. But when I got to the foot of the hill it had deserted me. Please publish "Shadowy Waters" at once, before any more changes are suggested by the changing Tatuas. Yours ever, George Russell

P.S. My wife wishes to be remembered to you and your sisters whom she met at Rosses.

P.S. 2. I have been hunting up old Celtic mythology and have got the skeleton of the Druidic philosophy and symbolism in my mind. I wish much to talk this over with you when you are next in Dublin.

TO STEPHEN GWYNN[1]   22 Lincoln Place
                                                                   14 Sept. 1900

Dear Mr Gwynn,

I just received your letter this morning on return from the country. I think your sketch admirable[2] and can suggest no alteration except the substitution of "Agricultural Banks" for "Land Bank" wherever the latter phrase occurs. A Land Bank on the continent has a meaning distinct from an Agricultural Bank and all our societies are Agricultural Banks. You might use the term "Rural Bank" instead, if you liked it better. Also I think you err in saying there are Land Banks in every parish in Denmark. I think Wurtemburg would be a better country to instance. There, in 1895 were 649 Agricultural Banks of the Raffiessen type and 574 Banks of the Schultz Delitsch type. I cannot suggest any further amendment. I think your article eminently readable and it is sure to help us. Yours sincerely, Geo. W. Russell

TO CHARLES WEEKES   22 Lincoln Place
                                                                   Tuesday 14.5.1901

My dear Charlie,

I am delighted to hear from you and offer my warmest congratulations on your marriage to ?. I hope to meet her some day if destiny brings me to England at any time. I am filled with the largest spirit of curiosity

---

[1] Stephen Lucius Gwynn, the Irish politician (1864-1950). (*See also* Biographical Notes.)

[2] Perhaps "Month in Ireland" which Gwynn contributed to *Blackwood's Magazine*, October 1900 (vol. 168, pp. 573-584).

concerning ?. I heard vaguely several times rumours of this but nothing definite, and indeed placed all these rumours to speculations based on your adventures in search of wisdom. After so long a search I suppose, or rather I feel sure, this is the real affinity, and therefore already feel a warmth in my heart concerning her. I hope you will bring her to Ireland sometime. Why not after the 25th? It is a changed Ireland, but it is the place of your birth and you must not forget the Mother who breathed into your soul the life breath which you are wickedly spending in a distant country. I grow more in love with the earth year by year and I have so much delight in my Mother Erin that I would like to bring back to her all her exiles. In the cosmopolitan you have everything and nothing, but here in a private plot of mountain the earth spirit yields to my endearments and whispers as sweetly as to her first children. And how unless the affinity has breathed the air of your land can she really understand you? Therefore, dear man, come over here, if not to Dublin, to Enniskerry or some place near where you will be visible to the eye. Why hang it, you have not even got common curiosity to remain away so long. Surely you have heard rumours even in London that Ireland is growing alive steadily, with immense waves of new ideas, Gaelic Leagues, Literary Theatres, music, art even business–the spirit of business–has opened a sleepy eye after long slumber, and won't be allowed to go asleep again. After your immersion in Saxondom surely this will appeal to you. Anyhow tell me something about the "affinity"? I congratulate her with more certainty than you not knowing her mental whereabouts. The "boy" is growing in beauty and impudence. With kindest regards to yourself and "?". Yours ever, Geo. W. Russell

TO KATHARINE TYNAN HINKSON   22 Lincoln Place
                                          Dec. 19th 1901

Dear Mrs Hinkson,

I have just returned from the country and have time to jot down a few ideas about Horace Plunkett[1] for you. The first time I got to know him fairly intimately was about four years ago when I was organising societies in the congested districts. He wrote to me before the Whitsuntide Recess that he would like to go round among the farmers with me and do what

[1] AE wrote an article "The Rt Hon. Horace Plunkett" in *The Gael* (New York), March 1902, pp. 81-82.

Thomas Elias Russell and Marianne Russell
(*AE's parents*) circa *1870?*

(i)

(iv)

Scenes fr

Performed privately in George Coffey's house (rehearsal) January 2, 1902: the first perforr
his son Diarmuid Coffey's 12th birthday. (See We Two Together *by J. H. Cousins an*
scenes to have been followed by The Craze for Gold *"By D.C." ("The wooing o,*
Deirdre and Naisi. (Followed by "The return of the Sons of Usna", from Act
(vi) Ainle, Naisi, Deirdre, and Fergus. The cast: Ainle *played by AE;*
Ainle *by R. I. Best;* Lavarcam, Ella Young;

(iii)

(vi)

re by AE

garden of G. Coffey's house at 5 Harcourt Terrace, Dublin, January 3, 1902, to celebrate
usins (1950) pp. 69-70.) The programme was printed on a duplicator, and shows these
from Act 1. (i) Naisi and Deirdre. (ii) Naisi, Ainle and Deirdre. (iii) Lavarcam,
isi, Ainle, Fergus and Deirdre. (v) Ainle, Fergus, Naisi, Deirdre and Buinne.
Miss Violet Mervyn [i.e. Miss Elizabeth Young, Ella Young's sister];
George Coffey; Buinne by James H. Cousins

67 Grosvenor Square.
Rathmines.

My Dear Miss Barrie

Before commencing
to talk of my own affairs I will go a little into
yours. I told Yeates of your idea of the tale
with the odd characters, the poetical princess
and the restless fairy, and he thinks it is
very good indeed as I expected he would.
Lipman is not yet back from Bray or I would
have asked his opinion also. I think you
should commence to write

Specimen page from letter AE to C. C. Rea [? June 1886]
Illustrated in water-colour

he could to aid in the work of organisation and to hearten up the congests. The average M.P. spends his holiday yachting but Plunkett went through Connemara, Achill Enis and part of Donegal with me day after day speaking to the farmers, going into their houses, trying to inspire them with the idea of self help and of cooperating together. I never knew a man so unwearied in helping others. No trouble was too great to undertake on their behalf. He is never downcast, his optimism is incurable. His belief in the capacity of Irishmen to elevate their country and their own condition is at least as great as that of the most unsubduable *intransigente*. He has achieved success because he never gives up an idea of which he is convinced of the truth. He had fifty unsuccessful meetings before he could get the first farmer's creamery started. Fifty meetings without result! I think most of us would be ashamed to face an audience after two dozen unsuccessful attempts to get a hearing. He is not naturally a fluent speaker but has by practise, and because he has something to say, developed into a really fine speaker with moments of passion and emotional depth. You always feel the sincerity of his speech. You always say "This man believes what he is saying." He has plenty of humour, and it never hurts. I never heard him say a nasty thing of his bitterest political opponent. At Galway where sixteen of our M.Ps slated him from morn to night as a place hunter, a dishonest politician, he never retorted by counter accusations. He always spoke of them with the greatest courtesy. "I have no word to say against men who for generations have clung to a cause they believe to be true and for which they have sacrificed so much." His hits are general and not personal but they are hits for all that. He said of the Orangemen who opposed him "They talk of lining the last ditch: myself I am of opinion they would be found climbing the first fence." While he is a Protestant by birth he has always worked without a trace of sectarian feeling with the most extreme Catholics. I don't believe he ever asks himself what a man's religion or politics are so long as he works for Ireland. He said a few weeks ago in Belfast at a public meeting where he tried to melt the obdurate sectarianism by a little humour. "We all know that those who differ from us on matters of religion will be adequately punished hereafter. So why harbour bad feeling now?" In all the work he has undertaken there is the same spirit forgetful and reconciling. The Organisation Society of which he was founder and president for five years gathered into its work the extremists of both sides and the societies are filled with Orangemen in the north and with United Irish Leaguers in the west, and no political or religious questions are ever raised in the industrial work which it is agreed

[37]

can be carried on amicably. A few years ago Plunkett went to a northern meeting with Father Finlay[1] to start a creamery. They were met by the Orange band with orange sashes and the Nationalist band with green sashes who gave them a hearty welcome, and by mutual agreement each side left out the more provocative items in their programme "Boyne Water" etc. etc. The Recess Committee was founded in the same spirit, and Nationalist M.Ps met with Unionists from Belfast at their meetings to take council on the economic condition of Ireland. The outcome of the I.A.O.S. and its work is about 600 societies of farmers continually increasing. The outcome of the Recess Committee is the new Department of Agriculture and Technical Instruction [*The rest of this letter is lost*].

TO SARAH PURSER   25 Coulson Avenue, Rathgar
                                                                                  5.3.02

My dear Miss Purser,

I have often wanted to write to you but have been nearly all the spring away in the country, and even the memory of my wife fades in the hurry of trains and impassioned orations to the Irish farmer to be up and doing. I suppose you are personally engaged in rummaging for Tanagra terracottas or are digging up ancient temples out of the bowels of Greece and will come back with trainloads of curios. I have had visions of your crossing the desert, fighting with Bedouins, weeping over the Holy Sepulchre and crossing the sea of Galilee. But cannot make up my mind whether you will be Egyptian Greek or Jew when you return. I find all my friends who go to Paris come back with an altered moustache and a new tie and a distinguished stranger air, so I am sure that when you go so far off the temptation will be irresistible to come back either as the Sphinx or something suitable and akin. I hope you are having a good time, Ireland stands where it did since you left, but I expect it will get a good lift when Miss Gonne appears as "Kathleen ni Houlihan" in Willie Yeats' little one act play which will be produced with *Deirdre* in Easter week.[2] I am designing dresses, colours, painting scenery and generally fussing about *Deirdre* in the odd evenings I am in Dublin. I really think it will be nice. The Daughters of Erin have flung their Aegis over us, and Yeats and I are being

---

[1] Thomas Aloysius Finlay, a Jesuit priest (1848-1940). (*See* Biographical Notes.)

[2] First performed on April 2, 1902 by W. G. Fay's Irish National Dramatic Company. Other performances: at Dún Emer, Dundrum (August 22, 1903); Abbey Theatre ("Theatre of Ireland"), December 13 and 14, 1907 (AE as Cathvah the Druid).

produced under their auspices. George Moore is giving an open air performance in his front garden to all Gaelic speaking Dublin. No English speakers allowed. It will be a new play by Hyde.[1] Please if you are in Greece or Athens when this reaches you pick up for me a pebble or stone from the Parthenon hill. I want to see if I could psychometrise it. I might find I was Phidias long ago or less [im]probably John Hughes may have been. I know I lived in the neighbourhood. Your paints are being transformed into faerys, gods, dewdropping twilights and Celtic dreams generally. I have your picture of the "Enchanted Pool" finished for you, and have now about thirty pictures for my exhibition which will take place sometime when I feel I have courage enough. Jack Yeats and the little Carribean Pixie Pamela Mamosetti Coleman Smith, bring out a broadsheet monthly[2] with coloured pictures. I like it. The first number has some drawings of Diarmuid and Grania and a picture of a green horse by Jack[3] "The Pookha", which is splendid. The Gore-Booth girl[4] who married the Polish Count with the unspellable name is going to settle near Dublin about summer time and as they are both clever it will help to create an art atmosphere. We might get the materials for a revolt, a new Irish Art Club. I feel some desperate schism or earthquaking revolution is required to wake up Dublin in art matters. The "celebrated Irish artist, Thaddeus" dominates the Academy. Whenever I see his pictures I hate him with a concentrated intensity of malignity which would allow him to sizzle in Hades for an aeon or two without pity. I wonder the law does not take notice of crime in art. It is just as wicked, more so, indeed, to harrow your soul than your body, and Thaddeus inflicts positive pain on me. I am sure you feel with me here,

> *Could you and I with Him conspire*
> *To grasp this sorry Thaddéus entire*
> *Would we not shatter him to bits, and then?—*

I have discovered a new Irish genius, and announce his name—Colomb:[5] only just twenty, born an agricultural labourer's son, laboured himself, came to Dublin two years ago and educated himself, writes astonishingly

---

[1] Douglas Hyde's play *The Tinker and the Fairy* first performed on Whit Monday, May 19, 1902.

[2] *A Broad Sheet*, monthly, 1902-1903 published by Elkin Mathews. See note in *The Letters of W. B. Yeats* edited by Allan Wade, p. 383.

[3] Jack Butler Yeats, the artist. (*See* Biographical Notes.)

[4] Constance Gore-Booth (1868-1927). (*See* Biographical Notes.)

[5] Padraic Colum. (*See* Biographical Notes.)

well, poems and dramas with a real originality. When he has three or four more years at his back he will be a force and I believe a name–He is a rough jewel at present, but a real one. I prophecy about him.

Hughes has never betrayed to anyone here any sign that he once lived in Ireland. Nobody has heard from him. I expect he is working from before dawn to bed time on his Irish fusiliers who are to guard the statue of the Queen. I wish the Queen had never died and we might have had another Orpheus and Eurydice. I feel sad over it, but I suppose it will turn out all right. I can't imagine John becoming an Onslow Ford. If I hear of any news I will write again. I suppose you wont be here before June. Lucky woman, With kind regards from Mrs Russell and myself. Yours sincerely George Russell

TO W. B. YEATS   25 Coulson Avenue
                                                                       [? April 19, 1902]

My dear W. B. Y.,

Arising out of the performance of *Deirdre* and *Kathleen*, O'Grady this week in *A.I.R.* tells us we may succeed in "degrading the ideals of Ireland and in banishing the soul from the land."[1] I think while we cannot say anything where the more literary or dramatic merit of our work is questioned, that a charge like this should be met and answered. I have addressed a vigorous letter to *A.I.R.*[2] and if O'Grady does not publish it I will send it to the *Freeman*, *Irish Times* and *Independent* with a letter accusing O'Grady of a mean slander on his Irish contemporaries and of cowardice in refusing to insert [the] reply. He needs to be pulled up and I have done it with a vengeance. I tell him frankly he has forgotten all he ever knew about the Red Branch cycle. I have degraded Concobar forsooth by emphasising the *only* tale in which he appears in an evil light. Shade of Macha, what a fib! I also inform him that he has lost the power to distinguish between what is heroic in literature and what is not, on account of a quotation he makes from Cuculain. He confuses the big and gigantic with the heroic. I have claimed for drama that no subject is too great for treatment. He says the Red Branch [cycle] is. I point out Prometheus, greater than Cuculain. I tell him frankly he is not great

---

[1] *All-Ireland Review*, April 19, 1902, p. 100.
[2] AE's rejoinder was printed in the *United Irishman*. See also his letter to Yeats, April 19, 1902 (II). AE's rejoinder "The Dramatic Treatment of Legend" was reprinted in *Some Irish Essays* (1906) and in *Imaginations and Reveries* (1915), pp. 22-27.

enough to issue fiats to other literary men and accuse them of decadence in a muddle of confused and contradictory sentences. If he publishes it and replies I hope we will have a gorgeous row. Please look up *A.I.R.* this week. The letter "Ichabod" was written by a hysterical lady who accuses me of practising the *Black Art* on the audience when I chanted!!! She saw three black waves of darkness rolling down over the stage and audience and it made her ill. She does not mention this in her letter but has raved about it since. I feel filled with the pride of wickedness, almost a demon. Isn't it a delightful audience we get in Dublin. If I write another play I'll work in more magic. If you would like to join in the fray you might take up O'G. on the point of keeping legends from the common people. He thinks the crowd should have nothing to do with legends. The aristocratic tendency of O'Grady's mind lays him open to a crushing rejoinder. Why, it was the common people who preserved these stories and who made the reputation of his aristocracy. I think the crowd would not follow O'Grady in thinking the legendary literature should not be given to them. Kind regards to Lady Gregory. Yours sincerely, Geo. W. Russell.

TO W. B. YEATS   I.A.O.S.
                                                                 19.4.1902

My dear Yeats,

I suppressed my letter to O'Grady, as I did not, on second thoughts, like fighting with a friend. His objection I find was our giving the traditions to the "Rabble". I will write in the *United Irishman* on this point. I don't know what to say about Martyn's letter as I know nothing about acting, and have only the slightest knowledge of the ways of the stage. I intend doing all I can for *U.I.*, but I have very little time, I am so much away from Dublin. I am trying in my spare time to get up sketches for exhibition later on. I have got, at last, the "Serpents of Wisdom", which I long wanted to see, and they are glorious beings. They were watching over my baby's cot one night, and I now understand the serpent myths. I have decided to take the legend of the Children of Lir for a dramatic subject and am brooding over certain structural difficulties just now, but I expect they will come out all right. I would weave in a whole lot of druidism into it, and I could get a fine end.

I will try and get some musical person to take down the chants. But when I get them taken down as they have been before and repeated to me from the notes I do not recognise my chant, and there would be no use in forwarding it. However, someone may succeed in doing it right. I will want several chants for the Children of Lir and choruses and I am going to do the music myself in my own way, if I can get a few girls to understand. Yours sincerely, Geo. W. Russell

TO JAMES JOYCE[1]   [Mid-August 1902]

Dear Joyce,

Could you come on Monday evening[2] next to see me? I think it would be better than Sunday. No one will disturb us and I want to have a good talk with you. Please let me know if you can come then. I am threatened with an invasion of other folk on Sunday evening and it is impossible to talk while there is a general gathering of odds and ends of acquaintances. Yours sincerely, Geo. W. Russell

TO SARAH PURSER   22 Lincoln Place
                                                        15 Aug. 1902

Dear Miss Purser,

Thanks for your letter and cheque which I shall hand to Fay[3] on his return to Dublin on Sunday. He is in Cork stagemanaging some Gaelic Plays today. I am sure the account will be good by then. The fiery youths of the company are rehearsing up to 12 o'c and they have every intention of making Dublin quake. I cant go and start a bank while you are at Mallenmow I am sorry. Norman[4] is away for a couple of days, and I am Editor and Miss Mitchell[5] rolled into one. The latter is getting better and is in good spirits. She seems to be having a good time and will be back here 25th about. I expect to see my young genius[6] on Monday and will find out more about him. I wouldn't be his Messiah for a thousand million

---

[1] Printed in *My Brother's Keeper* by Stanislaus Joyce. See Note 4, page 229.

[2] Monday, August 18, 1902.

[3] F. J. Fay and W. G. Fay. *See* Note 5, page 229. *See also* William G. Fay and Catherine Carswell, *The Fays of the Abbey Theatre* (London, 1935: Rich & Cowan), and Gerard Fay's *The Abbey Theatre* (London, 1958: Hollis & Carter).

[4] H. F. Norman, editor of the *Irish Homestead*. (*See* Biographical Notes.)

[5] Susan Langstaff Mitchell, sub-editor of the *Irish Homestead*. (*See* Biographical Notes.)

[6] James A. Joyce. AE's account of their first meeting exists in some typed lecture-notes (undated, but probably written in 1930-1931), used for lectures in America. That typescript is owned by Mr Diarmuid Russell.

[42]

pounds. He would be always criticising the bad taste of his deity. Yours ever, Geo. W. Russell

TO W. B. YEATS   22 Lincoln Place
                                                     Monday [August 1902]
Dear W. B. Y.,

I have been so busy here that I do not know what the Fays are doing except that they are rehearsing very energetically. I expect to see W. Fay in a day or so and will talk to him about the matters referred to in your letter with which I agree. I heard nothing about the comedy by "Mise" before. I think however it stands no chance of being acted at present as I know they will hardly be able to get through the programme already fixed. I have been so busy that I was unable to get at Lady Gregory's pastel but hope to do so this week. My Sundays are engaged sitting to your father who is working on a portrait some eccentric American[1] wants painted of me.

I want you very much to meet a young fellow named Joyce[2] whom I wrote to Lady Gregory about half jestingly. He is an extremely clever boy who belongs to your clan more than to mine and more still to himself. But he has all the intellectual equipment, culture and education which all our other clever friends here lack. And I think writes amazingly well in prose though I believe he also writes verse and is engaged in writing a comedy which he expects will occupy him five years or thereabouts as he writes slowly. Moore who saw an article of this boy's says it is preposterously clever. Anyhow I think you would find this youth of 21 with his assurance and self-confidence rather interesting. He is I think certainly more promising than Magee.

I am glad to hear you are working on a poem about Maeve. I have escaped from my brief folly of play writing and am working away at lyrics which come rapidly after a long silence of a couple of years. I will write you after seeing Fay. Kind regards to Hyde[3] and Lady Gregory. Yours ever, Geo. W. Russell

[1] John Quinn. This portrait was presented to the Irish National Gallery by Quinn's executors. (*See also* Biographical Notes.)

[2] James Joyce.

[3] Douglas Hyde (in Ireland called *An Craoibin Aoibin*, "The Little Branch"), historian, folklorist and poet, born 1860, died July 12, 1949. Educated at Trinity College, Dublin, Dr Hyde promoted the revival of the Irish language by his own scholarship, and through lecturing to collect funds, in America. He collected, edited and translated *Love Songs of Connacht* (London, 1893: T. Fisher Unwin), which remains his best-known book. From 1938-1945 he was President of Éire.

TO JAMES JOYCE[1]   [early October 1902]

My dear Joyce,

Yeats will be in Dublin all this week and will be at the Antient Concert Rooms every night. He would like to meet you, and if you could come here on Tuesday at 5 o'c. I will bring you to his hotel. I told him I would try to get you to come at that hour if possible. If this will not suit you you could call some other time on him yourself with this letter. He is staying at Nassau Hotel, South Frederic Street. He will be glad to see you. Geo. W. Russell

TO JAMES JOYCE[2]
                                                     [? November 1902]
Dear Joyce,

I have written Miss Gonne and Lady Gregory, and will let you know anything further I may hear from them. George Moore is useless. I saw him today and he was in one of his bad moods, irritable about everything, and as I expected before I went, he said his friends in Paris would wonder why the devil he sent anybody to see them who was not in their craft. I think Miss Gonne is more hopeful as an acquaintance there. Yeats may know more people in Paris than I and I think you should write to him now and give him time to meet people before you go to London. If I can think of anybody or anything likely to help you then I will write you and hope to see you again before you go. Yours sincerely Geo. W. Russell

P.S. There was a M. Dubois who wrote an article in *Revue des 2 Mondes* (I think) about Irish literature modern writers, who is a professor in some College. Could you get a letter to him?

TO W. B. YEATS   25 Coulson Avenue
                                              Monday [? March 2, 1903]
Dear W. B. Y.,

I was looking at a couple of rehearsals of the *Hour Glass*[3] and it struck me that it was a little difficult to understand why the Wise Man remains

[1] Published in *My Brother's Keeper* by Stanislaus Joyce, p. 182.

[2] Published in *My Brother's Keeper* by Stanislaus Joyce, pp. 191-192.

[3] *The Hour-Glass* was first performed by the Irish National Theatre Society in the Molesworth Hall, on March 14, 1903. Lady Gregory's play *Twenty-Five* was played in the same programme. Yeats lectured the audience during the interval: his topic, "The Reform of the Theatre".

lamenting in his room though there are crowds without. He has only a few moments to find his believer and he sends messengers and remains himself. It is a little hard to believe and is not quite convincing as I saw it. Could you invent some reason for his remaining? This point is not observable when reading but is to my mind noticeable when it is acted.

Another point which of course you might justify to some extent by the only half developed materialism of your wise man, but which I think is somewhat out of keeping with his character as a despiser of all spiritual influences, is his references to the planetary influences. Of course in astrology the planets are gods, and when he speaks of the "amorous star" he speaks of the spiritual power which it symbolises. I do not think it is logical to disbelieve in God and the angels and to believe in the divine influence of the planets. I think he should be sceptic of these things also and tell how men before he came believed in love coming from the "amorous star" but that now it is simply a comely presence and the promise of bodily beauty which awakens love. I just jot these points down for your consideration; a line here and there would make it right if you think the criticism is correct. Kind regards to Lady Gregory. Yours ever, Geo. W. Russell

Miss Gonne came here on Friday and went to Tralee Saturday. I expect her back tomorrow. She looks very well and says she is quite recovered from her illness.

TO W. B. YEATS
25 Coulson Avenue
[? Tuesday April 28, 1903]

My dear Yeats,

On Tuesday last when I returned there was a wire from Mrs. McBride[1] saying she would be home that evening. This was contradicted by another about nine o'clock saying that she was not coming. I understand she will not be in Dublin until the first or second of May. It is possible, probable, I will be away from Dublin on the 1st, but may get back on the second May. I cannot be here. Would you like me to leave a note for her if I have to go away? My wife told me that Miss Young had a curious dream about Mrs. McB., seeing her all grey with a darkness about her, and that she herself had a dream about ten days ago in which Mrs. McB. came to

[1] Maud Gonne MacBride lived in a house adjacent to the Russell's, at 26 Coulson Avenue, from 1902-1906 inclusive.

her weeping, and saying she did not know what to do or where to hide herself. My wife in the dream asked her was she not going to stay in her house in Coulson Avenue, but she said "no, he would find me there." My wife had not the faintest idea who was referred to, and only mentioned the dream because I asked her was Mrs. McB. coming back. I think it strange as she has not the slightest knowledge of Mrs. McB's past relations with anyone, or any knowledge of McB.

I have been trying with great pleasure to turn a woman of the Sidhe into a Virgin for your sister to embroider on a banner[1]. I think if I was allowed to, I would do all the Sidhe as archangels and seraphim, and get all the auras. I would dearly love to make a faery chapel and put mystical figures so that the good catholics who went there would become worshippers of the Sidhe without knowing it.

George Moore called to see me last night and I mentioned about the conditions on which he might work on *Diarmuid and Grania*. He thought them reasonable, but I think the clause empowering you also to rewrite rather took away his desire to do anything at it himself. He said then he would think it over. I think he is regretting the incident of the "spoons" and I do not think will talk about it much longer. I have got a severe attack of influenza for the last couple of days and don't feel fit to write or do anything except paint, which I can always do. I will be here all this week. If Robert Gregory is passing through Dublin he might like to see the sketches here. With kind regards to Lady Gregory. Yours ever, Geo. W. Russell

TO W. B. YEATS   25 Coulson Avenue
[May 1903]

My dear Yeats,

It is a good many years since I have read a book which pleases me more than your *Ideas of Good and Evil*. I like it better than the *Celtic Twilight* or *The Secret Rose*. I think it will do more than anything you have yet written to bring the mystical interpretation of life into literature, not because your prose is as good as your verse, but because it shows the long meditation out of which your verse springs. The lightest lyrics will lose their isolation and gather a unity from the background of philosophy which will glimmer behind them for all readers of this book. I have been away

---

[1] For St Brendan's Cathedral, Loughrea, County Galway.

and have not yet had time to read it all but just write this to congratulate you unreservedly. I did not think I would like the book so well as I do for I had only read one or two of the essays before, but read together they throw a reflected light on each other and the book has a perfect unity. I have seen one or two glowing reviews and gather that it will be a great success. But better than a wide circulation in England will be it will give aims to the few here who are making ready for Armageddon. I wish you would think when writing new essays of making them a criticism of orthodox religion from the standpoint of an artist and mystic and lover of beauty. The orthodox priest or parson has survived science because his religion is too woolly to be hurt by a club, and has survived materialism because he is on the right side though with wrong weapons, but to attack him with the scorn of the artist and mystic would, I think, do much more. You might make a new religion of beauty, and the more arrogance and contempt you display in your references to the churches the better. The religions of the grocer and the counting house must be killed, I think I would like to write something on this myself, but the devil having appeared to me in the form of a wife and family it would so far as I see have to be a posthumous book, though if someone put me in a rage I would do it.

The company have come back with the majesty which does befit kings after their visit to London. Frank Fay looks wiser and more dignified and has gained in some magical way the impression of being six inches taller and a foot broader. I am delighted they did so well from all accounts. I am sure it was an immense relief to you. Had you frightened the London critics or was it genuine appreciation, or was it due to the union of hearts which by the way Mrs. MacBride rudely shocked last night in the most gorgeous row Dublin has had since Jubilee time. The Rotunda meeting was a free fight and two M.Ps are incapacitated. The *Freeman* tries to depreciate the effect of the row, but the *Irish Times* and *Express* and *Independent* give good reports and do justice to the scrimmage. Martyn[1] has heroism thrust on him and his stay in the Kildare St. Club becomes one of the humours of Dublin. He says it is becoming serious for him for if they expel him he won't be able anywhere else to get a bed for 2/6 a night so comfortably. Yours ever, Geo. W. Russell

P.S. I think Macmillan will get poems in U.S.A. Quinn writes they want them.

---

[1] Edward Martyn (1859-1923), the author. (*See* Biographical Notes.)

TO JOHN QUINN
25 Coulson Avenue
17 May 1903

You are a good friend. I wish I could do something to show you how much I appreciate the trouble you are taking on my behalf. . . . I think your Literary Society will do well. The exiles appreciate Ireland better than most who remain. I know Charles Johnston. He is very clever, very vain and really a good fellow. He was at school with Yeats, and, I believe, turned Willie's attention first to mysticism. He ought to write a good deal better than he does, but he never goes beyond himself. I always wonder whether there is any real C.J. under that smiling, handsome exterior, or only a bundle of mental attributes. He will make a courtly President. Send him back to Ireland. He promised to return. After his long stay there he ought to be fit for this country and his angles gone.

With regard to the Dun Emer press, Yeats and I fought over one poem and, both being stiff-necked, he suggested that I should make a selection of all my verses[1] instead for his sister, and this I am doing. It enables him to get rid of the poem in *The Divine Vision* series which he disliked (he never got beyond the second verse) and I think it better, perhaps, for his sister's sales that the book should only contain about forty of the best lyrics I have done. I anticipate another struggle with Willie as to what are the best, but we will probably compromise. He is his sister's literary adviser, and I am afraid if he will not let them print anything which is not on the level of a sacred book the output will be small. I would probably have yielded over the omission of the lyric[2] he objected to on account of the one word "big", but it was an essential part of the sequence and next poem "A Summer Night", which is one of the best of all, depended for its effect on it . . . Anyhow, it leaves me free to make any arrangements I like with Lane, unless Macmillan or whoever gets the book in U.S.A. would like to have the English sale as well. If they would it would be much better, for I am not satisfied with Lane. If you think Macmillan would like this you can offer him the English sale, which would probably help him off with a considerable part of his edition.

[1] *The Nuts of Knowledge* by AE, published December 1, 1903 (200 copies).
[2] Evidently the poem "A Memory" ("You remember, dear") printed in *The Divine Vision*, p. 55, and in *Collected Poems*, p. 112. The line is "How God was a big kind brother". "A Summer Night" was omitted from *The Nuts of Knowledge*, which contains thirty-two poems.

I like the pseudonym AE which I have always written and which is much better known than George Russell, but if you like you can put it *The Divine Vision and Other Poems by "A.E." (George Russell)*

This, I suppose, will meet your views. John Yeats has made another sketch of me which he likes better than the last and has asked me to send it to you. I think it is better myself. I am fierce occasionally, but not so fierce as in the first sketch, and am vain enough to wish this more placid likeness which I send would appear instead. However, you can do as you wish about this.

I suppose you will have seen Yeats' new book *Ideas of Good and Evil*, which I think will greatly advance his reputation. While I cannot often agree with his opinions, I think he is always most suggestive, and less fantastic and extravagant in his criticism than he was some years before. I think it will have great effect and will do much for us in Ireland. I believe I will have to go to Germany in July, for 3 weeks about, to make a report on some German agricultural associations. I hope your visit here will be after I return.

There is a foolish union of hearts which occurs periodically between this country and England which is not likely to do much good. Our uneducated people suppose that the new land bill will stop emigration. I know Ireland as well as most, and I know that emigration goes on from districts where the farmers have bought their holdings just as they did long ago. A ten acre farm, even with the rent 5/- an acre less won't support six or seven strapping boys and 2 or 3 girls and off they will go as before. When this becomes evident the. . . . *[remainder missing]*. Yours very sincerely, George W. Russell

TO JAMES H. COUSINS[1]   22 Lincoln Place
                                          [September 23, 1903]
Dear Cousins,

Please excuse my not replying sooner. I have been in country for a week and am off on Friday again for another week of lecturing. I will *give* you a painting with pleasure. Don't be a fool and offer to improverish yourself for what you can get for nothing. When I return at the end of next week I will look up my sketches and give you one. With kind regards. Yours, in a hurry, AE

[1] James Henry Sproull Cousins, the poet and Orientalist (1873-1956). (*See* Biographical Notes.)

25 Coulson Avenue
                                                                      3.11.03

Dear Mr Mosher,

I have to thank you for the very charming little edition of Yeats *Land of Heart's Desire* and for other Bibelots.[2] I have been so busy during the past months that I have neglected all my correspondence and am just working off arrears. I notice you announce a new edition of *Homeward Songs* in the spring at which I am much pleased. I will never be so charmingly bound and printed anywhere again unless you undertake to improve on your past. I hope you reissue it because people want it. I have just corrected the proofs of a new book of lyrics *The Divine Vision*[3] which Macmillans are publishing over here. I think it is a more satisfactory book than *The Earth Breath* but it is very difficult to judge of one's own work. People who read any book of an author first are always inclined to like it the best because it first revealed a new way of looking at things. However, I think I have some good lyrics in the new book. I am also making a selection from lyrics written by young poets who are friends of mine here some of which I think are beautiful and all interesting from the historical literary point of view as showing the change of thought since the patriotic poets of Davis's time. The tendency here is to deal more with spiritual subjects and the spiritual side of nationality. One of the young writers Patrick Colum will I think be our next great literary figure in Ireland. He is only twenty-one and is teeming with ideas which crowd each other too much to allow of a perfect art at present. Another boy named Joyce writes with perfect art poems as delicate and dainty as Watteau pictures, and a curious young fellow named Starkey[4] has a strain of genius but is too shy and self mistrustful to ever take himself seriously. There is a girl named Alice Milligan[5] who has written better verses I think than any of our women writers but who is too lazy to publish them anywhere except in local papers where she forgets all about them. You could get an idea of her quality from a little play *The Last Feast of the Fianna* which is published by David Nutt and which was acted by the Literary Society here. It is worthy of a place in your Bibelot. Yeats thinks as highly as I do of its beauty. Miss Yeats book *The Nuts of*

---

[1] Thomas Bird Mosher (1852-1923), American publisher.
[2] Published serially at Portland, Maine. See this editor's *Bibliography*.
[3] Published January 1904.
[4] James Sullivan Starkey (1879-1956). (*See* Biographical Notes.)
[5] Alice L. Milligan. (*See* Biographical Notes.)

Knowledge will I think look nice, much better than her first printing of Willie Yeats' poems *In the Seven Woods*. The edition is already almost subscribed for before the book is ready. With kind regards, Yours very sincerely, Geo. W. Russell

TO THE EDITOR OF THE *ALL-IRELAND REVIEW*[1]

[March 1904]

Sir,

A RURAL LIBRARY ASSOCIATION FOR IRELAND

Will you kindly allow us to make known to your numerous readers that in view of the facilities given to Rural District Councils in Ireland by the Public Libraries (Ireland) Act of 1902, steps are being taken to form a Rural Library Association in Ireland with a view to spreading information on the subject, and promoting the formation of such libraries throughout the country. It is believed that such institutions, besides making the sources of scientific and technical knowledge more available to the workers of Ireland than at present, will have a valuable social and educative influence by encouraging the taste for and enlarging the facilities for reading wholesome literature. The powers given by the Act of 1902 have, as yet, been very slightly outlined; partly, in all probability, because they have never been brought to the knowledge of those concerned, and, partly, because Rural Councils are, in most cases, inexperienced in the procedure necessary to set the Act in effective operation. The Rural Libraries Association proposes, among its principal objects, to disseminate information as to the powers conferred on local government bodies, to outline a scheme of library organization applicable to almost any rural district, and to draw up a list of such books as might be considered indispensable for any Rural Irish Library. A meeting of the supporters of the project will be held about Easter, and in the meantime it is requested that any persons interested in the proposals and willing to join the association will communicate with the Provisional Hon. Secretaries at 26, Dawson Chambers, Dawson St., Dublin.

Provisional Committee. - Stephen Gwynn, Douglas Hyde, the Lord

---

[1] Text from the *All-Ireland Review*, April 2, 1904, p. 160.

Letters from AE

Monteagle, D. J. O'Donoghue,[1] T. W. Lyster, T. W. Rolleston, Hugh
Law, M.P.,[2] Rev. J. O'Donovan, C.C.
Hon Secs.–J. P. Boland, M.P.: G. W. Russell

TO W. B. YEATS   25 Coulson Avenue
                                          Wednesday [? April 1904]
Private
My dear Yeats,

I will alter rule[3] about reading committee to read "shall not be more
than five in number". This will leave you free to elect one or two if you
like. I think it better not to make W. Fay an ex-officio member but to
request his attendance at meetings as I have done in rules. The secretary
also attends but merely to record and has no vote. The mere fact of the
attendance of an officer being required does not entitle him to a vote,
and it would break through principle of not allowing any but general
members to take part in government or policy of society. You can get all
the information you want from him without making him a member. I
dont think Synge's suggestion about Gwynn is of any importance, as if
Gwynn is elected on business committee and will work he is practical
enough. You can't restrict the society merely to authors or actors unless
you want to have a business smash. What the dickens do you know about
accounts, or Synge, or Colm or Lady Gregory? I will take my "davy"
that not one of you could say whether a statement of accounts was
correctly made out or not. Keohler[4] could and so could Ryan,[5] if the
latter would work. It is the messy way business was done which was the
main trouble in the old system. I will alter the rule about the stage
manager being appointed by the actors. I don't feel very strongly one
way or the other about it. Of course what you say about never accepting
another stage manager is nonsense. If you found anyone better you would
want him. Anyhow he is the best you can get now and I dont think it
likely you will ever get a better actor at any time. By the way you will have

---

[1] D. J. O'Donoghue (1866-1917), librarian of University College, Dublin, from 1909.
He wrote *The Poets of Ireland, a biographical Dictionary* (Dublin, 1892-1893; new
edition, 1912), etc.

[2] Hugh Alexander Law, barrister and Irish M.P. (1872-1943). (*See* Biographical
Notes.)

[3] See Note 5, page 229.

[4] Thomas Goodwin Keohler, a company secretary. (*See* Biographical Notes.)

[5] Frederick Ryan; first secretary of the Society.

to define clearly the rules of stage-manager and secretary in the future. Under the rules the secretarial duties are those required of any secretary under the Act, but in a small society like yours where there is a lot to do and few paid people you must have some private understanding as to the *execution of business*. I have provided for the election of a *business manager* which office may be united either with the stage managership or the secretaryship. There is a great deal of work which Roberts[1] used to do, like getting advertisements for programmes, seeing about printing, posters, getting bills in, arranging advertisements none of which are strictly secretarial work. Roberts complained that Fay would never do any of these things, and when it was suggested at committee that Fay should do some of them as having more time Frank Fay burst into one of his rages at stage manager being asked to get advertisements, an unheard of innovation. There will be friction on this point. Personally I think that the paid people should do this, and that Fay should not refuse to do something as he did once to Roberts because it interfered with his painting lessons. I think you will have to instruct business committee to define the peculiar duties of each. I think all that work which Roberts did is too much to expect an unpaid official to do. He took it up when he was paid and he had to do it since. If you are paying three actors between them they should be made to do the kind of work I mentioned except perhaps the printing of the programmes where Roberts who has taste in such matters would do it far better. Remember you must define clearly and definitely or you will have rows and work undone. Personally I would make Roberts merely secretary with charge of the printing and let the paid people do the rest. Of course if Roberts will continue to do the work it would save trouble but I hardly think he could be asked to do so as it will increase greatly with the increasing number of performances the employment of paid actors will enable the Society to give. I have about ten years experience of the rows between managers and secretaries in eight hundred societies and I tell you the only way to get things done is to define the work of each in an agreement. Otherwise each will be laying the blame for things not attended to on each other as Roberts and Fay do now. I have heard them complain about each other for hours. Dont let their

---

[1] George Roberts, second secretary of the Society. Miss A. E. F. Horniman paid him one pound weekly for his duties; presumably after December 11, 1904, date of a letter to Miss Horniman, signed by the members of the Theatre Society (including Yeats, Synge, Lady Gregory, S. L. Gwynn, and AE and others): printed in Maire Nic Shiubhlaigh's *The Splendid Years*, pp. 199-200.

work depend much on each others work or there will be more. If Roberts is merely secretary keeps accounts, minutes, summons meetings, he will have no opportunity to row with Fay or Fay with him. It could not be bettered by either of them being out. Things like this always will occur when the duties of each are ill defined. It is human nature. I have told Roberts to summon meeting. I will speak to Norman[1] and Miss Laird[2] but not now. Norman is away for three or four weeks and I dont think Miss Laird is inclined at present to resign. I have not spoken to her about the changes but after they are through she may feel she is rather out of it and may volunteer. I will sound her later on and suggest it to her. I cant think either of them will ever bother about the Society in the future.

Your sister asked me about another work[3] to be done after Lady Gregory's. I drew up a rough list of poems, which I might alter as I did it in a hurry for her. I might possibly find better poems if I looked over what I have more carefully. George Russell

TO THE EDITOR OF THE *IRISH TIMES*   [December 1904][4]

A MODERN ART GALLERY FOR DUBLIN

We, the undersigned Irish writers ask our friends and readers to help us in a most urgent matter. We are most anxious to keep in Ireland the extraordinarily important collection of pictures by modern–chiefly modern French artists–now being exhibited at the Royal Hibernian Academy, chosen by experts from the Staats-Forbes and Durand-Ruel Collections, and admitted to be the finest representation of modern French art outside Paris.

Among the pictures there are twelve paintings by Corot, fourteen by Constable, sixteen drawings by Millet, and many works by Daubigny,

---

[1] Harry Felix Norman (1868-1947). (*See* Biographical Notes.)
[2] Helen S. Laird, a member of the Dublin Theosophical lodge. In 1905 married Mr Constantine Peter Curran, SC.
[3] *A Book of Saints and Wonders*, by Lady Gregory; finished at the Dún Emer Press, August 1906, published September 10. AE's *By Still Waters*, finished November 1906, published December 14.
[4] From a typewritten copy. See *Hugh Lane and his Pictures* by Dr Thomas Bodkin (1934 edn.), pp. 12-13. Printed in the *Irish Times* (Dublin), January 5, 1905. See other letters: December 2, 3, 8, 9, 21, 23, 1904 and January 13, 1905. Exhibition reviewed November 21. See also a pamphlet, *Proposed Gallery of Modern Art for Dublin. Report of Proceedings at a Public Meeting held 9th February, 1906* (Dublin, 1906); meeting attended by AE.

Diaz, Troyon, Courbet, Fantin-Latour, Whistler, Bastien-Lepage, Israels, Mauve and Marie. There are also the two great pictures by Manet, *The Strolling Musician*, and the *Portrait of Eva Gonzales;* the *Beheading of John the Baptist*, by Puvis de Chavannes, considered by him as his masterpiece, and three fine examples of Claude Monet.

Should it be impossible to raise the £30,000 or £40,000 necessary to buy all the pictures, we may at least keep some of the best of them, and some thousands of pounds have been already collected in Ireland.

Donations for the Purchase Fund will be gratefully received by any of us, or by the Hon. Treasurer, Modern Art Gallery, c/o The Hibernian Bank, Dublin.

(Signed): Jane Barlow, Augusta Gregory, S. H. Butcher, Douglas Hyde, Edith Oe. Somerville, Martin Ross, Emily Lawless, W. B. Yeats, Geo. W. Russell ("AE")

TO T. B. MOSHER   25 Coulson Avenue
                                    Wednesday [? April 1905]

My dear Mr. Mosher,

You are always kind. If you are as kind to all your distant authors as to me there must be at least one publisher for whom they have a good word. I am forwarding a copy of the little book to Miss Eva Gore Booth[1] who has published through Longmans a collection of lyrics *The One and the Many*[2] which have many good verses but which are now and then rather careless in technique. She is really of the order of poets. She is the daughter of Sir Henry Gore Booth, and has chosen to desert the most beautiful home in Ireland to work among the factory girls in Manchester. A tall slim defiant girl with enough ideas to stock half a dozen poetesses but too defiant of criticism of her technique at present to do the perfect things she might. I asked Seumas O'Sullivan to send you a little book of lyrics called *The Twilight People*[3] which contains some delicate verse with a real if faint beauty. If he forgot let me know and I will send you a copy. It might present you with a lyric or two for future anthologies. We have a young scamp named Joyce here who writes with a more perfect art than anyone except Yeats who is I believe going to publish a book of lyrics. He gave it to Grant Richards who collapsed, and I have not heard

---

[1] Eva Gore-Booth (1870-1926). (*See* Biographical Notes.)
[2] Published 1904.   [3] Published March 1905.

anything more of it as the poet has decamped to the continent with a barmaid. It will be a good book when it appears.[1] The little book *New Songs*[2] has to my astonishment gone into a third edition of 500. I picked up most of the poems out of mss lying about in my room, and which were given to me by young boys and girls who know I have a love for any kind of poetry. I hardly agree with you that Miss Gore Booth's verses charming as they were, were the best. Colum's poems rude as they are reveal a talent which I think one day Europe will recognise. I am rather sorry he is throwing himself into drama, I like verse better, but Yeats thinks with me that this boy if he lives has a great future before him. I am horribly busy organising agriculture, and inspiring farmers to do their business properly, when I am most melancholy in my soul, but an occasional lyric drops between the busy days. Most of our writers here are turning their attention to drama. I feel rather sorry I ever helped to get up the Irish National Theatre Society. If I had forseen the vortex it created drawing in half a score of good writers to it and [to] write plays which don't interest me I would have seen it perish in babyhood before I would have spent so much precious time and energy on it.

I heard great praises of you from a Mrs Simeon Ford of New York who was over here lately as the only American publisher of any independence who only published what he liked. With kind regards, Yours sincerely, Geo. W. Russell

TO CLIFFORD BAX[3]   25 Coulson Avenue
                                                  [*postmark* July 4, 1905]

Dear Clifford Bax,

It is a great pleasure to get a letter like yours. So many people care for one's work only because of the art in it that it is a real joy to find now and then someone who is more concerned about the life than the form. I have no interest in people who find in literature anything but an avenue to life. Every thought or mood is the opening or closing of a door to the divine world, and who is there we would not laugh at who went to a door and

---

[1] *Chamber Music*, published by Elkin Mathews (? May 1907). Professor Richard Ellmann notes: Joyce left Ireland first at the end of November 1902, stopped briefly in London, then went to Paris. He remained there until Good Friday, 1903, when he returned to Dublin. On October 8, 1904 he left with Nora Barnacle, for Zürich.

[2] Published April 1904.

[3] Clifford Bax (b. 1886) the English dramatist, brother of the composer Sir Arnold Bax. (*See* Biographical Notes.)

only admired or looked at it forgetting its uses. Art for arts sake is considering the door as a decoration and not for its uses in the house of life. I agree with you about English poetry for all its splendour that it moves in a world of illusion because of its lack of fundamental ideas. I except Shelley, Wordsworth and Blake. Myself, I prefer the Sufi poetry to any because of its intoxication with divine things; because romance and beauty and love which in our literature move on a path of their own are in Eastern mystical poetry rapt up into eternal things. I read hardly anything else for years when I was young but Eastern literature and I have never since been able really to enjoy the literature of Europe. I thought when I was young I would be able to bring into our literature in Ireland that interior life, but it needs a much bigger nature than mine and a better artist to do this. The book of my own which I like best is *Homeward, Songs by the Way*, which is published by John Lane, Bodley Head, Vigo Street, London, 2/6. There is another book of prose stories, very short, the first things I ever wrote almost, some of which I think good. It is called *The Mask of Apollo and other stories*, published by Whaley and Co., Dawson Chambers, Dawson Street, Dublin. 2/6. Both of these are in print still. I think you will like *Homeward Songs* better than *The Earth Breath* or *The Divine Vision*, most people do. I hope I will meet you when you are next in Ireland. With kind regards. Yours sincerely, Geo. W. Russell

Though I place this letter in Dublin I am writing on the top of a hill in county Donegal where your letter has followed me. I am here for a holiday. It is an enchanted country.

TO LORD DUNSANY[1]   17 Rathgar Avenue, Rathgar
                                              Saturday [1906?]

Dear Lord Dunsany,

I am sorry I missed you yesterday. I have taken a new house and therefore cannot come to Dunsany[2] this week. The rearrangement of books, pictures and the squeezing of my personality into its new surroundings will occupy my Saturday and my Sabbath. I will go next Saturday if the weather is fine. I am most curious about your new pastels.

[1] Edward J. M. D. Plunkett, 18th Baron Dunsany, born 1878, died in Dublin, October 25, 1957; the story-teller, poet and dramatist. (*See* Biographical Notes.)
[2] Dunsany Castle, county Meath.

There are a few more tricks which you can use in working them. The best effects are got by dividing the colours not by the flat use of them which I showed you first. I read your contribution to the new miscellany which I liked. I think all these stories would however gain greatly in their power if you mastered some one system of philosophic thought and used your own names, cities, countries, deities, &c, as the means of expression. At the back of the little book of stories[1] which I left with you there was the Vedantic system and I utilised it in all the tales. Any other system would do as well as the human imagination nearly always builds up the same formula, but it is a good thing to master the most complete as it enormously increases your appeal to thoughtful readers. You would not find much difficulty in doing this. Your city of the gods would correspond to Swargam in the Brahmin system, to Tir-nan-oge in the old Irish, to the Heart of the Heavens in the Aztec system and it has its correspondences in almost every system devised by the human mind. But in all these systems there was a kind of divinely logical necessity for the divine city and it is the logical necessity which gave the ideas of the old religion their power over the human imagination. When a man reads a fanciful tale in which he recognises a subtle undercurrent of reference to world old ideas he if he is an intellectual man settles himself down to enjoy it and respects the writer as being more than fanciful. But I can go into this better when I see you as I hope to next week. Yours sincerely, Geo. W. Russell

TO OLIVER ELTON[2]

17 Rathgar Avenue
Saturday [? May 4, 1907]

My dear Elton,

I was very glad to get your letter. I will see Starkey on tomorrow and will talk the whole matter over with him. I had already spoken to him and I think the real difficulty is one of ways and means. I know he would be glad to go. However he will write to you himself after consideration. He is a most lovable person but I feel in despair about his material circumstances as he seems utterly incapable of looking after himself. He seems like a kind of half incarnated being still more influenced by atmosphere, visions, winds, rythms [*sic*] abstractions, essences than by the

---

[1] *The Mask of Apollo*, by AE.

[2] Oliver Elton (1861-1945), Professor of English Literature at Liverpool University, 1900-1925. (*See also* Note 6, p. 230.)

world he moves in. He would busy himself to the verge of illness for a dream's sake but would not work an hour to advance his own position. The spirit will repay him but I expect his friends will always while he lives be anxiously speculating as to how he will live. I am a little afraid he is one of those who

> *long to travel back*
> *and tread once more the ancient track*

rather than one of those who would make this world into the likeness of the kingdom of light, and to whom its conquest is an object and who labour and work here for a future. It is the difference between the visionary and the hero. But I suppose they are all in the same army if we knew their work rightly. Your dream interests me. I think I would explain its origin otherwise. If I hear three English words, being a foreigner and know their meaning and use them, the three words are not the cause of my speech but the interior will. I know the words "door" "shut" "the". I hear them and somebody explains their meaning. Then I say writing them "Shut the door". The fact that I learnt the words is not the cause of my speech but the desire to have the door shut. The spirit is always speaking to us in sleep or vision and it uses the images of memory some-times but not so often as it uses images created by its energy. I could never believe that all vision or imagination was made up out of the images of memory. The creative will has other things to draw on. Try with one million photographs to make up one coherent image of a man, patch it any way you like and it will only be a patch work and will have no genuine illusion. The shadow will be wrong here, the proportions wrong there, this picture will not blend with that. But in my dreams I see vividly giants in brazen armour rushing up a hillside swinging great bells of brass by chains and the light dances on their armour, their faces glint like life, the shadows change on the ground, the blue hills beyond are full of variety and mystery. It is like life but I never saw anything like it in life. I have seen men mountains and perhaps a picture of brass armour but these pictures of memory are not fused in my dream picture. I recognise not one feature. All is [nearly *deleted*] new. If I tried to draw it I could not. It would be the labour of months. But the imagination projects it suddenly perfect like an image in the *camera obscura* and I feel imagination and memory are creatures dwelling in two different worlds, and if you brood patiently over your dream and try to picture to yourself what it is made your memories into one picture, how it was done without [your *deleted*] conscious effort of yours into a [coherent *deleted*] new coherency you will get troubled over your explanation and may try to explain it otherwise. But this is wandering away, and the speculation would lead us into the "Halls of Los" as Blake would call the memory of the Universe. I was glad to read your dream and was so interested that I speculated about it as I have written. I hope Starkey will be roused by your letter to think about his future. It is very kind of you to take so much interest in him. We all do and I don't know what conclusion the others have come to but I feel it is not for us. "God builds the nest of the blind bird." Yours sincerely, Geo. W. Russell

TO CHARLES WEEKES   17 Rathgar Avenue
                                                    [late May, 1907]
My dear Charlie,

This is Friday which I devote to clearing off my personal correspondence. I have so many business letters to write on other days that I have not the heart to write any on my own account. I guessed that Davis capitalist shrank from investing money on such a slender thing as my Watts essay. As a man of business I would have done the same.

I don't know what T. W. Russell[1] will be like. Anyhow I have nothing to do with him. I am not a Department Official I am a free lance in journalism running the *Irish Homestead* without lett hindrance or advice from anybody. I may possibly turn the paper into something important later on. I am devising plans for its future development.

My dear Honey, don't worry about me "coming along", I will never please you for between ourselves literature does not interest me enough to make me anxious to work hard at it. I simply want to live a natural energetic life and if a poem ever takes me along the way I will welcome it but won't go out of my way to look for one. If the Lord wants me to write anything special he will take me by the back of my neck and force me. I find no inward compulsion and take this as a sign that he has nothing special to do.

To tell the truth I am interested in new movements in Ireland so much and in pulling strings and in pulling red herrings along undesirable tracks that I don't feel I want to do anything else. I paint in my spare moments and keep an artistic soul alive. I have always an uncertainty

[1] T. W. Russell. See footnote to letter dated January 23, 1913, to A. J. Balfour, p. 80.

about ways and means but I can't say I have any bother. I suppose I am too placid to feel nervous about the future until I am actually hungry or out at elbows.

My dear boy, a man's success or failure is always with his own soul. You would like to see me well known, writing wise and beautiful books, hailed by the applause of the best critics. I might be all this and a failure in my own eyes, and wretched and unhappy. I am working for causes I feel to be good. I don't care in the least for recognition. In fact I loathe any personal publicity. I can't say that I have lived up to my highest possibilities. Nobody does, but I have not sunk to my worst, and many people do. I will go back to the stars without any flourish of trumpets, but I won't weep as I go back or whine about circumstances. Don't expect anything from me. I am not going anywhere I can be seen. But always think I have an affection for you which I hope you can feel. This is all very unsatisfactory but I have a conscience still and can't pretend I am going to do things which I can't do. Kind regards to Mrs. Charlie and Dan. Yours affectionately, Geo. W. Russell

TO SUSAN L. MITCHELL[1] 22 Lincoln Place
28.12.07

My dear Twilight auraed Slieveen,[2]
  Your accomplice told me you wanted me to write to you while you were in Sligo. But surely to write to one in the neighbourhood of the great mountain[3] would be as unfit as to retail the gossip of earth to a blessed angel. It is you who should write and shower blessings with a prodigal hand on those unhappy ones who have no mountain with a fount of gold and gods dwelling therein. However as we carry with us our own nature, and heaven and the nether world are really everywhere, I just send you this, hoping (what's the phrase?) hoping "that this will find you as it leaves me"!!–I mean in gay mood not any earthly comparison, as it leaves me clad in the garments of my sex, and I do not think you would look well in coat and trousers. But the "good people" have been truly good to me and have filled the "temple" with pictures of themselves and I wish you nothing better than the soft colours of faery around your heart. Speak to my friend the mountain for me. Say it was I who went by

---

[1] From a typed copy.
[2] Susan Langstaff Mitchell.
[3] The mountain: Ben Bulben.

hurriedly in a car and had no time to stay a week ago, but that I heard the melody floating out of the old house of the gods and it made me feel for a moment at home and in the heart and away from the arid waste of the world. Say I am trying to bring back its ancient day and that I hope it will be good to you. Ever yours fraternally, A.E.

TO LORD DUNSANY   The *Irish Homestead*
                                                    3 February 1908

Dear Dunsany,

I was talking to Hannay[1] and told him several plots for stories which I had invented and which I did not want to use myself. I told him he might use any of them. I believe the same evening I told him your story about Jones or Brown or Robinson having died and gone before his maker and about his having invented excuses and at last seeing God in his own image the one God he could not deceive and sinking back to the nether regions. You had told me this story some months ago and I was so delighted with it that I retold it to Hannay. Hannay got confused between my plot and your story and wrote two yarns using one of my plots and also the tale of Jones which was yours and when he came up to Dublin a couple of days ago he announced that he had written the two stories from my plots. I told him only one was mine and he got exceedingly agitated, and I believe has written to the magazine to stop it. Between ourselves, I think he also took a plot of mine which I don't remember telling him he might use. I am sorry about the confusion but it is not really my fault as I told him at the time the Jones story was yours and said I thought you could write delightful things in that vein if you tried. I told him so many stories that he must have got confused after a month or two when he began to write and could not remember which was which. I suppose he will let me know if he gets it back or will write to you. Probably he has changed it beyond recognition. Yours sincerely, Geo. W. Russell

Miss Mitchell who was with Hannay when I told him the Jones yarn remembers I told him it was yours, but his memory has got mixed up over it.

[1] Rev. J. O. Hannay (1865-1950) wrote many light novels under the pseudonym George A. Birmingham. (*See* Biographical Notes.)

1 *October* 1908

TO SIR HUGH LANE[1]

The *Irish Homestead*
28 Clare Street
22 Feb. 1908

My dear Lane,

Thanks for letter and enclosure. I cannot remember now what picture[2] of Madame Markievicz's I thought was good but I think I could find out and get it up to my house when you could see it without her knowledge and judge whether it is a picture you would like to put in rather than the doubtful "Madame Markievicz". I will begin writing about the pictures as soon as I feel well enough. I have to wash out the tunnel between my mouth and nose every day and it gives me a frightful cold for a couple of hours after. I think it is the lotion is very powerful, but it leaves my head so limp that my brains don't work. However I hope it won't be necessary for more than another fortnight or three weeks at the most. It is damned slow work massacring microbes in a hole in ones bones. There is always some Noah among them to escape the deluge and breed a new family.

I hope you will come back to Dublin soon. You are one of the few people alive in Ireland. Most of us are posthumous and ought to be buried long ago. Yours sincerely, George Russell

TO JOHN QUINN

17 Rathgar Avenue
1st October 1908

My dear Quinn,

Moore is still in Dublin, still bidding eternal farewells to Ireland, and I think he intends to stay here as long as he lives. The "farewell book" has been interrupted by the rewriting of *Evelyn Innes*, from which I have now disappeared, (thank heaven!) and the re-writing of *Sister Teresa*, but I think he expects to have it ready at the beginning of next year. He will certainly cause some amusement, as Moore says, "one half of Dublin is afraid that it will be in the book, and the other is afraid that it won't". Though I have never quarrelled with him and we are very good friends, I should be just as glad if I were out. I had to remonstrate with him furiously because he had attributed his conversion to protestantism to my influence, in one chapter of the book. He said that when he came over to

[1] Hugh Percy Lane, the art collector (1875-1915). (*See* Biographical Notes.)
[2] Hugh Lane exhibited sixteen paintings by French artists, from his own collection, in the Municipal Gallery, Harcourt Street, Dublin when it was opened on January 20, 1908.

Ireland "dear AE used to sit sadly looking at me out of his pantheistic eyes whenever I spoke of working in friendship with the priests." It is quite true I did, but I didn't want it mentioned. I don't know what other points his friendship may have packed up in the book. Willie Yeats, I think, feels a little uneasy about it, and I know a great many other people do, including Gill, Rolleston, Edward Martyn and a number of others. . . .

I am sending you a little book just published, *Aids to the Immortality of Certain Persons in Ireland*,[1] charitably administered by Susan Mitchell. I think you met my sub-editress when you were over here? I think it is very clever, although I do not know whether you will be able to follow the jokes, which depend so much on local knowledge of the little squabbles and rows in literary society in Ireland. The design on the cover, drawn by Miss [Beatrice] Elvery,[2] includes Edward Martyn, Yeats, Geo. Moore, Anthony MacDonnell, Douglas Hyde, myself, Plunkett, Hugh Lane, Billy Orpen and Shawe Taylor.

I had a very interesting accidental meeting with Bernard Shaw the day before yesterday. He talked for 25 minutes neither of us knowing who the other person was. I found a stranger in the National Gallery, who asked me a question about some picture,[3] and we got into an animated conversation. I thought this elderly gentleman, a very intelligent person. I hope to heaven he retained a similar impression of me, but I only learnt the same night that it was Shaw, who was passing through Dublin, not having been there for 35 years. He saw my portrait in the Municipal Gallery and told Jack Yeats, whom he met by accident there, that he had been speaking to a gentleman like the portrait while he was in the National Gallery. He was very amusing in his conversations; talked of Whistler a good deal, said that Whistler was frightfully stupid; that he (Bernard Shaw) was earning his living as an art critic at the time that the famous action *Whistler* v. *Ruskin* came off and he backed up Whistler in every way he could, but Whistler was so abominably stupid, standing on his dignity as an artist and all that kind of nonsense, when what he should have done was to have gone to a British Jury and said "I am a tradesman like yourselves, I am earning my money by hard work, and this man

---

[1] Published 1908. Inscribed on the half-title "John Quinn from one of the people who has received some slight 'aid'. 1 Oct 1908". (Quinn Sale, 1924: 8 dollars.)

[2] Beatrice Elvery, now Lady Glenavy.

[3] Hogarth's "Portrait Group" which includes King George the Second and Queen Caroline. See "A visit to our National Gallery" by Irene Haugh in *The Irish Monthly* (Dublin), vol. 60, no. 713 (pp. 693-8), p. 695 (November 1932).

Ruskin, wants to take my living from me." If he had made this appeal to the Jury, Shaw says Whistler would have got £10,000 damages.

Turning to the other matters which you mention, I quite agree with you that J. B. Y. is altogether past the time for any new adventures in strange countries. His daughters want him back and are alarmed about his long absence.[1] I think they have done their utmost to induce him to return, though probably he would not have told you. I see both the girls very often and they tell me all the news about their "Pilgrim Father" as they call him. I recommended them to cable "Family all dying. Come to receive last messages". But they said he would not come for that, and I don't know what will bring him. Yours sincerely, Geo. W. Russell

TO KATHARINE TYNAN HINKSON   28 Clare Street
Friday [*Postmark:* Dublin, December 19, 1908]

My dear Katharine Tynan,

I was delighted with some of the poems in *Experiences*.[2] I like "Memory" perhaps the best of any of them because I have a memory of your good father stored away. You have such a wholesome kind of heart. Nearly all the writers I know give one the impression of having a blight somewhere or a cancer in their heart and their sadness seems the melancholly of disease rather than the natural sorrow of life. I don't know how you manage to keep so sunny all through. I have not written more than two cheerful poems in my life and I would love to write cheerful poetry more than anything. But no matter how I begin or what ticket I get at starting, I am always in my verse, discharged at the town of Melancholy and can't go any further and personally I am cheerful enough. I have discovered a new young poet in a young fellow named James Stephens[3] who has a real original note in him. He has had the devil of a time poor fellow works about fourteen hours a day for twenty shillings a week and is glad to get it. Was out of work for over a year once and went hungry and homeless and was saved from starving by a woman who sold fruit on a street stall. Good education for the soul sometimes but bad for the body. I am going to try to get Maunsels to bring out a book of his lyrics next year. The greatest

---

[1] John B. Yeats remained in America from early 1908 until his death, February 2, 1922. See his *Letters to his Son W. B. Yeats, and others*, edited by J. M. Hone (London, January 1944. Faber).

[2] Published by A. H. Bullen, December 1908.

[3] (*See* Biographical Notes.)

pleasure I find in life is discovering new young poets. With kind regards from Yours ever sincerely, Geo. W. Russell

TO JOHN QUINN   17 Rathgar Avenue
                                                                    27th April 1909

My dear Quinn,

I think Yeats feels Synge's death very much.[1] He was much more Yeats' friend than mine. I did not know him very well, though I liked him much from the little I knew him. I was so completely out of theatrical matters for the last four years since Synge came to write for the Abbey, that I hardly ever met Synge or even Yeats. Yeats was up with me the other night and told me that Synge's executor is a Plymouth Brother and that he regards Synge's writing with grave disapproval. He threatens to go over all Synge's plays and to expurgate passages which he thinks are objectionable. He cannot injure what is already published, but the unpublished manuscripts he may be able to ruin. Vandalism of this kind arouses one's rage to the last degree, but I suggested to Lady Gregory that they might be able to look over the manuscripts and get copies made of them, so that whenever the Plymouth Brother departs this life and goes to the Hell he deserves for his religion and tastes, they may be reprinted.

I will send you the little book by James Stephens (*Insurrections*,[2] it is called) in a couple of weeks time. He is quite a boy, but I think he has great promise, and even since the selection made was set up he has done some half dozen things which are better almost than anything in the book, only it is too late now to have them inserted as the poems are with the printers.

There was no mask taken of Synge. There is a portrait in the Municipal Gallery[3] and I have no doubt that from photographs a relief might be done by Hughes, but I think all these after-death portraits are very unsatisfactory. I read your letter in the New York paper you sent and think it says beautifully what should be said. I think you have got a wrong idea about the politicians' hatred of Synge. Synge personally was never unpopular with them, or with anybody, and his plays were always received with great enthusiasm. The row at the Abbey was really a newspaper row, which got its ferocity to a great extent from certain defences made

[1] Synge died March 24, 1909.
[2] Published May 1909.
[3] The fine portrait by John B. Yeats. An iconography is printed in *J. M. Synge and the Irish Theatre* by M. Bourgeois, p. 297 (London, 1913: Constable).

by unpopular people like "Pat" the journalist, who would have it that the *Playboy* was a most accurate representation of Irish Life, and some of these apologies were put in such an offensive spirit that they helped on the row, and a lot of young devils, who like kicking up a shindy in the Theatre, helped it out. On the first night of the performance,[1] at which I was present there was a great deal of applause, and only just at the last a little hissing or booing over one or two of the phrases, and I am convinced that it would never have been much worse than that only for the defenders, who almost went to the point of stating that any Irish family would welcome a parricide. But Synge personally was never unpopular, and the fact was shown by the *Riders of the Sea*, which was performed every evening before the *Playboy*, being received with tumultuous applause. The *Playboy* is a miraculous piece of writing, but I think, owing to the subject it required to be acted with a great deal of phantasy, and this phantasy was in all the actors and the audience were carried along with it until the Playboy's father came in with his head bandaged and he looked so realistic and so like a poor battered old man that the audience got a chill and felt that they were really making a jest of parricide and father-beating. If in this 1st performance the father of the Playboy had been acted more fantastically and less realistically, I am convinced that there would have been no row of any kind. Synge has left a play *Deirdre*[2] one version of which is in Yeats' hands and the 2nd version in the hands of the Plymouth Brother. I hope he won't be able to amend it or rewrite it.

I do not suppose Yeats' "Pilgrim Father" is ever going to return to Ireland now. His family seems to have become resigned to his disappearance.

George Moore (who has been re-writing *Evelyn Innes* and *Sister Teresa* for the last year) has now turned with renewed ferocity to his farewell book. He told me a couple of weeks ago "Russell, I have just written over 2000 words about you." I nervously enquired whether I might see them, but he said: "No, you will see them later on," and I don't know what the fiend has written. Anyhow, we are good friends and I don't think he intends to say anything very hard. I think he is probably keeping most of his satire for the Church and W. B. Y. With kind regards. Yours sincerely, George W. Russell

[1] *The Playboy of the Western World* first produced at the Abbey Theatre, Dublin, directed by W. G. Fay, Saturday, January 26, 1907. *Riders of the Sea* was first produced at the Molesworth Hall, Dublin, directed by W. G. Fay, Thursday, February 25, 1904.

[2] *Deirdre of the Sorrows*, with a preface by W. B. Yeats, published by the Cuala Press, July 5, 1910 (250 copies).

TO H. G. WELLS   *Irish Homestead*
                                          Wednesday [? Summer 1909]
Dear Wells,

I will only thank you for the last book[1] which I have re-read with increased interest since it appeared in the *English Review*,[2] and wont criticise it now because Dunsany and Plunkett tell me you are coming here in a couple of weeks time, which is good news, and there are some most suggestive speculations I would like to talk over with you. By the way you make your folk talk such interesting philosophy I wonder you never thought of writing a symposium upon science like the *Banquet* of Plato. It seems to me, an outsider of your soul, that it would enable you to display one side of your talent to the greatest advantage one would require the slightest scenario, a secret society of advanced scientific men who know more than it was wise to reveal and who discussed the application of science to life; or, a group of them imprisoned in a revolution to be executed the next day who spend the night in hope and prophecy[3]–my [any?] thread would do to let your fascinating faculty of speculation have free play. To unite the ultimate dream of the biologist the chemist the engineer in one symposium would be rather a fine thing and it has not been done. But forgive me, we are all too prone to see how other peoples talents might be applied. It is such a relief from awaiting the crash of our own. I am looking forward to see you. Your sincerely AE

TO CHARLES WEEKES   20.III.10

My dear Charlie,

Many thanks for the Hamilton book[4] which I have been reading with the deepest interest.

I[t] came at a moment when I had almost decided to write a critical study of the problem of self-government for Ireland. Ireland has never

[1] *Tono Bungay*, published by Macmillan (London, February 1909). AE contributed an article, "The Diagnosis of Mr Wells" to the *Irish Homestead*, May 28, 1910, p. 442.

[2] *The English Review*, December 1908-March 1909.

[3] Russell used this setting himself for his story *The Interpreters* (1922).

[4] *The Life of Alexander Hamilton* (London: Constable), by Frederick Scott Oliver (1864-June 3, 1934). He was an early friend of Dermod O'Brien, PRHA. He wrote under his own name, and the pseudonym "John Draper".

given any thought to this question. It has been content to leave it to English statesmen but I am afraid any system of self-government they offer will leave us worse off than we are now and with the aid of Plunkett and some others, I hope this year to think out some alternative scheme to the English parliamentary system which I think would not suit Ireland, indeed would be disastrous for many years. The main points in my proposals are a gradual filtering of the representatives of democracy through successive elections, so that when a man gets on top he will have been five times elected, each time by a gradually decreasing electorate with a gradually increasing special knowledge of the subject the man has to administer or legislate about; take county councils as basis. Each will, under my scheme, have four committees, education, local government, agriculture, industries (or technical instruction). Each county committtee deputes two of its members on Central Councils of education, local government, agriculture or commerce. Each Central Council, once every three or four years, nominates twelve members on central boards of education, agriculture, local government and commerce. These forty eight, on election become, *ipso facto*, members of Parliament. This scheme would dissolve the party system, and substitute the expert for the demagogue who has power only over large masses but none when serving on committees. The scheme is really an attempt to solve the problem of intellect and character in the people's representatives. The co-operative societies will give their members a respect for the man of special or expert knowledge. The county committees which will administer the acts relating to Education, local government, agriculture and technical instruction, will be the first step in the education of the future legislator. He must, by his practical knowledge, convince his colleagues that he is a fit person to send forward to the central councils. At the central councils he will have to convince the picked representatives of the other councils that he is one of the best men before he comes on the Boards and has administrative and legislative power. I have a great many other ideas too long to write about now. But any how the scheme will force on Irish people thought on their own problems and the difficulties of self government which is what I want to do and Hamilton's Life gave me many ideas and more intellectual eagerness. With many thanks, Yours sincerely, George Russell

P.S. O'Grady still ill.

TO SIR HORACE PLUNKETT   The Plunkett House, Dublin
                                                 7th June 1910

My dear Plunkett,

I have come to the conclusion that the way in which we can affect
T. W. Russell most is by publicly embroiling him with the Liberal Party
in England. Therefore, I suggest that you should get Sydney Brooks[1] to
write an article on two Liberal policies to point out that in England the
whole Cabinet have decided on supporting and promoting agricultural
co-operation; that the Board of Agriculture subsidises agricultural co-
operation; that the Board of Agriculture issues leaflets on the subject; that
they introduce it into Bills. While in Ireland, a minor Member of their
Government is doing all he possibly can to fight against this policy; he
speaks against it and uses the forces of his Department to destroy it.
Brooks, to whom we can give all the facts, should ask, after contrasting
these two policies, whether the Liberal Government have any policy at
all; whether they have the courage to insist upon their subordinates
adopting the policy which they have decided upon in England; whether
agricultural co-operation is good for England and bad for Ireland. As all
the English Liberal papers (*Daily Chronicle*, *Daily News*, *Manchester
Guardian*, etc.) are advocates of agricultural co-operation, it will make it
very awkward for T. W. Russell. I think he will feel this even more than
he will feel criticism in Ireland.

I implore you not to forget this, for since you are in for a fight, you may
as well make it a good one and make any Vice-President of the Department feel that, when he works against the Co-operative movement, he is
going to arouse a hornet's nest which will make his life not worth living.
It should be done at once. Yours sincerely, G. W. Russell

TO CHARLES WEEKES   The *Irish Homestead*
                                          Thursday [? June 1910]

Dear Charlie,

I was delayed at Brooks with Plunkett until half past seven discussing
a campaign in the English press and had to rush for a train when it was no
use to telephone. I was sorry I did not get more of you alone. But it was
nice to see you anyhow. I had to rush back here to see proofs through
of what was written in my absence by my substitute. I am off on holidays

---

[1] Sydney Brooks (1872-1937), journalist. (*See* Biographical Notes.)

on Saturday but don't know this minute whether I go [to] Donegal or
Antrim first. We have already made Department climb down over the
most important conclusions of Butter Report and I hope we will get them
into a proper frame of mind. But I am going to dismiss them all for a
whole month with fat paints and flexible brushes and piles of excuses.
Economics be damned for a month. Yours ever, George Russell

TO SIR FREDERICK MACMILLAN[1]   17 Rathgar Avenue
                                                  [November 1910]
Dear Sir,
    One of our younger Irish writers James Stephens, at the suggestion I
think of Stephen Gwynn submitted to Messrs Macmillan a selection of
his poems. It was returned to him. I asked him to let me see the verses he
sent because I doubted whether he had yet acquired any faculty of self-
criticism. He has always seemed to me to be unaware how admirable he is
when he writes of his fellowmen and how far from admirable he is when
he writes about God. I thought a much better selection of his later verses
could be made than that which he submitted to you. Would you submit
again to your reader a new selection I have made which I think contains
some very original and vivid verses. Stephens has I think more talent than
any of our younger writers here. I think as a prose story teller it is likely
he will most win his way but I think the verse is well worth publication
and I would be much obliged if you would let me know whether you
would submit to your reader a new selection I have made and which I will
send if you would care to have them. Yours sincerely, Geo. W. Russell

TO CHARLES WEEKES   The *Irish Homestead*
                                               [early] Feb. 1911
Dear Charlie,
    I am so sorry to hear about your business worries. I vaguely guessed
from things you said when I last saw you that this gigantic concern of
yours had been shaky; but thought it was getting over its troubles. We in
the IAOS have always had the fear of bankruptcy before us during the
time I have been with it and I suppose I have got hardened and I go on
writing and living as if indeed our coffers were full to overflowing. A

[1] Frederick Macmillan, the publisher (1851-June 1, 1936), Chairman of Macmillan &
Co. Ltd. Knighted 1909.

movement depending to a large extent on voluntary support is always like that, but those whose nerves can stand it get hardened by exposure to troubles and sleep no less soundly at night than Carnegie I imagine. I suppose the Lord knows all our needs, and whatever we are all good for, and we get there somehow. Jennings[1] is very sick indeed and this troubles me more than anything else at present. He has a wife and some young children and if he does not get better there will be bad times for them. I have at various times thought of putting some of the *Homestead* ideas in book form but have found that my spare time is more profitably applied to painting, and painting is, as well, a relaxation from working and does not tire one's brain as thinking out articles sometimes does. I write easily, but sometimes do a lot of thinking or research work which does not show in the writing and this is fatiguing. Sometimes before I can write a simple sentence with confidence, I have to make enquiries on all sides about the facts. However, I enjoy it all. Plunkett is in U.S.A. at present trying to recoup after a breakdown. Cooperation, when it arrives will be built of our dead bodies and exhausted brains. It is always cheering to hear from you. The friends of our youth are the ones we belong to most in thought. I never hear of Dan[2] nowadays. Is he well? W. K. M.[3] is silent and writes nothing. I imagine he is becoming the bookworm. Give my kind regards to Mrs. Charlie. Yours ever Geo. W. Russell

TO JOHN QUINN   17 Rathgar Avenue
                                                 February 13, 1911
My dear Quinn,

   George Moore has gone! Alas, he has carried out his promise or threat and is going to settle down in Chelsea. I miss him very much. For the last 2 Saturdays I have wandered about trying to find a way of spending my Saturday night, which for 7 years I spent with Moore. I think George Moore ought to be a generic title, like Pharoah, King of Egypt, and when one goes, another qualified person ought to take his place and fulfill his functions. Moore was so much alive all the time, and the Irish people who write whom I meet here are anaemic people, or if they are not anaemic they have prejudices and no ideas. I suppose his book will soon be out, and the first volume will help to remind people of him while he is finishing

---

[1] John J. Jennings, first business manager of the *Irish Homestead*, died July 17, 1911. Plunkett gave his widow an adequate pension.
[2] Dunlop.   [3] W. K. Magee.

the 2nd. and 3rd. I have a faint hope he will return after a while, but it is very faint. His home is given up and he will never get as good a one in Dublin. I really don't know why he went. I told him I was going to spread rumours that he went off to marry an exceptionally good cook he had, so as to retain her service permanently, or his typewriter. There is nobody broad or bold enough to take his place.

There is a new monthly paper being started here, *The Irish Review*.[1] Colum and Stephens will have most to say to it and they have got a good business man to back them up. It will go on for a year, anyhow, and it promises well. The first number will come out in a week or so.

Jack Yeats is busy at Graystones now. He might be at the North Pole for all one sees of him, being so far out of Dublin, and what is worse miles from a railway station. The most prolific and amusing of Irish writers is now Lord Dunsany. Do you know his queer tales ... *The Sword of Welleran, A Dreamer's Tale*, and *Time and the Gods?* He is improving and has a great splash of genius in him. He writes a three act play in an afternoon, God forgive him. If he devoted three months to it, it might last three centuries. As it is, it lasts three days in the Abbey. But he has moments of great beauty in his tales. Yours ever, George W. Russell

TO CHARLES WEEKES   [? April 11, 1911]

Dear Charles,

Thanks for letter.[2] It is most amusing. I am going for you and "Efficiency" with impartiality this week. "Efficiency" is a clever fellow, Erskine Childers[3] who wrote *The Riddle of the Sands* an excellent book which led two English officers to spy in Germany and get into gaol. He also wrote a volume of the *Times*' History of the war. He is writing a book about Home Rule. He used to be chief clerk in House of Commons and is a son of Childers of Financial Relations fame. He is a nice fellow too. H. P.

---

[1] Edited by Joseph Mary Plunkett (1887–May 4, 1916). It ran from March 1911 until November 1914.

[2] Probably the brief letter signed "The Caterpillar", printed in the *Irish Homestead*, vol. 18, p. 292 (April 15, 1911).

[3] Born 1870; executed by Irishmen November 24, 1922. Mrs M. A. Childers wrote to the editor (July 11, 1957): "My husband's and my contacts with AE were occasional meetings until we established our home in Dublin, in 1919. He lived nearby and came often to see us and for long talks and later, after my husband's death, for some years he had supper with us once a week."

heard from Blair who promised to give your application full consideration. He said Smail was a candidate for same post. This is a strong man I believe so you have competition to face. I hope you will be successful. Yours ever, George Russell

TO MACMILLAN AND CO. LTD.   17 Rathgar Avenue
                                        20 February 1912

Dear Sirs,

I do not know Mr. Darrell Figgis.[1] He asked me for permission to quote "Refuge".[2] I told him that so far as my rights in it were concerned he could use it but I had no rights at all and that the copyright was yours and he must apply to you and that I had no doubt you would give permission freely as I believe had been done before with other anthologies. This is the sum total of my knowledge of Mr. Figgis except that I think he has written one or two clever articles somewhere I forget where and about what. It is always pleasing to an author to be quoted but beyond this faint sentiment which has not risen to a passion yet I have no feelings in the matter. Yours sincerely, Geo. W. Russell

TO JOHN QUINN   *Irish Homestead*
                                         May 26, 1912

My dear Quinn,

I was glad to hear from you again. I think I owed you a letter. I enclose a copy of my review[3] of Stephens' book of verses. I do not think his verses satisfactory. But he has a great splash of genius, and is poor and I wanted to help him. I think he will be a great story-teller, and he has got a masterpiece or 2 concealed in his skull. Anyhow he is one of the most vivid, vital and delightful persons I know in Ireland, entirely loveable. His story, *The Charwoman's Daughter*, published by Macmillans has got great praise from all reviewers, and he is writing an astonishing prose fantasy now. He read me one chapter which almost brought tears to my eyes, it was so beautiful. But he has also plans for a great book, a story of

[1] Darrell Edmund Figgis, poet and novelist (1882-1925). (*See* Biographical Notes.)
[2] AE, *Collected Poems*, p. 95 (*The Divine Vision*, p. 40). Perhaps Figgis intended using "Refuge" in his book *Studies and Appreciations* (London, November 1912: Dent); or possibly for an anthology, *The Lyric Cry*, advertised in 1915-1916, but not printed.
[3] In *Sinn Fein* (Dublin), March 23, 1912.

a young man, which if he writes it as he told me, and he has power to do it, will lift him up as our representative Irish novelist and he will take the place poor Synge was going to take before he died. Stephens is a bigger man in himself than Synge, with more brains, vitality, humour and imagination, though as a writer, of course, so far he is not in it with Synge. I place my trust in Stephens' personality which is astonishing, and I think you would like him. If you find your way to Ireland this year I am sure you would like to meet this queer little man, so charged with endless grit and fire. His story *The Charwoman's Daughter* is published on your side and I suppose you have read it. He is just beginning to get into his stride now. He may never be a great poet, but I will swear he will be a great story-teller, with one masterpiece at least to his credit. The English reviewers already have compared him with big names. "How differently Thomas Hardy and James Stephens would have written about this," says one critic, speaking, I think, about an Arnold Bennett book. Yours ever, AE

TO SIR HORACE PLUNKETT   17 Rathgar Avenue
                                          22nd July, 1912

My dear Sir Horace,

You asked for my opinion on *Criticism and Beauty*.[1] My first feeling when I read it through was of admiration for the literary strategy of the writer who seemed like a military chief advancing into strange territory, preserving himself from attack, throwing out scouts before him, digging trenches east and west of his lines of advance, laying down barbed wire entanglements, erecting concealed batteries on all sides to prevent surprise and capture. Mr. Balfour[2] has so generalised the whole subject by extending it over all the arts and back through all the ages that it is as difficult to grapple with his main contention as it was to catch a Boer Commando ranging over a thousand miles of country. I believe I agree with him in the main that we have no real criterion of beauty but somehow I feel he has no right to get to that right conclusion by such means as he employed. The Scripture speaks of people who do not come in by the straight gate

[1] Arthur J. Balfour's Romanes' Lecture *Questionings on Criticism and Beauty*, delivered November 24, 1909; published London, 1909. Rewritten as *Criticism and Beauty* (Oxford, 1910).

[2] Arthur James Balfour (1848-1930), statesman and philosopher. (*See* Biographical Notes.)

but leap over the wall illegitimately. The arts differ so much that criticism on them should not be generalised. They should be examined separately. It might be found possible to apply standards of excellence to painting, an art in which mimicry of nature enters which could not be applied to music, where the element of imitation is almost entirely absent. I have heard that the Greeks had fixed standards of proportion which were applied to architecture. I am not yet sure that the criterion of truth might not be applied to test beauty in literature and painting. We seem to be better able often to agree as to whether a statement is true than we are to agree about its beauty, if beauty only is discussed; but we might possibly arrive at a criterion of beauty by calling on truth to act as judge. Keats I think would have been satisfied to have his most beautiful lines appraised by that test for he said, "Truth is beauty", but I am almost afraid to suggest this because I feel sure that Mr. Balfour would ransack the ages to prove that there is no criterion of truth and he would do it so skilfully one would despair of escape from the maze of argument. I will only say for myself that "style" in literature, the quality of literary excellence which we can all see exists even if we cannot agree upon standards, seems to depend on truth telling, whether of telling truth about what one sees or what one feels. I think the subject could be more satisfactorily discussed by confining the quest of criterion of beauty or excellence to a discussion over one lyric, a few sentences of prose, or a single picture or statue. But I feel sure that if we did so we would come to Mr. Balfour's conclusions, because at the last analysis the fixing of standards of excellence in art or literature would be found to depend on one's conception of the nature of the being for whom art or literature exists, and we have not [discovered *cancelled*] decided yet whether man is material or spiritual in his origin. A right conception of the nature of man would not matter if we were discussing the beauty of a line like Keats's marvellous description of the world under waters

> *One faint eternal eventide of gems*

but it would matter greatly if we were to discuss a line of Dante's

> *In his will is our peace*

because the element of truth would inevitably be [unsolved *deleted*] involved in fixing criterions of the highest beauty in literature.

Again, it might be possible to argue that beauty is a purely subjective feeling, and is self discovery, a revelation of the self to the self, the lighting

[76]

up of some lordlier chamber of the soul than we had hitherto inhabited. The arts may simply be the means by which a light is flung on our subconscious nature. Many writers have felt that their highest imagination of things seemingly beyond themselves was in reality their deepest inroad into their own being. And their readers have also felt that in understanding the poem they understood themselves. The delight we feel in beauty may be the melting of our imperfection [into *deleted*] toward perfection, our incompleteness becoming more complete. Emerson says "I the imperfect adore my own perfect." If the poem, picture, or symphony is only a torch thrust into the darkness of the subconscious it would be difficult to fix criterions of excellence, because, as the soul grew more sensitive, it is possible that a half a dozen delicate touches of colour or a [dreaming *deleted*] drawing with a few lines might kindle in it a greater ecstasy than an elaborate beauty like the figures Michael Angelo painted in the Sistine. If the power of kindling beauty in ourselves is the criterion of excellence then on this assumption a little drawing by Blake might be deemed greater than the Bacchus of Titian. I like a little wood picture by Monticelli, a maze and miracle of melted jewels, with a white arm or neck emerging here and there, with suggestions of glimmering dresses in some sun splashed forest, better than the more defined art of Watteau with a more complete pictorial representation of the same kind of life, because I can imagine no more than the complete art of Watteau, while the magical haze of jewel-like colours where nothing is clearly defined sets my imagination creating where Monticelli's art ended. But all this simply means that I agree with Mr. Balfour's main contention that we have no criterion of beauty. I think we will get nearer to a discussion of standards as we get nearer to understanding ourselves. I think Mr. Balfour argues very fairly once you allow him to generalise, but I think he is not quite justified in the way he deals with the appeal to an aristocracy of taste. Because having admitted the seeming force of an appeal to a true aristocracy of intellect he proceeds to upset the appeal by assuming that they are not really experts at all, when he says some are inclined to assume an admiration which they do not feel for things which everybody round them thinks worthy to be admired. A real aristocracy of intellect would not pretend to admiration it did not truly feel, and I think the argument would have had more force if Mr. Balfour had admitted that there was a genuine aristocracy of intellect and had carried on his argument on the assumption that such an aristocracy of [truth *deleted*] taste was genuine. This point is the Achilles heel in an armour of argument otherwise impenetrable at least by me. I do not like closed doors in any direction of the mind and I intend to make some more subtle attempt to arrive at criterions of beauty than I have done in this letter, though I think artists and poets are not the best people to philosophize on their own [work *deleted*] art.[1] "If there be any gods," says Plato, "they certainly do not philosophize", and in so far as a man is artist or poet he is more capable of admirations and dislikes than of self-consciousness. His best moments are blind and dense with revelation and his intuitions are beyond his intellect. But he might have intentions about his intuitions and I will supplicate the oracle for an answer. Yours sincerely, Geo. W. Russell

TO JOHN QUINN   *Irish Homestead*
                                                 1 January 1913

My dear Quinn,

I suppose you saw Moore's *Salve*. His vision gets blurred as he recedes from his subject. I don't know why he wanted to leave Ireland. He is lonely and out of it now in London, I think. I have replaced Moore as a boon companion now by Stephens, whose last book *The Crock of Gold*[2] is the great literary success of the year 1912. He has suddenly leaped up to the fame which I had prophesied from the first writing, and now the enthusiastic reviewers are comparing him with all kinds of big men. I don't think, however, he has come to his best, by any means, yet. There are no younger men than he appearing. Colum is always hovering on the verge of first class work, but his family entanglements[3] and the difficulty of making a living prevent his having the leisure necessary to a slow working mind like his. He is quick with an article but slow with a poem or play. He knows he has to dig below surfaces and it takes him a long while. Do you know Dunsany's work? He has a good deal of genius but it is a pity he has £20,000 a year. If he were forced to write he would do great things. His very best tales are as good myths as anything I know, and his plays get better and more impressive. With kind regards, Yours ever, AE

[1] Plunkett's diary entry July 23, 1912: "My interview with Arthur Balfour was taken up chiefly with a letter AE had written upon his Romanes' lecture. . . ." On June 29, 1912 Plunkett's diary account of his meeting with Balfour concludes: ". . . we went on to talk of AE, and I failed to describe him as I should have liked. But Balfour was greatly interested in him and asked me to bring them together if I could."

[2] Published October 1912. AE's (unsigned) review was printed in the *Irish Homestead* October 12, 1912, p. 826.   [3] Mr Colum had a dependent family to maintain.

TO THE RT HON. A. J. BALFOUR, MP. The Plunkett House
23rd January 1913

Dear Mr. Balfour,

Since returning to Dublin I have consulted Lord Monteagle[1] and the Secretary of the I.A.O.S. and they both think no harm could be done by your referring to the case of the I.A.O.S. and the Development Commissioners in your speech, and that the reference would help to bring the matter to a head and get the Cabinet to decide one way or another. The delay is intolerable. The facts are, Sir Horace Plunkett first promoted agricultural co-operation in these islands. The success of the Irish Agricultural Organisation Society led England and Scotland to adopt the same policy and Agricultural Organisation Societies were formed there with general approval, and the promotion of agricultural co-operation became a national rather than a party policy in England, and Mr. Lloyd George made one of the objects to which the funds at the disposal of the Development Commissioners could be applied, the teaching of the principles and practice of agricultural co-operation. The three organising bodies applied simultaneously for funds. The applications of the English and Scottish bodies were granted and they are now in enjoyment of grants in aid of their work which is identical in every respect with the work carried out by the I.A.O.S. in Ireland. The Irish application has been held up for over two years and no definite decision has been come to. The main ground of opposition, so far as we can gather from reference to it by Irish members, is political. The I.A.O.S. is accused of having a party and political character. The other cause of opposition is interference with trade. We may dismiss the second cause. The Government can base no argument for refusal on this ground as every form of agricultural co-operation promoted by the I.A.O.S. has been sanctioned in Great Britain, and the Board of Agriculture has issued leaflets urging farmers to combine in the same way and for the very purposes denounced in Ireland. Returning [to] the first charge, that the I.A.O.S. is political rather than economic in its real objects, and was a device of Sir Horace Plunkett's to upset the Home Rule cause, the only evidence of this brought forward was a letter written

---

[1] Thomas Spring-Rice, second Baron Monteagle (1849-December 24, 1926). For some relevant information see *The Letters and Friendships of Sir Cecil Spring-Rice*, by Stephen L. Gwynn (London, 1929: Constable, 2 vols.). Monteagle was a member of the I.A.O.S. Committee.

to America by a Mr. T. W. Rolleston,[1] who was not a member of the I.A.O.S. but who told an American correspondent of his that the I.A.O.S. would get rid of "Dillon[2] and the Parliamentarians". This letter was sent back to Ireland and was published in the *Freeman's Journal*. Mr. Redmond[3] wrote at once denouncing the I.A.O.S. Therefore Mr. T. W. Russell[4] called a meeting of the Agricultural Board and struck off all friendly relations with the I.A.O.S. ostensibly on account of this letter, in spite of the fact that Mr. Rolleston denied positively that the letter contained any other opinions than his own, that he was neither member or official of the I.A.O.S., and that Sir Horace Plunkett denied, and truly as I know, all responsibility for Mr. Rolleston's opinions.

To refute these charges of partisan action it is only necessary to say that there are 97,000 Irish farmers organized in co-operative societies, that of these at least 80,000 must be Nationalist farmers, that on the Committee of the I.A.O.S. which controls its work and policy sit members of the Ancient Order of Hibernians, a member of the Council of the United Irish League and some presidents of local branches of that body, that the Nationalists on the Committee outnumber the Unionists, and that the I.A.O.S. to disprove the accusations which never weighed with the farmers, addressed openly a circular letter to every co-operative society in Ireland asking their Committees to state if the I.A.O.S., its officials, or organisers had ever introduced party politics in their work.

[1] Thomas William Hazell Rolleston (1857-December 5, 1920), a loyal disciple of John O'Leary, and life-long friend of W. B. Yeats with whom he was associated in founding the Rhymers' Club in 1891. He was active in the Irish Agricultural Wholesale Society for many years. Translator into English of the *Enchiridion* of Epictetus (1888) and *Selections from Plato* (1892), and into German Whitman's *Leaves of Grass*. He translated some Gaelic verse into English which won popularity. His original books included a biography of Lessing (1889) and *Sea Spray* (verse, 1909). His second wife was Maud, daughter of the Rev. Stopford Brooke. *See* the biography by his son C. H. Rolleston [1888-November 1950] *Portrait of an Irishman* (London, 1939: Methuen).

[2] John Dillon (1851-September 4, 1927) professional politician, follower first of John Mitchell, afterwards of Charles Stewart Parnell whom he succeeded as Chairman of the Irish Nationalist Members of Parliament, in 1890. During the first Secretaryship in Ireland (1895-1900) of Gerald Balfour (1853-1945) Dillon tried to obstruct the development of the I.A.O.S.

[3] John E. Redmond (1851-March 6, 1918), Chairman of the Irish Parliamentary party for several years. Nationalist M.P. for Waterford from 1891. See Stephen Gwynn's *John Redmond's Last Years* (London, 1919: E. Arnold) and Denis Gwynn's *The Life of John Redmond* (London, 1932: Harrap). He should not be confused with his brother William H. K. Redmond (1861-June 9, 1917), also a Nationalist M.P., from 1892.

[4] Thomas William Russell (1841-May 2, 1920) succeeded Horace Plunkett as Vice-President of the Department of Agriculture and Technical Instruction for Ireland on May 14, 1907, until 1918.

The replies received have been printed. I enclose a copy. Not a single society in Ireland could be found which made any complaint of the political attitude of the I.A.O.S. They all stated that it, its organisers and officials had never introduced politics in their work. These replies were published but had not the slightest effect on the opposition. The charges were also investigated by the Development Commissioners who took evidence both from those who opposed the I.A.O.S. claim and from those who were in favour of it. They unanimously recommended the Treasury to grant the I.A.O.S. application. Their recommendation has been held up for nearly two years.

I may say also that a very large number of Nationalist papers in Ireland are in favour of the I.A.O.S. The support is not only on the Unionist side. The Nationalist paper with the largest circulation in Ireland, the *Daily Independent*, approves of the work of the I.A.O.S. and even the organ of the most extreme Nationalists, *Sinn Fein* is a warm supporter of Sir Horace Plunkett's movement. If the I.A.O.S. had ever betrayed any partisan bias in its work this support would never have been given, the Nationalist members of the I.A.O.S. Committee would have resigned, and the movement would have been shattered in a fortnight. In Parliament the most monstrous charges have been made mainly by Mr. Dillon. His last speech on the I.A.O.S. made in the House early in July, I dealt with in an open letter[1] to him which I wrote at that time, and which you will find in the copy of the *Irish Homestead* which I enclose. There is nothing obstructs the I.A.O.S. except the influence of Mr. Dillon. The Liberal members are, I believe, as strongly in favour of the I.A.O.S. being supported as the Unionist members and the *Daily Chronicle*, *Daily News*, *The Nation* and, I believe, also the *Manchester Guardian* have expressed themselves as supporting the I.A.O.S. application.

This is a long letter but it gives you as briefly as I can, the main facts of the situation. We will be greatly indebted to you for your support of an Irish movement which is the only one which has succeeded in uniting Catholic and Protestant, Unionist and Nationalist in a common object. Yours sincerely, Geo. W. Russell

P.S. I do not, of course, want you to read the I.A.O.S. pamphlet but the open letter to John Dillon may interest you as an essay in political controversy.

[1] The "Open Letter to John Dillon" was printed in the *Irish Homestead*, July 13, 1912 (pp. 557-559). Dillon's allusion to I.A.O.S.: see *Parliamentary Reports* [Hansard] *Commons*, vol. 40 (1912), columns 1543-4, and see also columns 1540-7 (July 5, 1912).

TO CHARLES WEEKES   *Irish Homestead*
                                                       Friday [January 24, 1913]
Dear Charlie,

I have been caught into the usual vortex on my return. I don't know whether I have any sketches at present I would care to sign but will look up what I have on Sunday. You see I had neuritis in my painting arm and did not do anything for three months and was only able to use my arm again at the beginning of this year. Anyhow I can use it now and if I have nothing I can *make* something to send you. I was sorry I could not see you again. I was so rushed with one thing or another. I concluded my last day in London Friday, by lunching with Asquith and Birrell and dining with Arthur Balfour sandwiching between these two a visit to Orage Magee [?] and a long talk with Ralph Hod[g]son who is I think the best of the young poets on your side of the water. I felt like God holding no form of politics but benevolently contemplating all. I am very sorry I missed Dan. I will write you again if I find a sketch or when I make one. I have to write a long Memo on Home Rule for a friend of mine who wants to try and influence some of the lords not to be foolish over the present bill. But it is much more difficult to be sure. I would like to wring the neck of the present Home Rule Bill. Yours ever AE

TO JOHN QUINN   *Irish Homestead*
                                                         February 7, 1913
My dear Quinn,

    . . . I was over in London last week and saw George Moore. He has, I think, finally settled down between Steer, Tonks, McEvoy and Harrison[1] of the New English Art Club, and will never have any more adventures. His third volume, he tells me, is half finished. I tremble when I think of it. He gets every ounce of copy out of his friends that he can, regardless of their feelings.

    I saw a big post-impressionist exhibition. I think it is the second childhood of art, with Noah's ark, trees, houses and animals, only rather

---

[1] (Arthur) Ambrose McEvoy (1878-1927), English portrait painter. Henry Tonks (1862-1937), Charles Conder (1868-1909). Laurence Binyon (1869-1943). Ralph Hodgson (b. 1872) author of *The Last Blackbird* (1907), *Poems* (1917) and *The Skylark and other poems* (London, 1958: Hart-Davis, for Colin Fenton). Laurence A. Harrison (died 1937), a son of F. Harrison (1831-1923). Philip Wilson Steer (1860-1940). Herbert Asquith (1852-1928), Liberal Prime Minister, 1908-1916. Augustine Birrell (1850-1933), Chief Secretary for Ireland, 1907-1916.

more badly drawn than the Noah's Ark, trees and houses of first childhood. Gaugin and one or two others of the pioneers of this movement had a kind of talent, but now Picasso and Matisse have gone into a kind of hopeless drivel of line and colour and ideas which makes one feel unhappy as if one were in the society of lunatics. I saw a Conder exhibition-some lovely things there. He is of the same clan as Beardsley had a sharp and biting devil in him, while Conder had a soft lascivious devil in him. But at its best it is beautiful in a soft way, with delicately coloured little women surrounded by erotic auras.

The New English Art Club was closed just the day before I got over. I had four good days, saw Moore, Steer, Tonks, McEvoy, Harrison, Ralph Hodgson the best of the younger poets, Laurence Binyon, and F. S. Oliver, who wrote the *Life of Hamilton*. I had two hours with Asquith and Birrell at Downing Street, at lunch, and I had four hours with Arthur Balfour the same night and I sandwiched in between these two a couple of hours with the cleverest Socialist in England, probably in the world -a young fellow named Orage,[1] half Irish by the way.

I came back to Dublin loving Ireland more than ever. The size of London is appalling. The more humanity crowds together the more inhuman does it seem. I believe in the small communities. I think, with the Greeks, that a city should contain no more citizens than could be influenced by the voice of a single orator. I wish we could get self-government here and be quit of all the big imperial rascalities which draw us about like a small boat tugged by a rope after a mammoth liner. My ideal state would be about the size of County Sligo. But I am afraid I will never live to see Ireland divided up into independent county kingdoms, like the little Greek states. I believe in the intensive cultivation of humanity. But I won't go off into my special political theories. My writing is so bad I dare not inflict more of it on anybody than two pages. Yours ever, AE

TO JOHN HUGHES[2]   17 Rathgar Avenue
239, Avenue Raspail,   15th April 1913
Paris

My dear John Hughes,

This is to introduce to you a dear friend of mine James Stephens who is going to live in Paris for some months. He is the last and the best of

---

[1] Alfred Richard Orage, 1873-1934. Exponent of Guild Socialism; the most persuasive advocate of Social Credit Economy. (*See* Biographical Notes.)   [2] The sculptor.

the numerous band of poets and storytellers Ireland has been blessed with since our time. But he is better than a literary man, he is a real human being whom I am sure you will like as well as I do. I ask you first for my sake to do him any service you can. I am sure afterwards you will like him for his own sake. You come so rarely to Ireland, old friend, that your obligations to Ireland have mounted up. Please give this foolish child of song any good advice you can. Yours ever, George Russell

TO CHARLES WEEKES, *Irish Homestead*
Tuesday [? June 1913]

Dear Charlie,

Many thanks for the Lane file. I saw Roberts, a not unfriendly conversation as he stayed for two hours after it was over on Sunday night last. I heard all he had to say and I may mention that I was still less inclined to agree with his views when I had heard him, than I was before he came up. I had some faint prickings of conscience, that I might have misjudged him, but I have none now. Let there be an end of this disagreable subject.

I don't believe a word of what you say about my importance or my reputation. I believe there are a thousand or so people who have read my verses and perhaps like them, and that is all out of a population of 45,000,000 people in these islands. In Ireland I am getting more and more unpopular because of my ruthless economics.

I daresay I have friends in the Co-operative movement, but not ten of them know that I am either artist or poet, and I am jolly glad they do not know or they would have no confidence in me and would regard me as a mere "farmer of the pen". Get a proper perspective about things. You have lived so long in England that you have got their sentimental notions about literature and reputations. When I see the effect of these notions in an author like Yeats, who believes them, then I congratulate myself on my obscurity. Sorry for giving you so much trouble over the Lane affair.[1]

Yours ever, Geo. W. Russell

[1] AE's efforts to obtain release from his publishing contract with John Lane Ltd., The Bodley Head. Lane held the copyright in *Homeward, Songs by the Way* and *The Earth Breath* and had been remiss in furnishing Russell with annual accounts of sales. Russell wished to collect the poems from those two books, together with his later poems.

TO ERIC ROBERTSON DODDS[1]   17 Rathgar Avenue
[*postmark* August, 15 ? 1913]

Dear Mr. Dodds,

If you come to Dublin look me up either at the address above or at the Plunkett House, 84 Merrion Square, Dublin where I can be found during the day. The Hermetic Society is at present on holidays. That is it will not begin wasting the time of its members until October. But if you are interested in mysticism you can at any time meet the few people who are sincerely concerned about mystical things without going to the formality of joining the Hermetic. If there are any meetings of the society when you are here of course you could attend them. Dublin is interesting but the Hermetic is not worth while paying a visit to Dublin for. Yours sincerely,
AE

TO THE EDITOR, THE *IRISH TIMES*[2]   [October 6, 1913]

TO THE MASTERS OF DUBLIN

Sirs, I address this warning to you, the aristocracy of industry in this city, because, like all aristocracies, you tend to grow blind in long authority, and to be unaware that you and your class and its every action are being considered and judged day by day by those who have power to shake or overturn the whole social order, and whose restlessness in poverty to-day is making our industrial civilization stir like a quaking bog. You do not seem to realize that your assumption that you are answerable to yourselves alone for your actions in the industries you control is one that becomes less and less tolerable in a world so crowded with necessitous life. Some of you have helped Irish farmers to upset a landed aristocracy in this island, an

---

[1] Born 1893. Classicist. Regius Professor of Greek at Oxford 1936-1960. *Select Passages Illustrative of Neoplatonism* (London, 1923: Society for Promoting Christian Knowledge); *Euripides' Bacchae* (Oxford University Press, 1944); *The Greeks and the Irrational* (Berkeley, Calif. 1951: Univ. Calif. Press). He also edited the *Journal and Letters of Stephen MacKenna*. The postmark on this letter may be 1914 or 1913.

[2] Text from the *Irish Times*, Tuesday, October 7, 1913. Reprinted as a broadsheet, *To the Masters of Dublin* in 1913. Reprinted in *Labour in Ireland* by James Connolly (Dublin, May 1917: Maunsel). *See* J. R. White's *Misfit: an Autobiography* (London, 1930: Cape).

E

aristocracy richer and more powerful in its sphere than you are in yours, with its roots deep in history. They, too, as a class, though not all of them, were scornful or neglectful of the workers in the industry by which they profited; and to many who knew them in their pride of place and thought them all-powerful they are already becoming a memory, the good disappearing together with the bad. If they had done their duty by those from whose labours came their wealth they might have continued unquestioned in power and *prestige* for centuries to come. The relation of landlord and tenant is not an ideal one, but any relations in a social order will endure if there is infused into them some of that spirit of human sympathy which qualifies the life for immortality. Despotisms endure while they are benevolent, and aristocracies while *noblesse oblige* is not a phrase to be referred to with a cynical smile. Even an oligarchy might be permanent if the spirit of human kindness, which harmonises all things otherwise incompatible, is present.

You do not seem to read history so as to learn its lessons. That you are an uncultivated class was obvious from recent utterances of some of you upon art. That you are incompetent men in the sphere in which you arrogate imperial powers is certain, because for many years, long before the present uprising of labour, your enterprises have been dwindling in the regard of investors, and this while you have carried them on in the cheapest labour market in these islands, with a labour reserve always hungry and ready to accept any pittance. You are bad citizens, for we rarely, if ever, hear of the wealthy among you endowing your city with the munificent gifts which it is the pride of merchant princes in other cities to offer, and Irishmen not of your city who offer to supply the wants left by your lack of generosity are met with derision and abuse. Those who have economic power have civic power also, yet you have not used the power that was yours to right what was wrong in the evil administration of this city. You have allowed the poor to be herded together so that one thinks of certain places in Dublin as of a pestilence. There are twenty thousand rooms, in each of which live entire families, and sometimes more, where no function of the body can be concealed, and delicacy and modesty are creatures that are stifled ere they are born. The obvious duty of you in regard to these things you might have left undone, and it be imputed to ignorance or forgetfulness; but your collective and conscious action as a class in the present labour dispute has revealed you to the world in so malign an aspect that the mirror must be held up to you, so that you may see yourselves as every humane person sees you.

[86]

The conception of yourselves as altogether virtuous and wronged is, I assure you, not at all the one which onlookers hold of you. No doubt, you have rights on your side. No doubt, some of you suffered without just cause. But nothing which has been done to you cries aloud to Heaven for condemnation as your own actions. Let me show you how it seems to those who have followed critically the dispute, trying to weigh in a balance the rights and wrongs. You were within the rights society allows you when you locked out your men and insisted on the fixing of some principle to adjust your future relations with labour when the policy of labour made it impossible for some of you to carry on your enterprises. Labour desired the fixing of some such principle as much as you did. But having once decided on such a step, knowing how many thousands of men, women, and children, nearly one-third of the population of this city, would be affected, you should not have let one day have passed without unremitting endeavours to find a solution of the problem.

What did you do? The representatives of labour unions in Great Britain met you, and you made of them a preposterous, an impossible demand, and because they would not accede to it you closed the Conference: you refused to meet them further: you assumed that no other guarantees than those you asked were possible, and you determined deliberately, in cold anger, to starve out one-third of the population of this city, to break the manhood of the men by the sight of the suffering of their wives and hunger of their children. We read in the Dark Ages of the rack and thumb screw. But these iniquities were hidden and concealed from the knowledge of men in the dungeons and torture chambers. Even in the Dark Ages humanity could not endure the sight of such suffering, and it learnt of such misuse of power by slow degrees, through rumour, and when it was certain it razed its Bastilles to their foundations. It remained for the twentieth century and the capital city of Ireland to see an oligarchy of four hundred masters deciding openly upon starving one hundred thousand people, and refusing to consider any solution except that fixed by their pride. You, masters, asked men to do that which masters of labour in any other city in these islands had not dared to do. You insolently demanded of those men who were members of a trade union that they should resign from that union; and from those who were not members you insisted on a vow that they would never join it.

Your insolence and ignorance of the rights conceded to workers universally in the modern world were incredible, and as great as your inhumanity. If you had between you collectively a portion of human soul

[87]

as large as a threepenny bit, you would have sat night and day with the representatives of labour, trying this or that solution of the trouble, mindful of the women and children, who at least were innocent of wrong against you. But no! You reminded labour you could always have your three square meals a day while it went hungry. You went into conference again with representatives of the State, because, dull as you are, you knew public opinion would not stand your holding-out. You chose as your spokesman the bitterest tongue that ever wagged in this island, and then, when an award was made by men who have an experience in industrial matters a thousand times transcending yours, who have settled disputes in industries so great that the sum of your petty enterprises would not equal them, you withdraw again, and will not agree to accept their solution, and fall back again on your devilish policy of starvation. Cry aloud to Heaven for new souls! The souls you have got cast upon the screen of publicity appear like the horrid and writhing creatures enlarged from the insect world, and revealed to us by the cinematograph.

You may succeed in your policy and ensure your own damnation by your victory. The men whose manhood you have broken will loathe you, and will always be brooding and scheming to strike a fresh blow. The children will be taught to curse you. The infant being moulded in the womb will have breathed into its starved body the vitality of hate. It is not they–it is you who are the blind Samsons pulling down the pillars of the social order. You are sounding the death knell of autocracy in industry. There was autocracy in political life, and it was superseded by democracy. So surely will democratic power wrest from you the control of industry. The Fate of you, the aristocracy of industry, will be as the fate of the aristocracy of land if you do not now show that you have some humanity still among you. Humanity abhors, above all things, a vacuum in itself, and your class will be cut off from humanity as the surgeon cuts the cancer and alien growth from the body. Be warned ere it is too late. Yours, etc., "AE"

TO JAMES H. COUSINS   The Plunkett House
                                       [October 15, 1913]
Dear Cousins,

Many thanks for your kindness. I have not been photographed for twelve years, but there was a reproduction of an old sketch by J. B.

Yeats which my wife is sending to you. You are well out of Dublin these times. It is the most undrained swamp of humanity I ever heard of.[1] You will see by the enclosed what my views are on the labour trouble.

There has been gnashing of teeth over the open letter but I think it has awakened some consciousness here. With kind regards, Yours sincerely, George Russell

TO JAMES H. COUSINS   *Irish Homestead*
                                                      [October 29, 1913]

My dear Cousins,
    You don't call yourself a Theosophist after writing that article in the *Christian Commonwealth*,[2] to create vanity and egoism in the subject. I would be ashamed to show it to anybody. I don't mind AE ideas being talked about because they are not his but old as the world but G. W. R. is a thing of no importance and the less said about him the better. About the Indian project I don't know exactly how it could be set about.[3] It is very expensive getting adequate representation of artists the insurance packing &c cost so much, and the work over here would have to be undertaken by some person with lots of time on his hands. In the Whitechapel collection of Irish Pictures men came over and spent weeks going about. I will talk to Dermod O'Brien about it when I see him but really our numbers are a long way behind our writers. With the exception of old Hone, Orpen & Jack Yeats we have little distinguished work. The only person here who knows where the best work is is O'Brien and I will consult with him. With kind regards, AE

[1] *See* Note 7, p. 230.
[2] Vol. 34 (No. 1671) pp. 53-54 (October 22, 1913).
[3] "The Indian project" was a thought of mine that, when I would leave for Madras in the spring of 1914, I should carry a collection of paintings by Irish artists for exhibition. His quick glance over practical details of such an enterprise is the other side of his work. (*J.H.C.*).

TO SIR J. A. SHANE LESLIE[1]   17 Rathgar Avenue
                                              [? early November, 1913]

Dear Leslie,

Thanks for letter and enclosure. Why not join Roger Casement[2]. [and] Jack White[3] in their Home Rule Campaign in Ulster? Oh, I forget you differ on religious grounds and cant get on their platform. Myself I would like to make it illegal to mention the words Protestant or Catholic at a political meeting for the next five years in Ireland. When you are next in Dublin come and tell me about the local phantom.[4] When I was in Donegal I made a rough note of a creature with flames waving about him which I hope to paint but he had no clothes. He was playing along the ridges like a distraught thing. The Lord have mercy on him! I dont understand these things. I prefer the faery world to the world of the shades. Yours ever, AE

TO CHARLES WEEKES   *Irish Homestead*
                                              [Tuesday, November 4, 1913]

Dear Charlie,

I went on Saturday afternoon to your place of business but you work under good conditions of labour, I was told, and the Saturday half-holiday was your lot. I only made up my mind to go on Thursday and had no time to write. I have raised hell in Dublin; all the papers combine to attack me in leading articles. The *Freeman* both Monday and today spending itself on my poor soul. The church I daresay will conspire to drive me out of this country and out of the Co-operative movement. But

---

[1] Born 1885. Poet and biographer.

[2] One of the Governing Committee of the Irish National Volunteers, formed in October 1913. See *The Times* (London), October 25, 27, and 31, 1913. Roger Casement, born 1864 in county Antrim. Executed by order of the British Government, August 3, 1916. See Denis R. Gwynn's *The Life and Death of Roger Casement* (London, 1930, 1934: Cape). Perhaps for a book about Casement projected (but not written) by Henry Woodd Nevinson, AE planned writing a preface (*AE's Letters to Mínanlábáin :* New York, 1937: Macmillan) mentioned in his letter dated March 19, 1932.

[3] Captain J. R. White, born May 22, 1879, died February 2, 1947. He is survived by his sister Lady Gladys Napier, and by his widow, his first wife, and his sons. His *Misfit: an Autobiography* (London, 1930: Cape), contains interesting chapters on the 1913 strike in Dublin, on the Irish Volunteers, etc. *See* especially pp. 220-224.

[4] An eighteenth-century apostate priest, seen on Monaghan roads. (*Sir Shane Leslie's note.*)

I would find it impossible to live in Ireland if there was no personal or intellectual freedom, and my conscience compelled me to strike a blow for what I conceived to be right.[1] It is possible I may be looking for some other job in a little. But if the Church drives me out of the Co-operative movement, it will liberate my pen to write on many things in Ireland which I have refrained hitherto from touching on. I am sorry not to have seen you or Dan but my visit was only for a day and I went back at once to find thunder and lightning waiting for me. With kind regards; Yours ever, AE

TO W. B. YEATS   *Irish Homestead*
[Wednesday, November 5, 1913]

My dear Yeats,

Please let me congratulate you on your speech at the Peace Meeting and above all on your article in *The Irish Worker*.[2] I have differed from you in many things but I felt all my old friendship and affection surging up as I read what you said. It falls on us to make a fight for social and intellectual freedom. I have a long battle before me and the church is raging against me over Ireland and is trying to make my continuance in the co-operative movement an impossibility, and I am glad to see that you, Gwynn, Seamus O'Sullivan, Stephens are all on the same side in life. Please accept my assurance of my deep regard. Yours sincerely, AE

Dublin
TO THE EDITOR OF *THE TIMES*[3]   November 11, 1913

THE TRAGEDY OF LABOUR IN DUBLIN

Sir, It may seem an audacity on the part of one whose views on the politics of this city are obviously unpopular to attempt once more, through you, to influence public opinion. But the most unpopular council is not necessarily more filled with unwisdom. The masters of Dublin I have addressed in vain. I now ask the citizens of Dublin to consider what effect the policy

---

[1] Russell addressed a demonstration meeting in the Royal Albert Hall, London, Saturday evening, November 1. The object was to assist the Dublin strikers and to secure James Larkin's immediate release from Mountjoy Prison.

[2] "Dublin Fanaticism", printed in *The Irish Worker* (Dublin), November 1, 1913.

[3] Text: from *The Times* (London), Thursday, November 13, 1913. *The Times* immediately reprinted it as a broadsheet.

of the masters is going to have. What has been gained by this resolute refusal of the federated employers to meet the only body with which negotiations can be carried on? Are not the forces on the side of labour becoming more resolute and exasperated week by week?

Nobody in Dublin seems to realise the gigantic power the masters have challenged. As a disdainful attitude is manifested on the one side, the leaders of labour have settled into a grim determination never to submit. The labour leaders, men who have it in their power to do what they threaten, declare that they will rather hold up the industrial system of these islands than see the humiliation of the men completed. Are the citizens content? Do they think it right they should sit silent and have all this brought on them because the masters are too proud to meet the representatives of labour in Dublin? These people seem to read nothing, know nothing, or think nothing of what is happening in respect of labour elsewhere in the world. They do not know that organized labour has become one of the great powers, that its representatives are met by the representatives of capital in industrial countries with the respect that the delegates of great nations meet each other. In Great Britain, the Press, representing all parties, unite in condemning the policy of the employers. What is the position of the men? They have declared always that they wanted arbitration boards such as exist in hundreds in industrial centres where the representatives of organized labour and the federated employers could meet and to which disputes over labour could be referred. Agreements entered into after frank and free discussion as between equals the men will keep. They will not keep agreements into which they consider they are forced. Labour has a sense of honour of its own which is as high as the honour of the masters any day.

I will be met by the famous outburst about contracts and the nether world. That sentence was never uttered in the sense in which it was reputed. Mr. Larkin[1] was speaking not with reference to the contracts between masters and men, but about the masters' complaints that owing to strikes they could not carry out their contracts. It may have been an unfeeling remark, but it was not the defiance of all honour between master and employee that an abbreviated report made it.

Sir, if you will permit me to say something which may irritate the Irish press, but which, I think, is true and necessary to be said, if the Dublin

[1] James Larkin, the Irish Labour leader. He died January 30, 1947, aged 71. No letters from AE were among the scanty personal papers. See *Jim Larkin: the Rise of the Underman* by R. M. Fox (London, 1957: Lawrence and Wishart).

journals had not been so manifestly biased on the side of the employers, reporters would not have come to regard their work, not as the true gathering of strike news, but the making up of a case against the men. Nor would it have been so necessary for me to emphasize one side, as I did in my *Open Letter* and the much abused speech at the Albert Hall. I am charged with being a revolutionary, I who for seven or eight years past have week by week been expounding an orderly evolution of society. I am charged as being against religion, I the sole poet of my generation who has never written a single poem which did not try to express a spiritual mood. But I am not with those who wish to bring about in Ireland a peace of God without any understanding, and I and all free spirits will fight with all our power against the fanatics who would bludgeon us into their heaven, to bow to their savage conception of a deity. The deity of the infuriated bigot, call him by what holy name they choose, is never anything but the Old Adversary, who can put on the whole outward armoury of God. I have known, worked with, and loved many noble men, true priests of Christ, and they would not, I am sure assert that the spirit that drives a mob to bludgeon and kick parents before the eyes of their children is the spirit which is present at the elevation of the Host. What I say here of the hooligans of religion in Dublin I would say with equal sincerity of the hooligans of religion in Belfast.

But I do not wish now to explain or defend myself, but to point out the danger of allowing the present policy to continue. I tell the citizens of this city that, if the civil authorities, the masters, and their allies in the Press had been trying deliberately and of set purpose to make of Dublin another Barcelona, with the bomb of the Anarchist a frequent blazing terror in the streets, if they wished to empty the churches, and make of Dublin another Paris, they could not devise a policy more certain to bring about the result. The Irish are a gentle people, but history is thronged with evidence that in long exasperated men, suffering from real or fancied injustice, gentleness turns to ferocity. To know that is true we can find ample proof in the story of our own race, whether we begin with mythical Cat Head, in the first far-off uprising of the common people in Ireland, or come nearer our own time to the Dynamitards. Does no one read history nowadays? Is there not a single man in Dublin with knowledge of the human heart? Do not the most kindly and submissive natures change in character through what they believe is injustice or oppression? Natural good is transmuted by some devilish alchemy into hate, and forces are engendered which attract to them all that has been thought by the demoniac outcasts of society, so that the methods of the terrorists seem the only ones which can be adopted.

I ask my fellow-townsmen to think whether it would not have been better for the masters to treat the men as human beings who could be reasoned with than to issue ultimatums like despots to subjects who must be coerced without discussion? I ask whether it is most likely agreements will be kept and good work done if the men are starved into submission or if they are made after the most open interchange of opinions? The state has set up a tribunal which has given its judgement. Ought not public opinion to insist on the recommendation of the Askwith Committee being tried? How can the masters complain of the lawlessness of the workers when they themselves set an example by ignoring the verdict of the only legal tribunal which has tried the case? Dublin seems to be stumbling darkly and blindly to a tragedy, and the silence of those who foresee and do not speak is a crime. It is time for the Chorus to cry out to warn the antagonists in the drama. Yours, etc., Geo. W. Russell ("AE")

G. W. ERSKINE RUSSELL[1] London

[issue] Friday, November 21, 1913

TO THE EDITOR, *THE TIMES* (London)

Sir, I have no reason to be ashamed of any of my names; and I must esteem it an honour that I share three of them with the brilliant author who has been more generally known as "AE". But this honour has inconvenient accompaniments. I am assailed from all quarters by criticism of my supposed exploits in poetry, agriculture, feminism, and now "Larkinism".

An agitated lady writes, anonymously:

I am astonished and grieved to see that you, a Churchman and a professedly "Catholic" Churchman, should actually take part in a meeting to support the Syndicalist Larkin! . . .

I have read some of your writings with pleasure and profit, but I could not have believed till I saw it in print, and read your letter in The Times, *and the comments on it in the leader, that you could publicly support a demagogue, apparently carried off his head by vanity and ambition.*

---

[1] G. W. E. Russell, born 1853, died March 17, 1919, was an early friend of Horace Plunkett. He edited Matthew Arnold's published letters, besides writing many books himself, including several volumes of placid autobiography.

[94]

14 March 1914

As my correspondent withholds her address and reads her Times, *pray allow
me to tell her, through your columns, that I am innocent of the particular
offence which she lays to my charge. Your obedient servant, George William
Erskine Russell*

VIOLET RUSSELL TO   17 Rathgar Avenue
KATHARINE TYNAN HINKSON   22.12.13

My dear Mrs Hinkson,

    *I don't know how to thank you for your very charming present. It's
perfectly lovely, and George says the same. And your little note is just as
lovely as it could possibly be. George always told me you were the kindest
and dearest woman living, and he's always right you know.*

    *But I think I ought to scold you, because you really ought not to be giving
me these lovely things, and much as I like them, it really means much more
to me that you should like me one little bit even. I just wanted to say that
to you.*

    I have finished the Reminiscences. *That book is really an education to
me, because I am frightfully ignorant about that period. And I have been
positively gloating over your* Anthology.[1] *I never saw a book more gorgeously
produced. I like the poems very much too. Every one who was here last night
was wanting to go and get it straight away.*

    *I wish to you all a merry Christmas and a good new year. My love to you,
dear K. T. H. Yours ever, Violet Russell*

TO JOHN QUINN   *Irish Homestead*
                              14 March 1914

My dear Quinn,

    I have no intention of giving-in to the priests. I was not made that way.
At present I am trying to put some constructive ideas into the heads of
the unfortunate workers in Dublin. Nobody seems to care a damn in this
cursed country about the poor. Everybody tramples on them. They are
housed worse than swine. The Church bullies them. The press lies about
them. The law is weighted heavily against them. And with the exception .
of myself, and a Fellow of Trinity, a professor in the College of Science

[1] *The Wild Harp* (London, 1913: Sidgwick).

[95]

and a Professor in the new University, they can get no outside aid or advice at all. It is not my job but I have got to do what I can or be ashamed of myself. I am working slowly at a book with an Irish labour policy.[1] It seems odd that a person like myself, originally shy, intended to be an artist or a poet, should get caught into labour or economic movements. But I suppose it is all right and one won't go back empty handed to the stars.

We are all wondering whether Ulster will fight. They would at a word given by Carson. There are 100,000 of them drilled and armed with rifles, and there are, I believe two or three machine guns. And they are all stark, raving mad with hatred of the Catholics whom they regard as Hottentots. I wonder will the diplomatists stave the row off? There will be bloodshed, anyhow, whether much or little the Lord alone knows.

Moore's *Vale* is out, the most scandalous of all his books. I escaped with a halo, but halos fixed on one's brows by the wicked don't add to one's glory. I can't help liking Moore in spite of his bad taste. He is no hypocrite and is never afraid to say what he thinks. Everybody else here is cowed by all kinds of conventions, of religion or politics or society, and they are dreadfully shocked if you say anything outside of the conventions. Moore, having in *Vale* reanointed himself with the oil of his old sins until he appeared dripping with them, has gone on a pilgrimage to the Holy Land where he is collecting local colour for a romance about Jesus of Nazareth.[2] Having desecrated one holy island he is now going to desecrate the Holy Land in Asia. At least I imagine so. He won't come back to Ireland now, I think, ever. There are one or two folk here who would murder him.

I did not care much for Lady Gregory's book *Our Irish Theatre*, she centralises herself a great deal too much, and I think she gives too little credit to the Fays.[3] Yeats Martyn and Moore started the romantic movement so far as the writing of plays is concerned in modern Ireland, but the two Fays are entitled entirely to the credit of starting an Irish school of acting. Without them it could not have been done. They trained the actors, they established the tradition, and they worked at it for years without aid from Yeats or Lady Gregory. It was with a good deal of

[1] *The National Being.*

[2] *The Brook Kerith*, published August 1916.

[3] T[homas] G. K[eohler] reviewing *The Fays of the Abbey Theatre* by W. G. Fay and Catherine Carswell, expressed the same view in the *Dublin Magazine*, October 1935, pp. 89-90. The Fays left the Abbey Theatre in January 1908. Yeats dedicated *The King's Threshold* (1904) to Frank Fay, and *On Baile's Strand* (1904) to William G. Fay.

difficulty I induced Yeats to give them *Kathleen ni Houlihan.* I think historians of movements ought to be generous to those obscure folk who work at the foundations and did all the hard work, unthanked, when nobody looked on or praised them. I knew all about their work before Yeats or Lady Gregory came on the scene at all, and I always felt the Fays never got the credit they were entitled to get. It was at their suggestion, not Yeats or Lady Gregory's, that the National Theatre[1] was formed. I drew up the rules for it at Willie Fay's request, and for a year after the first performance of *Kathleen ni Houlihan* and my *Deirdre* the actor members of the Society subscribed 6d a week among themselves to hire a little hall for rehearsals. Of course they would never have made the society famous but for the writers like Yeats, Synge and Lady Gregory coming along. But they ought to get the credit for founding the Irish school of acting, as the writers founded the literary drama. I like Lady Gregory, but she does not know the origins of the National Theatre Society because she was not in Dublin. She writes pleasant gossip, but is as inaccurate as George Moore, almost, in parts where I can check it. . . . Yours ever, AE

TO SIR HORACE PLUNKETT   *The Irish Homestead*
                                          27th May 1914

My dear Plunkett,

I have received a full report of the conference at Tipperary and your speech. I have cut out the references to Home Rule because I could not have inserted them in the paper without making a protest in my Notes of the Week, or in the Leading Article against the introduction of politics by you at a co-operative meeting. All along, though I have been an extreme Nationalist, I have held loyally and faithfully to the principle that the movement should not intervene in party politics and that the Co-operative platform should not be used either as an argument in favour of one side or the other. If you refer again to this matter, I shall either have to make a public protest in The *Homestead* or resign my editorship of the paper. Your remarks, if correctly reported, are an argument in favour of Home Rule and, in my opinion, you have violated the principle of neutrality which you yourself set up.

I am sorry to have to write like this, but I just want to tell you that if you have any desire to split up the Ulster societies from you, another

[1] The early *Minutes* (incomplete) are now in the National Library of Ireland, Dublin (from George Roberts's papers).

speech of that kind reported in Ulster and commented on by the Ulster papers, will do for you what John Dillon could not have done, that is wreck your movement. Yours sincerely, G. W. Russell

TO THOMAS BODKIN[1] *Irish Homestead*
Thursday [September 1914]

Dear Bodkin,[2]

I think I have found a pleasant little spot[3] for our visit, Virginia in Co. Cavan. I could not get hold of our [*illegible*] and they remembered being at Virginia ten years ago when I was an [*illegible*]. There are woods and a large lake just behind the hotel. I propose to start on Thursday afternoon, I think 3 o.c. Thursday next week of course. We will return Saturday night and will have two whole days and I hope good weather. I have asked James Stephens to come along also and have secured permission to bring him from his keeper. I put it to her that I had to provide somebody to talk to you while I was painting and that I would be miserable if you sat gloomily doing nothing in a lone land which I was selfishly [*illegible*] my brush on canvas without [*illegible*] to you [*illegible*]. So I have secured James for you and of course for myself. Will this arrangement suit you. If so I will write off to the Hotel Boss to keep rooms and to have a car at Virginia Road Station as the village is six miles from the station. I do hope the weather will be fine because Virginia as I remember it was a pleasant spot and the woods were all along the lake with miles of bluebells. Yours ever, AE

TO CHARLES WEEKES *Irish Homestead*
Wednesday [October 14, 1914]

My dear Charlie,

Send along the mss and I will read them with the greatest interest and will give an honest opinion. I always do tell exactly what I think on literary matters as indeed I try to do on all other things. I used to think twenty years ago that you despised what came easily and naturally to you and desired to gain the qualities of other writers, and that that was a great mistake because all that a writer has to rely on is the natural mould of his mind and if he breaks that up or will not use it he is wrapping his talent

---

[1] From a typed copy.   [2] *See* Biographical Notes.   [3] *See* Note 8, p. 230.

in a napkin and stealing somebody else's talent to trade with and that literary law will force him to account to the true owner of the talent for every profit made out of it. You proved in your first book your natural wit, but there was a great deal of poetic felony in it and some fundamental brainwork, and I had hope you would leave some literary admirations, which appeared here and there, and revert to your own will and speak from your own centre. I am glad to hear you have been writing. So send them along. I want information about your pilgrimage. Though curiously I feel I know all about you by some inner certitude, just as I feel about Dan and some other friends of my youth.

You asked in your letter[1] why was I scared about Ireland. I can hardly tell you because I can hardly explain it to myself. I have a conviction deep inside me that we are going to have one more heart-searching trial, baring our lives to the very spirit, and that within the next few years. May be much sooner. The dragons of the past have not died and were only sleeping and recent events have stirred them. With the events in Ireland and the European war, I may be mistaken. The best thing which could happen to us would be a foray of about 2,000 Germans in the north and a rush of the rest of Ireland to rescue Ulster. But the Gods do not arrange things as in the story books or in the fairy land of imagination. Meanwhile, whatever you say about prose, I am working away at my book in such spare hours as I can get. I would like to leave a meditation over Ireland behind me. My poetic imagination has tempered itself by struggling with material forces so long that it is not likely I will go off in [*illegible*] . . . entirely. Yours ever, George

TO CHARLES WEEKES   *Irish Homestead*
                                          Saturday [October 17, 1914]

My dear Charlie,

I will read anything of yours with interest irrespective of date. Since writing to you before I have been reminded that I have to read a paper on the first Thursday in November and as I am preparing for an exhibition of pictures which opens the last Saturday of this month it might be better if you sent the mss about the first week in November as my mind will be freer then. Exhibitions especially involve a lot of work, and my colleagues

[1] Russell wrote to Weekes on July 21, 1914: "Lord, what a mess our politicians have made of their policies. I expect the hell of a row, if not this year certainly before the matter is settled."

generally leave all arrangements to me as the practical person in the group. I am often sorry I lost my old reputation as a dreamy unpractical man. It saved me a lot of work. Yours ever, George Russell

TO J. C. SQUIRE   84 Merrion Square
                                              Tuesday [December 1914]

My dear Squire,[1]

Alas, if you had written Saturday. I promised the verses to a famished little paper[2] here whose editor implored me to grace a Christmas number with an eleemosynary donation of poetry and I consented. Otherwise I would have sent them to you with pleasure. Lyrics and poetry have been pushed out of my mind because I am trying to write a prose book on *The National Being, some thoughts on an Irish Polity*, and I only write such rude lyrics as insist on pushing their way into my recalcitrant mind. *The Times* did understand I think, at least the editor did because I told him that I wrote the verses[3] as a protest against the bloodthirsty clergymen who wanted to go to the front to do their share of killing and who wrote to the papers complaining their bishops would not let them. The new Irish poet[4] has gone into the van. I heard vaguely that he had enlisted. I have not seen him for four months but that may be because he borrowed £5 from me on a promise to return it the next day. This singular silence which I have not broken by enquiry has made me think that his verse will lack something or other. However I believe it has been set up and Dunsany had the proofs. The poet is very young but I regret to say he shows this in common with many Irish poets that they borrow money and never mention it again. I would share my possessions with a fellow poet cheerfully but I object to them telling me a little tale always about their ship coming in the next day when they might have had what they wanted without straining an imagination better employed on their art.

---

[1] John Collings Squire (1884-December 26, 1958). Poet, parodist, journalist. He was literary editor of *The New Statesman*, 1913-1918, and edited the *London Mercury*, 1919-1934. Knighted in 1933.

[2] Not yet identified.

[3] *Gods of War: 1914* by AE, printed in *The Times*, September 30, 1914. (*Collected Poems*, 1919 ed., p. 236.) He contributed other poems to *The Times*, on January 28, March 5 and 18, April 5 (and August 9–in *The Times'* special *Poetry Supplement*), 1915. Collected with other new poems in *Gods of War*, privately printed (100 copies), 1915.

[4] Francis Ledwidge (1891-1917). (*See* Note 9, p. 231).

If I have any lyrics worth printing I will remember the *New Statesman;*[1] but war is a bad time for poetry. The Devil is the only supernatural power ready to inspire and he had a bad ear and worse style. You never came to Ireland as you intended. I am half way through Shaw's *Common Sense:* why has he not a touch of spirituality? With kind regards, AE

TO MRS A. S. GREEN[2]   The Plunkett House
                                                                                         Thursday Jan. 21, 1915

I see you are interested in the Tara title[3] discussion. You as a Nationalist have a right to protest. But that the *Irish Times* or the London *Times* should do so seems to me to deserve some ironical comment. I write a lot of satires but never publish them. They are only for private circulation. But as you are interested in this matter here is a copy of my complaint. Yours ever, AE

[The satire "complaint" is typed and *not* signed, tipped to the edge of AE's letter.]

TARA

They buried Tara underneath the grass
And herded bullocks o'er the graves of Kings,
And cursed us for the memory that clings
To our dead lions, not their living ass.
They joyed to see the Celtic culture pass
And all its glories, song and art, take wings.
And now, the dogs, they do pretend it stings
Souls hidden in impenetrable brass
Because some passing alien steals the name
Not they, but we, held sacred. Hush, you dogs!
Sorrows divine can touch you not. You may
Never be champions of our island's fame
Who changed its harp notes for the grunts of hogs.
Your Tara is Tara-de-boom-de-ray.

[1] Russell's sole contribution to the *New Statesman* was an article, "The Co-operative Movement", in its *Irish Supplement*, July 12, 1913 (in vol 1).

[2] Alice Sophia Amelia Stopford, widow of the historian John Richard Green. (*See* Biographical Notes.)

[3] Lord Aberdeen (1847-1934), the Lord Lieutenant of Ireland (first in 1886, then from 1906-1915), proposed adopting the title The Marquess of Aberdeen and Tara when he was promoted Marquess. He yielded to Irish resentment and varied his new title to the Marquess of Aberdeen and Temair. (*The Times*, January 16-February 6, 1915.)

TO CHARLES WEEKES   *Irish Homestead*
                                                Saturday [March 6, 1915]
Dear Charlie,

Thanks. I am glad you liked the Litany.[1] Words are a poor and cracked
mirror of one's feelings. One lives with a strained heart all the time. I
have so many friends in this struggle. Two dear boys, sons of Anderson,
both were killed, one a week ago and the other a few weeks before that. I
knew them since they were children. Other friends of mine are out both
on land and sea, some mine-sweeping, some in the battleships, some in the
trenches while some are missing; all friends of our movement here,
people who were about me often and the best kind of Irish. Our civilization
really does beget fine people with bodies, sheaths for the unrusted steel
of the spirit. There are many I knew and hardly expected that so flashing
a spirit would be drawn from the sheath of the body when there was need.
Kind regards to Mrs Charlie and Dan. With love, yours ever, AE

TO JAMES STEPHENS   The Plunkett House
                                                      [? March 1915]
My dear James,

I was wondering how long I would feel very close to you without either
of us giving a sign. It was an unfair advantage fate took because the book[2]
came and you felt you ought to send it, even if you did not feel the necessity
of communicating otherwise. Well you had to get the book out. There are
always beautiful things in your verse, but I can't disguise from you my
opinion that while your prose gets better and more poetical it has done so
by vampirising the poet in verse. I do not like this last book of verse as
well as the first two. I feel that your whole being is not in it as in the first
two. You have put your whole being into books like the *Demigods* and the
Crock, and I want you and not a section of you. I am too good a friend to
cheat you or allow myself to be cheated by you. You have of course got
ease and lightness in *Songs from the Clay* but you do not strike the same
full chord of feeling as in the other books of verse. It is not that you as a
writer are losing power but you are putting your increasing power into

---

[1] "A European Litany" by AE, printed in *The Times* (London), March 5, 1915,
reprinted in *Gods of War* (1915), p. 22 and in *Collected Poems*, p. 256 (as "To the New
Gods").

[2] *Songs from the Clay* (London, March 1915: Macmillan.)

other work. To write verse as good as your other things you would have to stop prose I think. Is this unkind? No, dear man, your *Demigods* shows that your literary power is getting greater and more mature. I think of it with more pleasure than any of your books and I don't care what other critics may say, it is a beautiful phantasy. Of course if any of the other young poets one has never heard of but are sure to be growing up in Ireland came to me with *Songs from the Clay* I would clap him on the back and encourage him and tell people I had found another poet. But you have chosen I think wisely to be a poet in prose and you are a unique prose poet, and you cannot expect to eat your poetic cake in prose and have it after in verse. Nobody can expect that. Of course there are beautiful things in the book which only you could write like my favourite (which is still my favourite) "The Snare". But it is not the side of your nature which moves me most which is in the new volume. I may be getting old and stupid over economics and incapable of appreciating a new point of view. Men at forty-eight are really on the shelf. They may go on talking and writing, but the Lord does not use them as prophets and forerunners; my bolt is shot. You, lucky man, have many bolts yet to shoot, good swift arrows I believe against the solidifying human matter the world calls the heart.

There is nothing interesting in Ireland now. The war has overflowed all ancient landmarks and Ireland is a Province of the British Empire. Thank the Lord there are still wild western places where no nationality or imperialism has tainted and life is wild and sweet and elemental as when Fion and his wild hunters pursued the deer.

I am damned tired of the world and want to go back to the stars. All the original starfire in me will die out if I stay longer. I hear you are forming ideas about Ireland, ambitious ideas, to be the Balzac of this museum of characters. If you could be the torpedo to explode them I would be enchanted. They are all dead in their bodies and the whimsies which delight you in them are posthumous vibrations. I have no news. I still write occasional verses which have appeared in *The Times*. People praise them which convinces me they are bad. When the world lends an ear it is sure to be something worldly. I always wanted to write for Gods. Damn them, they were deaf. Are you ever coming back? I suppose not. Well the world is a home anywhere for the imaginative man and your mind is not like the Lotus which is tied by a long stem to the mud of its native pond. I saw a very excellent article by you on Borrow, a very self-conscious old Bohemian I am afraid. But it was a good article. You write with great ease now and ought to be able to paint in words anything you imagine or think. I heard from Jack White that he saw you often. He said he had found peace in something or other. But it won't last more than a month. His peace comes in pieces. Give him my kind regards anyhow. I like him for all his quick silverness of his mind. Also remember me to Maud Gonne who is I hear in Paris. Kind regards to your household. As for yourself I am always Yours ever, AE

TO CHARLES WEEKES   *Irish Homestead*
                                               Thursday [? April 14, 1915]
My dear Charlie,

I think the poem you must have missed was called "Ares".[1] I have not a copy with me but I believe it appeared on Monday last week. Was that Easter Monday? You may have been holidaying then.

I thought the article[2] in *The Times* true: that is all I care about. The editor writes me tonight that he liked it immensely and so did others to whom he spoke. I do not think it out of place in a daily paper. I think all the other articles are out of place in a daily paper because they have nothing to say, as a rule. Robinson[3] has been wanting me for some time to write him articles. I will try what he will stand. I am quite aware that I have no popular ideas. I wish I could get on with my book on an Irish polity which, at the fifteenth chapter, is hung up because I don't know what the Home Rule Bill will come to and I must have some reference to Irish government in the future. I will be cursed enough in Ireland when it appears. I will have the press, the church, and the capitalists all against me. But I am a good Christian: I go one better than the Gospels. I pray not merely for my enemies but to have enemies to keep me alive. It is our friends we should guard against. They make us stiffen in the convention of ourselves they like. All my friends form conventional ideas of what I am and they are hurt if I don't act like their convention of me.

I wish the war was over. Ireland is quivering like a disturbed jellyfish and cannot act from its own will and its own centre. I wonder will

[1] "Ares" by AE, printed in *The Times* (London), April 5, 1915. It was reprinted in *Gods of War* (1915), p. 10 and in *Collected* Poems, p. 241.

[2] "The Spiritual Conflict: a coming recoil" was printed in *The Times* (London), Thursday, April 14, 1915. Reprinted in *Imaginations and Reveries* (1915), pp. 86-92.

[3] Geoffrey Robinson (1874-November 7, 1944), editor of *The Times*, 1912-1919 and from 1923-1941. Later changed his surname to Dawson. See *Geoffrey Dawson and our Times* by Sir Evelyn Wrench (London, 1955: Hutchinson).

any thing short of a German invasion or an earthquake rouse our sleepy folk to think for themselves. Kind regards to Mrs Charlie. Yours ever, AE

TO JAMES H. COUSINS   The Plunkett House
                                                        [May 3, 1915]
My dear Cousins,

Many thanks for your book which appears to me to contain the best work you have done.[1] I read poetry very slowly, a poem at a time, as it is the only way I can get any good out of it but the verses I have read I think are the best you have done. The poem you call "Awake" presents a true idea with real power. I like especially those lines with the recurrent ideas.

> *The deafness men call hearing*
> *The blindness that men call sight*

These are extraordinarily good. You are faithful to the spirit and you will get your reward. I hope you are getting on well in the land of the Saxon. The land of the Gael is in an awful state just now. We have had eruptions of publicans[2] over Lloyd George which disgust me with the name of Irishman. They say drink and nationality are bound up and *The Freeman* would make one believe it is the duty of Christians to fight for the licensed trade. You are well out of it, and I have no doubt you will like all Irishmen do well outside Ireland and will write better poetry about Ireland out of it than in it. Distance will give the glamour as it did to Yeats *Isle of Innisfree*. You say you like my *Times* poems but my days as a poet are past. Age (I am near fifty) destroys the lyrical in one. You are younger and have years of lyric writing in you yet. Gather your verses while you may. With kind regards, Yours ever, AE

[1] "Early in 1915 I was still in England, held up by the war. Grant Richards had published a small book of verse of mine under the title *Straight and Crooked*, reflecting my crossover from the fluid romanticism of renascent Ireland to the settled practicalism of a north English manufacturing town. AE's promise of reward for what he called my faithfulness to the spirit (vulgarly known as incorrigible idealism) was encouraging. Critics were most generous. What the 'eruptions of publicans' were I do not remember." (J.H.C.)

[2] The "Eruptions" were caused by the Chancellor of the Exchequer (D. Lloyd George) introducing heavier taxation on alcoholic liquor. See *Parliamentary Reports* (Hansard), vol. 71 (1915), columns 899–902, (April 29) for William O'Brien's (1852–1928) praise of the Irish distilled liquors, etc. *See* AE's leading article in the *Irish Homestead*, vol. 22, pp. 301–302 (May 8, 1915). See *The Irish Writers, 1880–1940* by Herbert Howarth (London, 1958: Rockliff), pp. 190–198, for a discussion of this.

TO JAMES STEPHENS   17 Rathgar Avenue
                                              Monday [? May 24, 1915]

My dear James,

I have not corresponded with you for some time. I was wondering
whether the absence of communications would incline your heart to come
back here. But I will not persist in this policy. Your letter shows that you
are disillusioned about France and French literature, French ideas. They
are really no better than English or German or any other; just the same old
things, "art thou there again, old mole?" There is a kind of average in
human life, a level we do not get away from no matter where we go. It is
like the sea which levels itself always even if a little wave here and there
gets its head above the other waves, the general level is maintained.
Ireland is just as good as any of them. Not in this or that special particular
but its "level", its "divine average" is the same.

Of course there is nothing to talk about. If one man was killed we would
talk about it. But when a million are killed we cannot think at all. We are
not ready for the infinitudes, an expert said no teacher could mistrust more
than twelve pupils. After that he could only deal with them by formula,
stupefy them. We can only get intimate with half a dozen or a dozen people
or ideas in a long life. It needs a Buddha to get intimate with the world soul
which is the multitude of souls. As a truth I hold that the way is narrow and
strait and when we wander about attracted by multitudes we lose our way.
The way is within and not without hence it is narrow, strait. This sounds
cryptic but you will understand it. I see you read the *Homestead!* I am
amazed. It is an unsavoury job. My task of the augean stables. Every
person gets such a job from his conscience but it is of no interest except
to the person who does it and the cows whose abodes are being made
sanitary. Anyhow I am clear of it. By the time you get this I will be off to
Donegal on my annual holiday. Dear God don't I hunger and thirst for
the pure hills and the sea! I go on Thursday after I finish this week's paper
and will for a month be at Dunfanaghy my address there will be c/o Janie
Stewart, Breaghy, Ballymore P.O., Donegal. Dermod O'Brien goes with
me. Seamus O'Sullivan is already there. I think Houston will follow and
perhaps John Eglinton. Our evenings will be long and conversational. Why
the blazes are you in Paris? Your own soul couldn't find an excuse for
you which would not be as shallow as the German excuse for invading
Belgium. Your letter seems to indicate financial difficulties. Is that so?
Can I help according to my means? You know, James darling, I would do

what I could if you let me know. What is that between thee and me? I guess it is difficult for all of our tribe to live now that the world has declared war on civilization, and Ares is trying to whip us into heroism and sternness and disregard to beauty and love. I explain him in the verses herewith[1] one of several I puzzled the readers of *The Times* with. It is the dregs of my flask and filled out of Castelay on the springs of Helicon. It is [*word indecipherable*] hard when the vintage is good we won't drink it and when it is in its dregs people will pay heavily for it. Ireland is rotten with drink but it has its old courage and love of a fight and it is enlisting for the army and dying on battlefields not its own in the good old Irish fashion. The net result of the war will be that we will exchange characteristics with the Germans. We will have an ancestral bureaucracy organising industry and life to manifest power. That is if we win. If we don't we will be a crippled timorous decaying old race like Spain after its day of glory. When I say "we" I include all the British Isles unless we Irish have enough fire in us to rise on our own account out of the general ashes. I could talk for hours upon the psychological effects of the war, its good and its evil results. But I daresay you have heard all the speculations and are bored with all the virtues of good and bad they open. We devour our cake of the imagination before it is baked, we human beings, and hence our lethargy. But let me not be philosophical with you.[2] May the Lord have you in his keeping and bring you out of that city of exile home to your own people. Kind regards to Mrs. Stephens. Yours ever, AE

TO DERMOD O'BRIEN[3]   [? July 1915]

Dear Dermod,

Here are some copies of the little book.[4] You said you would like a couple to give away. I think you would rather send them away than read them but I don't mind that. The basis of friendship is mutual unintelligibility which excites a pleasant curiosity and so long as we are unintelligible

---

[1] "Ares" printed in *The Times* (London), April 5, 1915, p. 7. Reprinted in *Gods of War* (1915), p. 10, and in *Collected Poems*, p. 241.

[2] *See* Note 10, p. 231.

[3] Dermod O'Brien (1865-October 3, 1945), the painter. He was long a member of the I.A.O.S. Committee. From 1910 he was President of the Royal Hibernian Academy. His wife, Mabel, predeceased him, in 1942. O'Brien was a member of the Irish Conference Committee, which later led to the Irish Convention. See *Palette and Plough* by Lennox Robinson (Dublin, 1948: Browne and Nolan).

[4] *Gods of War.*

to each other so long we are interested. Very glad we fixed date for show[1] because the day after you added a week the sketching club made up its mind to exhibit and made great moan that we had a fortnight of November. This will teach them the truth of the proverb that the early bird catches the worm napping. Yours ever, AE

TO SARAH PURSER   *Irish Homestead*
                                                   Friday [? 1915]
Dear Sarah Purser,

A thousand thanks for your note. You aimed straight at my vanity and got home. I don't mind whether people like my poetry or not. My own conscience in that is the only critic I care about much. But the *Homestead* is an intellectual adventure on perilous seas, and it is full of excitements hard blows, kicks and no laurel wreaths, and whosoever with brains to their account likes it[2] or is interested in it anyhow is a friend indeed. Yours ever, AE

TO CHARLES WEEKES   84 Merrion Square
                                                   [September 14, 1915]
My dear Charlie,

I had a few copies printed of verses written since the war broke out.[3] I don't like to publish them or ever include them with earlier poems as they are different in mood, and I am afraid they are poor stuff, the children of literary old age. Anyhow I got a few copies printed for myself to give away to my friends and I send you a copy "for your information". Mrs. Charlie sent me a photograph of you in uniform; a uniform which was half of a military and half a culinary character and suggests that you were the head cook of the regiment. I believe in reality you are an aeroplanist or something electrical and engineering in the way of warfare. Anyhow you look very fine in spite of the white cap, and I am sure you are putting every ounce into it. I am only fit for agricultural economics, painting and things of that kind, and a machine is an unknown creature whose brains

[1] Pictures by Frances Baker, William Crampton Gore, Dermod O'Brien, P.R.H.A., and G. W. Russell, exhibited at the Hall, 8 Merrion Row, Dublin, from Monday, November 1, to Saturday, November 13 (1915).

[2] Minna Wagner placed a laurel wreath in Wagner's bed after the triumphal first performance of *Rienzi!*

[3] *Gods of War, with other Poems.*

are foreign to my character. The only machinery I understand is dairy machinery. I am glad my elder boy is only sixteen for he would enlist, sure as fate. I am getting excited about the war because when it ends I think we are bound to have social revolution all over Europe. See "Apocalyptic".[1] Don't trouble to reply. I know you are busy. Yours ever, AE

TO MACMILLAN AND CO. LTD   17 Rathgar Avenue,
                                                     Monday [October 25, 1915]
Dear Sirs,
    I would be glad if you would allow the "Fianna Company" permission to use the poems they ask for. The "Fianna Company" I believe is really an enthusiastic lady who believes in boy scouts and has organised companies of them and wishes to combine poetry and scouting and make her boys into poets as well as heroes. She is certainly not looking for profits. I believe she is a sister of Sir Josslyn Gore-Booth,[2] at least I surmise that that is the "Fianna Company". Her boy scouts are called "Fianna". I don't think her experiment will be a success but I wish it well and I like the idea of boy scouts with a pocket book of poetry, so please let them try. Yours sincerely, Geo. W. Russell AE

TO GEORGE A. MOORE[3]   [April 6, 1916][4]

    Your account of Yeats is very amusing, quite in the *Ave Vale* mood, but I don't think you have dealt seriously with the psychology of Yeats. He began about the time of *The Wind among the Reeds* to do two things consciously, one to create a "style" in literature, the second to create or rather to re-create W. B. Yeats in a style which would harmonise with the literary style. People call this posing. It is really putting on a mask, like his actors, Greek or Japanese, a mask over life. The actor must talk to the emotion on the mask, which is a fixed emotion. W. B. Y. began twenty years ago vigorously defending Wilde against the charge of being a poseur. He said it was merely living artistically, and it was the duty of

[1] A poem in *Gods of War*, p. 37. In *Collected Poems*, p. 251.
[2] A member of the I.A.O.S. Committee.
[3] Text from John Eglinton's *A Memoir of AE*, pp. 110-112.
[4] Conjectured from the allusion in *Letters of George Moore to John Eglinton*, p. 35 (privately printed, 1942).

everybody to have a conception of themselves, and he intended to conceive of himself. The present W. B. Y. is the result. The error in his psychology is, that life creates the form, but he seems to think that the form creates life. If you have a style, he argued once with me, you will have something to say. He seems to have also thought, though he never said so, that if you make a picturesque or majestic personality of yourself in appearance, you will become as wonderful inside as outside. He has created the mask and he finds himself obliged to speak in harmony with the fixed expression of the mask, and that accounts for the lifelessness of his later talk and writing. His memories of his childhood are the most vacant things man ever wrote, pure externalities, well written in a dead kind of way, but quite dull except for the odd flashes. The boy in the book might have become a grocer as well as a poet. Nobody could be astonished if this had been issued as a novel, part one, to find in part two the hero had for some reason given up thinking of literature and become a merchant. Why does he do it? We are interested in Yeats's inner mind, whatever it is, but not in anecdotes of things he saw and whose effect on his own mood is not clear. He bores me terribly now, and he was once so interesting. You are a humorist and a novelist, and he is subject to your art. I want life and thought, and he talks solemn platitudes under the impression that this nonsense is arcane wisdom. Any bit of pedantry a couple of hundred years old seems to him to have a kind of divine authority. But in a way we are interested in him still because of his past. We go to hear him as we go to see the tomb of Shakespeare or the Italian garden where Keats lies. The only difference is that Yeats is his own coffin and memorial tablet. Why can't he be natural? Such a delightful creature he was when young! And at rare moments when he forgets himself he is still interesting as ever almost.

TO EDWARD MACLYSAGHT[1]   17 Rathgar Avenue
                                    Monday [April 17, 1916]

My dear Lysaght,

Yes I will go with pleasure. Please tell me what station I go to. I could get off any time after 12 o'clock on Thursday before Easter.[2] You said

---

[1] Edward E. Lysaght. Now Chairman of the Irish Manuscripts' Commission. (*See* Biographical Notes.)

[2] Thursday, April 20. AE began his return journey from Raheen, Tuamgraney, Co. Clare, to Dublin, on Tuesday, April 25. *See* the *Memoir*, p. 115.

there was a late train I think but I can't remember the station. The later it is on Thursday the better for me as I get the paper off and don't throw work on others. I will be very glad to see Clare. With kind regards. Yours ever, AE

TO EDWARD MACLYSAGHT   *Irish Homestead*
                                    [Monday ? May 22, 1916]
My dear Lysaght,

I discovered yesterday the balance of the stretchers in my painting room. They had come and my boy without telling me about them had placed them in a corner where I supposed they were the first lot because they were made up in the same way. They have been there for weeks so you must not blame your staff. I write this to take all the blame upon myself and my careless household. Now it only remains to get the bill. But perhaps I will find this inside the parcel yet unopened. There is a committee meeting tomorrow of our budding Constitutionalists.[1] Hope you are feeling well now. Kind regards to Mrs Ned. Yours ever, AE

TO CHARLES WEEKES   *Irish Homestead*
                                           25 May 1916
My dear Charlie,

If any honest man expressed his views on the Irish revolt, with absolute lucidity and fearlessness, whether he was Unionist or Nationalist, he would find, first, that no paper would have the courage to print what he wrote and secondly, if it was printed he would find himself in jail. I asked my own soul about all this trouble and got, not opinions, but a direction of feeling, and what I wrote under that inspiration I do not intend to make public simply because I am in a movement which is non-political and I am an important figure in it and any statement made by me might create a split and cause intense anger in a movement hitherto free from political passions, and in my opinion the only hope of Ireland. I am quite ready to give my opinions on the economic cause of the revolt, as I did in the first number of the *Homestead* which appeared after the rising, but I am not going to deal with the spiritual causes of it, not, at any rate until the passion has subsided somewhat and I myself can write without passion. You want dramatic and spectacular utterances and at the moment everybody is excited. I believe in speaking when the excitement has died down.

[1] The Irish Conference Committee was the unofficial forerunner of the Convention.

I am a philosopher and do not believe truth is best uttered in a highly charged atmosphere. The fact is I am not big enough for the post for which you would cast me, and I know my own limitation, and I have also a hatred of publicity, which is perhaps wrong and personally I would rather a thousand times go into the woods and paint than write about Ireland and it is a small portion of conscience keeps me thinking of it at all. You have given up writing drama but you have not given up casting your friends for parts in the drama of life. It is a mistake.[1] Yours ever, AE

TO THE RT. HON. A. J. BALFOUR, M.P.   84 Merrion Square
1st June 1916

Dear Mr. Balfour,

You probably forget, among the innumerable persons you come into contact with, having met an Irishman introduced to you by F. S. Oliver, under the pseudonym of AE. I remember most vividly a statement you made that evening, with which I agreed then and now, that there were only two possible solutions of the Irish Question. One was complete union with Great Britain and the other was Colonial self-government. Half settlements are no settlements any more than half payments of debts will satisfy creditors and it is pure folly to think that a settlement which excludes Ulster will satisfy the Ireland whose dissatisfaction has created so many Imperial difficulties. Mr. Redmond cannot speak for the Irish people on this matter. He has lived so long out of Ireland that he cannot gauge the feelings of the present generation and his ignorance of the power of the Sinn Fein movement is proof of this. He and his colleagues may now agree to some settlement excluding Ulster but they will never bind Ireland to accept such a settlement as final and any future war in which the Empire was engaged might find the three southern provinces thinking it a good opportunity for the re-conquest of Ulster. A settlement should be a settlement from an English point of view as well as from an Irish. Imperial policy requires guarantees that a self-governing Ireland will be friendly to the Empire. Ireland, on the other hand, will never be contented either with the Empire or a scheme of self-government which divides Ireland and does not allow complete control over Irish affairs, and Ulster will not accept any scheme which does not provide guarantees that it will not be oppressed in respect of religion or by legislation or

[1] *See* Note 11, p. 232.

administration which would be unfair to its economic interests. Ulster will also require some assurace that the self-governing Ireland it is associated with will be friendly to Great Britain. Can these conditions be met in one scheme? I venture to suggest to you that they would be met under a scheme of self-government for Ireland where, instead of the Senate proposed in the Act now on the Statute Book, a House of Lords with a veto would be substituted. The Irish Peers are mainly Protestant. Their loyalty as a class to the Empire is undoubted. They have been allies of Ulster during my lifetime and the possession of a veto by them would be almost equivalent to giving Ulster a veto on legislation for this generation at least, and the power over administration which such a veto would entail. Their traditions would impel them to be friendly to the Empire and this sentiment would continue, for in all probability their sons would be educated in Public Schools and Universities in England, and the younger sons would seek employment in Imperial service.

This scheme could hardly have been proposed by the Liberals fresh from their exploit of limiting the veto of the Lords and the irony of it would have been too great. But if a coalition ministry is going to settle the Irish Question, this difficulty would be greatly diminished. If Unionists agree to it, there are pressing reasons in world conditions why Liberals should also assent. They would have no grounds for opposition if Irish representatives agreed among themselves. It is, obviously, not a scheme Mr. Lloyd George with his political traditions could be the proposer of, and so I write to you who have always been trusted by Ulster Irishmen to suggest that, if you think such a solution possible and desirable, and fitting Imperial policy, you might pass the suggestion on to the Ulster leaders, and, if they approve, the suggestion for such a settlement might come from them in the Conference as the sole condition under which they would feel their own interests and Imperial interests safe in a scheme of self-government for Ireland. Mr. Redmond and his colleagues would I am convinced accept this solution if it was intimated to them by the Ulster leaders that acceptance of it was the sole condition on which Ulster would come in and that failing acceptance they would resist inclusion as before. Ireland would accept it with relief on the whole. There might be ultra democrats but their voices would not be listened to. I am an ultra democrat myself and I sacrifice a good many ideals in making this suggestion and postpone them for the millenium. Irish Nationalists would accept hungrily and with gratitude any measure which Ulster would accept and which would include Ulster. The fact that the scheme was an Ulster

[113]

scheme proposed by Ulster men would go far to make Ulster predominant in a self-governing Ireland. They would have the prestige of finding a solution which the Nationalists could not find.

I may mention that the last time I met Mr. Arthur Griffiths,[1] the founder of the Sinn Fein policy, was just after the introduction of the Home Rule Bill. He thought it bad and said this which is worth remembering, "If a good Bill accepted by Ulster had been introduced I and my party would have disappeared from Ireland. Nobody would have listened to us."

I write this to you as the sole public man in Great Britain whose views count for much in Ulster. If there is anything in the suggestion I beg you for the sake of this unhappy country to consider it and pass it on. Yours sincerely, Geo. W. Russell AE

TO KATHARINE TYNAN HINKSON — *Irish Homestead*
2 June 1916

My dear Mrs. Hinkson,

We are all well here and at home, we had bullets pretty near us but they had other billets. I would like to have locked Sir Horace up. He is too valuable a life to risk in the streets but anyhow he escaped. Ones heart is very heavy. Everybody seems suffering from a kind of suppressed hysteria but it will go off I suppose. I think Ireland is in a bad way and I see no hope at present and Lloyd George is no good. He is a sheer muddler. But we can talk when you are here. It is well you were out of the trouble with kind regards to Hinkson and Pamela. Yours ever, AE

---

[1] Arthur Griffith, born in Dublin, 1872. Until Parnell's fall he worked in a newspaper office: he then went to South Africa to work as a compositor, and returned to Ireland in 1899, founding the weekly *United Irishman* which he wound up in May 1906 after a legal action against him for slander had been won with an award of £500 damages. Immediately he opened another paper, *Sinn Fein* in which similar political opinions were expressed. Griffith, Russell and P. T. Daly, TC., were constituted the Council of the Sinn Fein Co-operative Peoples' Bank Ltd (Dublin), December 1908-January 1909. Horace Plunkett recorded in his diary (January 29, 1908), "AE and Griffith, the editor of *Sinn Fein*, a remarkable young revolutionary, dined. We had an interesting evening." Griffith was one of the five plenipotentiaries sent to London to negotiate the Anglo-Irish Treaty in 1921: his colleagues being Michael Collins (1890-1922), George Gavan Duffy, Robert Barton and Eamonn Duggan. On January 14, 1922 Griffith was provisionally appointed President of the Irish Parliament, with Collins as Chairman. He died (natural causes) August 12, 1922. See George A. Lyons's *Reminiscences of Arthur Griffith and his Times* (Dublin, 1923: Talbot Press), and Padraic Colum's biography of him (Dublin, 1959: Browne & Nolan).

TO EDWARD MACLYSAGHT   *Irish Homestead*
                                                  8 June 1916

Dear Lysaght,

Which would Thursday or Friday next week be most convenient for
you and Mrs Lysaght to receive a wandering artist with a heap of paints
and canvases and an interminable power to talk? My canvases have come
and I could get away either Thursday or Friday next. I will be glad to get
out of this city with its passions which make me ill. Yours ever AE

TO EDWARD MACLYSAGHT   *Irish Homestead*
                                                  Monday [July 18, 1916]

Dear Lysaght,

I have just heard that Sir Horace Plunkett who is now in a nursing home
is going to summon a conference of unofficial folk to consider the Home
Rule question. So that any ideas you and O'Brien[1] and Monteagle may be
working up will come in handy. I have been trying all morning to write
but I have been so stuffed up with food for the past month that I am not
yet hungry enough to be able to think apart from the lazy overfed body
which Mrs Lysaght was so energetically building up around my soul. I
daresay it will take at least a month for me to get underfed enough to let
my soul speak in its usual exasperating way. I don't blame Mrs Lysaght.
She probably thought that the more my soul was clouded over with good
meals the better for other peoples' souls and she worked patriotically to
this end. I find the conference I came up for which was to take place
tomorrow was postponed because of Sir Horace Plunkett's illness. I was
right about the conference but his illness put it off so I might have
remained until Monday and got a leader out of your inexhaustible optimism. I spent a whole day yesterday feverishly working on the pictures and
have improved some of them greatly. I had a very happy time at Raheen.
You are the kindest and most natural folk. Your boots on the cushion was
a great moral act. I admired it and still admire your determination to be
natural. I have put my own boots up in the presence of visitors and am a
comrade. But I had not the courage to put my boots up along with yours.
I am only brave in my own trenches. I shall yield to you if I see you put

[1] George O'Brien (*b.* 1892), the historian. *The Economic History of Ireland* (3 vols.),
vols. 1 and 2 published by Maunsel's, October 1918 and 1919; vol. 3 (1921), published
in London by Longmans Green.

your boots up on my mantlepiece, and will follow you as my leader. You are an Irish reincarnation of a Chinese Taoist. The tao being the gospel of being natural. Let us two start an Irish or Celtic code of manners, liberate us from the despotism of what the English call good taste; that being their accumulation of rusty chains wherewith they chain themselves. As Curtis says in his *Medieval History* the Irish chiefs were most natural people until the English came. I jogged Maunsel about your book¹ and Miss Mitchell's: that is I spoke sternly to Hone who listened with that air of listless agreement which distinguishes him from all other Irishmen. Everybody here is in a rage about Home Rule, and I think the more we rage against it the more eagerly will the Government thrust it on us, like a dose of disagreeable stuff which children must swallow for the good of their stomach. I hope you had something of interest in Limerick on Sunday. I write this mainly to tell you about Plunkett's plan as I thought it would interest you, and to thank you and Mrs Lysaght and Miss McVey and Bobby and Booby² for a delightful holiday and much kindness. Yours ever, AE

TO EDWARD MACLYSAGHT   *Irish Homestead*
                                                 Monday [July 25, 1916]

Dear Lysaght,

I am sorry I have made your naturalness unnatural,³ but even Buddha recognises that the first steps to completely being in accord with nature must be self-conscious. To tell the truth, on that famous occasion when you lifted up your boots while Miss Knox⁴ was there I suspected self-consciousness and an effort to get over it. I admired your conquest over convention because you were conscious of the convention. There is no use in a man doing heroic things if he was endowed by nature with a total insensibility. Heroism is disregard of one's cowardice. I hope Ireland in the future will be natural and that every decent home will provide rests for the feet of men and women rather higher than their heads or that tables will be recognised as the proper place for feet—or as an alternative every person will be entitled to two chairs, one for his body and the other

---

¹ Lysaght's biography of Plunkett: Mitchell's *George Moore*.
² Nicknames of two dogs.
³ *See* letter July 18, 1916 to E. MacLysaght.
⁴ Dora Knox, associate of Mary Spring-Rice, and strong nationalist.

for his feet. I always claim two chairs myself. James MacNeill[1] went over to England a week ago. I saw him on the Sunday before he went and I don't know how long he will be as he was trying to see what could be done about his brother and that's a long business I imagine. But I will speak to him when he returns. I see him fairly often. Plunkett is very poorly and is not picking up as we hoped and he could not get back on Saturday as he expected, but is thinking of returning to Dublin this week. I think he is really ill poor man and won't be able for much. Dermod O'Brien should get into touch with Samuels, K.C.,[2] who is working up a unionist conference with some of his friends, and whose ideas and Dermod's are fairly close, enough to make them natural colleagues. I don't think Miss Mitchell[3] has got any of her proofs yet. She is on holidays however and they may have been sent to her direct and not here. I am correcting page proofs of *National Being*. I am glad your Plunkett book is through. It is devilishly hot and heavy here and I have no brains and energy. The heat saps my wits. I hope you are all well and that Mrs. Lysaght had not to chloroform the Red Rover[4] on account of his [*sic*] misguided affection. Please give her my kind regards also Miss McVey if she is still at Raheen with the small boy. By the way Boyd has a book coming out through John Lane in America, a history of the modern Anglo-Irish Literary Movement and he says Maunsels could arrange for sheets for an English edition. He says he would like to do Standish O'Grady for your Irishmen series. You might talk this over with your co-directors?[5] Yours ever, AE

TO CHARLES WEEKES   *Irish Homestead*
                                                    [August 18, 1916]
My dear Charlie,

I don't believe half a dozen persons in England and America care one farthing what my opinion [is] upon the recent revolt in Ireland. Nobody, Unionist, or Nationalist, agrees with my opinions. Personally I believe

[1] From 1928 Governor-General of the Irish Free State. His brother was Eoin McNeill.

[2] A. W. Samuels, KC (1852-May 11, 1925) was President of the Social and Statistical Society of Ireland, 1906-1908. He took a prominent part in Irish political financial and social affairs; was M.P. (Unionist) for Dublin University, 1917-1919; Attorney-General, 1918; Solicitor-General for Ireland, 1917-1918. He was a pronounced anti-Nationalist.

[3] Susan Mitchell, *George Moore* in the Maunsel series *Irishmen of Today*.

[4] A bitch hunting-dog.

[5] Dr MacLysaght was a Director of Maunsel's from February or March 1916 until 1924.

F

there would have been no revolt if the employers and authorities had not been so unmerciful and unjust during the great strike. They left labour inflamed. I wrote then a letter, suppressed here, but which appeared in *The Times* in which I said "if the authorities were wanting to make Dublin a place with the bombs blazing in the street they were going the right way about it." It was labour supplied the personal element in the revolt. It had a real grievance. The cultural element, poets, Gaels, etc. never stir more than one per cent of a country. It is only when an economic injustice stirs the workers that they unite their grievance with all other grievances. The stirring element in this was labour. Connolly[1] was the strong man and intellect in the rising and he, I believe, was firing at the Sinn Feiners as people who talked and did nothing for many months. But our politicians all want to make party capital out of the trouble and they hate labour questions being discussed as they are all equally inhuman in regard to them. I may write later on. I won't write now. I am not going into well-timed hysterics. I am too much troubled over Ireland to write hastily and I won't write at all if I don't think I can do any good. I don't think I can now. Everybody wants blood at present, except a very few people who know that the seed of the martyrs – Yours ever AE

TO MISS J. FORTUNE[2]   17, Rathgar Avenue
                                          [*Postmark* November 1916]

[*Chicago postmarked receipt* 28 November 1916]

My dear Miss Fortune,
    I don't mind what titles are put on the pictures. It is my greatest difficulty finding titles. "The Foam Dust of the Wave" seems all right for the Bathers. The children playing "Tig" might possibly be described in two lines of a little lyric called "Frolic" page 21 *Collected Poems*.

[1] James Connolly, born in Glasgow, June 5, 1868: executed by a firing squad, May 8, 1916. From 1898-1916 he edited, in Dublin, the *Workers' Republic*. Keir Hardie inspired him, early in life, to visit Ireland and America. A prominent labour leader from 1912 his execution after the Easter Rising in Dublin aroused Irish resentment, for he was so weakened and wounded that he was propped in a chair to be executed. See Connolly's *Reconquest of Ireland* (Dublin, April 1915: Liberty Hall), and his collected writings, *Ireland and Labour* (Dublin, 1959. At the Sign of the Three Candles. 4 vols.). *See also* Desmond Ryan's *James Connolly* (Dublin, 1924: Talbot Press) and Nora Connolly O'Brien's *Portrait of a Rebel Father* (London, 1935: Rich & Cowan).

[2] *See* Note 12, p. 232.

> *A glimmer of dancing shadows*
> *A dovelike flutter of hands.*

but this might be too long and "Frolic" might be a better title. For the "Twilight on the Hills", the lines

> *Dusk, a pearl grey river o'er*
> *Hill and vale puts out the day*

seem all right, or you might use another line:

> *Twilight, a blossom grey, in shadowy valleys dwells*

For "Enchanted Ground" a quotation from "Dust" page 34 *Collected Poems* might suit:

> *Mother thy rudest sod to me*
> *Is thrilled with fire of hidden day,*
> *And haunted by all mystery.*

But you can put any names to the pictures or any lines you think suitable.

I received last night together with your letter the photographs of Tagore and the pictures of Sessiagh Lake and the children in the woods for which I am very grateful. The pictures came out better than I thought they would as I use so much violet a bad colour for the camera that it is difficult to get the tones in a reproduction. You are really one of the kindest of human beings and the only Chicago I knew about the Chicago of *The Jungle* by Upton Sinclair is getting obliterated. Why did I ever think because of that book that it was more inhuman than any other city?

I am very glad to have the photo of Tagore whose *Gitanjali* I have a great affection for. I had for some time a reproduction of Rothenstein's chalk drawing of Tagore[1] but it disappeared. I hope to send you in a week or two an account of a co-operative society among the rocks in Donegal[2] as you are interested in this work which is near to my heart. This particular society is the most wonderful instance of self-help by the poorest folk in Ireland in the most barren region and it may interest you to read about it. A little pamphlet I am writing about it is going through the press. With kind regards, Yours sincerely, Geo. W. Russell. AE

[1] Perhaps he meant *Six Portraits of Sir Rabindranath Tagore* by W. Rothenstein, with a Prefatory Note by Max Beerbohm (London, 1915: Macmillan). *See* John Rothenstein, *The Portrait Drawings of W. Rothenstein, 1889-1925* (London, 1926: Chapman & Hall).

[2] *Templecrone.* First published in the *Irish Homestead*, vol. 23, pp. 709-713 (November 11, 1916). Reprinted as a pamphlet. The Manager of the Templecrone Agricultural Credit Society, Dungloe, Co. Donegal, was Patrick Gallagher ("Paddy the Cope"). See *My Story, by Paddy the Cope*, i.e. Patrick Gallagher (London, 1939: Cape).

TO JAMES STEPHENS [? November 1916]

Dear James,

I went to bed last night early after a hot bath having a very bad cold, so could not get round. It may be too bad for me to get round tonight. I only drop this note to say that I had a letter from Darrell Figgis writing from the

"Place of Internment",
Reading

which I suppose his address, and he wonders whether you would send him your new book. He asks me for mine[1] and Susan Mitchell for hers,[2] reading being his only occupation. So I pass on his request to you. I wonder whether they will let him have Irish books. I will try him with *The National Being*. Yours ever, AE

TO MACMILLAN AND CO LTD 17 Rathgar Avenue
[Saturday] 14.1.17

Dear Sirs,

I came to an understanding with my namesake Rt. Hon. Geo. W. E. Russell[3] some years ago that he was to accept the credit of my verses when the young ladies in poetry clubs wrote to him congratulating him on his poetic genius, and that I, living in a poor neighbourhood, was to accept without protest the glory attaching to the title of "Right Honourable" by which I am frequently addressed. But I distinctly made no agreement with him to pay his bills when by chance they came to me. I doubt if he has paid any of mine. I am shocked to find that he has not paid for books bought before the war and has stretched the moratorium to cover two trifles of 7d. each. He got the books and I the bill and the obloquy of not paying. Please send this letter to my namesake and tell him I am open to a deal about paying his Dublin bills if he will engage to pay my London bills for books. Yours sincerely, Geo. W. Russell, AE

P.S. Please note that in my case the "E" is not sandwiched between the W. and R., but comes after my name AE. This is the minute difference between my namesake and myself. It is like the pink and blue ribbons nurses put on twins to distinguish them, AE

[1] *The National Being*.   [2] *George Moore*.   [3] *See* letter, November 21, 1913, p. 94.

TO DR. BETHEL SOLOMONS[1] 84 Merrion Square
Monday [*Postmark* 13 March 1917]

Dear Solomons,
I would like to have a talk over Stephens any time you have a moment to spare if you are passing here morning or afternoon. I think he ought to get away for fortnight or so to recruit when he is able. I don't think he can have any funds for this and if a dozen of his friends contributed two or three pounds apiece we could hand Mrs Stephens the money for the purpose and let her go with James to some good hotel in a mild quarter of Ireland. I would like your opinion. Your ever, Geo. W. Russell

DR. BETHEL JACOBS[2] 42 Fitzwilliam Square, Dublin
TO E. MACLYSAGHT 15th March 1917

My dear Ned,
I was speaking to AE the other day about James Stephens and having consulted his doctor, who considers that James should go away in order to recruit his health, we found that it would be necessary to collect £21 so that he might have this holiday. We decided therefore to ask seven or eight of his intimate friends to give £3 each. You are one of those we thought we might bother.
Stephens as you know had heavy expenses. His royalties are down and his salary is small. I might suggest that if you felt so inclined you could ask your father to give part of the above amount. The best to you both, Yours ever, Bethel Jacobs
P.S. James of course knows nothing about what we are doing.

[*Circular letter*][3] 70 Harcourt Street, Dublin
March 17th 1917

Dear Sir,
Within the last few weeks a proposal has been gradually taking shape to refer the question of an Irish settlement to the Imperial Conference or to a

---

[1] The surgeon, Bethel Albert H. Solomons, born 1885. Author of *A Handbook of Gynaecology*, with Edward Solomons (London, 1944: Baillière) and of an autobiography, *One Doctor in his Time* (London, October 29, 1956: Christopher Johnson).
[2] The surgeon.   [3] From a typed copy.

Commission consisting in great part of representatives of the Colonies and Mr. Asquith's speech during the recent debate and Mr. Lloyd George's response have made this more and more likely. Whether this proposal be adopted or not, there is no doubt that the opinions of the Dominion statesmen will exercise a considerable influence on the future of Irish Government and it is most important that these gentlemen, who are strangers to Irish ideas, should be informed of the views held by men and women of Independent thought in Ireland, not prominently identified with any political party. Their opinions will not be expressed, either by the official Nationalist or by the official Tory Parties, who are already organised and represented in London, and can readily state their respective points of view. If the opinions of these sections only were placed before the Commission it might lead to grave misunderstandings, friction and perhaps disaster, when the committee's report is laid before the country.

We, the undersigned have carefully considered the various points that are likely to be raised and have drawn up a statement which we believe represents in outline the views of a large number of Irishmen, but which have not yet been formulated or put forward in a concrete shape. We do not believe that anything will be gained by attempting a plan, which has already failed many times, to induce an agreement between the two hostile sections represented by the Orange Party and the Irish Parliamentary Party; we have therefore confined ourselves to considering the opinions of those who we think may possibly agree with the general terms of the statement enclosed.

We propose to get into communication with the Colonial Premiers and to discuss the matters with them at a private meeting which it is hoped can be arranged. In any case it would be useful to have a document stating the considered opinion of numbers of Irishmen who are independent of existing parties: so that if an interview is not possible, the document might be sent to each member of the Commission. We believe it will have a certain effect in clearing their minds as to the real claims of the Irish Nation. Later on if it is considered wise to publish the document we think it will have the effect of consolidating public opinion which has been in a fluid condition for the last two years.

We ask you to read the enclosed paper carefully, to make any remarks or amendments you may consider advisable, and, if you are satisfied with the general terms we hope you will attend a meeting to consider the suggestions that have been made by others, and to make arrangements for a meeting with the Colonial Premiers. The meeting will he held at

Allen's Hotel, 70 Harcourt St. Dublin 4 p.m. on Friday March 23rd. next.

Meanwhile we trust you to treat both the general proposal and the suggestions in the enclosed paper [as] very private and confidential; they are only being communicated to a few persons.[1] Yours truly, (signed) Maurice Moore[2], Geo. W. Russell, James G. Douglas[3]

TO COLONEL MAURICE MOORE   *Irish Homestead*
                                                            April 10, 1917

My dear Moore,

I have just heard from Kerr[4] who writes "Your letter of the 5th only reached me yesterday, Sunday morning. Adams[5] is not here today, but I am sure he will be glad to meet Col. Moore and Mr. Douglas[6] any time they come over here. They ought not of course to come and see us in any sense as a formal deputation because we should have no status to receive them as such: but personally and I am sure Adams also would be glad of an opportunity to talk the whole matter over with them. I wish you could come over too because I should like to have a talk with you about these things. Will you let me know when they expect to arrive?"

Kerr writes from 23 Cambridge Sq W and I think you and Douglas should write to him there to fix up the day or get on to him on the telephone if he has one. I received your letter also the cheque. I will retain this for the moment because I do not yet know whether I can or cannot get away this week. I will return it if I cannot, and perhaps in any case as I think I ought to pay my own expenses, if I can get off. Anyhow write to Kerr and I will write him also. There might be much more chance of my getting over next week than this and I could do some propaganda if it was any use then. This week is very dubious. Yours ever, Geo. W. Russell

---

[1] *See* Note 13, p. 232.

[2] *See* footnote 2 to letter May 8, 1899, to Horace Plunkett.

[3] *See* Biographical Notes.

[4] Philip Henry Kerr (1882-1940), 11th Marquess of Lothian, journalist and statesman. From 1916-1921 he was Private Secretary to David Lloyd George (1863-1945). See *Lord Lothian, 1882-1940* by J. R. M. Butler (London, 1960: Macmillan), and *D.N.B.*

[5] William George Stewart Adams (b. 1874) was Superintendent of Statistics and Intelligence in the Department of Agriculture and Technical Instruction (Ireland), 1905-1910; Gladstone Professor of Political Theory and Institutions (Oxford), 1912-1933; Secretary to the Prime Minister (Lloyd George), 1916-1918, and editor of the War Cabinet Reports, 1917-1918.

[6] James G. Douglas (1887-1954). *See* Biographical Notes.

TO COLONEL MAURICE MOORE   *Irish Homestead*
                                                   April 13, 1917
Dear Moore,

Owing to a stupid blunder of a maid at the Plunkett House who told Robinson[1] of *The Times* I was out when I was in I missed the long talk we had arranged. But I have written Robinson at length and with the utmost seriousness on the Irish question on the lines of our memo. If you can get Northcliffe[2] you will get a great power on your side. Oliver[3] would naturally object to control of customs. His idea is a federal union of Ireland not with the Empire but with Great Britain and a common trade policy. He will have to be educated out of that view. I was speaking to a prominent American judge a couple of days ago who said that the Senate would vote anything for France but owing to English treatment of Ireland anything proposed for England would be resisted by many Senators to the last man of Irish extraction. The price for Anglo-American friendship is political freedom for Ireland. *The Times* Washington correspondent wrote much the same thing a few days ago. The argument is nothing less than the memo policy will win Ireland's friendship and slake the anti-British feeling among Irishmen the world over. Is it worth Great Britain's while to win that friendship? We are too politically educated now to be fooled by half-measures and it will only result in bitter disappointment if half measures are adopted. Was Adams friendly, or Kerr? What are the chances of your seeing the Prime Minister? Yours ever AE

TO COLONEL MAURICE MOORE   *Irish Homestead*
                                              Saturday May 29th 1917
Dear Moore,

There is no more to be said. I was deeply offended at the time when you talked about "legal rights" as if I was a thief of ideas trying to make away with them. For my own view is that none of us contributed any original ideas at all, for the Ulster Council, National Civil Service, expenditure to balance revenue & etc. while the Anglo-Ulster-Irish question has lasted, and the only originality anybody can claim is a manner

[1] Geoffrey Robinson (1874-November 7, 1944), editor of *The Times*, 1912-1919 and from 1923-1941. He changed his surname later to Dawson. See *Geoffrey Dawson and our Times* by Sir Evelyn Wrench (London, 1955: Hutchinson), and *D.N.B.*

[2] Lord Northcliffe.

[3] Frederick Scott Oliver. *See* footnote to letter dated March 20, 1910, p. 68. His printed discussion of *Ireland and the Imperial Conference* (1917) was widely circulated.

of presenting the facts and the arguments and the tone employed. I am incapable of patchwork and feel as distressed at different rythms [*sic*] from my own as Yeats would be if he was forced to admit a line of mine in every verse, so I refashioned the whole memo[1] leaving out arguments I agreed with, facts I felt sure were accurate and much excellent work simply because I could not fit them in with the facts which personally appealed to me and the peculiar tone I wished to pervade the document once I was made responsible for its drafting. It was I know annoying to those like yourself and Lysaght and Coffey and Johnston who have worked so hard on the various methods of treating the suggestions to seem to ignore what was carefully thought out, the historical references & etc. But it was not in my nature to be moved by them so as to make an article with a moving and personal appeal. I should have been much more apologetic about this but it is the natural egoism of people when they have written something to be obsessed by it. So far as I am concerned I have no desire for political notoriety at all. It is out of my world. I forsee [*sic*] endless waste of my time if my name is appended at all to a political document when I would very much prefer to be at other literary work I have on hand, but have been unable to touch for months. I have probably annoyed you as much as you annoyed me. Let us forget it, my dear Moore. I have a villainous temper but it does not last long. Yours AE

TO EDWARD MACLYSAGHT *Irish Homestead*
Monday [July 1917]

Dear Ned, Its all right. I understood. We are in for the job now. I think there is a chance of doing something, but that will be made clearer when we get to know these Ulster folk. I hear three of the Southern Unionists want our colonial settlement. Mrs Green[2] writes me this morning that Lord MacDonnell wants it also. If so I hope he will be on. Yes come by all means to see me when you come up. I think the first few days will be merely formal fixing of procedure but really I know nothing of how long these matters take: I am making preparations to see how one can meet the Ulster delegates in a friendly fashion not merely across tables at Committee meetings. You are announced as a Conventionalist in today's papers. We will in all probability end by being denounced but what does that matter? Yours ever AE

[1] *Thoughts for a Convention*, Joseph Johnston, FTCD, and Diarmuid Coffey.
[2] Alice Stopford Green.

F*

TO KATHLEEN KYLE[1] (MRS MCCLOY)   *Irish Homestead*
Friday [? July 1917]

My dear Kathleen Kyle,[2]

Why should you not write to me if you think I have been unjust to Ulster. It was the very last thing I would wish to be. I am an Ulsterman by birth and retain many associations with the province though I have not lived there for many years, but for the past fifteen years I have always spent a month in Ulster because I like it and go there in my holidays. The difference between Ulster "settlers" and the Spanish, Norman, English and Danish settlers elsewhere in Ireland is that the latter accepted Ireland wholeheartedly became Irish in fact and ceased to be settlers. Many Ulster people still regard themselves as settlers, saying openly that they feel more akin to England than to the Irish. They have been almost uninfluenced by the intellectual or cultural traditions of Ireland. As one leader of Ulster politics told me. "I and my family have lived [here] for three hundred years but I always feel that I belong to a conquering race and I always mistrust these fellows." Now that man was a settler and it is his opinion which pervades Ulster too much. A man ceases to regard himself merely as an Englishman or a Scotsman earning his living here. Of course I know there are thousands, many thousands of Ulster people, who are not settlers but as Irish as Connaught. But political Ulster has more and more emphasised its division from Ireland. It prefers England to Ireland and so long as it prefers England to Ireland that party must be regarded merely as a party of settlers. If they had any genuine culture it would have expressed itself in literature. I refuse to believe in a culture which does not express itself in literature or art or music and where can one point to an Ulster Unionist whose name has been heard of in literature or art or music. I believe myself there is a diversity of intellectual and cultural traditions and Ulster will not be able to express its soul or its Irish character so long as it looks to Great Britain for its cultural ideals.

[1] From a typed copy.

[2] Kathleen Kyle, born in Belfast, 1890; educated in schools in France, and at Wycombe Abbey, England, before admission to Trinity College, Dublin, where she graduated in philosophy (1912); continuing until 1916, to read law, "Merely for the sake of learning", as her father could maintain her indefinitely. In August 1918 she married Dr J. M. McCloy, later Chief Medical Officer for Health (Northern Ireland) who died in 1943. When she wrote to AE (they did not meet), Mrs McCloy was a disciple of Maurice Barrés. Mrs McCloy is a friend of Miss Edith Shackleton Heald, the hostess of W. B. Yeats in his declining years. Since 1953 Mrs McCloy has been living in cultured retirement with her family, in London; occasionally lecturing for the National Book League.

Unionism in Ireland had produced no literature. There is not a single name famous in literature or art which is not identified with Irish nationalism, Yeats, Synge, Shaw, Orpen the artist, Colum, James Stephens, Seamus O'Sullivan, Ledwidge, the elder Yeats the painter and father of the poet, Katharine Tynan, Ethna Carberry, Alice Milligan, J. O. Hannay, Pearse, MacDonagh and going back, Davis, Mangan, Fergusson and the rest. Even Standish O'Grady one of the greatest, ostensibly a Unionist was so passionately national that he gave the greatest impetus of any Irish writer to modern nationalism and I know him very well and his unionism and it was for reasons which would have endeared him to every Fenian heart that he was Unionist. He thought Ireland could dominate Great Britain if it wanted and he desired an Irish domination of the empire. I desire myself the widest diversity of culture and in my suggestions for an Irish settlement I would have Ulster, or such portion of it as desired that separateness, have control over local education, marriage laws, police, judiciary, public institutions, etc., so that its regional characteristics might be preserved if it desired such protection. I never heard in my life any southern nationalist expressing the slightest desire to oppress Ulster or to deprive it of its regional character, but Ulster or North East Ulster continually vociferates its hatred of the rest of Ireland of which it has not the slightest knowledge and it accepts the opinions put before it by the meanest and most lying press in these islands, about their fellow countrymen. Everything an Irish Nationalist says is distorted out of all likeness to the truth. For example, the *Northern Whig* reviewing my pamphlet[1] said I offered Ulster nothing but the Gaelic League when I expressly made provision against a Gaelic ascendance and left Ulster full control over education in its own area. How can you believe such lying papers? I who have lived all my life in the rest of Ireland being of a different religion from the majority never anywhere saw any religious intolerance, but only, I am sorry to say in my own province did I find these wild opinions and mediaeval religious obsessions. It is my firm conviction that Ulster Protestants are far more dominated and directed by their clergymen than Southern Catholics. The first have theoretical freedom but their ministers direct their minds. In the second case there is theoretical domination by the clergy but the whole history of Irish Catholicism during the past quarter of a century shows that the church follows the people after trying in vain to restrain them.

[1] *Thoughts for a Convention.*

I personally never objected to the Ulster Volunteers except in the sense that I have an intellectual objection to the use of force when reason and sympathy and imagination are more powerful agencies to bring about an agreement. But I recognised that when Devlin started the Hibernians and the Nationalists were weak enough to recognise them and practically made them the party machine that Ulster was justified in organising itself in opposition to a party weak enough to be dominated. What I think Ulster Unionists did not know was that the Hibernians were execrated by Nationalists and that they rapidly lost power once they were organised and today they have little or no power of any kind. What is bad in itself is contrary to Irish instinct and the innate good sense and idealism in the Irish character revolted against a sectarian and semi secret society. The Sinn Fein revolt against the Party was largely a disgust with the Hibernian element and the adhesion of the people to Sinn Feiners expresses their disgust with Devlinism in politics. I knew it was there and that it would assert itself as soon as Hibernianism became a kind of Catholic orangeism. But on the whole I approve of the Ulster Volunteer Movement for this that it taught the baser elements in nationalism that Ulster could not be dominated by mere voters and Ulster will be treated with all the respect it is entitled to in a self governing Ireland. Your papers may not have informed you that the Irish Volunteers called for cheers for the Ulster Volunteers and they were heartily cheered because the ideal nationalist hated Hibernianism just as much as Ulster did and it has now crushed that malign machine and made it powerless. It will in future have little political power and will survive only as a society under the insurance act and not a popular society. I do not myself wish for a "spurious unity". I hate uniformities and love diversities of culture and I believe only in common sense unities of a practical kind relating to government, justice, etc., but leaving the greatest possible freedom of thought. I wrote in an Irish paper that I would prefer 4,000,000 Irish people all thinking differently to 4,000,000 Irish people all thinking alike. I always think with envy of the Attica of Pericles where as he said "they never turned sour faces on those who disagreed with them."

My main criticism of Ulster is that it is not yet itself. It does not express itself but a party in Great Britain which dominates it. If it was within an Irish state with a provincial freedom to develop its own life without looking to English Tories for its ideals but looked to itself it would be able to express the idealism in it which I know is there. It is as impossible for Ulster to express its soul in the style of English Toryism as it would be for Yeats to express his soul in the style of Milton. It must find itself. It has formed its own will in the Volunteers. It has not yet found its soul because it looks beyond itself not within itself. But I have let myself run on much too long. I had an idle hour and your letter moved me by its sincerity. Don't believe the Ulster papers, do not believe *any* Irish paper. They are all lying and cursed. The only knowledge of Ireland which is true can at present be got from personal knowledge and that I acquired during fifteen years when I was through every county living in cottages meeting every kind of person organising them in societies. You can also get a knowledge from the latter [-day] Irish literature but the press is the devil. I know it well. The Editors rarely write what they believe but what they must write to keep their posts.[1] They confess so much in private conversations. They regard themselves as barristers paid to plead a case and the truth of their side is not their concern. So it arises that privately the editors and staff of many Unionist papers are nationalist and they curse the ill fate which brought them to be what they are. They know too much as journalists to believe what they write about the other side. Beware of the press. Yours sincerely, AE Geo. W. Russell

TO EDWARD MACLYSAGHT   84 Merrion Square
                                                  12 July 1917

Dear Ned, I got a letter from Duke[2] this morning asking whether I would go on Convention. He tells me he has written a similar letter to you. I thought I would hear from you by wire today whether you would accept. If you do I will. Will you please wire me tomorrow as early as possible "accept" or "refuse". Plunkett[3] is urgent that I should go on. He says there will be at least five or six serious people on the Convention and they ought [to] be able to affect it. Please confirm me in any action. I wrote Duke today saying I was taking twenty-four hours to consider. As I did not hear from you before post time I thought this best. I told

[1] For a recent example see the truthful record of a controversy: *Observer* (London), July 13, 1958 (p. 12), and more dangerously the deceptive double-speak of Dr Verwoerd, Mr Louw and Mr Erasmus of the South African government throughout 1960.

[2] Henry Edward Duke, born 1855. Called to the bar, Gray's Inn 1885, QC 1899. Chief Secretary for Ireland, August 1916-May 1918; knighted 1918. Lord Justice of Appeal, May 1918; President of the Probate Divorce and Admiralty Division, 1919-1933. He was created Lord Merrivale of Walkhampton, 1925. Died May 20, 1939.

[3] *See* Note 14, p. 232.

[129]

him I would wire him sometime tomorrow. If we go on East Clare[1] will deprive the "Party" of any authority to speak for Nationalist Ireland and those who press more extreme views will even if few have the ear of the Convention as people who speak for a multitude. Yours ever AE

TO EDWARD MACLYSAGHT   *Irish Homestead*
                                                 Friday [October 1917]

Dear Ned, I have just read your proofs and I think your memo[2] splendid the best, much the best statement of the Irish case on the business side made by anybody in the Convention. I hope you will get it out and have it sent to the members so that the Ulster people will have it before the Grand Committee meets and will have been influenced by it when consulting with their employers the Ulster Council as to how far they may go in committee to meet the Nationalist demand. I had begun a memo myself on Irish control over customs and excise but I hardly think it necessary to go on with it as you have put the case so well.[3] I congratulate you. It is admirable and businesslike and the Pollocks[4] will find it a hard nut to crack. You will make them feel that Sinn Fein is not brainless idiocy. AE

HORACE PLUNKETT   *Kilteragh, Foxrock, Co. Dublin*
TO LORD MIDLETON[5]   20th *December 1917*

My dear Midleton
    We must think ahead a little in the interval during our Christmas holiday.
Your intervention and the fine backing you have received from the best
elements in the party you lead have immensely improved the prospects of a
compromise settlement. Already we are assured of the co-operation of a

---

[1] East Clare: Mr de Valéra was elected there, in 1917. *See* Biographical Notes.

[2] *Self-government and business Interests*, published as a pamplet in March 1918, by Maunsels. It was first, in 1917, a memorandum circulated to all members of the Home Rule Convention.   [3] *See* Note 15, p. 233.

[4] Hugh McDowell Pollock; first Minister of Finance in the Northern Ireland Parliament, 1921. He was a prosperous business man, and member of Parliament for many years. He died, aged over 80, on April 15, 1937. In the Convention he represented the Belfast Chamber of Commerce, being the financial expert for the Ulster Unionists.

[5] *See* Note 16, p. 234. Lord Midleton (1856-February 13, 1942) led the Southern Unionists at the Convention.

considerable number of moderate Nationalists with the Southern Unionists. . . .
I have, however, banked upon Dunraven[1] for a genuine Federal scheme.
I had long been familiar with the case for a Dominion status and fiscal
...lders' Framework of Home Rule and
...AE. I did not in the least mind having—
...nd every other plan presented in the strong-
...of getting a compromise accepted by the
...he Convention into it, unless the divergent
...and fairly stated by their best exponents.
...fulfilled this requirement in the Convention

RISH TIMES[2]   December 25, 1917

...EW NATION

...er have told me how impossible it is to
... I, on the contrary, assert that it has
...t only possible, but natural, for us to do
...e depths and not on the surfaces, and is
...n, and not otherwise. Before the most
...uttered, even in the pagan world, in
...pths revealed. Our own bardic literature
...ually find affection for the foe expressed.
...he ancient Irish epos, could weep over
...d in the famous combat between those
...l each other, perhaps made suddenly
...ing above the body in each other. They
...eyes their brotherhood in eternity. All
...reathes a spirit which must cry out its
...en when these advance towards it armed
...er days, in plains that are wider than
...e realm of air where epic and heroic

[1] ...d Dunraven (1841-June 14, 1926) was Under-
...and Chairman of the Irish Land Conference,
1902-1903. On the Convention he advocated a Federal solution. He was nominated by
W. T. Cosgrave to serve in the first Senate of the Free State, June 1921.

[2] Text from the *Irish Times*, Thursday, December 27, 1917. The earlier letter on this
theme was reprinted in *Imaginations and Reveries* (1921, 1925).

deeds have scope, the winged warriors laugh at each other while dealing death, and drop wreaths commemorative of the bravery of the dead.

It is natural to love our enemies. In so far as fear of the body is cast aside, in so far as for the moment man is fire and spirit, he can discern only what is akin to his immortality, and he thrills in recognition of those, who like himself, have overcome mortality and its fears. I remember at the beginning of the war how that deep nature was stirred in the correspondent of some paper, and he asked how we were to interpret Christ's command, "Love your enemies"; and I think it was an archbishop[1] who gave a plenary indulgence to the spirit of hate by saying, "It is true we were told to love our enemies, but we were nowhere told to love other people's enemies," and we heard no more of that Commandment. It is not those who fight who violate most that high law of human nature, but the interpreters of Scripture who remain at home trying to effect some economy of meaning in difficult texts. I can imagine a soldier, watching the oncoming of the enemy, saying to his neighbour, "Are they not grand fellows?" without any fear of being misunderstood. Men who, by facing death, make clear their loyalty to their nation are always strong enough to show their loyalty to humanity. It is those who are conscious they are doing little for their nation who are most apt at lip-fighting. The soul has an instinct of balance as well as the body, and lack of deeds is instinctively balanced to empty words, or the soul would not even to itself have the appearance of standing erect.

The inspirer of Christendom said, "Love your enemies" because He knew it was natural in the life of the spirit. If it be not the mode of our being, then it is vain to preach it to us as it would be to expect the eagle on the high rocks to bring forth doves. I might go further and say that our enemies hold more for us than our friends, and we can learn more from those who think differently from us than we can from those who agree with us. One of the greatest of English poets said, "Standing water breeds reptiles," and if we remain fixed in opinions too long, we breed reptiles in the mind. I am not going to dispute the law which meted out death to Pearse and Connolly, but I say that there are few of their opponents who would not profit greatly by reading the books in which these

[1] His Grace the Most Reverend John Baptist Crozier, DD, (1853-1920), Archbishop of Armagh (1911-1920). Not to be confused with the Roman Catholic Archbishop of Armagh (1887-1924), who was Cardinal Logue (1840-1924). Dr Crozier's pronouncement was printed in the *Freeman's Journal*.

placed on record the ideals by which they stood and for which they lived. Men gain more a thousand times by enlarging the boundary of their thoughts than they do by reading books which echo back to them beliefs they already hold. Both parties in Ireland have much to learn from each other, Nationalists from Unionists a practical efficiency in the affairs of life: and Unionists from Nationalists that idealism and love of beauty which has blossomed in a thousand songs. It is strange to find the genius of writers of Nationalist character fully recognised in other lands, even in Great Britain, while in their own country a partisan spirit so dominates our Press that Unionists will hardly allow for a moment there could be any rightness or intellect or nobility of character in those who oppose them, and they hate, being ignorant of what they condemn.

I am convinced also that it is not by such as Pearse or MacDonagh or their following that the practical genius of their countrymen can be guided, and that this group might, with great benefit to their policy, study the methods and opinions of the captains of the great Northern industries, where also, for lack of that idealism, wealth is being created and a civilisation being built up which is barren of culture or beauty. Beauty, which our national idealists possess so abundantly, is flying from the grey cities in which we live, fading from the lives and imagination of workers in factories and mills, for they do not hear, they are not permitted to hear, the idealists who are the almsgivers of the gold of Paradise, and whose gifts might make the grey of life to glow to that gold. I do not wish to be controversial. The sphere of the argumentative intellect is the world where all things exist by way of balance of opposites, where for every black there is a white, and for every *pro* a *con*; and, if we lived only by the intellect, there could be no progress, for argument could be met by equal argument. "An eye for an eye and a tooth for a tooth" is the justice of the intellect, and that warfare may go on for ever. We can only escape from an eternity of opposites by rising above them like that spirit which fixed the balances in the heavens and made equal centrifugal and centripetal. It was that spirit which would fain have admitted man to Its own sphere, showing us how to escape from the dominion of the opposites by rising above them. It counselled forgiveness until seventy times seven — a hard saying, no doubt, to those who have just cause of offence. But it is the only way by which we can be melted and made one in the higher spheres and work out the destiny of our nation. Yours etc., "AE"

TO EDWARD MACLYSAGHT   84 Merrion square
                                                 or 17 Rathgar Avenue
                                                 Friday [December 1917]

Dear Ned,

I suppose you have seen the Government reply to Dunraven in today's paper. I agree entirely with Dunraven and Curzon's[1] reply seems to me to conceal something sinister beneath its hesitations and vagueness. I always supposed that the decision or agreement of the Convention would be referred to Irish people for approval and that the only theory to which the Government was committed was that Ulster would not be co-erced. That did not necessarily imply that what Ulster agreed upon would be agreeable to the rest of Ireland. If the Convention was representative truly of all sections, Sinn Fein Nationalist and Unionist its agreement might be regarded as a pact binding the country and it would be unnecessary to have a general election or referendum. But it is representative truly only in respect of Ulster delegates, and the rest represent nothing certainly, so that the Convention from my point of view could only be regarded as an unrepresentative committee trying to draft an Irish constitution to be submitted later on to Irish people for approval. Curzon's refusal to accede to the request for a referendum puts me in an unpleasant position, for in the Convention's agreement, if there is one, is not submitted to Irish people either by way of general election or referendum then the agreement has no power to bind the party now not represented. Any Sinn Feiner can say "we are not bound by the Convention agreement. It was never submitted to Irish people for approval, this scheme of theirs. We will work on for our own solution." Now if the pact of the Convention is submitted to the people of Ireland and if they agree to it it is a pact with the people of Ireland and should give the new Irish Government moral power in dealing with disturbances. I see no hope if the Government does not openly declare the Convention scheme will be submitted to Irish people. I was strongly tempted to write this morning and resign from Convention but do not like doing anything hastily. So please tell me your views. I will see Plunkett tomorrow on his return from London he may know what lies beneath Curzon's reply. I get to hate the Convention more every day. But I will not withdraw if I think there is a ghost of a chance of it doing any good. With regards to Mrs Ned, AE

[1] George Nathaniel Curzon, Marquess Curzon of Kedleston (1859-1925).

[134]

EDWARD MACLYSAGHT TO
G. W. RUSSELL

24 *Upper FitzWilliam Street*
Dublin
Sunday [*January 20, 1918*]

Dear AE,
  I am sending you a copy of the letter[1] *as it went yesterday. Redmond's*[2] *amendment asks the Government to co-erce Belfast into a bad scheme of self-government. If I attend the Convention again, my inclination is to vote against it. That means voting in the same camp as Barrie;*[3] *a horrible prospect. In my opinion the proper course is to get the pledge (for what it is worth) from the Government first, and with it to work for a better scheme than Midleton's, one to which, if such a pledge existed, the S. Unionists would be almost obliged to agree. A no-customs-cum-fancy-Parliament settlement will be repudiated by the country.*
  My own view is that abstention from the Convention till a reply is obtained from Lloyd George is the right course.
  My advice to you would be to send off your letter of conditional resignation. You could make your speech in support of Murphy[4] *against the Midleton proposals in the Convention on Tuesday and explain at the same time what you had done. I think that would reinforce my action tremendously and prevent the Convention from making a fool of itself. It is certain to pass Redmond's amendment unless what I have done is followed up by more striking move on your part.*

[1] To Plunkett, resigning from the Convention, with effect from January 22, 1918. (*See* Note 17, p. 234.)
[2] John E. Redmond. *See* footnote 3, p. 80, to letter dated January 23, 1913 (to A. J. Balfour).
[3] Hugh T. Barrie (1860-April 18, 1922). Conservative M.P. for North Londonderry from 1906; sometime Vice-President of the Department of Agriculture and Technical Instruction for Ireland. Dr MacLysaght's contemporary diary records AE's observation that Barrie's "company was degrading". Possibly that was prompted by Barrie's support in the Convention for partitioning Ulster from southern Ireland.
[4] William Martin Murphy, born in county Cork, 1844. He founded the Dublin daily paper the *Irish Independent* in 1905. He was M.P. for Dublin (St Patrick's) 1885-1892. He retaliated against the syndicalist strikes in Dublin, in 1913 by forming the Employers' Federation. He was President of the Dublin Chamber of Commerce. From February 1915 he was Chairman of the Finance and General Purposes' Committee of the Red Cross Committee, Dublin Castle. He was a member of the Home Rule Convention, 1917-1918. Died June 26, 1919.

TO SIR HORACE PLUNKETT   84 Merrion Square
                                                            1st Feb 1918
Dear Sir Horace,

I have been brooding much upon the state of Ireland and I have come to believe that the Convention, constituted as it is, and hampered by the pledge of Ministers to the people of Belfast, cannot be the instrument by means of which an Irish settlement can be attained. I have no belief that the Government will rise to the higher statesmanship required for a real settlement of the Anglo-Irish question. The Midleton scheme which you have to some extent favoured and which seems to have Government support, would not, if put into operation, assuage the feeling against Great Britain here for a week. A much bigger measure is required, giving Ireland complete control over Irish affairs. If that compromise were put into operation, there would only be harassing and exhausting agitation for an Irish control over Customs, a full Irish use of Irish Revenues and for an Irish Territorial Force controlled by an Irish Parliament for the defence of Irish interests. I view with the greatest foreboding the future of Ireland and I do not think I have any part to play politically in a country ravaged by such passions, and I intend to devote such energy and thought to other movements with which I have more affinities.

I tender to you, as Chairman, my resignation as a member of the Convention. I do so with regret, as I entered it with some hope. I have not now the least hope that anything in the nature of a settlement will come out of it either by its own agreement or by reason of the War Cabinet's intervention. World circumstances must finally bring about the conditions which the wisdom of men could not bring about. I have no desire to make any public explanation of my reasons for withdrawal and will quietly drop out of its deliberations. Yours sincerely, George Russell

HORACE PLUNKETT TO AE   *105 Mount Street, London, W1*
                                                    2nd February 1918
My dear AE,

I was distressed at Lysaght's resignation at the time he chose and am, of course, much more deeply so by your proposed withdrawal. It is true that I have "to some extent favoured" the Midleton scheme because I, personally, believe that, when the alternative of an All Ireland parliament in immediate operation and a break-up of the Convention with the Irish Question, no doubt more clearly defined than ever before but obviously incapable of settlement without a very drastic treatment of Ulster (which might not be successful and would, in any case, be a most inauspicious beginning of Irish self-government), all the same opinion in Ireland, where I have always felt public opinion should be tested, would, after two or three week's public discussion, decide by an enormous majority in favour of the former alternative. Of course, you may say that Midleton's scheme does not carry with it the immediate setting up of an Irish Parliament, to which I reply that I do not expect Nationalists to go beyond committing themselves to that alternative on the distinct understanding that Government finds means of bringing Ulster in and fulfilling the condition.

If you must resign, certainly your method of silent withdrawal is far the most considerate to those who wish to continue the effort to make the Convention fruitful. But I hope you will at least postpone any such action. I do not, myself, believe that Ministers have yet closed their minds to any course which could be shown to have some prospect of success. I should not feel that they had plumbed the Irish situation of today unless they had heard your views as well as those of the other clear minds among the protagonists in our recent negotiations and debates. Therefore, I hope you will come over next week, arriving here on Tuesday. I would suggest travelling by day as it is much safer and less exhausting, and if you arrive on Tuesday night you would be in ample time for the preliminary negotiations. But do let me beg of you not to come to so important a decision until you have had an opportunity of ascertaining the real mind of the Government. Remember that, rumours to the contrary notwithstanding, neither the Cabinet nor any of its members have sought to influence the Convention, its members or its Chairman in any way whatsoever. They have simply said: "Bring us the invaluable assistance of an Irish agreement and we will do our best to give effect to it." To the Government I think you ought to say what you are saying to me and from the Government you should get your answer. Yours ever, Horace Plunkett

TO SIR HORACE PLUNKETT   17 Rathgar Avenue
                                3rd Feb. 1918

My dear Sir Horace,

I am very sorry I cannot do as you suggest. I have come to the conclusion that the Convention, constituted as it is, is simply an obstacle to an Irish settlement, and that the only thing to do is to let the new forces of Nationalism manifest themselves in their full strength. I think, in spite of South Armagh, that they will grow stronger and I think nothing but the most determined opposition to British Government in Ireland will have any effect on that Government. I have no affinities with extreme methods and while I see their inevitability I am not one who can take part in them, and if I said what I thought about Irish politics, it would only make it impossible for me to continue working with profit to the I.A.O.S. whose work is far more important than the Convention. I am confirmed in my intuition that the Convention is futile by the speech of Sir Edward Carson reported in this morning's papers. He is obviously going to oppose any inclusion of Ulster in any scheme of self-government Ireland would accept and, that being so, the only thing to do is to let the new National forces gather strength. It is a lamentable thing but the entire responsibility for the state of Ireland is on the shoulders of the English politicians. Asquith, Law[1] and George gave Belfast pledges and, after having inflamed them to the last degree possible against their fellow countrymen, the English arm them with promises and send them in to humbug us and tell the world they are allowing Ireland to settle its own destiny. The Sinn Feiners were right in their intuitions from the first. If I had followed my intuition from the first I would have remained away also. A man must be either an Irishman or an Englishman in this matter. I am Irish. Yours sincerely, George Russell

TO THE RIGHT HONOURABLE DAVID LLOYD GEORGE, M.P.[2]

84 Merrion Square
5th February 1918

Sir,

I resigned my membership of the Irish Convention last week explaining my reasons for so doing in a letter to the Chairman. I have come to believe that, constituted as it was, and hampered by pledges of ministers to the people of Belfast, pledges which I think were unreasonable in the form in which they were made, nothing in the nature of an Irish settlement can come out of the Convention. The Ulster delegates in my opinion were relying on those pledges and this conviction has been deepened by recent speeches of the leaders in Ulster. I shall not be

---

[1] Andrew Bonar Law (1858-1923).
[2] (1863-1945). Liberal Prime Minister, 1916-1922. His papers are owned by Lord Beaverbrook.

present at the meetings in London. As I have never belonged to any political party and have no following, my absence can leave no gap in the representation of sections. I am unfitted for the practical business of bartering bits of my convictions in meetings obviously arranged for compromise. I can only state what I believe would affect the ostensible purpose of the Convention which is to arrive at a settlement of the Anglo-Irish question, and I am certain that a policy of half-measures will earn no gratitude from Ireland and will relieve Great Britain from not one of its anxieties in respect of it. I wrote before the Convention began its work a pamphlet which had a very wide circulation in Ireland.[1] Of this I enclose a copy. Nothing which has happened since has led me to alter opinions there expressed. They are not the opinions of a party politician but of one who for thirty years has been on friendly terms with men of all parties and whose desire to understand all led him to friendship with Pearse, Connolly, McDonagh and other leaders of the revolutionary movement, some dead, others still living. This personal knowledge of the national extremists is not, I believe, shared by any other member of the Convention. It is my reason for drawing your attention to the pamphlet. I do not think any of those you will meet could give you an account both accurate and fair of the ideals of the national extremists now making a conquest of the Irish mind. Longing myself for brotherhood between peoples; believing that race hatred corrupts the soul of the nation, and being desirous of a settlement, I want to warn you that any scheme of self-government which does not meet them to some extent will not relieve you from a single anxiety about Ireland, nor for a year even make it more friendly. I believe friendship is possible on the terms indicated in the pamphlet and I say this after consulting with many Sinn Feiners. I know in spite of the fact that Lord Midleton has induced the representatives of Southern Unionism to adhere to his proposals that nine-tenths of them believe that fiscal autonomy ought to be the basis of a settlement and they have said this openly in the Convention and privately also. Ulster at different times through its prominent spokesmen has declared that if self-government was to come its only chance of success depended on its being full self-government of a dominion character and not a half-measure, and that also is the openly expressed belief of constitutional Nationalists however ready they might have been to accept instalments. I think with regard to Unionist Ulster's interests, all that it is reasonably entitled to demand, could be met by such

---

[1] *Thoughts for a Convention.*

representation in an Irish Parliament as Nationalists are prepared to give and have offered; by an administrative council with local control over education or other matters where it might feel a Catholic majority with every wish to be fair might prove unsympathetic; and by a commercial treaty attached as a schedule to the Act providing that no duties should be put on goods the growth produce or manufacture of Great Britain or Ireland by either parliament, and so ensuring that free trade which Ulster regards as essential to its economic prosperity. There is no Ulster interest which would not by such means be effectually safeguarded; and in my opinion the unreasonableness of the pledge to Ulster was that it was not a pledge to safeguard its interests but an unconditional pledge that it would be supported against the wishes of the vast majority of the Irish people. I have said now all I wish to say, except this, that we have for the first time in Ireland a disinterested nationalism not deriving its power from grievances connected with land or even oppressive Government but solely from the growing self-consciousness of nationality, and this has with the younger generation all the force of a religion, with the carelessness about death, suffering or material loss which we find among the devotees of a religion. Any Government established which does not allow this national impulse free play, will be wrecked by it. I feel it my duty to say this and I say it as one personally unconcerned, for my own interests are literary and economic and not political at all. I am, Sir, your obedient servant, George Russell

HORACE PLUNKETT TO AE
Confidential

105 Mount St, London, W1
6th February 1918

My dear AE,

Whenever a calamity threatens to overwhelm me I always look for some devious way of turning it to account and, while your resignation may be a very serious blow to the Convention in Ireland, in England, and perhaps most of all in America, I am using what I can sincerely say of your character, intellect and knowledge to bring it home to the Government that they must deal seriously, radically and immediately with the situation. Your letter to Lloyd George may be helpful and, indeed, if it were not for the brilliant part you played in the Convention, I should say that nothing became you in it like leaving it. Of course, I should have liked you to keep your resignation from the public for a day or two in the hope that, after Carson's interview with the

Prime Minister tomorrow, something might turn up that would fully justify you in reconsidering it. But, as you say, you have done the next best and, events may show, the best thing. Yours ever, Horace Plunkett

TO THE EDITOR, *MANCHESTER GUARDIAN*[1] [*Dublin*]
[May 8, 1918]

Sir, Undeterred by any warnings from those who know us, our rulers seem determined to force military service upon the Irish people. The people of England should realise the danger, not merely to Ireland but to the Empire, of the policy of those they maintain in power. The situation is full of such tragic possibilities that truth should be spoken now as if men were speaking to God and not to one another. I write as an Irishman interpreting my own people, but not, I hope, without understanding and sympathy for the people of England. I would not willingly wound any in this crisis of their history, for I know there is hardly a household in Great Britain to which death has not drawn nigh, and its people are bitter at heart about my people, are judging and condemning them. They have cried out against the law which left Ireland free to act as it willed in this war, while with them everything from boyhood to the verge of age was summoned for the need of the State. In theory Ireland is part of the United Kingdom. In theory it has obligations to the Empire. Acting now on that theory, the State imposes military service on behalf of the Empire on the manhood of this country. It is met at once by Irish Nationalism everywhere in unanimity in refusal to obey that law. It is this opposition I wish to interpret. I would not have any think it is either factious or ignoble. However painful it must be for English people to hear it, the truth must be told.

What is opposed to our rulers, what they are trying to overcome, is the soul of a nation.

They have never understood the subjective life of Ireland, because they were contented with domination over all that was apparent. Your people in their schools and universities have been taught that Ireland was an integral part of the United Kingdom. You made a law, and it became so. Ireland as a nation disappeared for you, but never so to its own imagination. It never accepted the Union. Never at any time was there a psychic tie

---

[1] Text from the *Manchester Guardian*, May 10, 1918, p. 3. Reprinted as a pamphlet for the Anti-Conscription Conference, Mansion House, Dublin, May 1918.

corresponding to the physical fact. British authority at all periods in Irish history, as today, rested solely on superior power. There was never a year in the seven centuries of that domination when the vast majority of the people were not opposed to it. When overcome in rebellion they waited sullenly, silently, and steadfastly for the hour of doom falling upon this as upon all empires in history. They desired to manifest their genius in a civilisation of their own. That feeling has been as deep, indeed much deeper, and more selfconscious since the Act of Union was passed; and to-day, partly through a recovery of the ancient culture, partly by the reaction against State policy, that self-consciousness of nationality is more vivid, passionate, and dominant than at any period in Irish history.

It is at this moment the Irish nation is denied rights over either soul or body. The principles for which Great Britain is contending in this war may be right. Many who most bitterly oppose British policy in Ireland think they are right. But the enemies of Ireland would not have free service. Their agents here, as I know, and as it was confessed to me, objected to Nationalists and Catholics enlisting in the army, as it removed the main argument against self-government on which they relied. They wanted Nationalists dragged as slaves and humiliated, and this at a time when self-consciousness and pride in nationality had become a burning flame. Sympathy was turned to indifference. Indifference was fanned into hostility and I am afraid hostility is changing to bitter hate. I see all this with grief. I have always believed in brotherhood between peoples, and I think hatred corrupts the soul of a nation. This last exercise of authority over us is not merely bringing death to the body, but to all that is spiritual, gentle or beautiful in the Irish nature. Our people look on this last act of British power with that dilated sense of horror a child might feel thinking of one who had committed some sin which was awful and unbelievable, as the sin against the Holy Ghost. What power, they wonder, except one inspired by spiritual wickedness would weave this last evil for a land subdued, force it to warfare to uphold a power it hates, that has broken it, that has killed its noblest children, overthrown its laws, taken the sceptre. They turn in appeal to the Master of Life and supplicate Him, and they believe by conscience they are justified in resistance even to death.

I cannot expect many in England to sympathise with Irish feeling, but I may ask them to consider it in relation to the future weal of the Empire. If they persist in forcing military service upon Ireland, if they insist on breaking the Irish will, there will not be a parish here where blood will not be shed. There will grow up a hate which will be inextinguishable, lasting from generation to generation. It will be fed by tradition every-where, and our people live by tradition. "Here this man fell." "There that group made their last stand." No expression of regret after the deed is done will wipe out those memories. They will be like that stain upon the hand of the Queen in the darkest of all tragic dramas–the stain which was ruddy to the spiritual sense, and no purifying water could cleanse it. It will spread over the Empire. It will invade that great Republic where so many millions of our exiled children have their home. The Irish are capable of the most bitter as of the most gentle speech, and the darker side of that eloquence shall be turned against you. Millions of the bitterest tongues in the world will be incessantly wagging, breeding sedition in your dominions, and hostility against you in whatever alien State they may live. There are already many burdens laid on the weary Titan of empire. Will this burden be laid on it also? I ask English people to consider in connection with this question what may be the effect on the dominions of an unsatisfactory and inconclusive peace. When they go back, in the moral revulsion which comes on all communities after prolonged shedding of blood, when they think of the deed they have done, how life and treasure have been wasted, and have not even–for this is possible–the pride in victory to uphold them, will it not lend force to those already numerous voices which hold that the tie of Empire is a danger, involving young nations in ambitions and policies which hinder their growth? Rightly or wrongly, such things will be said, and none will argue them, none will lend force and fire to them more than the Irish in the Empire.

I ask how, in face of this, State policy in respect of Ireland can be justified? The State has listened to bad counsellors. It consulted those who hated Irish nationality and not those who loved their country, and who might have won it, through freedom given, to befriend and defend yours also. The State listened to the few in Ireland, and turned a deaf-ear to the multitude. Now it needs the multitude; and what use to the state are those counsellors who opposed Irish nationality, who have no respect from it, and who, as that memorable day of national protest showed, had not even respect from their own employees, for in three-quarters of Ireland no train ran, no work was done, no shop was opened, no newspaper appeared?

You speak to a wide public. Through you I wish to make clear the feeling among my countrymen ere the deed is done, and there remains nothing but a destiny. I have encroached much upon the space a paper can allot to its correspondents, but if this deed is done you will have many columns recording things which will horrify whatever conscience remains in the world.

What moral strength can come to you from a nation broken in its pride, shamed and bleeding ? What aid to military power will be those who would now as readily turn their arms upon your officers as the enemy, for to such a pass has the unwisdom of our rulers brought this country ? I say to the English people, drop this thing and seek the way of friendship. It is not yet too late. Allow Ireland the freedom in government the majority of its people ask for, and trust to those who are free to defend a freedom guaranteed by Imperial law. Yours, etc., Geo. W. Russell ("AE")

TO JOSEPH KING[1]   17 Rathgar Avenue
                                                        Thursday 15.8.18

Dear Mr. King,

I was glad to hear about Madame McBride. I had a letter from her also. I have been trying to arrange about the education of her boy. I am afraid what you say is true that until the war is over there is not much hope for the business. With regard to your visit to Ireland I doubt whether you would learn anything by a fresh visit which you do not already know. Sentiment and conditions remain unchanged here. I think if the government start conscription that things will happen here which would require some witnesses, not merely fresh members of Parliament, so that people in Great Britain might know what was going on. The country is quiet because the Sinn Fein leaders before their internment sent round a message that on no account was there to be any action leading to violence. They were to reserve themselves for resistance of conscription if it was enforced, and as far as I can gather this advice has been and will be followed. I do not know the intentions of the Government about conscription. I think sometimes they are scared about possibilities and at other times they are impressed by the military who tell them that conscription could easily be enforced and with little loss of life. But until Parliament meets I imagine things will remain very much as they were when you were here and I doubt whether you could do much or learn much that would be useful. But if the Government decide finally to issue Orders in Council and to start conscription I think it would be well worth your while to see

[1] Joseph King (1860-1943). Labour Member of Parliament for North Somerset, 1910-1918. Author of *The German Revolution* (1933), etc. He was a friend of E. D. Morel. *See* the *Memoir*, p. 121.

at first hand what was going on here because certainly the press in Great Britain will not be allowed to report or will get gulled versions with the worst things slurred over. That is my opinion. I am inclined to think that if the Government wants Ireland to be in the war it should allow American regiments to recruit from Ireland and Irish American regiments might be sent here to rest and recruit. The young men are so angry over the treatment of the Home Rule problem that they won't enlist and they will resist conscription. I believe that numbers would go in under America. It is a strange situation but I doubt whether our government will take any advice from any people who know Irish feeling or if they do they will take it with so many reservations that the policy would be spoiled in adopting it. I believe if the Home Rule Bill had been put in operation when it was passed that the Irish would have been conscripting themselves in their anxiety to show they deserved it. But that chance is gone and I don't know, as the country is so sick, whether even self government would produce much change of feeling. At least that is my opinion. With kind regards. Yours sincerely, Geo. W. Russell

TO WILLIAM O'BRIEN[1]   17, Rathgar Avenue
                                                   14th November 1918

Dear O'Brien,[2]

I hear that a meeting has been arranged in Dublin at which some form of recognition or salutation to the Russian Revolution will be made. I hope the mists which have obscured that mighty upheaval will soon be cleared away and the real character of the revolution made known. I have no doubt that much to be regretted or deplored has taken place, but I have come to the conclusion, partly from personal statements made to me by people who were in Russia during the revolution, and from confirmation of their statements, which have been made public, that the stories of violence and bloodshed have been greatly exaggerated. A Canadian acquaintance who was in Russia for four years, returning this summer, told me that he had seen since his return minute, precise, and detailed accounts of massacres and the destruction of buildings in Moscow. "I was

---

[1] Text from *The Voice of Labour* (Dublin), New Series, vol. 1, no. 52 (November 23, 1918).

[2] William O'Brien (b. 1882). Not to be confused with the well-known Nationalist M.P., William O'Brien (1852–1928). Secretary of the Irish Transport and General Workers' Union for many years. (*See also* Biographical Notes.)

there at the time," he said "and there was not a single shot fired and the buildings were intact." Colonel MacCormack, President of the American Society of Engineers, who witnessed the Revolution, wrote this spring in a New York paper that nine-tenths of the stories of outrages and murders were pure inventions of the old régime, and that they were circulated by the German Government, accepted by the Allied Press, and this helped to increase the gulf between Russia and the Allies, which it was the aim of the German Government to widen. I was aware some years ago of an Irish journalist in the West of Ireland who fed his young ravens by inventing stories of outrages in Ireland and sending them to the English press, the demand for such stories in certain quarters stimulating the supply. That Irish journalist has cosmopolitan kinsmen, and they have indulged in war profiteering, I fancy, in their line of business. Even if these stories were true, this could be said in extenuation, that the autocracy kept the people of Russia ignorant and they could not be blamed much if they did not act with wisdom. The Russian peasants and workmen were regarded by the ruling classes as little above the brute, and were treated accordingly and if men are treated as brutes it is too much to expect when aroused they will act with gentleness. The leaders of the Revolution had the heritage of a country desolated by war and wrecked economically by a corrupt and inefficient bureaucracy. Swift action was necessary if worse was not to happen, and I doubt whether any Government—English, French or German—in a similar position, would have dealt more mercifully with minorities which obstructed them. It is said the Revolution is not democratic, that general elections were not held to give a moral sanction to the new régime. This is a strange criticism arising in countries like our own where a practical dictatorship has been established since the war began, where the most revolutionary changes were made without any reference to the electorate. When victory is sure our rulers begin to think of elections, and in Russia no revolutionary leader has made any pretence that the existing system of Workers' and Soldiers' Committees could be permanent. When the revolution is safe they will act as our own rulers, who have waited until victory was secured before they spoke of seeking the approval of the country.

We do not know enough yet to praise or blame the leaders of the revolution in respect of their dealing with those who opposed them. But we do know enough from dispassionate observers to see that heroic efforts are being made to reorganise Russia, to build up a new social order on democratic and co-operative lines. The leaders of the Revolution were, I believe, Marxians, and they would, only the genius and tradition of the Russian people opposed it, have built up the new social order as a highly organised piece of state socialism. But the vast mass of the Russian people, with ideals of life begotten in the Mirs and their great co-operative movement, desired a social order combining more freedom with democratic solidarity; and, as the promoters of co-operative societies almost alone had the practical economic experience required for the work of reconstruction, the Revolution, through their guidance, is tending to make of new Russia a vast network of co-operative, industrial, and agricultural societies to which the central government is more and more delegating the work of production and distribution. About sixty million people are already connected with these great and growing organisations. They own and manage co-operatively flour mills, soap factories, oil mills, printing works, factories for manufacturing agricultural machinery, leather works, boot factories, saw mills, iron foundries, sugar refineries, rope works, dye mills, tile works, dress workshops, co-operative stores, creameries, bakeries and banks, and, in fact, they are attempting to make co-operative production and distribution equal to the whole range of necessities in the Russian Republic. Their efforts are appreciated by foreigners living in Russia, for the American Russian Chamber of Commerce recently passed a resolution to the effect that they believed in the permanent responsibility of the Russian Co-operative Societies, and they, as representing American business firms in Russia, advised the Government at Washington to support financially and in other ways these powerful democratic organisations. These developments are not noticed in the press here, which selects all that is sensational, whether accurate or rumour, and ignores the work of reconstruction. I have read papers which in the same article denounced Lenin and Trotsky as paid agents of Germany and also commented on the disastrous effect of their propaganda on the morals of the German soldiers and workmen. These men could hardly be paid by the German autocracy to undermine its influence over its own people. On the Eastern front Trotsky and Lenin, the men of ideas, won against Hindenburg and Ludendorf, the men with guns. We begin to suspect that the *Daily Mail* for once allowed truth to be printed in its columns when its correspondent in Russia wrote that, strange as it might appear to people in England, Lenin and Trotsky were men of real intellect and probably knew more about international politics than Mr Arthur Balfour. We can see over the smoke of conflict the scaffolding of the new Russia arising. The conflict over its foundations will pass, but the building will be continued, and the democracies in other countries should see that their Governments allow the Russian people to work out their own destiny. Even those who are enemies of the Revolution have to admit that ninety per cent of the Russian people are supporters of the present Government. And no League of Nations, however armed with self-righteousness, could have a moral right to overturn the social order in a country which is supported by the people themselves.[1] We do not hear of Russians rising in masses against the rule of the Soviets, but Czecho-Slovaks and Japanese and other foreigners deputed to punish the Russian people for their crimes against humanity. Their crimes I believe to be twofold. They desired to be at peace when the rest of the world was at war, a very serious offence, as we in Ireland know. They also desired to have economic democracy when the Great Powers had got no further than a desire to make the world safe for political democracy and were, I believe, even a little dubious about that state of society, though experiment has proved that pure cultures of capitalism can be cultivated in a political democracy and develop there with the rapidity of bacteria in a jug of Dublin milk. Yours sincerely, Geo. W. Russell

TO EDWARD MACLYSAGHT   *Irish Homestead*
                                                    Wednesday [1919]

Dear Lysaght,

   Your handsome young man[2] called today to know if I got the mss. Yes, I am sorry. I write most of my letters on Friday and forgot that you might not know that. Please excuse me. It came all right without censorship on the contents. Yours ever, AE

   [1] So, the Chinese People's Republic not admitted to membership of the United Nations' Organisation. Nor material aid sent from the Western Hemisphere in quantity sufficient to ease the starving Chinese millions in the 1960-61 famine. See Graham Greenc's superb letter on a similar topic: *The Times*, January 4, 1961.
   [2] Conor Clune, employed by Edward MacLysaght to run The Irish Book Shop in Baggot Street, Dublin. Dr Maclysaght employed only Irish speaking staff, before that had become customary. Conor Clune was captured by British Officials in Dublin, in November 1920, and was shot there, with Peadar Clancy and Dick McKee, on Sunday, November 21, 1920. Clune had done no wrong. *See* the unpublished memoirs of Dr MacLysaght, *Master of None*, chapters 7 and 9, in the National Library of Ireland.

(Postcard)   *17 Rathgar Avenue*
FROM MRS G. W. RUSSELL   *Tuesday March 22nd 1919*
TO MRS THOMAS BODKIN[1]

Dear Mrs Bodkin,
    I couldn't write to thank you before for your invitation, as I didn't remember your address. I am so sorry neither of us could go. George is dining out, and I can't go out at night.
    I hope you are taking care of yourself, and that both you and the babies are flourishing. I do hope to find time to go down to see you when the days are warmer, and I have my seeds in. I have done practically nothing in the garden yet, and I am fearfully bothered with neuritis in my right arm too. I suppose you have your garden very nice now. With kind regards, Yours very sincerely, Violet Russell

TO HUNTLY CARTER[2]   84 Merrion Square
                                                    29.1.20
Dear Mr. Huntly Carter,
    I do not think George Moore has serious views about anything except his own writing. The only person I know here who has much personal experience of spiritualism is Lennox Robinson,[3] the dramatist a letter to the Abbey Theatre, Dublin, would find him. The centre of spiritualism in Dublin is a Mrs Travers Smith,[4] FitzWilliam Street. I believe she has published something about it which attracted attention because she got a message from Sir Hugh Lane who was drowned in the *Lusitania* and there was considerable controversy over it. She is quite honest and a clever woman a daughter of the late Professor Dowden. She might have something interesting to say from her experiences. I hardly know her as I dislike Spiritualism though I have discussed their experiences with spiritualists

[1] From a typewritten copy.
[2] A book-reviewer (in *The New Age*, 1911, etc.), apparently interested in sociology. Author of *New Spirit in the Russian Theatre, 1917-1929* (New York, 1929: Brentano's). Evidently he had asked AE to contribute to *Spiritualism: its Present-day meaning. A symposium*, which he edited (London, July 1920: T. Fisher Unwin).
[3] *See* Biographical Notes.
[4] Hester Dowden, Mrs Travers Smith (May 3, 1868-February 16, 1949), author of *One Step Higher, Automatic Writings* (London, 1937: Rider & Co.), etc. See *Far Horizon: a biography of Hester Dowden* by Edmund Bentley (London, 1951: Rider).

G

and have not been attracted and most of those I have talked to are doubtful themselves as to whether it is the subconscious mind of the medium which is the control or whether it is a disinterested entity. Lennox Robinson if he would write should probably have something of interest to say. There are many people in Ireland with developed psychical faculties but few of them adopt the methods of spiritualists. They are generally clairvoyants of a spiritual nature and are much more interesting to me personally. I believe in survival after death but prefer to investigate spiritual matters otherwise. Yours sincerely, Geo. W. Russell

TO EDWARD MACLYSAGHT   84 Merrion Square
                                              Friday [February 1920]

Dear Ned,

I will of course suggest Raheen if any person comes my way wanting agricultural education.[1] Good luck to you in your holidays.[2] I envy you seeing any places with the word "Indies" in it. It recalls the tropics, Columbus, colour spices, gold, ivory, apes, peacocks, romance, guava jelly (Swiss Family Robinson) buccaneers (Stevenson and Marryat) Eldorado and the Fountain of Youth of which I hope you will both drink. My ideas summed up in this drawing [*humorous pen sketch*] of palm trees, a hammock, a señorita, a lover, and a ruffian rival with a dagger. It is an enchanting dream; the survival of a youth of penny dreadfuls: my advice founded on a vivid memory of that reliable literature of the tropics is "shoot at sight" and don't forget this if you meet a pirate. Kind regards to Mrs Ned. Yours ever, AE

TO JOSEPH O'NEILL[3]   17 Rathgar Avenue
                                              12th August 1920

My dear O'Neill,

I am glad you were able to see Tagore. You must tell me all about him when you come back. The political atmosphere is probably thicker than when you left the government military tribunal bill having led everybody to believe we are in for the devil of a time. The Southern Unionists are

---

[1] Farm pupils.   [2] To the West Indies.
[3] Joseph O'Neill, the novelist. (*See* Biographical Notes.)

flocking more and more into the Dominion camp and if the Republicans could imagine anything more to the left than a Republic they would set it up. The Dominionist of today will be the Republican of tomorrow. Except for this heightening of the feeling there is no particular news except that old Unionists are trying to fraternise with Sinn Fein to see whether they could really get along with them as they feel they cannot get along with Lloyd George. I watch the Polish trouble with intense interest. If England and France go to war in Russia I believe it will secure the success of revolution all over Europe. It will be the last straw on the European camel's back and I fancy a Labour Government would be in power in Gt. Britain sooner than anybody expected. It is a wild world and I have not been at a cinema for a dose of sensation for a year. I would really like to see as an anti-toxin to the present mood a good old senti- mental love tale with a vicarage garden and a quiet love affair and no villain only knitting and sewing by the maiden aunt and talk about flowers and apples, pure golden age placidity. I meet all kinds of strange journalists whose eyes have looked on revolution in Russia and elsewhere and who look on Ireland as experts and think it is unique. But I fancy we are a [*illegible*] lot compared with the Russians. I hope you are getting sunlight there is none in Ireland. "The good deeds of men make the sun to shine" say the Todas[1] and there are not enough good deeds here to make even the gilt edge of a cloud. Kind regards to Mrs O'Neill who I imagine is laying up a store of novel ideas for her collection. Yours ever, AE

TO MISS E. J. SKIPWORTH[2]   84 Merrion Sq
28.12.20

My dear Miss Skipworth,

Here I am today as I was yesterday grinding out my Leader and Notes and was very glad to get your note. I hope you will soon be all right again and coming in to disturb the Editorial sanctum. Susan is moving to a flat in Rathmines and is excited about her change of residence which takes place in a few days as her nieces are breaking up house. I have not seen R. A. A. for some days but hear he is golfing sensibly, the most sensible

[1] Todas: a strange ancient tribe, living in the Nilgiri Hills, S. India.
[2] Eleanor Jane Skipworth (1866–June 1, 1956) was private secretary to R. A. Anderson, probably throughout his career in the I.A.O.S., and to Sir Horace Plunkett.

thing he has done for a long time, as he never tries to make himself well. Had two hours with a political agent of Government trying to find out what settlement would settle Irish question! I told him but said we were convinced Lloyd George could not deliver the goods. Which I am afraid is true as he has no power in his new Cabinet about Ireland though he would like to do the right thing. However I believe the end of 1921 will see us through the worst of our troubles and we will begin to cheer up. Most of us are more melancholy over Ireland than we are over ourselves. If the disease of Ireland was cured we could begin to enjoy our own private diseases properly and get the good out of them the Lord intended us to get. With best wishes for the New Year Yours ever AE

TO THE EDITOR OF *THE TIMES*[1]   March 25, 1921

IRISH FINANCE. EFFECTS OF THE ACT

Sir, I dread lest through the coming year, as though the year which has passed, controversy about Ireland should rage only over those incidents which are now the bitter daily bread of the Irish soul; that the apologists for Government will continue to plead the death of many servants of the Crown; that these will be countered by tales lamentably just as true of many atrocities committed by agents of the Government, and that the fundamentals underlying the struggle in Ireland will be ignored.

It is the policy of Government spokesmen to deny that the Irish people have real grievances, or, if there are any, they are removed by the recent Act. But I assert that the Act inflicts on us and makes permanent deeper grievances than those it removes. I will take but one out of many, an economic grievance, for I know how vain is the endeavour to make an alien people understand the spiritual or cultural moods which have with us the strength of religion. I wish to show how inevitable it is under this Act that there must be economic stagnation and decay as there was under the Act of Union.

---

[1] Text from *The Times* (London), Monday, March 28, 1921. Russell also wrote a pamphlet, *The Economics of Ireland and the Policy of the British Government*, published as one of the *Freeman Pamphlets* by B. W. Huebsch Inc., New York, 1921, with an Introduction by Francis Hackett.

After 1800 a transfer of wealth from Ireland to Great Britain began. The aristocratic classes moved to the new centre of political power, and their revenues, raised in Ireland, were spent in Great Britain, with the result that many industries, previously sustained by the expenditure of that wealth in Ireland, began to decay. Then there came the amalgamation of the exchequers, and the surplus revenues of Ireland again were spent in England. At present the excess of revenue over expenditure is £21,394,000, and under the new Act the tribute which Ireland must pay annually to Great Britain is fixed at £18,000,000. Every economist knows that the fund out of which production is maintained in any country comes from wages, salaries, and profits or dividends. If the sum of these is lessened consumption must fall. This affects production, and there is consequent unemployment. Now the effect of the annual payment to Great Britain of so huge a tribute, fixed in a time of inflated prices and profits, must be exactly the same as if wages, salaries and profits had been decreased in Ireland by that amount. Consumption must fall; production be correspondingly affected; and unemployment be inevitable. Great Britain benefits by the purchasing power transferred from Ireland, which, whether dispensed in orders for ships, equipment, salaries, or interest on loans, helps to sustain production and consumption, while with us there must be stagnation and export of population to which export of revenue always leads. What can Ireland do but cut down its standard of living, which was what took place in the early part of last century until the Great Famine thrust on it the alternative of casting off its children? Emigration begins again with us; and I believe from statements made publicly by the present Viceroy and other Irish administrators, that this emigration is not unpleasing, is in fact just what is desired.

The apologists for the Coalition speak of the prosperity of Ireland. They can only do so by ignoring the interpretation placed on Irish statistics by the officials who collect them. The deposits in the banks have increased, but the official statistician warns the reader that they represent less purchasing power than half the amount in 1914. The nominal values of imports and exports have increased, but the volume remains very much the same as in 1904, when the statistics were first collected. The flooding of a country with depreciated paper money adds nothing to the wealth or comfort of its people.

That the transfer of purchasing power from one country to another must bring about economic stagnation in the country vampirized is so obvious that one reluctantly comes to the conclusion that the effect is aimed at. I do not suppose British Ministers are so unintelligent as not to know the simpler facts in economics. They can well realize the effect on their own economic system if Germany had conquered in the late war, had annexed Great Britain and transferred half the British revenues to Germany to pay for the building of ships in Germany for its navy, to provide munitions and clothing for its army. English Ministers understand such things quite well, and I have no doubt they understand thoroughly the effect on Ireland of the yearly transfer of almost half the Irish revenue to Great Britain. If the stagnation of our industrial life and the continued emigration of our people was not directly aimed at there would have been provision in the Act that the Irish contribution to Imperial services would be spent in Ireland, that it should be paid in kind, in ships, in clothing, munitions and equipment manufactured in Irish workshops, so that, however high the tribute was, it would not in the manner of its exaction bring about industrial stagnation and the improverishment of Ireland. The revenues transferred would maintain a population of seven or eight hundred thousand people in Ireland. Is it any wonder that the volunteers say "If we continue fighting we could not lose yearly 5 per-cent. of the population we must lose annually by emigration if this iniquitous Act comes into operation? The war as we carry it on does not cause Ireland as much economic loss as the peace the British Government would enforce on it."

Ireland is the only country in Europe which has lost half its population within the memory of men still living and that is because it is the only country in Europe whose revenues and the purchasing power connected therewith have been systematically transferred to another country. If the volunteers in Ireland were all imprisoned facts like these would rankle in the heart of Irish patriots, for they would feel they belonged to a nation whose doom had been decreed. It is this knowledge that is making those who once were Unionists move more and more to the left. I was asked lately by one who would enquire into Irish conditions for introductions to Irish Unionists. I tried to think of some. I used to know many, Deputy-Lieutenants, Privy Councillors, and the like, who were the bulwark of the British connection. I could not now think of one who did not feel as bitterly about British policy in Ireland as Sinn Feiners do, though they still desired to remain in the British Commonwealth as a Dominion. There was not one I knew who desired any further interference in Irish affairs than such a status allowed. Yours sincerely, George W. Russell ["AE"]

TO LIONEL CURTIS[1] 84 Merrion Square
31 May 1921

Dear Curtis,

Joseph O'Neill is travelling for the Intermediate Board and I do not know his present address, but I have sent *The Round Table* to the Board to be forwarded to him. I am going away for a holiday tomorrow and am going to forget, if I can, the political situation. I do not feel people like myself can do anything to ameliorate the conditions in Ireland at present. The militarists on both sides have things their own way, and the people are so exasperated that I doubt greatly whether any settlement such as you suggest would lessen the hatred of British rule to any extent. As I have told you before, I do not care myself what government I live under—if the people are happy. I simply repeat as a student of the psychology of Ireland, that it will not be content with any settlement which will leave Great Britain power to bully it with army or police or interfere with its economic system or trade policy, or which partitions Ireland. While they [*sic*] things remain, Ireland and the Irish throughout the world will work for the destruction of the Empire I am afraid, so far as bitter tongues can assist in creating a sentiment for its downfall. To what extent such bitter propaganda of an exiled people numbering twenty millions, and fed from their native island, can affect its purpose finally, I do not know. All I can say is that Lloyd George has made most Nationalists feel so intense a loathing of the British Government that it would take a generation to lessen it, even with the complete freedom of a Dominion and it will always be likely to spring up again for another half-century unless you can get a set of politicians of nobler character than those who run your Empire at present.

I feel you try to be fair, but you really are not. Why, for example, do you balance my statement about the attacks on Co-operative Societies by referring to an anonymous letter minimising the number of attacks? You were at the Plunkett House and must have known that every attack reported there had been investigated by our dairy and other experts who were sent to assess damages, that the files of the I.A.O.S. contain reports

---

[1] From a transcript in Mr Dermot Morrah's custody. Mr Curtis wrote to the editor that AE's letters to him were among the early records destroyed by the fire in his home in 1933. AE's letter probably refers to an unpublished minute by Curtis circulated to the editorial committee of *The Round Table*.

of evidence before County Court judges who considered the claims.[1] Yet you try to make it appear that I was not stating the truth when I have spoken to managers, organizers, read the affidavits, the reports of cases tried before County Court Judges . . . and you want to offset this by the letter of an anonymous correspondent. That is not playing the game, Curtis. You ought to know that Dublin Castle has a set of journalists hired by it to issue statements. They publish a sham bulletin, as if it was the *Sinn Fein Bulletin*, and send it out hoping to disgust people by the violence of its statements on behalf of Sinn Fein and trusting that those who receive it will not know it is faked. I have seen this sham *Bulletin*, and the Government Department which will descend to such depths will do anything. . . . Greenwood first denied that Crown forces were responsible for the attacks. He said (a) Agricultural Labourers did this out of hostility to farmers (b) that the attacks were by trade rivals (c) that it was done by the Sinn Fein Army–and lastly, he now admits it was ordered by the military because the Societies were "fortresses." Another lie! He said at Ballymacelligot[2]–where the worst attack was made, two men killed and two wounded and the creamery burned–that there was an ambush and shots were fired from the creamery. We saw the full evidence at a military court martial held on five men arrested at the time and it came out from the evidence of the military that there was no ambush and no shots fired from the creamery, and the men were released. But the assistant manager was shot, a member of Committee also, two milk suppliers wounded and the creamery destroyed. I would, though a poor man, willingly forfeit £100 if you or anybody else can prove that a single one of the attacks referred to in my statement, did not take place. What do you know of me to lead you to suppose that I would, that the I.A.O.S. would, make up a faked case? Do you think County Court Judges are going to award damages for property which has not been destroyed? I feel annoyed over this statement of yours because it is put in as if I was a dishonest journalist and you were trying to discredit what I said.

I am afraid matters are going to get worse here and the complete ruin and rapid depopulation of Ireland will follow the government attempt to hold Ireland against its will. I am too sad about it all to write any more. . . .

[1] Detailed reports of Co-operative Societies' premises destroyed or damaged by armed forces of the British Crown were printed in the *Irish Homestead*, vol. 27, pp. 901-908, following AE's Leader *A Plea for Justice* (December 18, 1920); and in vol. 28, pp. 297-298 (April 30, 1921). *A Plea for Justice* was reprinted as a pamphlet in 1920.

[2] In county Kerry.

If I was not too old I would clear off to America or some other country, to get out of the Empire whose treatment of my country and the movement I have spent my life in trying to build up makes me sick. You have not yet got over the idea that you, as British, have a god-given right to Ireland, and until you can base your claim on moral ideas and the will of the governed it is impossible to argue. I think the Irish problem will be settled by world circumstance and not by British statesmen and it will be settled before ten years are over. You might keep this prophecy for I think if you do you will find I am right. For you personally, my dear man, I have nothing but friendship.[1] But you will have to polish up the Irish element in your nature more, to understand Ireland. Yours ever, AE

TO B. P. WADIA[2]   17th October, 1922

[AE coupled a condemnation of the Theosophical Society] "which seems to me now in some moods to be a nursery of the Black Art", [with words of appreciation of] "that great and wise man, William Q. Judge whose very memory seems to have been forgotten by present day Theosophists. I think he was a true adept in that sacred lore and I have never found in those who came after H. P. B. and Judge the same knowledge, wisdom and inner light.

"The Theosophical Movement has overflowed from the Theosophical Society and I think better work can be done by Theosophists in working in other movements and imparting to them a spiritual tendency. I have tried to do this in the economic and cultural movements I have been connected with in Ireland. But I retain membership of a little mystical group here which works on the lines of the old T.S. before it became the home of psychism and dogma. I have watched with interest so far as I could the economic and spiritual movements in India, a country which I regard as a kind of spiritual fatherland and whose influence on the thought of the world must, I think, grow greater because in no literature is there such a reservoir of divine truth as in the Indian."

[1] *See* Note 18, p. 235.
[2] Mr Wadia was then Editor of *The Aryan Path*. This text is taken from that Bombay journal, vol. 6, no. 12, pp. 721-722 (December 1935). Mrs Sophia Wadia (b. 1901) is the present editor.

TO THE EDITOR OF THE *IRISH TIMES*[1] December 27, 1922

OPEN LETTER TO IRISH REPUBLICANS

If I intervene in a conflict, my natural desire is to take part with the under-man. If I do not do so now, it is because you are where you are only by reason of a mentality which may be changed. You are not like the poor in the slums–held there by inexorable pressure from a social order not yet beneficent enough to secure comfort for all in the national household. You have only to speak a word and active hostility against you is ended. Can you say that word without dishonour? I believe you can.

My friends among you defend to me your warfare on the Free State on spiritual grounds, asserting the natural right of our people to complete independence, and that they had no freedom of choice in taking the decision they did, being under threat of a war to extermination if the Treaty terms were not accepted. I do not deny the right asserted. I could not without self-contempt condemn those who desire full independence for their country any more than I could blame those who would bring about a revolutionary change in the economic system so that none might be neglected or starved in mind or body. But there may be discussion over the means to those ends. I think, with your employment of force, the ideal you stand for tends to recede and become more and more remote in the affections of your countrymen. They cannot dissociate the ideal from the acts of those who uphold it and the ruinous consequences of those acts. Now, the certitude of the soul that its ideal is right too often begets a moral blindness with regard to conduct and its purity of motive is taken as absolution for its sins. Ideals descend on us from a timeless world, but they must be related to time; for this world has its own good and, if we do not render to it its lawful rights, neither will it receive our message, and Heaven and Earth are divorced and both are wronged.

There is much may be said in defence of a small nation contending for freedom with a great empire when it adopts the method of guerilla war-fare. It is dangerous; for only an internal light, hard to keep, prevents degeneration into the methods of the assassin. Yet a nation may only have that choice or complete submission. But you continue the same methods of warfare against your own countrymen, though by doing so you admit

[1] Text from the *Irish Times*, Friday, December 29, 1922. Reprinted in the *New York American*, March 4, 1923. A reply in the form of an "Open Letter to Mr. George Russell" was written by the editor of the *Irish Republican Daily Bulletin* (Dublin), and was printed in its issue dated December 30, 1922.

you are outnumbered in relation to those you attack, as the nation was against the empire; and your moral authority to act as you do is thereby diminished. Some of you assert the conflict was begun by the Free State, though it has seemed to many onlookers it began with those who without authority seized public buildings, filled them with armed men, and interrupted national services.

But the country has come to such unhappiness that it is not judgment on the past which is imperative, but consideration of the future. The wisdom of the world is not great enough always to secure a peaceable settlement of disputes between nations. But the most highly evolved have found a means of preventing the greater horror of civil war among their citizens by their common assent to the principle that questions at issue between them must be decided by majorities. It is admitted that majorities may be, and often are in the wrong. They may err because of ignorance or decide because of fear, as you assert the majority has done in accepting the Treaty. If there was fear on the people, I cannot think it was therefore justifiable for you to work on that fear and hold a terror over your countrymen to force them to yield to your policy.

Some of you argue that it is only by suffering and sacrifice a people come to the highest in them. But that crown comes to those whose sacrifice is willing, not to those on whom suffering is forced. They feel only the wrong that is done to them and lose too often the belief in any ideal; and I think this country through civil warfare is lapsing into a bitter materialism, and at another election it may be those disillusioned who will have power to make Ireland in their own image. I believe in the democratic solution of national differences, and think it is better to wait for recognition of the error and the righting of the wrong later by a democracy persuaded thereto by reason and experience rather than bring the most morally ruinous of all conflicts on a country.

In civil war more hateful passions are let loose because greater natural affections have first to be overcome. The effects of the conflict cannot be confined to the organism of the State which is assailed, any more than a fever can be confined to one limb in the body. The whole body politic suffers–the people far more than the State, which can only topple when the ruin of the people is complete or their mood is changed with regard to it. But in this conflict I think the majority regard you, not the Government of the Free State, as the cause of their suffering; and, while they may be turned from it because they think more of its acts harsh or unwise, they are not therefore moved to support of your policy.

In sickness the germs which cause the illness multiply and run right over the whole body. So when violence is relied on rather than reason the impulse to violence is intensified on all sides, the most powerful mood evoking its likeness in characters with any affinity to it. Those who are normally restrained from violence in a settled order break out and we have violence everywhere. It is not you and the Free State troops alone who employ force, but every rascal in the country, and many, alas! who were not rascals, but merely morally weak, and who are impelled thereto by the prevalent mood. The bandit, the bully, the lecherous, all use violence; and they do their deeds under the aegis of your ideal, and you cannot, while employing force in guerilla warfare, evade popular attribution to you of your responsibility for many of their acts. For some of the most terrible deeds done, whether your leaders approved or not, they must accept responsibility; for in this guerilla warfare men are split up into small groups acting on their own initiative. If the power of death-dealing is given to hunted and passionate men, not disciplined by long training, as the armies of States usually are, this leads to assassinations, and in the minds of such men personal hatred tends to become indistinguishable from political antagonism.

And, still more, because of this warfare those opposed to you who form a great part of the nation, are led into a violence equal to your own and a harshness of policy; and so the whole national being is degraded in its imagination of itself and in the regard of other nations. No ideal, however noble in itself, can remain for long loveable or desirable in the minds of men while it is associated with deeds such as have been done in recent years in Ireland. I believe that Christ and His Kingdom would have been execrated by humanity if His followers had sought to impose their religion on the world by a warfare such as has been waged in the name of Irish freedom.

I think the best of you existed in a dream of the high character of our people. But a true psychology of national character is impossible in a suppressed nationality. It lives by imagination of the high things its children will do once they are free. This mood begets poetry and the literature of dream; but there can be no true understanding of character until the depths are sounded as the heights are known. Because of this conflict a hateful illumination has taken place of the brute nature which exists among us. You must know now, if not before, where the path the nation is treading leads with the Dark Immortal as shepherd. But, you will say, it is as great a spiritual evil to swear allegiance to what the soul abhors.

[160]

It is not demanded of you that you must swear allegiance to the Free State or the titular head of any empire. There are few in any nation who take such vows to the State or its rulers. It is not demanded. If they kill no men, violate no woman, steal no person's goods, they are free as you would be to live their own lives, worshipping such gods, heroes and ideals as they choose. I do not like to think of you that the only service you can render to Ireland is to shed blood on its behalf. Much of the best service rendered to humanity was by those who were not members of any parliament or servants of any State. Our own cultural and economic movements made Ireland more truly respected by foreigners than our military activities, and they endeared Ireland more to its own people.

Can you not find ample work in those fields where too little has been done, and win respect for your political ideals by the genius, wisdom and energy you exhibit? Not the least of the disadvantages you now suffer from is the ignorance of your countrymen in regard to your capacity. To be ready to sacrifice life is not of itself evidence of statesmanship. Few know what images of an Irish civilisation are in your minds. Before a nation surrenders itself to those who would lead it on to revolution or war it requires, I think rightly, evidence of their capacity and wisdom. It asks what are their cultural ideals, their economic ideals, and the social order and civilisation they stand for. It is by these a nation justifies its existence and its struggles for freedom. Padraic Pearse and James Connolly, before they were chosen as leaders, gave evidence of imagination or a power of constructive thought. It is not enough for you, who ask your countrymen to risk everything under your leadership, merely to refer to the ideals of those who went before you. Men, to be followed with devotion, must themselves seem more to the nation than mere followers of a tradition. They must be known by their own thought and be deemed intellectually and morally equal to the enterprise. There may be men of that stature among you, but how are they to be known to be so?

Most of you have come to prominence as militarists only during recent years. A man who is now dead, a man who was dear to me, Erskine Childers, had great ability—greater, I think, for peace than war—but can you name those who, if you were all killed, would have left behind, as Pearse or Connolly, MacDonagh or Childers did, evidence of constructive thought or imagination? Which of you are architects, master-craftsmen in the art of nation building? How do you expect your nation to answer to a horn blown by those who are unknown to it for aught but desperate courage and readiness for sacrifice? You have yet to create cultural,

economic and political ideals which the nation can brood over and take to
its heart.

You consider the Irish a nation because they spring from the Gaelic
root, and are not merely a colony established by our neighbours. It is
for this Gaelic State you strive. But you ought, I think, to realise that the
majority in Ireland hold by the slenderest tie to a Gaelic civilisation. That
character was almost obliterated by a century of alien culture imposed on
us. It survived in most not as a character in the heart, but as a word on
the lip, and that national character must be allowed to take root again
before too great a strain is imposed on it, or the Government Irishmen have so lately abjured may, in their wretchedness and ruin, seem
more desirable than the unexplained future to which you would allure
them.

I do not ask you to give up any ideal. I think, if your cause alone is to
be considered, a non-military Republicanism would win you more adher-
ents. Your ideas would take deeper root in men's minds because they
would be well-considered, accepted because of their superior beauty or
fitness for Irish needs. Adherence to them would not be passional only,
arising out of the antagonism between races. I ask you to take as companion to that principle of liberty which you champion the principle of
brotherhood; for they are nothing apart from each other, and it is because
of their severance that lamentable cry has gone over the world about
liberty and the things that are done in its name. The wisdom of hell is to
divide and conquer the divine principles, and its religion is to uphold
one half of heavenly law so that by that lure good men may fall into the
pit.

I would not dream of seeking you out to arrange terms of settlement or
surrender. I do not like to think of you as being defeated by aught except
the best in yourselves, or as to be allured by offer of employment or a
share in the power of government. I prefer to imagine you as retiring
generously from a civil conflict whose continuance you realise would be
disastrous to the nation. I would like to imagine you, with no lessened
love for Ireland, attempting by patriotic activities of another character to
make a new conquest over the Irish mind. There is no dishonour in
raising the conflict from the physical to the intellectual plane; for it is
there the only victories which do not leave the spirit desolate and bank-
rupt can be won. If you win these, if you gain the soul, you may have the
body also. Even one of you there by creating noble images of society
may conquer millions. Until you have been worsted in that field you are

still undefeated. It is only when you have failed there you can sing the
Song of Defeat:

Shaun O'Dwyer a glanna,
We're worsted in the game.

George W. Russell, "AE"

TO JOHN QUINN   84 Merrion Square
                                                          5th April 1923

My dear Quinn,
    I should like to be in New York for a week for the pleasure, among other
things, of diagnosing your psychology in regard to the arts. I think you are
suffering from art fever. I have seen it in others, I surmise it in you at a
distance. A genuine love for painting, then an absorption in the pleasure
it can give, then comes the stage when, somehow, the pleasure is lost and
one only wants the abnormal. The drug-taker is satisfied at first with a
small dose, then he has to take bigger and bigger doses to give him his
original sensations. So you have travelled from the normal to the abnormal
in art.
    I remember mention of Picasso and the cubists in your case, and I see
you have Seurat. I do not deny he is an artist. I only say he, Gauguin and
Van Gogh are spiced art for jaded palates, and so are many others. You
remember Yeats' poem or folk song, so wise, "She bade me take love easy"?
Well, I fancy one has to take art easy to keep in constant enjoyment of it
in all its forms. If one expects impossible delights out of love it will end
in the asylum. And if one expects eternal excitements from art, it leads to
the futurists, post-impressionists, cubists and all those in whom a
delirium of the fancy or imagination leads to abnormalities of colour or
design. I get modified pleasure myself from the abnormal in art, because
the sane, academic mind is tiresome in its products. The real thing which
excites in art or literature is imagination and we don't tire of it. The fault
with the academicians and the faultless painters is that they too often have
no imagination but only a science. I am afraid your Seurat is only a
scientist. So is Picasso. Van Gogh had more imagination. I guess much of
the charm of colour is lost in the black and white reproductions, but I
think I would like "Landscape" and "Le Crotoy" and the "Boat at Dock".
The "Bathers" seems to have decorative value. "In the Park" is wooden

and dull. Your "Lady with the Powder Puff" has merit, but as I would not like to meet this plump lady in life so I am not particularly desirous of making a more intimate acquaintance with her in art. I think Degas did dancers kicking up their legs better than Seurat. Degas was a real draughtsman and the drawing of his figures was superb as well as the design. The "Vaudeville Dancers" has little distinction and I cannot find the classic root in it as Pach surmises the classic root in Seurat. I can see it in "Bathers" or the landscape. "The Three Models"! Oh, dear John! I defend you by surmising colour, because I have a sense of justice. But why have you no sense of justice? Why let a colourist be transplanted into black and white? It is like taking the bandages off a wound and exposing the sores.

I fancy, however, you get great pleasure out of these pictures. Certainly one can talk over them. They excite controversy. You cannot get excited over Michelangelo, or rather you cannot have controversies over his art. So it is with Velasquez, and a score of other mighty men. But you can have delicious conversations over Gauguin, Van Gogh, Signac,[1] Seurat, Picasso, Matisse and their compeers, and you go to bed feeling you have had an enjoyable evening. I have no real doubt the horror of the orthodox adds to your enjoyment of your pictures, and I fancy orthodoxy in U.S.A. has reached heights unknown elsewhere in the Universe. I should think there are good people who would like to bring in a bill at Congress prohibiting these artists' works being imported, just as they would prohibit alcohol or cocaine. Yes, one might have delightful controversies over these men, just as James Joyce gives the jaded literary taste a stimulus, and we start fighting and analysing until the effervescence goes and there is no more controversy and alas, little pleasure in the Seurat or the Picasso.

Do I horrify you, dear John, by analysing so cynically the pictures which give you so much happiness? But you are right to get anything which pleases you, and I hope you preserve in the bottom of your soul a little impish knowledge that it all need not be taken seriously. . . . Yours ever, AE

[1] Paul Signac (1863-1935). French painter, with Georges Seurat (1859-1891), regarded as the founder of neo-impressionism. He frequently painted landscapes and marine subjects. Paul Gauguin (1848-1903), Vincent van Gogh (1853-1890), Edgar Degas (1834-1917), Pablo Picasso (b. 1881), Henri Matisse (1869-1954), Walter Pach (b. 1883). See *Cubism* by Guy Habasque, English trans. by Stuart Gilbert (Lausanne, 1959. Skira).

TO VAN WYCK BROOKS[1]

c/o Janie Stewart,[2] Breaghy, Ballymore P.O.
Co. Donegal, Ireland
[June 1925]

Dear Van Wyck Brooks,[3]

The Pilgrimage of Henry James[4] followed me up here where I am taking a three weeks holiday, and I have been reading it with more concentration than would be possible if I was back in Dublin and up to my neck in the business of my life.[5] I have read it with the greatest admiration for the subtlety of the analysis. You explain Henry James to me. He was never one of my heroes partly because I first came across one of the difficult later books, *The Sacred Fount*, and I would like to have sent him that wise Chaldean oracle which has this wisdom: "Deepen not a superficies." He seemed to me to make intricacies in the shallows, subtle yes, but I felt like Thoreau looking on at the labourers, "I wish as you are brothers of mine you could find something better to do." Partly also I was prejudiced a little because I had perhaps wrongly the idea that he was a snob, that there was something of the spirit in him which made less cultivated story tellers of America and England delight in bringing a young American or Briton into a foreign court where they marry a princess. But I feel now that he had a mission pursued in spite of himself, the mission of Mark Twain, Walt Whitman, Vachel Lindsay, Carl Sandburg and other American writers, which I think is to cut the umbilical cord connecting spiritually the new world to the old. Twain did it with irreverence, James through disillusionment, Whitman by new forms and by being a positive creator. Whitman and Emerson seem to me your positive men who had a basis of their own, and I do not think you have got their spiritual equals since. I am always looking for the great American genius who will do what Whitman prophesied. I feel sure that the mingling of races which makes your people will bring about a more complex mentality than the world has known before. At present the noise of building state and civilization draws men too much from central depths to surfaces and I miss the element of dreams in your later literature. But I feel certain there will be a

[1] From a typed copy.
[2] *See* Note 19, p. 235.
[3] Van Wyck Brooks (b. 1886) the eminent American literary critic.
[4] *The Pilgrimage of Henry James*, published by Dutton (New York), 1925.
[5] *See* Note 20, p. 236.

revolt against the external; new individuals will break away as Whitman and Thoreau did to find their own centre. I think Europe is tired out and one cannot expect more from England, France or Italy than they have done. Russia may create a literature after its ferment. But my instinct is to look to America for the literature and art of the future. Nobody here sounds new deeps. Of course Europe is a great continent and it will go on emitting sparks of genius like Wells' atomic bombs in his romance of *The World Set Free*, but with dimming lustre. Your book starts me on all kinds of speculation and I am grateful for the gift of it and am glad to think you found something to like in my own work. We in Ireland are reacting against the idealism which led us to war and civil war and I fear we are in for an era of materialism. Our new government is however honest and energetic and from a romantic conception of Ireland is being evolved the idea of the highly efficient modern state. I would like to live for fifteen years more because I think we will react again to the imaginative and spiritual and we shall probably begin a fight for spiritual freedom. Our religions are outworn and we must find cultural substitutes. But Ireland is a very small and unimportant part of the planet and I don't share the egomania of my countrymen who think the whole world is staring at them. But it is a lovely country to live in, and here in a little cottage on a hill farm I can see seven seas as I look round through gaps in the hills and rocks, there is a lake in the valley below me, beyond are Breaghy dells and bay and [beyond] that the mountain [*illegible*] and the people here are fine, hardy and natural. I wonder have they a future of brilliancy. Sometimes I think there is plenty of genius but unkindled. Anyhow I would be melancholy if I had to leave Ireland and I cling to it with a consciousness that it is my spiritual home and my soul would wither out of this atmosphere. I knew from the beginning that where I was born was my fertile field and was wiser than James who thought he could take root in a new country. But I have no typewriter here and my writing is the despair of my correspondents and I won't inflict more of it on you. I wish sincerely to thank you for your book which has given me plenty to think about when I am not painting which is my way of spending a holiday happily. With kind regards, Yours ever AE

TO E. A. BOYD[1]   17 Rathgar Avenue
                                              2 Aug. 1925

Dear Ernest,

Many thanks for review. I was very dubious about the poems. They
were all with the exception of the MacSwiney poem and *Michael* written
within the last year. I found myself making verses though I had a feeling
that when one is within a year of sixty one must have lost a great deal of
the sensitiveness which is necessary for the writing of lyrics. I think two
or three of them are good, am not sure about the rest. But then I never am
sure about the merit of what I do write. I have heard nothing of Stephens.
He has not turned up here nor written nor do I know anybody who has
heard of him. I am afraid he is pulled out of Dublin by Mrs Stephens.
But perhaps there is a pull in him also and he may come back here. I was
glad to hear he was a great success. Many people told this of him. I find
the *Statesman* a horrible grind, have no leisure for anything else, and it is
not much pleasure writing it as the country is insensitive in the re-action
against all the excitement. I am sensitive enough to know that all idealism
in politics or economics would be wasted in the present Irish mood of pure
realism and I tune myself to it. It will be a generation before we get a new
idealistic wave I think. Yes I saw your articles. I suppose this business of
overturning old idols has to be done in America. Walt Whitman began
the business of cutting the umbilical cord connecting infant America with
Mother Europe. Mark Twain in his tramps abroad did it not as a creator
of new things but as an irreverent iconoclast. Vachell Lindsay is another
with the scissors. So I imagine is Carl Sandburg and you join in the
turning of the boat which carried you up to where you are now. I suppose
the umbilical cord must be cut but I wonder who will follow Whitman
in creating a new soul for the States. I do not find as much pure literature
in all the States with one hundred and ten million people as came out of
Ireland in the last thirty years. Wilde, Shaw, Moore, Synge, Yeats, Hyde,
Lady Gregory, James Stephens, Padraic Colum, Séan O'Casey, Standish
O'Grady, Corkery and the rest. Perhaps it is only ignorance of American
writers makes me think this or national egomania. We are perfectly quiet

[1] Ernest A. Boyd, born in Dublin 1887, died in New York, December 30, 1946. From
1917-1920 he was literary adviser to the Talbot Press, Dublin. He worked in the British
Consular Service from 1913-1920, when he moved to New York, working as a journalist
and writer. From 1932 he edited *The American Spectator*. He also edited the works of
Guy de Maupassant (1850-1893). He was reputed to have a sharp eye for human weak-
nesses, and a caustic wit describing them.

here politically. You rarely see a reference in the papers to the Republicans. The country turned them down at Dáil elections and even more in the later local government elections. On the whole the politicals the conflict threw up have turned out competent. O'Higgins, Blythe, Gilligan, Hogan, are hardworking and I believe honourable. Cosgrave has panned out better than one could have imagined possible. O'Neill and Mrs O'Neill went off on a holiday yesterday. She was for six months under the care of Rolliers at Leyden [?]. I think she is better. She came back at Easter and has remained fairly well. I am in fairly good health with only the increasing stupidity of age to worry me. Diarmuid goes off in September to India to join Bryan who has been there for three years. Violet is keeping fairly well. Figgis I never meet. He I think fears he won't be selected as Deputy and is trying to get elected as Senator. He has brains but no character I am afraid, and I do not think his brains are at their best in politics. Egomania is his curse. Who else were friends of yours. Con Curran, well as usual. Yeats takes himself very seriously as senator. I wish he would write poetry. He is getting out a big philosophical mystical work[1] this autumn. John Eglinton is still sulking in Wales hiding away from the world. I think he is cursed by the "Dusk of the Perverse" which Poe imagined sheer opposition to everybody and everything ordinary. I fancy his wife has driven him to isolate himself in a wretched Welsh village far from everybody and everything, and I do not believe he is happy. I imagine he knows he is a fool in his heart but he would never confess it. Moore I never see. He is still in London and is writing a medieval love story. I fancy it will be a poor thing. I doubt his talent for creating historical atmosphere and I am sure he will have historical howlers. But perhaps he will be wise enough to concentrate on characters and love affairs and not try to display a knowledge of medieval Ireland. I thought of you long ago as an American correspondent.[2] I had suggested it to Plunkett and between ourselves he was alarmed lest your radicalism might upset the Americans who contributed the funds to start the *Irish Statesman* and from whom he hopes to get more. You see they promised to pay in three yearly instalments quite a big sum and they are very touchy. He knew them better than I did but I know one of them is very conservative. So I left it to him to find a correspondent but I did not think he was any good myself, so finally I dropped him. I think in about two months or so

[1] *A Vision* by W. B. Yeats. First published January 15, 1926. He largely re-wrote it for the revised edition published October 7, 1937. *See also* Bibliography.

[2] Boyd never wrote for the *Irish Statesman*.

the last instalment should be handed over and this appears cynical, there will not be the same necessity to soothe feelings, and there is nobody I would like better than you. I have quite a number of American readers some hundreds. I occasionally get an Italian letter from Hone, a French letter from Simone Téry. You never met her, an enchanting little girl who came from France to Ireland to write it up in French papers a couple of years ago. She wrote a book on our politics and a second book *The Island of Poets* a couple of months ago dealing with Yeats, Synge, AE, Stephens, Moore and James Joyce. I heard it was very successful in Paris and the first edition was sold out in a month. I understand she is very enthusiastic. But she has a little malicious humour which licks off the over-sweetness of the enthusiasm. She is off to India this autumn to explore it, a most adventurous young lady and as clever as a girl could be. My French is too fragile to read her works in French but O'Neill tells me they are very good. I am finishing this on the first Monday in August a holiday. As Miss Mitchell and my typist are away I would not have time to write anything if I left it over. I am sure you will do a best seller some time the thing you hated. But you know my theory that we become what we hate. I am wise and do not hate anything for fear of the law getting me in its noose. You I am afraid are not so wise and your fate is to do a best seller. I wont cast it up at you if it enables you to pay a visit to Ireland again. Kind regards to Mrs Boyd. Yours ever, AE

TO OSBORN J. BERGIN[1]   84 Merrion Square
                                                      14.1.25[*for* 1926]

My dear Bergin,

I like your Ballade.[2] If I had it yesterday it would have gone to the printer, alas I sent a grey poem by young Wilson[3] in, but your ballade will make things gay the week after. Your verses set my mind dancing and I had almost constructed a reply to your note in verse before my breakfast interrupted the flow of soul. Here is the fragment addressed to you.

[1] Osborn Joseph Bergin (1873-1950), "regarded as the supreme authority on Irish liguistics" (D. A. Binchy). (*See* Biographical Notes.)
[2] "Ballade of the Relapsed Philistine", signed N.I.A., was printed in the *Irish Statesman*, vol. 5, p. 649 (January 30, 1926).
[3] R. N. D. Wilson (1899-1953).

> *Here's an editor ready for song*
> *Or, if you wish it, satire or rann,*
> *On a diet all texts you can't live long*
> *Eat your share of the world like a man.*
> *Heads to thwack at, hares to start,*
> *Ballades to write, and girls to woo*
> *Why should old Irish have all your heart?*

It is very inferior, but this is the fate of all imitations. What does N.I.A. signify? Why not O.B.? It is nothing to be hidden under a bushel that ballade. Yours ever, AE

TO E. A. BOYD
Irish Statesman
15 March 1926

My dear Ernest,

It was not forgetfulness which caused no review to appear of your book[1] but the long illness of Susan Mitchell during which I was doing double work with a very heavy heart and had no time to write anything to which I must devote thought. Finally I asked Walter Starkie to do an article and he tells me he has it almost finished. I suppose you saw in the *Statesman* that Susan died, a great blow to me, indeed the heaviest I ever felt in my life because she was the kindest and most unselfish of colleagues for over twenty years. I never lost any friend with whom I had been in daily association and it leaves a terrible gap in my life. I suppose time will cover this up by degrees but since last Christmas up to the present I am more oppressed in my mind and heart than I ever had been and I have to drive my pen to get an article written. In old days my thought ran before the pen.

The Quinn executors asked very high prices for the O'Leary portrait by Yeats and the W. B. Yeats portrait by Sargent, and I had to wire back after consultation with the director of the National Gallery here that we could not go beyond first offer. It may be that after trying to sell them at higher prices there they will offer them to Dublin again, at the price we

[1] *Studies in Ten Literatures* by E. A. Boyd (New York, April 1925: Scribners) was reviewed by Walter Starkie in the *Irish Statesman* vol. 6, pp. 126-127 (April 10, 1926) as "Tendencies of Contemporary Literature". It was unfairly indexed as *Indecencies of* . . . etc. A misprint comparable with *Who Was Who's* note for George Moore's last book; listed as *A Communication to* Fly *Friends*; it is *to* My *Friends*. Susan Mitchell died March 4, 1926.

first suggested and anyhow I will tell O'Callaghan the Director what you say and he will be able to find another way of getting at the Executors. I asked James Byrne to bid for interim[?] giving him a letter of indemnity by the Director, for the payment.

I am so sorry to hear about Stephens. He has a delicate constitution and he had pneumonia before. I hope he won't die. I do not believe he has the physical strength for prolonged activity and he would have done better to remain in Dublin at the Gallery. I fancy he was driven out of it by Mrs Stephens. Do let me know if you hear how he is.

I read with interest what you say about your life. I am sure America will squeeze every drop of Ireland out of you for its own amusement but the squeezing will probably give you the sensation of being alive and I suppose you will be able to live comfortably while the squeezing goes on. I fear America and thank God or Karma or destiny that I live here not there whenever I meet returning writers who tell me their experiences. But I suppose it is not so bad after all. Human beings have to live there and they make their surroundings human there as elsewhere. The "movies" are a new employment for you. I do not think O'Casey's *Plough and Stars* is at all as good as *Juno and the Paycock*. It is moving of course and controversial, but I do not wish to see it again for all its power. He is writing a new play *The Red Flower* about prostitutes in Dublin which I expect will either never be acted or will cause an infernal row. Perhaps London or New York may be kind to him as Paris was to Joyce. His *Juno* has been running in London for five months, so I suppose he is now independent while the royalties last.

I read Orage's articles.[1] Not very interesting but then I imagine he was a little hampered by the Catholic atmosphere of the *Commonweal*. Orage is at his best preaching big ideas to a little clan. I fancy in the States he has to cut out subtleties and quarter tones in his magazine articles, though I read one good one I think in the *Atlantic Monthly*. If you see him please remember me to him.

This is a very dull letter, dear Ernest, but I am very sad, and have no spring in my mind at the moment, but I may get it back after a while. My wife keeps fairly well and Brian is still in India, his last letter says getting on well. Things are dull here. The Republicans I think are collapsing and

[1] Perhaps an error. Orage contributed three articles to the *New Republic* (New York) between December 1924 and February 1926; "On Religion", "On Love," etc. The article in the *Atlantic Monthly* (Boston, Mass.) was "New Standards in Art and Literature," vol. 135 pp. 204-207 (February 1925).

quarrelling. I am glad you think *The I.S.* has some interest for you. I wonder how it has I have been so heavy at heart, but now my poor Susan's long and painful illness is over I may come back to normality as we all do. It was blood poisoning infection from a bad eye caused perhaps by an operation. Please give my kind regards to Mrs Boyd and any other friend of mine you come across. I hope to be more cheerful when I write next. I will then have new aid for my editorial work and won't be overworked as well as sad. Yours ever, AE

TO SÉAN O'FAOLAIN[1]   84 Merrion Square
                                                            [Spring 1926]

My dear O'Faolain,

I have posted on today some more books and magazines to Michael.[2] I sent them to his mother as I did not know the address of the hospital. My feeling about O'Flaherty is that he is a genius when he imagines and creates and a goose, a delightful goose, when he thinks and reasons. He is too young to have sound ideas about politics and economics and his inclination is to talk wildly. I do not mind anybody being an extremist if he has an intellectual basis for his extremist doctrines. I can take off my hat to Lenin and say this was a truly great man, but the communist who has not thought out his communism is no more tolerable to me than the old tory who has nothing but prejudices. O'Flaherty is a clever fellow and in ten years time his intellect will have developed and then if he keeps his genius he may do something really big. His short stories so far are his best work some of them really fine. Of the long books *The Informer* is the best but very gruesome. Personally he is a most likeable companion. I do not think O'Sullivan knows Gaelic, but in this I think he would rely on the advice of his Secretary Joseph O'Neill who is a native speaker and one of the ablest of all Civil Servants in Ireland. Perhaps when Bergin goes to Cork for his holidays you could pick his brains about the proposal to introduce the publication of texts. When are you off to U.S.A. ? Yours AE

[1] Séan O'Faolain, born 1900. Irish novelist, biographer and critic. He was Commonwealth Fellow in America, 1926-1928; Harvard Fellow, 1928-1929; lecturer in English at Boston College, 1929. He returned to England, teaching at St Mary's College, Twickenham 1929-1933. Since then Mr O'Faolain has resided in Ireland. His essays on AE were printed in the *London Mercury*, vol. 32, pp. 361-364 (August 1935); and the *Virginia Quarterly Review*, vol. 15, no. 1, pp. 41-57 (winter, 1939) ("AE and W.B.").
[2] Michael O'Donovan ("Frank O'Connor").

TO L. A. G. STRONG[1]   c/o Janie Stewart, Breaghy
                                                    [? June 1926]

Dear Mr. Strong,

If you had written to me earlier I could have given you permission to quote and would have done so with pleasure. But the poems are now in a volume *Voices of the Stones* and Messrs Macmillan own the copyright and it is to them not to me that permission to quote must be sought from. So far as I am concerned I give permission with pleasure. Personally I prefer "Promise" to "A Hillman." I like "Outcast" as well as any. I will read any poems you send me with interest and I am sure with pleasure. Though I am close on sixty I still retain a love for poetry and like Herbert "relish versing". I will be here for another fortnight but if you write better send letter to 84, Merrion Square as the posts here are uncertain but I will probably be back in Dublin before you write. With kind regards. Yours ever, AE

TO JAMES STEPHENS   The *Irish Statesman*
                                          Tuesday [September 7, 1926]

Dear James,

I just got your wire. Many thanks. I do not know the station but as it is the line from Calais to Paris I suppose it is easy to find out. Con Curran wrote me that he would be in Paris on 13th. His address is Hotel Jacob St. Angleterre, 44 rue Jacob, Paris. My information here is that I get to Paris 6.16 from Calais. I have written this to Curran telling him if he does not meet me here I will loudly commit suicide leaving a note that it was due to him that I arrived alone in Paris not knowing a word of the language but relying on false and fickle friends. Possibly Simone Téry will look me up if she is in Paris. She was my second line of defence against being friendless and without a guide. Please fix up anything with Curran who is my monitor and will agree with delight.[2] It is so pleasant the thought of seeing you again. Yours ever, AE

[1] Leonard A. G. Strong (1896–August 17, 1958), poet, novelist and critic.
[2] C. P. Curran contributed an account of their holiday in Paris to John Eglinton's *A Memoir of AE*, pp. 184–188. Arrived Paris, September 14.

TO SÉAN O'FAOLAIN

The *Irish Statesman*
November 19th 1926

Dear Séan O'Faolain,

I was very pleased to get a letter from you, though I am a little perturbed by the "dread temptation" you speak of to remain there after your
years of study are over. The intensity of work which you describe has I
think hardly any parallel in Irish universities, though odd students here
and there from some inner impulse do work very hard. I should say that it
is very good for O'Rahilly[1] to be in a place where they take very little
notice of him. When he returns to Ireland it may lessen that infallibility
of judgment which was so obvious about him. Yes, Colum's address is New
Canaan, Connecticut. I had a visit yesterday from your friend, Michael
O'Donovan[2] who is working very hard on his book on Celtic Culture and
on his translations. I think he hopes to have the manuscript ready within
another two or three months. It should be a very interesting book, he has
such a talent for verse translation and he may be something of a stylist in
his prose. He has certainly a sense of style. I note you have been reading
Spengler. His *Philosophy of History*[3] is exciting and interesting but I
always feel life much more complicated than even Spengler would make
it out to be, and that generalisations on history which seem when you
read the book to be sound, the moment you turn from the book and make
original observations for yourself you discover that you could make another
generalisation the exact opposite of the one about which you had been
reading and could get ample evidence to prove it so. I think myself that
the reactions do not take place within such periods of time but begin at
once; that the moment one powerful idea is made manifest at that very
moment the opposite idea or energy is called into being, and they go on
warring in society; "one lives the other's death, one dies the other's life."
Some followers of Spengler, because there has been such a development of
engineering and mechanics, think that life itself has become mechanical,
whereas I believe there was never more freedom of thought than there is
at present, and that the moulds of mind of serfs under the feudal system

---

[1] The Irish scholar T. F. O'Rahilly (1882-1953), like O'Faolain, in America at that
time.
[2] Michael O'Donovan (b. 1903) the distinguished Irish short-story writer. Generally
known by his pseudonym "Frank O'Connor".
[3] Oswald Spengler, *Der Untergang des Abendlandes* (2 vols., 1918-1923). Translated
by C. F. Atkinson as *The Decline of the West* (vol. 1, 1926; vol. 2, January 1929). The
translation was reissued in one volume, by Allen and Unwin, London, April 1934.

were much more a prison for the soul than the moulds of mind of mechanics in, let us say, one of Henry Ford's factories. I have no evidence to bring, but I think my proposition is arguable. I think Yeats had lectured at Harvard when he was in America before. I doubt whether they could get Bernard Shaw to go over. Drop me a note now and again and let me know how you are getting along. Yours sincerely, AE

TO JAMES H. COUSINS   84 Merrion Square
                                        May 31st 1927
My dear Cousins,

Many thanks for you letter of the 6th. As I wrote to you some days ago I had got the information I wanted. You are getting plenty of experience of the world and are fortunate in living in a country where philosophical and mystical ideals still appeal to a great number. I have written mystical poetry all my life long in a country where I do not suppose ·605 of the people have the slightest interest in such ideas. I imagine that Europe will finally evolve its own spirituality, but it must get through its Tamas and Rajas states before it comes to Satva. By the way, have you read Oswald Spengler's *Decline of the West*. If not it is well worth reading, for if you take what Spengler calls cultures and relate them with the sub-races of theosophical literature the conception of the latter will be greatly enriched in the imagination.[1] Yours sincerely, AE

TO W. B. YEATS   The *Irish Statesman*
                                        17th Aug. '27
My dear Yeats,

The National Library has opened and I looked up the passage in *Laws of Manu*. It is rather lengthy and I could not copy all,[2] and the passage should be correlated with some more mathematical statement of the Indian doctrine of cycles and Yugas which are like the Hesiods. This is the passage I copied:

the sun divides days and nights, both human and divine, the night for the repose of created beings and the day for exertion. A month is a day

[1] *See* Note 21, p. 236.
[2] *See* "Sacred Books of the East" series (London: Kegan Paul), vol. 25, *Laws of Manu* trans. by J. Jolly, which includes a chapter on Yugas or cycles. An older translation, by Muir. Sanskrit texts in Trübner's Oriental Series (London: Routledge and Kegan Paul).

and a night of the Manes, but the division is according to fortnights. The dark fortnight is their day for active exertion, the bright fortnight their night for sleep. A year is a day and a night of the gods, their division is the half year, during which the sun progresses to the north will be the day, that during which it goes southwards the night. But hear now the duration of a night and a day of Brahman, and of the several ages (of the world, Yuga) according to their order. They declare that the Kuta age consists of four thousand years of the gods, the twilight preceding it of as many hundreds, and the twilight following of the same number. For the other three ages with their twilights preceeding [*sic*] and following the thousands and the hundreds are diminished by one (in each). These twelve thousand years which have been just mentioned as the total of our human ages are called one age each of the gods.

But know that the sum of the thousand ages of the gods makes one day of Brahman and that his night has the same length.

The doctrine is expanded in other books and as usual in India one has to search many books for the complete doctrine. I understand it to mean that our consciousness runs up through all planes of being to Brahma. On this world our day and night is twenty-four hours. In the mid-world the day and night, or its contraction and expansion, make a lunar month, thirty days; our psychic being is affected by this darkness or this light in the mid-world. On the heavenward or third plane man is the deva (translated gods). Its day and its night are a year of our time, "when-ever it is winter here it is summer in Tirnanoge"[1] you remember Lady Gregory's old man's tradition. In the fourth world Turya or spirit waking, there is an immensely longer day and night. I think it corresponds to the Great Year of the Babylonians and the being of man there has become almost impersonal and reflects the *anima mundi*. I cannot prove this last but that is my intuition from reading much about the cycles when the doctrine is carried further to Kalpas and Maha Yugas and up to the nights and days of Brahman. I cannot follow as it deals with metaphysical abstractions too tenuous for me. The Government escaped by a hair's breadth from defeat. I do not know what is best. A fresh election would annoy the country and no party could afford it. I think the policy is to unmask the intentions of Fianna Fail by discussion in Dail so that the country will be in no doubt

---

[1] In Celtic mythology Tir-na-nog is the existence ideally unaffected by time; a "Land where even the old are fair, and even the wise are merry of tongue". *See also* the unsigned editorial "Lunar Journey" in *The Lancet* (London), no. 7134, pp. 1117-1118 (May 21, 1960), an informative and brilliantly lucid report on the physiological and psychic hazards of rapid propulsion remote from the earth.

about what De Valera and his party intend. Behind the smoke screen of
Labour and National Party nobody really could find out. Now that there
is no coalition they must act for themselves and for a few months ought
to have an X-ray of them in the popular imagination. Yours ever, AE

TO JAMES M. PRYSE[1]   [New York]
                                                     January 27, 1928
My dear James,
    I have already come to your country–landed two days ago–and one of
the attractions which brought me to America was the hope that I might
visit the Pacific Coast and look you in the face again. . . .

TO MISS L. R. BERNSTEIN[2]   84 Merrion Square
                                                     [? July 1928]
My dear Leah,
    How nice of you not to forget me! I miss my pretty model very much
and wonder will my Karma, as the Indians say, be good enough to bring
her into my circle of things again. Yes Wales is the nearest thing to Ireland
in Great Britain but it is not so lovely as the west as Sligo Donegal or
Kerry or Connemara. I hope you are having the most delightful holiday
and good weather. I myself think all weather good except very hot weather.
I have settled into my rocket here and it will take an earthquake to get me
out of it again for a year at least. The quietude of my own country is
wonderful after U.S.A. and my last hectic week there with conferring of
degree, dinners, night clubs, aeroplane journey, theatres and all that
American kindness could cram into me. But I regret my pretty model most
of all. I think if I could paint you every day for six months I would become
quite a good painter for good art is born out of the affections. I hope you
will find some younger artist and poet who will delight you with his praise
and whom you will make happy. Good bye my dear Leah Rose and drop

---

[1] Text from *The Canadian Theosophist* (Hamilton, Ontario), August 15, 1935, p. 165.
[2] Miss Bernstein was accompanied by about twenty other Wellesley College girls, on
shipboard for Europe, and met AE during the voyage. She was nineteen. Miss Bernstein
married Bernard Werthan of Nashville, Tennessee, in 1930. She writes, "This was a
beautiful romance. . . . AE and I adopted each other–I as a model, he as *my* inspiration!
We painted all day, and talked all night. I regret, now, that I did not go to Ireland with
him; but I was young, modest and afraid."

me a line now and then if my image ever comes up before you. You made
my voyage home delightful to me. There are all kinds of sweet things I
would have liked to have whispered into your ear to awaken the Psyche
but I was slow and old and shy. Yours sincerely, AE

TO MISS L. R. BERNSTEIN   84 Merrion Sq
                                                              28.8.28

My dear Leah Rose,

   If I meet James Stephens who is in Kerry now writing a new book I
will tell him how you read his *Etched in Moonlight*. I like the *Crock of
Gold, Deirdre*, and *The Demigods* better than the last book. If you are
reading Irish writers try first of all W. B. Yeats the *Collected Poems*. There
are also lovely things in F. R. Higgins[1] *Island Blood* and *The Dark Breed*
and in Padraic Colum's *Wild Earth*. You will find beautiful poetry in
Lennox Robinson's *Golden Treasury of Irish Verse* (Macmillan) the best
Irish anthology which you can read if you can't get the other books. I am
glad you have had such a good holiday. I hope some time you will find your
way to Ireland which has scenery as beautiful as any country in the world.
I felt sad not having a pretty model to draw every day. I was cheered up
for the last fortnight by the visit to Ireland of an enchanting French girl
Simone Téry who has written books about Ireland and I have made one
good drawing of her and one bad, alas. My sight makes me blunder in my
portraits. Nevertheless if you were here I would try to make a new drawing
of you every day and if I was a magician I would multiply images of you
as ornaments to woods and fields and hills and houses. You see dear Leah
Rose I am a poet and I fall in love with every pretty face and I am not
fickle for I remember them all and never turn away from them. If you ever
read the *Banquet* of Plato and Socrates' speech, you will understand that
there is only one master of the beautiful in the world and that that magician's art is in all lovely things and we are to love them all. I am afraid I will
not be at Wellesley next session. I am too elderly for this strenuous business of lecturing and travelling, though I love the States and the people I
met and thought them the kindest folk in the world. I am to meet your
Secretary of State, Kellogg,[2] who comes to Ireland this week, and I met

---

[1] Frederick Robert Higgins, the poet (1896-1941). (*See* Biographical Notes.)

[2] Frank Billings Kellogg (1856-1937), U.S. Secretary of State. (*See* Biographical Notes.)

Gene Tunney the boxing champion also here. Symbols of peace and pugnacity both here in the same week. I am afraid Gene Tunney has set more Irish boys shadow boxing in their homes than Kellogg will set dreaming of world peace. However as America supplies the pugnacity it also supplies the antidote.

Padraic Colum on a visit here from U.S.A. has just interrupted me and I forget what I was going to say. I hear that Robert Frost may come over next week. I hope he will. He is your nicest American poet today.

No I have never been in Switzerland or Italy or Germany. I love my own country too much to leave if for holidays elsewhere. I was in Paris to see pictures and my dear Simone Téry. But only lovely pictures or a lovely face could draw me away from Donegal or Kerry or Sligo on holidays. I met so many lovely faces in U.S.A. that they may draw me back there some time.

I hope you will find something to like in my poems—they are very serious. The AE who is in the innimical [?] who writes poetry is a very solemn person not at all like the vagrant and jesting person he is incarnated in. Dear Leah Rose, it was nice of you to write to me. You are young and I alas am sixty-two and it is real friendship to give so much of your time to somebody forty years older than yourself when there must be so many handsome boys wanting to say adoring things in your ears. I hope you will find some one who will marry you and appreciate you as I do, and a great deal more, for sixty-two can never appreciate twenty-one as it ought to be appreciated. Here is a little picture of Donegal drawn specially for you, dear Rose Leah. That is the country which keeps me here, all hills and hollows and such kind folk. Give my regards to any of my Wellesley friends you may meet, and I send my love specially to my pretty model. A.E.

TO W. B. YEATS   The *Irish Statesman*
Hotel Mignon, Rapallo, Italy   9th November 1928

Dear Willie,

I am sending you the issues October 20th, 27th, November 3rd. and 10th.

The libel case[1] is still dragging itself through the courts, where it has been for a fortnight. It is the most astonishing case Dublin has any

[1] *See* Note 22, p. 236.

knowledge of for a generation, in which a day's jury heard the evidence of
scholars like Dr. Bergin and Rahilly on the proper construction of Gaelic
sentences. Musicians like Sir R. Terry and Herbert Hughes spoke on
minute technical points of musical notation. Singers went into the impossibility of singing various consonants. Such unintelligible evidence was
supplemented by comments on the morals and politics of the defendants.
I am half way through my cross-examination at the moment and on
Monday I will be again like a butterfly with a pin stuck through its middle
for exhibition. There is no doubt that all the weight of evidence is on our
side, the scholars, the musicians and the singers have all declared that it is
a bad book and many of them that if they wrote the review they would have
made it worse than Donal O'Sullivan, who was a superb witness. I do not
know how it will turn out. The legal expenses must amount to about
£2,000 already.

I hope that you are finding your new home and surroundings pleasant.
Yours sincerely, AE
G.B.S. writes a devastating article on the censorship.[1] I will have it [in]
next week.

TO MISS L. R. BERNSTEIN   84 Merrion Sq
                                                              5.2.29

My dear Leah Rose,

Why did you cut "him" out of the photo? I discern a hand over your
shoulder and I guessed it must be him. Was it? and if so how unkind to
cut him out. I hope you will be very happy with him, my dear. I was glad
to get the fragment anyhow with your laugh and dimples in it though I
drew you often enough to remember them quite well. He should have been
an artist. But after all business men are entitled to have pretty things as
well as artists. "Eben de poor business man–he hab a soul." I was
perhaps too emphatic in saying I would never go to U.S.A. again. It is of
course possible, but when you are in your sixty-third year a lecturing tour
is rather exhausting and I was near the end of my tether last April after
nearly four months of it. It was meeting so many young people kept me
young enough to go through it. If you were my daughter I would paint
you and keep young looking at you until I was seventy or eighty and then

[1] "The Censorship" by Bernard Shaw, printed in the *Irish Statesman*, vol. 11, pp. 206-
208 (November 17, 1928).

I might get a fresh lease of life if you had a little girl as paintable as your-self, and I could start getting young again painting her, or she might suggest poems instead of paintings. The girl in *The Strange City*[1] suggested poetry to me though I have drawn her several times. She is an enchanting French girl who was in Ireland for some months, four years ago, a world roamer. I get letters from her from Paris, Italy, Algiers, Suez, Saigon, Japan, China, Honolulu, all within six months, and when I was in New York our paths crossed for a day.[2] She was going back to Paris from China and I was just beginning my American trip. We were so delighted at meeting in that big strange city that we took a motor car and drove round the park for four hours, holding each others hands. She is very young, very pretty, very clever, and has written three books and some plays. One of her books was *The Isle of Bards* and it dealt with Irish poets, Yeats, "AE", James Stephens, George Moore and James Joyce. I expect I knew her from the beginning of the world, we made friends so quickly in spite of nearly forty years between our ages, and she writes me about her young man who is also very noble as yours is. They always are. But she is so mercurial that I fancy he will have a lively time as she is bound to run away from him for months and he will get a letter from Peru or Fiji asking how he is and that she will come back again to him when she has travelled up the Amazon or found the source of some river. You would not run away like that. "He" could rely on you beaming every morning from the breakfast table. There are some girls who are fixed stars and some who are erratic comets and my lovely friend Simone is an erratic comet, and more fit to inspire poetry than painting which requires a sitter. You can't paint people who run away from you but you can follow them with imagination.

I suppose you will leave Wellesley with mixed feelings. You must have made many friends there, and had a good time. The College built halls for you all as if you were young queens which of course you are. I am not in good spirits at the moment dear Leah Rose because one of the re-viewers of a book in a paper I edit let me in for a libel action which we had to defend at enormous cost and it may bring the paper to its end, although the other side lost their case the costs of defence were gigantic. That may mean I must go to U.S.A. again. There is a University would like me to become a professor of literature, and if I went I would become a country-man of yours. But I may be extricated from that trouble. I hope so, as I am

[1] *Collected Poems*, p. 418. First printed in *Vale* (1931), p. 48.
[2] *See* Note 23, p. 237.

too old to be uprooted though it would be pleasant to see you again and to congratulate the lucky man. With much affection dear Leah Rose. Yours sincerely, AE

[*crayon sketch*]

TO MISS L. R. BERNSTEIN
84 Merrion Sq
11.6.29

My dear Rose,

How nice of you to remember my existence in the midst of these examinations and with the excitement of that fortunate young man to whom you are to be married. I think you must really have liked me for my image to come up before you with all those other delightful distractions and sensations. Anyway I do not forget you. I made so many attempts with bad chalk and impossible paper to draw you that I will have a very clear image of you, my dear, so long as I live. I only wish you were a daughter of mine so that I could have gone on drawing and painting you for years until the young man came from America as he inevitably would—one cannot escape destiny—and taken you away. I would have painted quite nice pictures and paid for your education and [*illegible*] out of the sales of Rose Leah as child, girl and young woman. Maybe you would have got bored sitting. But I would have shown you yourself better than the mirror. Maybe you will think of me when you come to choose your next life and say Please I want to be born near AE this time. Next door if possible.

I am glad you liked my *Deirdre*. I wrote it in a few days about twenty-five years ago, though when I wrote it I had not been in a theatre twice in my life and I knew nothing about stage craft, just imagined the people talking to each other. It was popular here for a number of years, was played too in the open air. Dudley Digges the star actor in your New York Guild Theatre acted the part of Naisi. He was in Ireland then. I never wrote another play though I was the Vice President of the National Theatre Society for four years. I preferred writing lyrics. I did start once to write a romantic comedy but was interrupted half way through by something and never went on with it. It was about a feminine Avatar of beauty who set the world crazy.

I am afraid I am not going to U.S.A. this year or next. I am busy here, tied to my work. I am off on holiday next month to Donegal in northern

[182]

Ireland, to the wildest loneliest and loveliest country I know, a country of
hills and hollows, of lakes and woods, of cliffs, mountains rivers, inlets of
sea, sands, ruined castles and memories from the beginning of the world.
From the cottage I stay at I can see seven seas between hills, and I paint
all day long and at night I go to my friends Hugo Law and his wife Lota
Law, and talk poetry and painting or go by the moonlit sands to Ards,
where Arnold Bax the musician, and myself saw years ago the silver fires
of faery twinkling all along the ridge and the tall phantoms dancing below
us in the sands.[1] I would be there now only I have to wait to 2nd July here
as Trinity College are following the example of Yale in your country and
are conferring a "D.Litt" upon me.[2] Aren't you envious that I could get
degrees without working for them or passing examinations? You have to
work hard for your degree my pretty Rose, but I simply wrote a few lyrics
in my spare moments and lo, I get degrees! I have a nice young poetess
here as an assistant in my office.[3] She writes quite good lyrics, and she
helps correcting proofs etc., all the work of an editor's office. She was
really awed the first day when she came in and in two days had forgotten
her awe and told me I was "silly", at which I was greatly delighted
as I like people to be natural. I have discovered half a dozen poets and
poetesses in my time. I think poetry is an infectious disease for when
they come near me, they begin to write verses. I wonder would I have
infected you if I had talked to you more. No I think you were better cast
by nature to inspire the artist. Come to me in Tirnanogue when you are
dead and I shall paint the ideal portrait of you there. Do you
not know about Tirnanogue. It is the Celtic Heavenworld the Land
of Heart's Desire where whatever the heart imagines comes true.
Nature and life changes instantly as we desire it. Once I wrote a poem
Tirnanogue[4] about a dead friend, a lovely girl who died and I dreamed
about her.

[1] See *Farewell my Youth* by Arnold Bax (London, 1943: Longmans).

[2] President J. R. Angell (1869-1949), by W. L. Phelps (as Public Orator) conferred
the Yale D.Litt. on Paul Claudel (1868-1955), J. L. Lowes (1867-1945) and AE, on
June 20, 1928, at New Haven. Bruce Rogers received an Hon. M.A. at that ceremony.
The TCD degree was conferred by Sir Robert Tate (Public Orator) on M. Franz
Cumont (1868-1947), John Galsworthy (1867-1933), Sir T. Little Heath (1861-1940),
and AE on July 2, 1929.

[3] Miss Irene Haugh, born 1906, in Dublin, poet and journalist. Her article "*Study
of AE (G. W. Russell)*" was printed in the *Ireland-American Review* (Dublin) (quarterly:
ed. Maurice Leahy), vol. 1, no. 1, pp. 36-49 (September 1938).

[4] *Collected Poems*, p. 392. First printed in the *Irish Statesman*, vol. 6, p. 232 (May 8,
1926), and in *Vale* (1931), p. 22.

> *We were happy and dead, you and I,*
> *With the gay light footfall of dream,*
> *We followed the moor through the hills*
> *By a quivering jewel of stream.*
>
> *We were happy and dead, you and I,*
> *For all things ran at our will,*
> *The genii of earth and of sky,*
> *Blue night, and moon-coloured rill,*
>
> *And the mountains crouched by our side,*
> *Were a pulse of the spirit more gay,*
> *Would arise and shine with delight*
> *In the gold and the silver of day.*
>
> *In the valleys Death gave us for joy*
> *There were voices and lights that we knew;*
> *Earth's fables of love and of beauty*
> *That Death had brought to be true.*

I wonder whether you could think of death so gaily as I do. I expect when this old body opens its doors an aery child will go out in the wind and run to the wonder worlds and to meet its friends made young again. I hope to meet you there in an airy body, with all your curves more shining. Don't choose any other Heaven world but the Irish. None of the others are any good. With much affection dear Rose, Yours ever, AE

TO IRENE HAUGH   c/o Janie Stewart, Breaghy
                                                         [July 1929]

Dear Irene, I hope you are not overworked or in any tangle. This is merely to say that if you are hunting in the copy box for more articles do not use Liam O'Flaherty's story as I believe it has been published elsewhere. My old bones are aching walking over these hills. Trams and buses are no preparation for Donegal. Good bye, dear young person. Half a week has gone. A few more and I will be back again. AE

Don't forget to send on new *Statesman*, AE

TO CHARLES WEEKES   The *Irish Statesman*
                                                    July 26, 1929

Dear Charlie,

I have just returned from holidays and got your very kind letter. I am glad that you still remember the friend of your youth. It is possible I may be in London for a few days this Autumn and I hope to see you there. Sorry, I have so many letters waiting my reply I cannot write at more length. Yours sincerely, George W. Russell

TO IRENE HAUGH   *Irish Statesman*
                                                    1 Aug. 29

Dear Irene,

Here is the cheque. I am sorry it did not come yesterday. I hope you will have the happiest of holidays and that you will have time to study other methods of bobbing hair when you are in Paris. Though I dread lest you might return with some ultra-modernist cubist-futurist cut in which the whiskers will grow out like this. [*simple crayon sketch*] There is nothing impossible with your generation. Your subservient editor, AE

TO RICHARD CAMPBELL[1]   The *Irish Statesman*
                                                  September 13th 1929

My dear Dick,

I am very sorry indeed to hear that you had to go to a Sanatorium. I can sympathise with anybody who has suffered at the moment, for a week I have had a very bad attack of lumbago and I feel sympathetic for anybody suffering. I have practically got over my trouble and I hope that you will also. You always seemed to me to have a healthy and vital personality but I imagine there is wear and tear in New York life which we in drowsier countries do not experience.

The pictures are on way to Mrs Hackett. I have to take the risk along with others who are also sending pictures to her—she seems a nice woman anyhow.

[1] Richard Campbell, the American lawyer (1872-1935). (*See* Biographical Notes.)

[185]

Between ourselves I think that Dermot has fallen in love with somebody in New York, and you are sufficiently young to know what that means, and how any difficulties in meeting are regarded as an injustice inflicted upon them by the governing powers in the universe. He will have to put up with it.

I am sending you herewith a letter from the Manager and copy of the balance sheet up to March when it was last made, together with some copies of letters which were sent to the treasurers of *The Statesman* fund which gives some kind of idea of the feeling the writers had about the paper. These letters could have been multiplied. I hope the letter and the Statement of Accounts gave you the information you want. You have taken a great deal of trouble over the affairs of the paper for which I and the other directors are very grateful. I did not imagine that the controversy over the National Anthem would excite any feeling in America. Here, nearly everybody is sick of the *Soldier's Song* which has bad verse and inferior music and they hope to get some genuine Irish air of which we will not be ashamed whenever it is played, but I am all for the *Soldier's Song* as against *God Save the King*. The sentiment which inspired the southern die-hards is rapidly fading away and in another few years it will be practically extinct.

Please give my kind regards to any of my friends you may meet, Ernest,[1] Mary Rumsey[2] and George Moore[3]. I hope by the time you get this you will be yourself again and there will be no necessity for the intervention of any surgeon. Our friend Sir Horace Plunkett is trying to learn flying and get a pilot's certificate. I never met such an astonishing man: he goes up in the air, comes down, goes to bed for several days in a half state of coma and when he is better goes up again, and says it stops his insomania from which he suffered for many years. I am terrified of his latest hobby and look at the morning paper to see whether he has crashed. His last letters were written from a sick bed and when I think of the dangers of his being in the air I almost prefer his being in the sick bed. Yours sincerely, AE

[1] E. A. Boyd.
[2] *See* Biographical Notes.
[3] Probably George Godfrey Moore, President and General Manager of the National Reserve Life Insurance Co., Topeka, Kansas, from 1920. Politically a Republican, and a Baptist, he was a large-scale collector of rare books. Born Philadelphia, November 28, 1872, he died March 15, 1939.

TO SARAH PURSER   17 Rathgar Avenue
                                    Friday [September 20, 1929]

My dear Sarah,

My wife and I are both very sorry indeed to hear of the death of your brother.[1] The death of those who have been part of our lives for many years seems to take part of our own life away. I have always felt when any I loved or worked with died that something died in myself, and the leaves were falling from my own tree of life and I know you must feel deeply the departure of one you have known since you can remember life at all. Please accept my sincerest sympathy for your loss. Yours ever, Geo. W. Russell

TO THOMAS BODKIN[2]   *The Threefold Movement*
                                          Union of East and West
                                          League of Neighbours
                                          Fellowship of Faiths
                                    16 S. Frederick Street, Dublin
                                       Dublin 6th August 1930

Dear Dr Bodkin,

Sir Francis Younghusband, of England, and Mr Charles Frederick Weller, of America, have asked me to give my signature for this letter inviting you to become a Member of the Dublin Committee of One Hundred of the Threefold Movement–Union of East and West, League of Neighbours, Fellowship of Faiths.

In fifteen cities, in nine countries, this Movement has Committees of One Hundred, formed or forming,–

> For the Realization of Peace and Brotherhood through Under-standing and Neighbourliness – between people of *ALL* Nationalities, Races, Cultures, Classes, Conditions and Creeds.

In Dublin, one of the early activities will probably be a Dublin meeting similar, somewhat, to the London meeting described by the enclosed

---

[1] John Mallet Purser (1839-1929) died 18 September. He published a *Manual of Histology* (1884) and numerous papers on physiological and pathological subjects. Added to his practice as a physician he held professorial appointments at Trinity College, Dublin. He had lived with his sister at Mespil House.

[2] Typed circular letter, signed. The editor has been told that Russell apologised to his offended Catholic friends for this unique breach of his diplomatic habits.

Programme. (About 1,200 people attended this meeting in the London City Temple–in which "World Unity" was discussed by representatives of Eight Religions and Seven Countries.)

A Dublin letter-heading is to be printed with the names of Dublin Committee members and Officers (similar to the London letter-heading upon which this letter is written).

By kindly permitting the printing of your name on the Dublin letter-heading as a Member of the Dublin Committee, you DO NOT pledge yourself to attend meetings or to do active work or to assume any financial responsibilities–beyond your own personal, voluntary Membership contribution (for which a Dublin subscription envelope is enclosed).

We all hope, earnestly, that you will be glad to endorse this Movement and to lend it a little of your influence by kindly accepting Membership in the Dublin Committee of One Hundred.

Will you please address your reply to the Secretary of the Dublin Committee at 16, S. Frederick Street, Dublin. Yours sincerely, Geo. W. Russell, "AE"

Appreciation (The Quarterly Journal of the Movement) will keep you in touch with its development, in Dublin and elsewhere.

FROM THOMAS BODKIN AND OTHERS TO G. W. RUSSELL

[August 1930]

Dear AE,

We received your letter of the 6th with surprise. You show a sad misunderstanding of the Catholic position in sending it to us.

As Catholics we are as anxious as you are to promote "the realisation of peace and brotherhood throughout the world". But we do not, for an instant, admit that such a consummation can be brought about by "a fellowship of faiths". We believe in one true church, out of which, save for the comfortable doctrine of "invincible ignorance" there is no hope for humanity. We regard our faith as the only God appointed way to real peace, here or hereafter. Our efforts towards peace can only be made under the guidance, and by the authority of the Catholic Church, universal and apostolic.

Membership of your association would, therefore, mean for us an admission that mankind's highest aspirations can be realised outside the Church.

So, while recognising the good motives which, no doubt, prompted your invitation, we must decline it, as we have no pretentions to "the appreciation" of other faiths. With kind regards we are, Yours very sincerely,

[188]

TO MACMILLAN AND CO LTD.   17 Rathgar Avenue
                                                      30.8.30
. . . May I supplicate attention for his mss.[1] He is a young man of very great talent, an admirable poet and something of a scholar. His translations from Gaelic are the best I know. His stories are I believe about the civil war in Ireland and he had exceptional opportunities for gathering intimate knowledge of this dark period in our history. But his interest in writing these stories is not political but human. That is his interest is in the characters not in the political situation. I recommended James Stephens to your attention a good many years ago. I have come across no young Irish writer since in whose future I have more confidence. . . .

TO MISS E. J. SKIPWORTH   Thursday [? September 11, 1930]

My dear Miss Skipworth
    I am sorry I could not find you when I came to say goodbye. There are two photographs on my mantelpiece one of Sir H. P. one of R. A. A.[2] and a sketch of Susan[3] in the corner of the room beside the mirror. I wonder would you keep these in your room until I return. The other portrait of Susan by old J. B. Yeats will be called for by her sister. Miss Tipping [?] will keep it for her. With best wishes, Yours ever, AE

TO DR FRANK PURSER[4]   *North Western Hotel, Liverpool*
32 Fitzwilliam Place, Dublin   Friday [September 12, 1930]

Dear Frank,
    I have been so hurried these last few days clearing things at 84 Merrion Square and trying to prepare for U.S.A. that I did not say to you what I felt about your kindness to myself and my wife and what a deep down good

[1] Probably *Guests of the Nation* by Frank O'Connor; published by Macmillan, London, in September 1931.
[2] Sir Horace Plunkett and R. A. Anderson.
[3] Susan L. Mitchell, a pencil sketch given to AE by Dr Thomas Bodkin, to help console AE after Susan's death. AE gave the sketch to Mr C. P. Curran when he dispersed his possessions in 1933. Miss Tipping (?), not identified.
[4] (September 16, 1876-February 28, 1934). He practised in Dublin, specialising in nervous diseases. Dr and Mrs Purser became friends with AE about 1915. "Young philosopher", his child Séan Purser.

H*   [189]

fellow you are. I go off with a warm feeling in my heart for you and all the friends who made my last days here so memorable. There is no place like Ireland. I will come back to it and my friends with a deep sense of satisfaction. Good bye my dear fellow and with kind regards to your wife and the young philosopher. Yours ever, AE

My boat goes tomorrow

TO JAMES M. PRYSE[1]   [Missoula, Montana]
                                                           November 1, 1930

I expect to be in Los Angeles on the 17th of this month. I have two lectures to deliver, one in the morning and the other in the afternoon. I shall seek you out that evening about 8 o'clock, and I hope to see you again, dear James, after so many years. . . .

TO OSBORN J. BERGIN   (*Sunset Limited*)
                                          Letters sent to me c/o Mrs Rumsey
                                             152 East 40th Street, New York,
                                                            will be forwarded
                                                                   29.11.30

Dear Osborn,

I am writing in the middle of the desert in California on my way to Arizona. Don't the names thrill you, you old reader of Wild West stories. I look out of the windows on cactus and sage and sand and stones and distant mountains of a kind of wrinkled pink colour. I have seen no cowboys except in Los Angeles and I suspected they were made up for cinema. It is hot as the hottest day in our summer here close on December. I have gazed on California for a fortnight, palms, cactus, desert, orange and nut groves, mountains and sea all marvellously beautiful. San Francisco is the most romantic city in the world set with white or golden buildings and hills with bays and a blue sea to enchant you and blossomy with flowers. It looked most magnificent and mysterious from the mountains above it in the evenings with shine and shadow for leagues of land locked bay and islands and shipping. When I first came to it across the ferry the city rose at night like a city out of the Arabian Nights all glittering with rose and

[1] Text from *The Canadian Theosophist* (Hamilton, Ontario), August 15, 1933, p. 165. AE was in Los Angeles for three days; each evening from 8 o'clock he spent with Pryse.

golden and silvery lights, and I said I am getting into Paradise. Then as I came closer I knew the jewelled lights were passionate appeals to smoke particular brands of cigarettes or to eat particular brands of tinned fruits. But there is a romance about the city in spite of that. I have been whirled about ever since I landed and life is an unending series of railway journeys and lectures with an odd day or two rushing off to see national parks and glaciers and forests and canyons, all inconceivably vast. Ireland seems as remote as the Pleiades or Orion. But by the time you get this I will be half through my pilgrimage and ready for retreat into a hermitage. It is too much for my sixty-four years all this but I am bearing up well and I hope to see you in April and tell you all about it. Good luck. Yours ever, AE

TO SIR HORACE PLUNKETT   152 East Fortieth Street
                                                     January 28th 1931
My dear Sir Horace,

I was glad indeed to get your letter, but was sorry that you were not feeling in good health. I think the best thing you could do would be to throw up any kind of work in England, which has the most detestable climate on the planet, and go to Algiers or some sunny place and let the sun which is the great doctor work his miracle upon you.

I expect to be back sometime the end of April, and if I come through London I will let you know, and I can tell you all about the agricultural situation over here, for I have been amassing volumes and volumes of facts. My life is a bewildering one going around from place to place, and my impressions are a little blurred, but I will disentangle them when it is all over.

Do take my advice about easing up on any kind of work. I recall what a Hell of a climate you had when I was last with you. There were five hundred and sixty square miles of fog, and your motor which met me at the station had to crawl, not knowing whether it was going for a ditch as everything was invisible. Fly from that climate! Fly! Fly! Sincerely yours, AE

TO JOSEPH O'NEILL   The Blackstone
                                  South Michigan Avenue, Chicago
                                                          14.2.31
Dear Joseph,

Here I am just arrived from Detroit one of those gigantic new cities built largely round Henry Ford's enterprise but with huge skyscrapers like all the big American cities making you dizzy and awed when you look up at them. I have come here for a conference with some agriculturally interested folk who want to start an agricultural foundation to save American agriculture on my lines. I think they are a great deal too ambitious. They want to raise five million dollars. I don't know where I go after that. My schedule comes to-morrow from New York. I have been doing some wild travelling during the past ten days. I lectured at Lansing February 6th, left it same day and lectured at Grand Rapids went to Detroit on 7th and lectured there. Then on 8th went to Wooster University and did my turn. Left Wooster and went to Buffalo stayed there a night and went to Ithaca, where I lectured at Cornell University 12th talked again next night and after that took a night-train at 12 o.c. for Detroit where I lectured on 13th and again on 14th and arrived here tonight rushing off after lecture to train. It is the hell of a life. But I am standing up against it very well and I hope by the grace of God to wind up all my business here at the end of April and start home at the beginning of May. I was in Montreal in Canada before I went to Lansing. I like Montreal where I talked twice and found delightful folk. The world was white for thousands of miles and the temperatures below zero which makes one's blood tingle. It is a dry electric cold not like our damp cold. But oh Lord won't I luxuriate in idleness when I get back and rise up in the morning with the heavenly feeling that there are no trains to catch or speeches to make. I have become the expert lecturer by practice and face my audiences without turning a hair, I who used to be terrified at speaking a word before a crowd. The restless unceasing energy of these people is amazing. They are heaping up economic dangers for their own civilisation by over-energy resulting in overproduction. Fewer and fewer people are required to do the work, science and mergers and rationalisation and more efficient machinery creating unemployment. The country is filled with relief schemes. Every state and city has them. I guess there must be about six million unemployed or five million at the very least, they try to minimise it. I think there is going to be tribulation in this great country and that it will deepen national life. They are big enough to pull through. But it will be a pull. I hear nothing of Ireland in the papers. We are not murderous enough to interest the cable companies. I think de Valera's stock has slumped over here. At least I found no enthusiasm about him as I did before. It will take me some time to make up past history when I get back. Seven months of Irish life and I not knowing about anything! I who used to keep track of all that went on. I fear the censors are active. Michael

O'Donovan[1] says at first their activities were a genuinely important guide to immoral literature but that now they have taken to censoring books that would not be a temptation even to a parish priest. I would have had great fun commenting on the censors if the *Irish Statesman* was still in being. Do you miss it? Does anybody? or is it forgotten and gone behind time like Griffith's *Sinn Fein* and the *United Irishman*. I hope Mrs O'Neill is well. Give her my kind regards. I am too perambulatory to have ideas or intuitions. They will come later. Yours ever, AE

TO VACHEL LINDSAY[2]   [June 1931]

I am staying in a remote mountainy district in Donegal. Before the cottage door I see this [*Sketch*] The mountain is Muckish, one of the twelve sacred mountains in Ireland . . . I amuse myself painting. I had eight months in your country and feel empty after talking all the time, and came here to fill the empty psyche. Why were you not born here? You would have upset all our old traditions over which we have brooded too long. I see nobody. I read nothing. I eat griddle bread, drink buttermilk, sit by a turf fire, and walk over hills and sands, and try to empty my mind so that Mother Earth may come into it and talk to me a little. She used to breathe in me, and I have hopes she may sing a little song through me again.

TO C. M. GRIEVE[3]   17 Rathgar Avenue
                                                26.9.31

My dear Grieve,

Yes I am back from America. Had a very long and exhausting tour: after that eight weeks in Donegal to try and get back to myself and have

[1] The transcripts of letters printed in *A Memoir of AE* (p. 226), are in many places inaccurate.

[2] *See* Note 24, p. 237.

[3] Christopher Murray Grieve (b. 1892) the eminent Scottish poet whose books have been published under the pseudonym Hugh MacDiarmid. His work in the Scottish vernacular and in English is widely read. Mr T. S. Eliot and the late Dylan Thomas have written appreciatively of his poetry. Thomas called him "the greatest Scottish poet since Burns". Mr MacDiarmid's fragmentary autobiography, *Lucky Poet* (London, 1943: Methuen) promised two subsequent volumes which have not yet been published. He promised to discuss in them AE and A. R. Orage, among others.

started writing a book but find my mind very flabby except at rare moments. The trouble is head-aches which began about two years ago and which come and go and leave my mind with no cutting edge to it. To answer your questions (1) Yes there was a complete bibliography of my books pamphlets etc. published in the *Dublin Magazine* about a year ago. (2) No I never got a copy of [*To Circumjack*] *Cencrastus*. What is this? a book? a pamphlet? Yours? Many letters went astray while I was in U.S.A. as I was travelling all the time. I read little or nothing while I was moving about and do not know what books were published and I read hardly any papers now so am completely out of information about current literary activities. I think because I had to keep abreast of such things when I was an editor that I rather gladly give my mind a holiday about them and renew my reading of the ancients. (3) Will you send me mss of the poems and I will see what I can do. About some things I can write and about other things my mind remains lethargic. I could not if you offered me a thousand pounds write about let us say *Tom Jones* while I could write easily about literary work of one fifth the talent if the ideas had any affinity with my own. So please send them along –I promise I will reach with a microscope for any germ of an affinity. You know I like your poetry and thought your verses had much more vitality than the verse published by your English contemporaries. (4) If you think the sketch[1] worthy of reproduction you can use it. Better ask some artist about it. You see I am an amateur and was never taught to draw and when I try painting sometimes it comes off because of an idea or imagination and sometimes it is pretty feeble. But if your artist friends think the drawing would reproduce and not disgrace the Press by all means use it. A drawing I did of James Stephens was reproduced in *New York Times*[2] and I was astonished to see how well it came out. Have I answered all your queries? I wish success to the new enterprise. I think that five short lyrics are a little short measure for an edition all [*illegible*] probably expensive. The Fountain Press in New York which printed poetry of Yeats, Stephens, myself and others in expensive editions required about fifteen lyrics or thereabouts giving a little quantity as well as quality for the money they asked. The number required was essential. But probably you know the ropes better than I do. Yours ever, AE

[1] A sketch of the author, by AE, was reproduced as a frontispiece in Hugh MacDiarmid's *First Hymn to Lenin and other poems* (1931).

[2] *New York Times*, June 22, 1931. Section 5, p. 13.

TO J. M. HONE[1]   17 Rathgar Avenue
                                                 Tuesday [? October 1931]
Dear Joe,
   Yes I have been reading your admirable book on Berkeley.[2] I am not
sure yet that I understand the philosophical part. In a sense it is simple
enough but it does not recreate itself in the imagination. I had always this
trouble about Berkeley. I have no such trouble about Plotinus who super-
ficially is more complicated. The real trouble I have about the Berkeleyan
system is that even if I accepted it I would not know how to live or act
by my philosophy. I have not this trouble with Plotinus, Sankara,
Patanjali. I know what I ought to do, by what threads I climb inward to
their light and to an expanding consciousness. But Berkeley is opaque to
me. I am glad you and your collaborator are not complete enthusiasts.
If you were I fancy Yeats would have tried to make all his friends
Berkeleyan and have conceived of Ireland as the Vatican tendency of that
Pope of the spirit. I am not writing any articles now. The only article I
wrote and for the last year was a review of Humbert Wolfe which I was
supplicated to write, and I did it badly because I am suffering from
headaches which blur the edge of my mind. This may be because I had
a very strenuous time in U.S.A. and had to be keyed up all the time, as
I was lecturing day after day to Universities and Chambers of Commerce
and travelling by night and I wonder I did not collapse. Once the room
rocked up and down before my eyes as if it was an Atlantic liner in a
storm, and I am hoping if I rest from work I will get back to normal and
the headaches will go. If I do get back to normal I may ask Seumas
O'Sullivan to let me do it for the *Dublin Magazine*. I could do nothing
now that would not be stupid. I hope I will see you sometime. I am going
on Friday to Galway for a week or thereabouts. Yours ever, AE

TO PADRAIC COLUM,   17 Rathgar Avenue
                                                               29.3.32
Dear Padraic,
   You are always kind. You are as good as you were when you were young
which is saying a great deal about anybody. I am trying to keep myself

[1] Joseph Maunsell Hone (1882-1959), the eminent Irish literary critic, thinker and
biographer. (*See* Biographical Notes.)
[2] *Bishop Berkeley, his Life, Writings and Philosophy* by J. M. Hone and Mario M.
Rossi. Introduction by W. B. Yeats (London, October 1931: Faber).

alive by writing a book. But it goes slowly. Maybe after a month in Donegal in the Summer it will go swiftly as things once used to flow from me. But as one gets older that swiftness of mind cannot be maintained. Anyhow I hope to write the book. I did not expect to find you back in Paris after so short a stay in U.S.A. Is Paris to be your spiritual and actual home in the future? I know when good Americans die they go to Paris. I did not know that it applied, this affinity, to Irish Americans also. We are all wondering here what is going to happen. When the boy scout kind of mind gets into power it is like Bernard Shaw's romantic soldier having a mind. The boy scouts of last generation are growing up and they are the Fascists in Italy, the Hitlerites in Germany and the I.R.A. in Ireland, a dread phenomenon. Ask Molly[1] who is studying psychology about this. I really dont understand the psychology of the generation after mine. When de Valera says he is going to remove the oath and abolish the Governor General and keep £79,000,000 the yet unpaid land annuities and lay claim to £30,000,000 wrongly paid in the past, and then says calmly if any bitterness should arise in the controversy it will not be the Irish fault! Lord what an obtuse mind. What would you feel if I insulted you and picked your pocket as well and said if there is any bitterness over the incident it won't be on my side it will arise? Oh for a lodge in some vast wilderness (nice to paint) with canvas and paints in plenty, a nice friend or two, and I would be glad to exchange 17 Rathgar Avenue for that lodge. If you should see Simone Téry tell her she is a little beast. She will know why I say this. She has not written reply to a letter. But don't tell her. Perhaps I addressed it wrongly. Give my kind regards to Molly. How is her book getting on? Are you coming over to Ireland or will you wait to see whether England declares war and blockades our ports. Good luck to you dear Padraic. Yours ever, AE

TO W. B. YEATS   17 Rathgar Avenue
                                          Monday [May 23, 1932]
My dear Yeats,

I have just heard of Lady Gregory's death.[2] Though you must have expected this for a long time the passing of one who had been your best friend for the best years of your life cannot but move you deeply and I am

---

[1] Mary Colum.

[2] At Coole Park, on May 22, 1932, aged 80. *See* Yeats's *Letters*, p. 287. See also *Lady Gregory: a memoir* by Elizabeth Coxhead (London, 1961: Macmillan).

Violet Russell (AE's wife), with Sara Allgood and others, 1911

Photograph taken by Lady Glenavy at the wedding of Miss Ruth Pollexfen (a cousin of W. B. Yeats) at St Columba's College, Rathfarnham, county Dublin. Mrs Russell to the left of the photograph; Sara Allgood in the centre

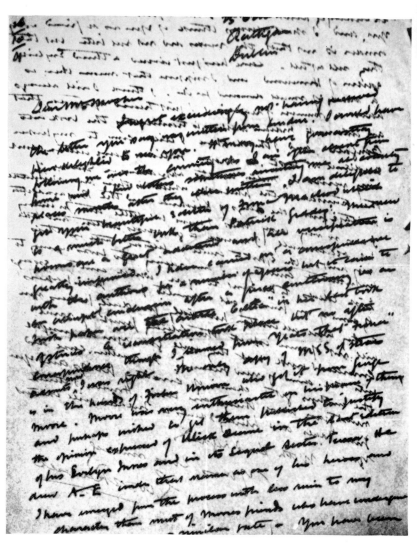

Specimen pages. AE to

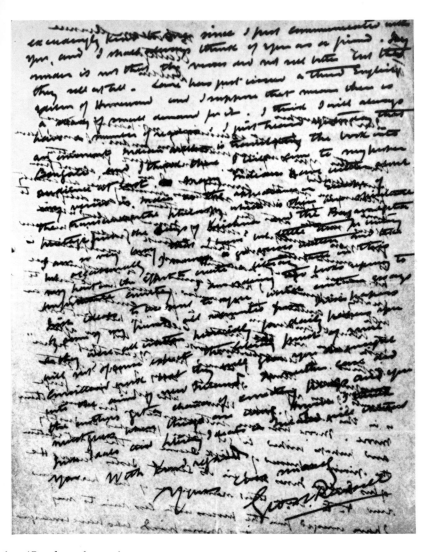

her (October 26, 1901)

G. W. Russell, February 21, 1935

Photographed in Washington, DC *for the Department of Agriculture
by their staff photographer Mr E. C. Purdy*

sorry for you that from this on your life must be lonelier. She was a very noble old lady. The generation to which she belonged was I think a rarer and finer breed of life than those who came after. I think of her, of Horace Plunkett, of Louis Claude Purser,[1] of Mrs. Green,[2] and others like them who thought in the noblest and most disinterested way about their country, going deeper than those who came after them in time. My own acquaintance with Lady Gregory was comparatively slight for I was absorbed in other things but I always appreciated a workman doing beautiful things though in a field of effort far apart from my own. The Anglo-Irish were the best Irish but I can see very little future for them as the present belongs to that half crazy Gaeldom which is growing dominant about us. I am very sorry for the loss of your friend. Yours sincerely, AE

TO VAN WYCK BROOKS[3]   17 Rathgar Avenue
                                         15.8.32

Dear Van Wyck Brooks,
    There is no biography of a man of letters which I desired to read with more eagerness than a life of Emerson. I have always loved him since I first read his poems and essays a good deal over forty years ago and I find he is one of the few writers who last so that I can take up his essays and find new profundities in them. I have sometimes thought that a great book could be made by taking aphorisms out of the essays and commenting on them as one might comment on a verse in a sacred book. He was of that order of genius whose daemon utters through him wiser things than he himself knows. He must have known they were wise or he uwold not have written them down. But I doubt if he saw all the implications psychological, philosophical and spiritual of many of these sentences. He requires to be explained at some length by the reasoning mind which yet has insight enough to feel that there are divinations of truth above reason to discover but which when stated reason may defend or make clearer. The schoolmen made a philosophy for Christianity out of the transcendental utterances of the gospels, and an American philosophy might be made out of a rationalization of Emerson's transcendentalism. He says things so swiftly that a slow mind passes on to the next sentence without having

[1] L. C. Purser (1854-March 20, 1932), a brother of Sarah H. Purser.
[2] Alice Stopford Green. *See* Biographical Notes.
[3] From a typed copy.

seen all the implications of the one it has just read. No American writer needs a commentator more, for his mind went into occult depths and had kinships with arcane fragments like the Chaldean Oracles or with the hardly less arcane Plotinus or the Upanishads. There are deeps and profundities in these which he saw, and knew that they were of the eternal order of truths which are not for a time but will not cease to be illuminating to the spirit until man becomes more than man. If I was younger and had more energy of mind I would like to write that commentary on say a hundred of the Emersonian aphorisms just to let Americans know how great a man this was whom they have learned from, but who was I think the spiritual germ-cell of American culture. You see how much in love with him I am, and can guess with what eagerness I read your life and how pleased I was to have him personally conjured up for me as you have done. In a sense he does not seem merciful to his biographer because he did not run away with his neighbour's wife, nor did he fight on any barricade or have any of these picturesque incidents which make the lives of Byron and Shelley such exciting reading. He was based in himself in the sense in which the Upanishads say "the soul is its own witness and its own refuge" and his adventures were largely spiritual and removed from our vision unless we have insight to follow him into his reveries and illuminations and surprise him waiting on the gods. So in a sense it was a more difficult biography to write than the study of Mark Twain. But you have placed before us a serene personality and I hope your life will make the present generation of Americans who have gone from central depths to surfaces turn to read so wise a sage. I was staying for three weeks with an American friend[1] in Donegal and he pleased me by saying that Emerson's writings were the American sacred books. He had only begun to discover Emerson though he had read him long ago being a Bostonian and a professor in Harvard. What is your next book? I think the deeps in Whitman have to be rescued from his surfaces. Sometimes he utters cosmic revelations and sometimes he is betrayed by surface vitality to be a mere booster of the land of pork and cotton. Few people understand how a man can sometimes be inspired and sometimes will shout nonsense. The tide of being rises and falls in us in ways we do not ourselves comprehend. I have seemed to myself in meditation to be near the Oversoul on

---

[1] Mr and Mrs A. Kingsley Porter, at Glenveagh Castle. After AE's death Mrs Lucy Kingsley Porter edited the letters written to them by AE. The collection was published by the Macmillan Company, New York, in February 1937, as *AE's Letters to Mínanlá-báin*.

the next day I would be shouting or excited over some of our ephemeral politics. And whoever writes of Whitman must always have in mind these exaltations and descents from the energy of spirit to the energy of body. Or does Whitman not attract you as Emerson, Henry James and Mark Twain did. I think Emerson and Whitman have more permanent value than James or Clemens for they had something of the element of infinity in their being without which writers lose their hold over the imagination and which makes them belong to one wave in time however subtle or prodigal in humour they may be. I am probably talking nonsense as all men do when they get to be sixty-six and the mind gets blurred a little and exists in its own conventions rather than its illuminations. I was sorry I did not have some long conversations with you when I was in America.[1] But I was projected all over the country for eight months and was in a state of perpetual circulation. I thank you dear Van Wyck Brooks for the gift of your book. I wish I was again Editor of a paper that I might have written about it and Emerson. But I have dropped out of all journalism and indeed out of most people's minds because in this age if you are not saying something every week people forget you are alive. I am glad you have not forgotten. Yours sincerely, George Russell "AE"

TO HEINZ HÖPF'L[2]   17 Rathgar Avenue
                                                              [December 1932]

My dear man,

You must not place me on any pedestal in your mind or look to me for any universal wisdom, or for insight into the contrasts between Catholicism and Protestantism, or for any considered opinion about Christ. All my life since I was a boy and first began to think has been less devoted to study through reading than the development of vision or intuition. I very early came to the belief that it could only lead me into a Maya if I began to think about things of which I had no vision or had no intimate spiritual knowledge of. So I began trying to track consciousness to its

---

[1] AE never met Van Wyck Brooks.
[2] Dr Höpf'l, born 1908, educated at Bonn University. Author of *AE, Dichter und Mystiker* (Bonn, 1936), based on his doctoral dissertation. He spent much time with AE in 1933, during his long visit to Dublin. Dr Höpf'l also wrote *Kleine Geschichte Englands* (1953). He is at present London editor of the *Frankfürter Allgemeine Zeitung*. Other German books about AE were written by Friedrich Biens (1935) and Martin Plass (1940). Dr Höpf'l also wrote a pamphlet on AE, in *Kleine Beitrage* (Leipzig, 1936).

fountains in the spirit through meditation and concentration. I have told something of the method in *The Candle of Vision* and also in a later book *Song and its Fountains*. As for Catholicism and Protestantism while I was yet very young, about fourteen years of age, I escaped from their influence, and really knew very little about Christian dogma until when I was about thirty-five or thereabouts I began to read the books which to my contemporaries were scriptures. But I came to them after reading the sacred literatures of other religions, Brahmin, Buddhist, Tao, Hermetic and Platonist and Neoplatonist literature and then I began to see things in gospels and epistles which I could not see when I was a boy and turned from them. All these scriptures I have mentioned and the Christian scriptures as well I read for sentences which come out of a deep life. I brood upon a sentence rather than upon a book, carrying it away in my mind until I have realised all its implications, spiritual and psychic and material, until in fact I have come to some kind of glowing realisation of spiritual life or law which was implicit in the sentence. You see my life has been made up of a series of visions and intuitions, and each of these have appeared to me so precious that I never thought of making a system out of these intuitions. In *The Candle of Vision* I tried to explain the method, and in *Song and its Fountains* a particular exploration of the psyche and in *The Interpreters* I put together some other intuitions about the relation of our politics to the Archaeus or Soul of the World. In the poetry I have tried to make a record of moods which became transparencies into soul or spirit and I have written no poetry without this idea. I am rather elderly now but I still retain this ideal of writing nothing which has not some relation to the spiritual life. I enclose a little booklet[1] of my last verses which I got printed a week ago to give to friends at the New Year. You can see in the varying moods that each one touches in some way on the presence of the spirit. I am trying to write a sequel to *The Interpreters* a book which I call *The Avatars* which is a symposium on the nature of avatars. I hope I will have inspiration and energy to complete it. When one gets nigh to the seventies there is a little lessening of physical energy. One has no less ideas but rather less power to state them with beauty and vigour. I do not know whether I have enlightened you in your quest, I feel always how slight a thing I am in the universe and have I believe but little variety, but I cannot help being pleased that you should have found something to light your way in my books. If I have held a light even for a little it is something. Yours sincerely, Geo. W. Russell, AE

[1] *Verses for Friends.*

11 *April* 1933

TO OLIVER ST J. GOGARTY[1]   17 Rathgar Avenue
                                              Wednesday [early 1933]

Dear Oliver,

You have nominated Shane Leslie as for a "member" rather than an "associate" of academy. Members have to have some creative work Irish in character or subject, see rules. Could you send me a list of books he has written which justify his nomination as member rather than as associate. All these nominations will be discussed at the Council meeting. Of course you will receive a notice of this as a member and you can explain there. But if you are not able to come you had best give me names of books. I think he has written some novels Irish in character or subject which would get him in where his biographies would not. I am sorry for troubling you but so long as we have the two classes the Council will discuss the reasons for recommending anyone for one class rather than another. I write because Yeats asked about this. Myself I see no reason for two classes. My only "ist" would be literary activity. Yours ever, AE

TO MACMILLAN AND CO. LTD.   17 Rathgar Avenue
                                              11.4.33

Dear Sirs,

I have received agreement about *The Avatars*[2] for which I thank you. Please insert a dedication.[3]

To
W. B. Yeats,
my oldest friend and enemy.

and on the title page insert this as a parable of the meaning of the book.

The light is the real person in
the picture. Claud Monet.

Yours sincerely, Geo. W. Russell, "AE"

[1] *See* Note 25, p. 237.
[2] He sent the manuscript on March 30, 1933.
[3] On May 21 he returned final batch of page-proofs and asked to revise the dedication "To W. B. Yeats". Published October, 1933.

17 Rathgar Avenue
[*postmark* May 24, 1933]

Dear Best,

Here is the other copy promised in case the one to Leeson Street went astray. If both came keep and give to reporters as the one Maurice Moore had copies made of first is by this superseded. AE

[*Enclosed with letter to R. I. Best, May 24, 1933*][2]

It would be unseemly that the ashes of George Moore should be interred here, and the ritual of any orthodoxy spoken over him. But I think he who exercised so fantastic an imagination in his life would have been pleased at the fantasy which led his family and friends to give him an urn-burial in this lake-island which was familiar to him from childhood.

Whatever may be the fate of his spirit it will never be the fate of the Laodiceans, he who was always hot or cold. There could be no fitting burial for one who always acted from his own will and his own centre, in cemeteries where the faithful to convention lie side by side.

However he warred upon the ideals of his nation he knew it was his Irish ancestry which gave him the faculties which made him one of the most talented and unfilial of Ireland's children. His ironic spirit would be pleased at urnburial in this lonely lake-island so that he would be to Ireland in death what he had been in life, remote and defiant of its faiths and movements.

He loved the land even if he did not love the nation. Yet his enmities even made his nation to be as much admired or loved as the praise of its patriots. He had the speech of the artist which men remember while they forget the undiscriminating voices which have nothing but love.

If his ashes have any sentience they will feel at home here for the colours of Carragh Lake remained in his memory when many other of his affections had passed.

It is possible the artist's love of earth, rock, water and sky is an act of worship. It is possible that faithfulness to art is acceptable service. That worship, that service were his. If any would condemn him for creed of

[1] Richard Irvine Best (1872-1959), the illustrious Irish scholar. (*See* Biographical Notes.)
[2] *See* Note 26, p. 238.

theirs he had assailed let them first be certain that they laboured for their ideals as faithfully as he did for his. AE

TO CHARLES WEEKES 17 Rathgar Avenue
4.7.33

Dear Charlie,

I write to ask your advice as you are the most practical of my friends living in London. Since my wife died last year I have felt it a burden keeping up a house here too large for one person, and I have given it up. I intend to live in London for a year at least, perhaps longer. I am going on Saturday to Donegal for a month where I will be c/o A. Kingsley Porter, Esq., Glenveagh Castle, Gartan, Co. Donegal. Now what I want your advice about is this. I could afford to spend about £5 or £6 a week rent and subsistence. Could I get a sitting room and bed room with use of bath in any livable locality where I could be fed as well as housed? I could furnish an unfurnished flat, but I don't want to see after my own meals. I would not mind making my breakfast if there was a restaurant below the building where I could get lunch or dinner without trouble. Or are there flats where the proprietors are prepared to feed as well as house, to make beds? I am rather ignorant about these matters as I have been looked after all my life long. But you lived so long in London that you could advise me what to do. I could of course live in a hotel but don't like that idea. I would have to until I got rooms. I intend to bring myself over to London about the middle [of] August. Will you like a good man give me advice. I hope to have many talks with you, our interchange of wisdom being interrupted early in our lives. I am at the moment a *little over-saturated with Irish ideas and want to breathe another air for a while*.[1] Do think over my plight and when you have thought send me a note to Glenveagh Castle, Gartan, Donegal before the end of the month. If you knew of rooms by that time which would meet my modest needs I would send a cheque for three months rent. I have an account at the Westminster Bank and I think they would say I was safe as I have over a thousand with them. Please think and give me your practical wisdom. You gave up being a poet to be a man of affairs. You owe something of your practical wisdom to poetry which you deserted, and I think what is owing might be paid to me in advice. Yours ever, Geo. W. Russell

[1] Underlined by Weekes.

TO CHARLES WEEKES

Glenveagh Castle, Gartan
County Donegal
8.7.33

Dear Charlie,

I came here last night: Kingsley Porter[1] sent his motor to Letterkenny with a note to me to call for him and his wife on the way to the Castle. They had been spending a day or two at Inishbofin. When I came to the appointed [?] place I found Mrs Porter in agony. Kingsley had been drowned in the afternoon and his body had not been discovered. It will probably float off later into the Atlantic. I will be here for a day or two. I do not like leaving Mrs Porter alone until some American friend of Kingsley's comes, to whom she wired to England. So please do not write me until I let you know where I will be. I will try to find a place to stay in Dunfanaghy possibly. It is kind indeed of your wife to think about my case. I really know nothing about London and where it would be best to stay. You are right to suggest furnished rooms at first. *I got rid of all my things in Dublin keeping only a few pictures and some books.*[2] I will write as soon as I clear my movements up. The *Chelsea district sounds attractive.* I think I have a few artist acquaintances there. But I would just as soon be near you. I only know James Stephens well, of all my London friends, except you and Dan. All the others are acquaintances Helen Waddell, Orage, Steer, Tonks, Clifford Bax, Arnold Bax whom I know more or less well, the latter best of these. I *want like Tennyson's Ulysses* to start *something fresh.* I won't write more now as Mrs Porter and I are going to motor to the place where Kingsley was drowned to see if the body was discovered. Yours ever, AE

TO CHARLES WEEKES

[Glenveagh Castle]
Thursday [July 9, 1933]

Dear Charlie,

Many thanks for your message. I am staying here until the middle of next week as Mrs Porter wished me to stay. The body has not yet been discovered and it may be washed into the Atlantic, as Porter fell on the far side of the island with an outgoing tide. I am trying to fix things so that *I will get to London about the beginning of August*, and will go to some

---

[1] Arthur Kingsley Porter, archaeologist. (*See* Biographical Notes.)
[2] Charles Weekes's crayon underlining.

hotel until I can get rooms. I will be most grateful for any guidance in this matter. I will look you up and collect from you your wisdom on this matter. *My house is at present being emptied and all in it is sold. I am keeping only a few pictures and a few books. I dont want to gather possessions. I want to be mobile and not tied to things. I had begun to feel I was in a rut and I want to break up the mould of mind in which I was decaying. I think the change will re-invigorate me and it will be a relief to get away from Ireland in its present mood which is one of smugness.*[1] I feel sad over the death of Kingsley Porter, one of the best friends of my later life. He was a very distinguished man in his own line. His volumes on Romanesque architecture are the best things of their kind. He was something of an artist in thought, wrote plays [for] reading not acting and was very understanding and with a sense of humour. His wife was devoted to him, and I remained on to help to bring her back to normal. Now she has got one of her husband's secretaries here, a nice fellow, it will not be necessary for me to keep her from brooding and I return Dublin Wednesday next. I don't know where I shall stay there until I go to London. Two friends want me to stay with them. But I think I will go to a hotel to be freer and anyhow a note to my old address 17 Rathgar Avenue will come to me wherever I am. I am looking forward to seeing you. Yours ever, AE

TO OSBORN J. BERGIN   41 Sussex Gardens, Hyde Park
                                          Wednesday [August 2, 1933]

Dear Osborn,

I called round to bid you good-bye for a year[2] but found the windows down and the knock brought no answer and I guess you were away on one of those mysterious professorial holidays which Walter Starkie's book has led us to surmise in our scholarly friends. Here I am looking out over trees down a long street after a day of trying to find a way through this prodigious jungle of a city and I know no more about it than when I started exploring in the morning though I have a map to study. However people of lesser minds within the law have mastered the ritual of travel by bus and underground train and I think I should be able to do it. I was sorry I did not see you for you are a good friend and your humanity has survived ancient Irish which suggests that there is some tough incorruptible spiritual atom in it. When I get more settled I will start a new book.

---

[1] Underlined by Weekes.   [2] He arrived in London, August 2.

The Avatars is printed but Macmillan are uncertain whether to issue it in September or October. I will send you a copy when it appears and it and the pictures may keep me in mind until you see me again. I went round to see Michael [O'Donovan] also at his library, but it was closed and dark and blind as your house, and I could not find him so I suppose he is taking more holidays. It is very hot here. I will be ready to face Hell if that is my punishment for ill-doing, having experienced its worst heats in the streets of this city and nothing much hotter can exist in the universe or it would melt. The stupidest detective ever invented would have tracked me by the perspiration I shed as I walked about. What about a book "The trail of the drops of perspiration?" It seems obvious as a clue but I do not remember it in any of the books I have read. Should I copy-right the idea until I am ready in my second childhood to write the story of our dreams? This is merely to tell you I am alive and have my friends very much in my mind, and you and Saturday nights and the odour of coltsfoot. So sorry I did not see you, but will in Sushupti if my psychology is true and my psyche limber in deep sleep. Yours ever, AE

TO GEORGE SANTAYANA[1]   41 Sussex Gardens
                                                              19.9.33
Dear Mr. Santayana,

Just before I left America a couple of years ago I saw in the house of a friend your volume *The Realm of Matter*. I had just time to read the preface where you referred to the verses I called "The Virgin Mother".[2] I wished to get the book but had to return to Ireland where I found my wife very ill, and the book passed from memory until a few days ago I came across it and read it. What I wish to say is that the "questionable line" was questionable by my own intellectual conscience. I wished to contrast a power moving within nature with the power existing in the heresy of separateness outside nature, i.e. the orthodox deity of which I heard in boyhood. You being yourself a poet know how we are cramped by the intricacies of the craft and often cannot come to the precise expression of thought possible in prose by the use of many more words. So having committed myself to rhymes I substituted the contraries of earth underfoot and heavens overhead, for within and without, hoping that the

---

[1] George Santayana (1863-1952), philosopher. *The Life of Reason* (1905-1906), *Realms of Being* (1928-1940), *The Last Puritan* (1935), *Dominations and Powers* (1951), etc.

[2] *Collected Poems*, p. 35.

spirit of the poem would incline the reader to the full meaning of the last lines. And I had when I was a boy of about twenty[1] written about the same mystery.

> *I heard them in their sadness say*
> *"The earth rebukes the thought of God.*
> *We are but embers wrapped in clay,*
> *A little nobler than the sod."*
>
> *But I have touched the lips of clay.*
> *Mother, thy rudest sod to me*
> *Is thrilled with fire of hidden day*
> *And haunted by all mystery.*

But in neither poem did I get so near what haunted me about the substance of nature as in one of my last poems[2]

> *This was the heavenly hiding place*
> *Wherin the Spirit laughed a day,*
> *All its proud ivories and fires*
> *Shrunk to a shovel full of clay.*
>
> *It must have love, this silent earth,*
> *To leap up at the king's desire,*
> *Moving in such a noble dance*
> *Of wreathéd ivory and fire.*
>
> *It will not stir for me at all,*
> *Nor answer me with voice or gleam,*
> *Adieu, sweet memoried dust, I go*
> *After the master for the dream.*

"It must have love this silent earth." It is the mystery of the obedience of matter to spirit. What was shapeless becomes a shape of beauty. What was a shape of beauty becomes again shapeless. What made it fall into the mould of beauty? What was it, in atoms, electrons, to make them desert that cycling about their own centre, as in the diagrams of scientist and mathematician, to fall into the mould of beauty? Do they live also? Have they desire? Is what we speak of as affinity a kind of consciousness of living? It was with such thoughts intuitions and guesses in my mind I wrote "The Virgin Mother" and many other poems. If I had what

---

[1] *Collected Poems*, p. 34.   [2] *Collected Poems*, p. 373.

Wordsworth called the philosophic mind I might have come to greater precision of statement. But the years do not bring this to me only more intuitions and surmisings. I ask your pardon for intruding into your own reverie. But as you found the line "questionable" I only wished to say that that line and many more I wrote are questionable by an exasperated consciousness which can never make its moments of intuition or vision clear to the moments which follow of reverie and reason. Yours sincerely, Geo. W. Russell, "AE"

GEORGE SANTAYANA   *Hotel Royal Danieli, Venezia*
TO G. W. RUSSELL[1]   *Sept. 22, 1933*

Dear Mr. Russell,

   It is interesting to know that you have noticed the quotation from your poem, "The Virgin Mother", in my Realm of Matter. *The devil notoriously quotes scripture for his own purposes, and you must forgive me if I used your words to point a moral which (as I now see) was not the one you intended. The immanence of "love" or potential "beauty" in the material world is, in one sense, a truism. When anything arises or happens we may say that there was a "mysterious" tendency in the conditions to produce just that thing. The God of Platonism and Christianity is simply a hypostasis of this tendency in nature towards the good, and is perhaps less "external" than we may think: if the tendency is a distinct power working in things, it is a part of nature. Perhaps this was exactly what you meant by saying that we should reverence earth and not heaven: the real motive force towards the beautiful is inside the world and not beyond.*

   The centre of my own interest is at a somewhat different point. I don't know, and I don't much care, what the existing motive force is that makes for the beautiful: in any case it it very imperfectly successful. What I care for is the beautiful itself and the vision of the beautiful, in so far as they manage to exist, or to be suggested: and this frail, intermittent, but actual realization of the beautiful I call the spiritual sphere. All life is, intrinsically, a part of it; but horribly interrupted and perturbed. Yours sincerely, G. Santayana

[1] Printed in *The Letters of George Santayana*, edited by Daniel M. Cory (New York, 1955: Scribners), pp. 283-284. This text is taken from the original letter. Mr Santayana told this editor he could not distinguish any real difference between AE's interpretation and his own.

TO FRANK O'CONNOR[1]   [? January 1934][2]

. . . I live a peaceful life without troubles, getting my three square meals and my sleep, every 24 hours, and I write occasional verses and am trying to complete my longest poem. And I go to picture exhibitions and spend much time at the Burlington House exhibition of British Art, and I ascribe the dullness of three-quarters of the pictures to the drinking of much beer by the British painters, and their brains got so muddy that pure colour is hardly ever visible. Oh, but there was one mighty picture, "Salisbury Cathedral" by Constable, a universe created by a titan. . . .

It is this sensation of emptiness which frightens me here. The poets like Eliot and Spender have no light in their minds. They are the dead end, and when Eliot writes a volume of criticism of poetry the effect is to make me never want to read poetry any more in the world, the criticism is so dry and joyless. I think there is a revolt beginning against his influence. But what will the revolters do if they cannot intoxicate us with exuberant imaginations themselves. It will be like ghosts electing new leaders, leaders who are ghosts themselves. It is really a dead country, but there are very nice people among the dead, and if they were only alive they would be the best people in the world. . . .

TO HERBERT E. PALMER[3]   41, Sussex Gardens
                                                    1.2.34 [*sketch*]

My dear Palmer,

Why the devil do you suppose I should write to you and tell you any defects I find in your verse. I don't read poetry for defects, I read it for its virtues. If my spiritual eyesight was like this, that it saw only defects I would not read at all. There would be no pleasure in it and I have not come to the stage where it is a pleasure to see how many faults the other man has. I read you because I like you and when I read I surrender myself to what I imagine was in the mind of the writer.

[1] *See* Note 27, p. 238.
[2] "Winter Exhibition of British Art, 1000-1860" at the Royal Academy, January 6 to Saturday, March 17, 1934.
[3] Herbert Edward Palmer, the eminent English narrative and lyric poet. *Collected Poems* (1933), *Summit and Chasm* (1934), here acknowledged by AE, etc. (*See also* Biographical Notes.)

Yes, I like the "Autumn Ode", a very original and changeful rhythm which when one murmurs it to oneself recreates the mood of the poet in oneself as an Indian Mantram and I like too, in some remote kinship of mood with the Autumn poem the "Two Songs" written in one of those moods of quiet desperation in which so many of our days are spent. There are two points in our lives never to be spoken of, the highest which is sacred, and to speak of it would turn earthwards the soaring meditative spirit; and there is the depth in us which we never speak of for pity's sake. It "Must never, never be sung".

I like the way in which queer assonances quiver in the verse and give its rhythm a unity. It is by this unity of tone and rhythm one knows the sincerity of the writer. Other things can be faked but some strange tone welling up out of the heart or soul can't be learned or faked.

I admired very much the fresh picturesque vigour of your François Villon "Ballade", where there is a verbal character in every verse. It is sustained from beginning to end. I am full of envy of your vocabulary, and it is most moving too, it seems to speak of the secret romance of redemption which somewhere exists in every lost soul.

I like too for its humour and its self criticism "God's Response". Of course, my dear fellow you will be in Paradise, but in one of its sanatoriums for a while, to prevent you clapping archangels on the back too roughly, or digging too solemn saints in the ribs, or perhaps until they have been educated up to such pleasant intimacies. I sometimes feel the martyrs will take some time to learn how to laugh after their experience at the stake or on the rack.

My way of reading poetry is not to go through a book completely, but to take one or two poems at a time, the way the Japanese bring out their pictures, so I have not got through your book, but these and some others I read I liked very much and note you have lost nothing of your freshness, and I have more to read.

Yes, please come and see me again. Drop a postcard. The only afternoons I am generally engaged in are Wednesdays and Thursdays. My mornings are always free for friends. So when you can come send a card and I will be sure to be in then and will bring you out for lunch, and I am grateful for the book of your poems. You are one of the few people singing today who suggests that he has a soul alive in him even if it has occasional heartaches or toothaches. Yours sincerely, AE

[210]

TO LORD DUNSANY   41 Sussex Gardens
                                   5 April 1934

Dear Dunsany,

I would sit for you[1] with pleasure if I was in London when you come.
I am leaving this place on Monday morning April 23rd and going to Donegal
where I have taken a cottage for three months. If you come to London
before that and let me know I will come and sit while you turn me into
one of the sinister gods of your mind country or if not into a god or daimon.
I thought your Irish tale most beautiful and fresh. It has all the phantasy
of the old stories with the added beauty of precise and lovely word
painting of this world. Your staying power is great. Most writers who had
written as much as you would have nothing new to write and could not
surprise us with a fresh beauty; congratulations. Yours ever, AE

                    [*crayon sketch*]

Did you ever try these coloured chalk pencils for sketching? They are
very good.

TO JAMES H. COUSINS   c/o Mrs O'Donnell, Parkmore
                                   Ballymore, Donegal
                                   16.6.34

Dear Cousins,

Your publishers have sent me your *Study in Synthesis*, a very remarkable
and stimulating book, your very best work in prose.[2] You have gathered
together the threads of your life and experience and have woven them into
the pattern of world thought and I think your mind has never moved so
clearly and at times your writing is full of vivacity, a difficult thing to
achieve when one has such a subject, and it could only happen because
you have made your ideas part of character. I am glad to think of your
intellect opening and widening in this way. You must have learned a great
deal from your wanderings in India and America? probably most of all
from meeting in India good interpreters of India's traditional wisdom. It
has stimulated me here where I came with no books except eleven
volumes of the *Mahabharata* which I ordered from India and which I
find in parts of extraordinary interest. I have been finishing a book of
poetry the last I shall write. When one gets to my age the body does not
melt over ideas, and unless there is a melting of the whole being the verse

[1] *See* Note 28, p. 238.   [2] *See* Note 29, p. 238.

must be only intellectual. I do not know whether I shall write anything in verse. My publishers want me to write reminiscences. But all that was really interesting in experience I had put into verse or in prose books like *Candle of Vision, Interpreters, Song and its Fountains* and *Avatars*. But it will probably depend on the state of spiritual or intellectual activity I find in myself. One must express what one feels or imagines not to get praise or profit but because it is part of the cosmic activity in which the spirit becomes subconscious in the manifestations of the universe. "The universe exists for purposes of soul." I am close on seventy and it is time to stop writing anyhow, unless for private amusement or occupation. You are younger and at the best of your mental activity, and doubtless will go on doing good thinking for some years yet. I am here until end of July. I do not know where I shall be after that, but Macmillans London will always find me. I wrote them about the quotations and they wrote they had given permission. They are generally decent about such things but like to be asked first for permission. Seumas O'Sullivan and Keller are both here now in next cottage but return to Dublin on Sunday leaving me to my solitude. But I have other friends here when I feel lonely which is not often. I keep up an intimacy with nature and it speaks to me as it always did since I was a boy. There is no other God but Nature as the Master wrote. With kind regards and congratulations on your latest book. Yours ever, AE

TO RUTH PITTER[1]   c/o Mrs O'Donnell, Parkmore
                                          Tuesday [? June 1934]

Dear Ruth,

How well you caught the speech of the old priest. I can imagine you giving off in triumph to K. to show her how much more Irish you became in a fortnight than she with all her Irish ancestry. Have you put up the scaffolding of a dramatic representation of me and my accent? It's damnably lonely here without you. We have to pay for all our delights. But I would gulp down a month's dreariness for another week's rambles with you. I went for a long walk to-day and remembered with deep self disgust that there were lots of beautiful places I had not shown you, and

[1] Ruth Pitter (b. 1897), the English poetess. She was introduced to AE by A. R. Orage who had early befriended her by publishing her poems in the *New Age*. Between their introduction, probably in 1933, and AE's death, they met "several times". *See* Note 30, p. 239.

then I reflected that if I had crammed them all into that fortnight your young legs would be aching and my old legs would be paralysed, and may be the gods will be good to me and bring you over here again if I am here. You really do not know how lovely the west of Ireland is. Every five miles from this down to Kerry will stand comparison with this and every person swears by his own bit of country. I only regret you did not see Erigal and the lakes there. But if you had you might have pined away in London thinking of it and been no use at business any more. I am so glad you and your mother liked this place. I had all kinds of qualms when I wrote you to come whether I could really make you comfortable, and then I said Damn it she's a poetess, a genuine one, not a made up one and she's bound to be happy once she gets into the open air! I was selfish and did not let you brood enough alone. I should have said, there's that ridge, go to the end of it. Be alone for three hours or as long as you like, and you might have come back with your face shining as Moses with his tables of the Law, you with a sheaf of verses caught out of the air.

By the way I woke up Sunday night or perhaps better to say Sunday morning in the dark and saw you clearly. I suspect when you went asleep your what do you call it thought-body went back to that dark ridge at Breaghy to look at it. Your eyes were quite recognisable only more ultra-marinely bluer and more brilliant than their physical counterparts. You seemed to be near me yet curiously you were not in the room but carried about you the phantasm of the rocks as if you were dreaming of them. I looked at you moving about for a while, quite interested, with your shadowy rocks. I should have tried to set up communication but I was shamelessly sleepy and went asleep myself or maybe that was my only way of going for a ramble with you over Breaghy cliffs after midnight. No accidents seem to happen [to] thought-bodies, they do not tumble down out of the air, or stub their feet against stones, and they are airy and do not weary as old physical bodies do. We had a generous downpour of rain since you left. It would have done your Anglo-Saxon heart–pining for wet in plenty–good to see. Now it is sunny and cool again, and the air enters ones lungs as if it had been delicately prepared for poets use by the genii. Poor Ruth, breathing London mist. If I go over to London this autumn I will bring a bottle of Atlantic air and uncork it after dinner under your nostrils instead of champagne. What about a scheme for scooping up an Atlantic gale in vast funnels and forcing the air through pipes so that it could go uncontaminated to London and be laid on in poets houses. Would it pay? Alas, I cannot imagine it. But think of lying

I

back in your chair with closed eyes and open mouth in Chelsea and gulping in huge lungfuls of this intoxicating aether. But I must not waste your time now you have got back to business and its worries. I only want to say you were an angel to come here. You are one of the best of companions. You have the airy element in your nature predominant so that you never get entangled in things like those with the watery nature. You will rise above London and its fogs and its business because of that airy element, which makes you a free creature as far as mortals may be free. All my friends whom I love have that airy nature, all I loved. If you ever come across James Stephens you will find he has it. If you ever meet my delightful French friend Simone Téry you will find she has it. I have only enough of it to adore it in others. Forgive this letter which is stupid for I had a devilish long walk and only my fingers are not tired. I picked out of my little book a scribble of the bay at the end of the ridge and another of the sand hills at Dunfanaghy seen from the top of Breaghy cliffs. I make these scribbles to look at later in dreary hours. But I really know them by heart. I pass these to you Ruth dear. From yours ever, AE

TO OSBORN J. BERGIN   c/o Mrs M. O'Donnell, Parkmore
                                                        15.7.34

Dear Osborn,

I have taken the liberty of dedicating to you a new book of verse[1] which Macmillans are bringing out this Autumn. I send you the dedication[2] in which you will see I have carefully protected your repute as a scholar so that nobody can say you are responsible for my perversion of an old Irish myth. But as I have taken the liberty of publicly calling you my friend[3] I do not wish to shame you by misspellings, so will you like a dear write down for me a proper spelling of the following remembering that the spelling must not seem to the initiated English reader to suggest sounds which cannot be fitted into blank verse. The names are, Mananan, Ogma, Dana, Fintan, Angus, Diancecht, also the names of the four cities from which the Tuatha de Danaan came, Murias, Goreas, Findrias, Falias.

[1] *The House of the Titans.*
[2] "In the book he dedicated to me . . . one word is mine. Happily he sent me a type-script of pp. 1-2. I objected to his addressing me as *'impeccable* scholar' as there is no such person, and sent a list of substitutes, 'inaccurate' . . . 'incredulous' . . . etc. . . . He chose *'incredulous'.*" (*Osborn Bergin to the editor.*)
[3] "I did not make AE's acquaintance till about 1914." (*Osborn Bergin to the editor.*)

This is the nearest I can remember to the sound as I am far from books, and if you do not reply telling me I shall put a footnote at the end of the book with the misspelled names and say what an inestimable advantage it was to me to have the benefit of your scholarship when trying to spell the names. I have been here from 1st May and have to leave end of this month. I am trying to find another house here to stay on until September or October but don't know if I can. I have had divine weather and my face is as red as my hair once was. I hope you are well and enjoying from a distance the Celtic Congress. Yours ever, AE

TO JOSEPH O'NEILL c/o Mrs Dickinson
1 Brunswick Square, W1
Saturday [1934]

Dear Joseph,

This is not a letter but simply to acknowledge the three bales of literary merchandise, which I will proceed to unroll and investigate and will issue a report on the quality of the goods, which will be sent to you in due course. I like getting shockers without having to buy them. If it is a good shocker I will say so, if it has a goodness beyond shocking I will say so. If it is a bad shocker I will send the bales back marked "freight will be paid by consignee". Kind regards. That is all for the present. Yours ever, AE

TO A. R. ORAGE 1 Brunswick Square
Tuesday [November 6, 1934]

Dear Orage,

I called at Cursitor Street this morning and heard the so sorrowful news about your wife. At such times there is nothing to be said that in the least lightens ones burden. I have twice lost those I loved and trusted most in the world, and found no comfort except in the depths, in some profundity of belief in a fulness or holy sepulchre in which everything was merged, we, those we adored, stars, stones and all that is,–too strange, too remote to offer to others as solace this conviction. But I do indeed feel sad for you, dear Orage, with your children so young, and their Mother and your companion gone. I found two with wet eyes in your office and I know you will have many to feel for you, but what is any sympathy that it will compensate for a dead companion, it is only time the enemy we hate that can do anything for us. Yours affectionately, AE

TO MRS JESSIE ORAGE   1 Brunswick Square

Wednesday [November 7, 1934]

Dear Mrs Orage,

When I called in yesterday at the *New English Weekly* I was met by two distracted people who explained Orage's absence and being rather deaf I thought they said his wife had died so suddenly and I went out distressed greatly and wrote to my friend, and now I find it was he was dead, and I have no words to speak about him who had the most luminous mind I met in this country and whose friendship to myself I valued so greatly. Dear Mrs Orage, can you forgive the letter written yesterday in misapprehension. It was my deafness, and know that my sorrow is sincere and I feel as all his friends and readers must feel that a great light has gone out and a guide to those whose way was uncertain has been parted from them. I am but a late friend in his life but I was not late in perceiving the magnitude of his mind and do not know where I shall meet his like, and it is dreadful for you and for us all. Yours sincerely, Geo. W. Russell

TO C. C. RIDDALL[1]   1 Brunswick Sq

1.12.34

Dear Riddall,

I would be much obliged if you would send me a copy of the I.A.O.S. *Rules for Agricultural and Dairy Societies*, as I may have to write something about agricultural co-operation, and would like to keep my memory fresh about fundamentals of organisation. I will remit cost if you will let me know. I would be glad if you could send this soon as I will be going to U.S.A. in a week or ten days time where I will be for two or three months –not lecturing, thank heaven. I hope you are well. Give my kind regards to any of my friends who are at the Plunkett House. Yours ever, Geo. W. Russell

JUDGE RICHARD CAMPBELL   *17th January 1935*
TO M. L. WILSON[2]

. . . When AE first arrived, what with the shock of Mrs Rumsey's death and an increasing sense of the magnitude and diversity of the problems which

---

[1] Charles Coates Riddall. (*See* Biographical Notes.)

[2] Text from *The Oriel Review* (New York) [1943], pp. 89/90. *The Oriel Review* (no. 1, April 1, 1943) superseded the *Ireland American Review*. It was edited by Maurice Leahy (born in county Kerry, 1900).

confront us here in America, he felt, I think, somewhat inadequate to what he thought you expected of him. I spent as much time with him as I could spare from my office while he was here in New York and told him . . . in many letters which have passed between us, what Mr Roosevelt and his Administration were trying to accomplish, and I outlined especially what I conceived to be the programme of Secretary Wallace.

I then led him on to talk of cooperatives and agricultural economics . . . and I had forgotten how fascinating these subjects can be when AE talks about them. I soon found, in other words, that his mind had lost none of its sweep and that he was as mentally and physically alive and vigorous as ever. I gradually encouraged him as he went on to undertake the work. . . . Even after he reached Washington he was restive for the first two weeks, but before leaving for Chicago he wrote telling me that he was pleased with his reception and with his contacts with the various groups. . . .

He is positive, as I knew he would be, that he does not want compensation, but on the other hand, he is anxious not to draw on his little capital for his expenses while here. Now I have some seven hundred dollars the balance of one thousand dollars which Mrs Rumsey had her secretary send me while she lay ill and which was intended as an advance to take care of his immediate needs when he arrived in America. This seven hundred dollars ought to take care of him at the Cosmos Club for two or three months. Then before he leaves for Ireland I think we ought to bring the matter to the attention of Mr Averill Harriman, brother of Mrs Rumsey, with the view to raising some small sum to re-imburse him for his passage out here and back to Ireland, and this sum should include some moderate compensation, say 200 dollars or 300 dollars per month for the duration of his stay in America.

In all probability he will refuse compensation, but I think we ought to insist on his accepting some nominal sum at least. There has been a time when I could meet these deficits myself but the time is not now, and we will have to carry it to Mr Harriman. . . . I have no misgivings whatever as to the outcome.

TO M. L. WILSON,[1]   Cosmos Club
Friday [February, 1935]

Dear Wilson,

I think tomorrow must end my conversations at the Department of Agriculture unless you have already made engagements for me early next week, in which case I will meet them. I find I over-rated my energies

---

[1] Text from *The Oriel Review* (New York) [1943], p. 94.

which even a couple of years ago answered to almost any demand on them. I feel an old man, rather stale and repetitious. . . . But it has been the greatest pleasure to me to meet you and your colleagues. . . .

I think at the end of next week I will go to New York and find a ship to bring me back to my own country where I can sink into the meditation which the Eastern Sages say is proper for the ageing, and try to finish a book I had begun before dear Mary Rumsey cabled me to come over from Ireland.

I will try to see you on Monday morning next and only wish I was thirty years younger that I might really carry the torch about the U.S. I think you have the root of a real humanity in you and what you do must be for good, though God knows I fear there are going to be more troubled times before this country before it discovers its real destiny.

TO JAMES STEPHENS   Paradise Flats, 14 Tavistock Place
                                     Russell Sq., London, W.C.1
                                     18.3.1935

Dear James,

It would be an act of human kindness if you could come to see me some afternoon. I am an invalid. I would ask you to dine with me but I could not ask you to share the pallid foods to which I am condemned, rennet, junket, soda, milk, barley water and the like. I returned from U.S.A. on Wednesday last. I got some inflammation of my insides and had to break away earlier than I thought; as I dreaded getting laid up in a strange city and thought I had better be an invalid among friends. I am getting somewhat better under the drastic treatment, but it may be two or three months before I am quite normal, and I had wanted to go to Donegal and bring you there to the cottage I had last year with a spare bedroom. But I am wondering now whether Donegal which provides honest natural fare can provide the diet my doctors may condemn me to. Anyhow I have lots of things to tell you about Washington and my life there, so find your way here some afternoon like a good man. AE

TO CHARLES WEEKES   Paradise Flats
                                                         22.3.35

Dear Charlie,

Not having copies of *Homeward Songs* or *Earth Breath* with me, (my books are packed up in a case) I wonder whether you have copies and you could look in for a little on Saturday afternoon and let me check the correctness of selections from these. I can give you tea. My maid was out last Saturday afternoon hence my inhospitability. Yours ever, AE

If there are any poems in *Vale* you think might be included please let me know. What about "Dark Weeping"? The bacteriological examination shows nothing out of the way.

TO CHARLES WEEKES
Paradise Flats
28.3.35

Dear Charlie,

I see you have entered into a temporary partnership with Dr. MacDonald and Dr. Munro.[1] Many thanks. The sour milk is a welcome addition to my dieting. I will settle with you for this when I see you next. Yesterday was the best day I had for months. I felt quite gay as if I was on the hills in Donegal in a cool sunshine and I think I have got the selection almost complete. There are three or four things I am still pondering about. But a week should see them all weighed in the balance and found to justify their places or to be condemned to the outer darkness of the complete edition. Yours sincerely, AE

M. L. WILSON TO
CHRIS. L. CHRISTENSEN[2]
May 10th 1935

. . . Secretary Wallace and myself are interested in bringing AE–George W. Russell–to this country this Fall, to be available for a series of country life and extension worker meetings in which he sets forth his philosophy of life in general, and particularly his philosophical interpretation of the deeper meaning of agricultural cooperation and community development.

I believe that the Country Life Association would like to use him; if we could get him, we should like to arrange a speaking tour for him throughout the country.

[1] *See* Biographical Notes.

[2] Text from *The Oriel Review* (New York) [1943], p. 92. Chris. Lauriths Christensen (born Minden, Nebraska, 1894), special investigator for U.S. Dept. of Agriculture on Co-operative Agriculture, in Europe 1922-1923: and Chief of the Division of Co-operative Marketing, 1924-1929. He was Dean of the College of Agriculture, and Director of the Experimental station at the University of Wisconsin, 1931-1943. He is a Trustee of the Rural Youth Foundation and other helpful youth organisations.

Mrs Mary Harriman Rumsey was greatly interested in AE and Secretary Wallace and myself had a verbal understanding with her to the effect that she would finance AE for any such inspirational and educational use that we might make of him in this country. Our plan provides for bringing him over on the first of the year and keeping him in this country for a year or more. During the early Winter and Spring he was to confer with the workers in the Department of Agriculture, and during the Summer and Fall with the people in the Colleges of Agriculture. He dislikes formal lecturing, or anything in the nature of formal Chautauqua lecture tours. For this reason our scheme proposed sending him as a kind of itinerant from one agricultural college to another . . . to stay around the place a couple of days and to visit and talk informally with members of the faculty and students.

. . . [re death of Mrs Rumsey] . . . He stayed at the Cosmos Club, but after being here for a couple of weeks began to suffer from a stomach disorder. He returned about the first of March to England. Now Secretary Wallace would very much like to have AE brought back . . . provided his health is such that he can stand the trip, to be available as a sort of catalizer both to workers in the Department and to the colleges. I am wondering if it might be a legitimate project to be financed by what I call the Alex. Legge Foundation. I know that you are very close to this and that you could give me advice as to whether or not it might be well to make a formal application to its Board, or whether its plans are somewhat crystalized, and it would be useless to bring the proposition to their attention.

M. L. WILSON TO AE[1]   *May 10th 1935*

. . . Much regret was expressed by the Cooperatives that you would be unable to attend the Institute of Cooperation meeting at Cornell; also Mr John Collier was over the other day and expressed his regret that you were not returning immediately. . . . We are now considering plans for the holding of special Institutes with extension people throughout the country during the late summer and early Fall months. There are about five thousand extension workers, such as county agricultural agents, home demonstration agents who work with farm wives, Smith-Hughes high school teachers, who teach agriculture in the high schools. A plan is being considered to bring these people together in groups of about one hundred or more to the group. It would be a

[1] Text from *The Oriel Review* (New York) [1943], pp. 100-101.

wonderful thing if you could be made available to meet some of these important institutes.

I realise your dislike of speaking at such public gatherings any more, but if you could be tempted in any way to participate in this movement, I should immediately begin casting about to work out some plan of financing the same. Secretary Wallace and myself are both agreed that just now our people need philosophy and something which lifts their eyes and spirits a little above the horizon. . . .

Mr Averill Harriman seemed very appreciative of you. Secretary Wallace often speaks of you, and not so very long ago said: "M. L. see if you can't find some way of having AE with us again this Fall; we need that touch of beauty and interpretation of reality which he alone can give". . . .

TO CHARLES WEEKES 14 Tavistock Place
[Sunday] 16.6.35

Dear Charlie,

My friend Mrs Jacobs[1] has told me of a nice place kept by two ladies at Bournemouth near some fine woods and there is a garden where I can sit in the sun if there is one and I have written today to ask if I can go Thursday or Friday. I understand there is a fast train leaving Waterloo at 4.30 getting into Bournemouth at 6.30 and I could go by that. If the reply comes that I can go I would like to know Magee's Bournemouth address. Would you send it to me. I think the change of air would do me good. Mrs Jacobs has already written to these ladies and I think it will be all right, and I think I will have solitude as it is not an hotel or a big boarding house. Yours ever AE

TO CONSTANCE SITWELL[2] 14 Tavistock Place
17.6.35

Dear Constance,

Please call me AE. I am unfamiliar with the name I was born with. I am sorry indeed I will not be in Donegal when you are there. I am going at the latter end of this week to Bournemouth for a fortnight: a friend told me of a nice house beside June woods and with a garden where I can sit

[1] Mrs Bethel Jacobs (*née* Sophie Solomons; b. 1887), a gifted singer; sister of Dr B. A. H. Solomons and Mrs J. S. Starkey. AE's last *Will* was signed on June 14, 1935, in the presence of Mrs Jacobs and [Miss] K[athleen] Goodfellow; sworn before Mr P. A. Knight, Commissioner for Oaths. [2] *See* Biographical Notes.

and soak in sun if there is one and I will be able to renew my friendship with John Eglinton whom I have not seen for fifteen years, a charming writer and a boyhood friend of mine. I am glad indeed if you found anything I said spiritually exciting. I only wish I had not been so limp in soul and body after six months of my trouble. I was once a creature with some electrical intensity but now seem to myself to be in a state of *pralaya* or decay. Wentz[1] after his stay in Ireland went to India, travelled in Thibet, found many wonderful mss. *The Thibetan Book of the Dead, The Tale of Mela Repa* which he edited and which were published by Oxford Press. He went on pilgrimages, lived with Yogas in their caves to understand them better. I saw him in London last autumn just before he returned to India. He had all the old determination to get at truth, which made him force his way into the nursing home where he heard I was dying, to get from me before I died answers to some questions. I like him very much. In the little book *Vow of Poverty*[2] there is a reprint of an Essay "Purposes of Soul" which I read when I was very young and it influenced me more than almost anything I had read before or since. I was keyed up to meet its intensity and I felt I could not write poetry or mystical thought if I could not hold on to its truth in the face of death. I do not know whether anybody else could be so moved as I was for everything in it was related to what I was then thinking or striving for. I wish I could be so made of wrought steel of will and spirit as I was in those years. Ones energies uncoil gradually like a wound-up spring and we gain breadth rather than intensity, at least it was so with myself. But my work apart from the mystical adventure forced me to think of many things, economics, politics, labour problems, art, literature and this again affected my meditation. I suppose it was all right as I did not feel spiritually unhappy as I would if I had been off the path. We have to go in and out of ourselves. We go out to get new elements to transmute into the substance of light; we go in to discover the pilgrim of eternity.[3]

[1] W. Y. Evans-Wentz dedicated *The Fairy Faith in Celtic Countries* (London, 1911: Oxford University Press) to AE and to W. B. Yeats. Dr Evans-Wentz kindly supplied the following information: "p. 59-66 was dictated to me by AE in his Dublin home." The pages referred to are a dialogue, question and answer. In the book it is printed anonymously. AE reviewed Dr Evans-Wentz's *Tibetan Book of the Dead* in the *Irish Statesman*, vol. 8, pp. 620-621 (September 3, 1927).

[2] *The Vow of Poverty, and other essays* by Jasper Niemand (pseudonym of Mrs Julia Wharton Lewis Ver-Plank, *née* Campbell; later Mrs Archibald Keightley). Mrs Sitwell's copy (London, 1904: Thomas Green, publisher), was bought at AE's request, in May 1935. "Purposes of Soul" is at p. 14. James M. Pryse may have drawn AE's attention to it.   [3] See also *The Avatars*, pp.175-188.

9 *July* 1935

Like you I have always loved light and I was most excited by the *Upanishads* which spoke of the eternal thought being joy in me, and hailed it with exultation. It was so different from the pathos and penitence in Europe where it seemed easier to most to read the mystery told in tears and to understand sorrow better than joy. I hope when I see you next I will have got rid of the colitis and come to normality. If I don't I will resign myself to gradually dwindling into the other world and will look out for some place where I can fade out peaceably and quietly and where I can bid a gay good-night to the world. But I would like a few more years to knit myself when living to that vast spiritual unity, for it is while we are here we struggle and progress, after death we only enjoy[1]. I am praying for fine weather for your Irish holiday. Yours ever, AE

TO CHARLES WEEKES   18.6.35
[Postcard]

Miss Myers can have me. Wrote saying I was going Friday.[2] Station Bournemouth, W. She will have me met there outside booking office. Blue car–Green hat. I told Magee that you were coming with me. Perhaps you and he could come round to Miss Myers that evening after I have my unappetising meal. Unless I hear otherwise I expect you here 15 to 4 p.m. Yours ever AE

TO JAMES STEPHENS   c/o Miss Phoebe Myers,
                                                                    Havenhurst,
                                                              Canford Cliffs,
                                                                 Bournemouth
                                                                      9.7.1935

Dear Seamus,

My doctors had their final consultation over me this morning and told me my trouble was not curable either by medical means or by operations but that an operation could make things easier for me while I last. They allow me a year or thereabouts. Don't think I feel anything melancholy. I hold to the spiritual verities I have believed all my life and indeed would be glad and more cheerful if my time was shorter. I have had good friends I loved like yourself. This news is for you. I don't want it spread or to get

---

[1] See *Letters of G. Santayana* (ed. D. M. Cory), pp. 294-295 for an acute comment on this orthodox notion of immortality.   [2] June 21.

[223]

into papers. After the operation I am told I will have an easier time, and if I pick up I will write at more length. I am too limp now to write more. Yours ever affectionately, AE

P.S. Thank Cynthia[1] for her kind letter.

FROM MISS P. MYERS   *Havenhurst*
TO RUTH PITTER   *11.7.35*
Dear Madam,

   Mr. Russell was operated on yesterday afternoon. He had a bad night and altho' weak, he is holding his own this evening, when my partner rang up to enquire. She saw him for a couple of minutes this morning when he spoke to her. Dr. Munro came down and arranged everything with the other two doctors here yesterday morning. Yours sincerely, P. Myers

TO HENRY A. WALLACE[2]   "Stagsden", West Cliff Road,
                                                         Bournemouth
                                                          15.7.1935
My dear Henry,

   This is to say goodbye to you. My doctors have diagnosed my trouble as one that cannot be cured either by medical or surgical means. Will you convey to my good friends Wilson and Collier how much I appreciate their kindness to me when I was in Washington. To you, dear Henry, as to myself, death does not make much matter. We understand each other. I hope for you a great career in your country. Give my kind regards to your wife. Collier and Wilson will understand I was not trying to escape from any work I could do. It was really that I felt incapable. Yours ever, AE

TO ELEANOR SKIPWORTH[3]   "Stagsden"
                                                          15.7.1935
Dear Eleanor,

   This is really to say good bye to you.

   I had a severe operation and my doctor holds out no hope of recovery either by medical or surgical treatment.

   [1] Mrs Stephens.
   [2] The Hon Henry Agard Wallace (b. 1888), Vice-President of the U.S.A. 1941–1945. This letter was dictated to Miss Pamela Travers. Mr Wallace kindly sent the editor a typed copy.   [3] From a typewritten copy.

Will you say goodbye for me to all my dear friends of Plunkett House. I look back upon my years spent with them as the best years of my life.

I am asking my friend Pamela Travers to write this for me. You have been one of the kindest friends to me. AE (*pp. P.T.*)

C. P. CURRAN TO W. B. YEATS Havenhurst
Tuesday night 16.7.35

Dear Mr Yeats,

I arrived at Bournemouth this evening at 8.45 and went straight to Stagsden Nursing Home. AE was quite conscious and only complained of being very limp. He was not in pain and his face except in so far as it was thinner and seemed more elongated, showed no sign of suffering or distress. His hair and beard were brown as usual indeed the greying hair appeared more golden. His voice grew weak at times but was perfectly clear and so was his memory. He gave me Diarmuid's address in the States and details of that sort.

He was aware that his condition was beyond recovery and since he was so tranquil I had no difficulty in asking him his desires in regard to burial in the event of his dying in Ireland. I said that we felt strongly that his place was between Violet and Thomas Davis—using Keohler's phrase. He at once agreed and said that the bank, his executor, would, he supposed, arrange it. I said that his friends would see to it. Having said I would write to Diarmuid he then enquired for you and I told him I had been speaking with you last evening and gave him your messages of affection. I mentioned the enquiries of his other friends Osborn Bergin, Fred Higgins, Keohler and others and he made corresponding enquiries. He was obviously very glad to see me and I tried to convey to him the affectionate concern of his friends in Dublin. We were together for I imagine a half hour and I left him when the nurse came to make provisions for a quiet night. All through he was perfectly conscious, tranquil in mind but weak though quite clear and intelligible in speech. I mentioned the Academy medal and also took it upon myself to say that at its meeting on the 31st steps were to be taken to obtain for him the Nobel award. This gave him pleasure; I mentioned some dates and he smilingly said it would be of little use to a dead man.

I have not yet seen Magee who calls each day. I have met Dr Hector Munro and Pamela Travers. Miss Travers who was down in Sussex came over here on Saturday and dealt with his correspondence. Dr Munro gave me his medical history. He suspected the presence of trouble before AE's last visit to the States and doubted the diagnosis of colitis on his return. AE has apparently been in Bournemouth about a month. Trouble developed a week ago with an obstruction and the surgical examination showed a cancerous affection with secondaries which render his recovery impossible. He has been a week in this condition but without serious suffering.

We are staying together and ready for a telephone call during the night. It is possible that AE will survive tonight and tomorrow but the end is not far off.[1]

I am writing this hurriedly and I am afraid very illegibly after midnight. But I think you will like to have any account of our dear friend. Sincerely yours, C. P. Curran

[1] He died whilst sleeping, soon after 11 p.m. Wednesday July 17, 1935. Charles Weekes, C. P. Curran, W. K. Magee and Oliver St J. Gogarty were with him when he died. A. R. Orage's widow visited him soon after death.

Appendices

Notes

1. *page* 18. Charles Weekes did not preserve any letters which he had received prior to his marriage. Similarly the early letters from AE to Yeats have not survived among the papers in Mrs Yeats's possession. W. K. Magee and Weekes constantly corresponded throughout life. Dr Magee admitted to the editor his regret that they agreed, after Russell's death, to destroy all their letters in which Russell was referred to. Dr Magee assured the editor that in his opinion Weekes's letters were inimitable, and all should have been preserved. During the Second World War Weekes destroyed vast quantities of accumulated correspondence, AE's letters alone surviving.

Note 2. page 23. From a typed copy kindly supplied by Professor David H. Greene of New York University. Professor Greene's biography of Synge (using the late Edward M. Stephens's papers), was published in 1959 by the Macmillan Co., New York. Professor Greene advised the editor that this is the only AE letter among Synge's papers, and added: "Synge's *Diary* records four evenings spent with Russell; first with Yeats and Russell, November 8, 1897; second 'at Theosophical Society with Russell', November 26, 1897; third, and fourth merely 'evening with AE', October 12 and 30, 1898. Yeats, Synge and Maud Gonne were all active in the Irish League, in Paris." Synge wrote a comparison between Yeats's and AE's poetry–unflattering to AE–in *L'Européen courrier international* (Paris: 1901-1906), May 31, 1902.

Note 3. page 24. Horace Plunkett's diary entry, November 11, 1897: "Saw one George Russell, a £60-a year clerk in Pim's, but a poet, mystic, theosophist, etc. I am going to train him as an organiser and I think he will be a success." Plunkett sailed to America a few days later, arriving December 2. Russell left Pims's employ on November 3, 1897. See also Yeats's letter to Lady Gregory, November 17, 1897, in Wade's edition of Yeats's *Letters*, pp. 290-291.

Note 4. page 42. Printed in *My Brother's Keeper* by Stanislaus Joyce (London, and New York, 1958: Faber & Faber: Viking Press), the unfinished *MSS* edited by Richard Ellmann, p. 176. James A. Joyce 1882-1941), author of *Dubliners* (1914), *A Portrait of the Artist as a Young Man* (1916), *Ulysses* (1922), *Finnegan's Wake* (1939) and the tenuous verses *Chamber Music* (1907), and *Pomes Penyeach* (1927). See also *The Letters of James Joyce* [vol. 1] ed. Stuart Gilbert (London, May 24, 1957: Faber & Faber), vol. 2, edited by Richard Ellmann (Faber), and the *Joyce Bibliography* by J. T. Slocum and H. Cahoon (London, and New Haven, 1953: Hart Davis, Yale University Press), and the biographical and literary masterpiece by Richard Ellmann, *James Joyce* (1959: O.U.P.).

Note 5. page 42. The *Rules of the Irish National Theatre Society* were drafted by AE, and registered in Dublin, December 30, 1903. In the Secretary's copy an amendment slip, written out by AE, was pasted-in at the end, and dated April 6, 1904. The amendment was signed by W. G. Fay (1872-1947), H. F. Norman, P. Colum, G. Roberts, F. Ryan (who later emigrated to Egypt, and died there), A. Wright, Maire Nic Shiubhlaigh, Prionnsias Mac Shiubhlaigh [Frank Walker], F. J. Fay (1870-1931), Sara Allgood (1883-1950), J. S. Starkey, M. Ni Gharbhaigh [Miss Garvey, later the first Mrs George Roberts], witnessed by AE. The signatories promised to continue members of the Society for at least one year, provided they continued residence in Dublin. The Original draft of the *Rules*, by AE, is now owned by the Theatre Collection, Harvard University Library, together with the secretary's copy. A copy of the printed *Rules* is included in the National Library of Ireland, W. A. Henderson's *Theatre Collection*, vol. 1, p. 236. [S. Allgood's sister, Maire O'Neill (1885-1952) married Arthur Sinclair.]

Note 6. page 58. Mr Leonard S. Elton kindly wrote to the editor in 1954: "I don't know what dream of A.E's produced this reply. He once related one to me, in which he was inside an egg-shaped room with a large cricket or grasshopper. Every time it jumped it took a year off his life. He made wild efforts to catch it but couldn't, and finally just as the last year of his life had vanished he woke up in a state of much agitation! . . . he rather disliked dreams being described, but used to try to explain them rationally, as having been occasioned by actual occurrences to which they could be traced back. (This idea always seemed to me to spoil the charm and pleasing idiocy of most dreams.)"

Note 7. page 59. "Undrained swamp" to which AE refers in the foregoing letter was the mess-up of feelings of growing antipathy between Ireland and England and their partisans in Southern Ireland

and Ulster, out of which came the armed movement led by Sir Edward Carson *against* the anticipated passing of a Home Rule Bill. This provoked a similar movement in Nationalist Ireland *in support* of the British Government, a queer twist of allegiances that probably only Ireland could hand out to History. To this add a labour army that added economics to politics, and remember AE's long work for citizen co-operation in materials of life and his ideal of mutual understanding and toleration in religious and cultural matters, with a strong desire for the elevation of the worker as expressed in the open letter to which he refers, and you will begin to get at his sense of fermenting stagnation at the time. But there was more movement working up in the swamp than he was aware of. Yeats too was not alive to what was developing. He wrote "Romantic Ireland's dead and gone. . . ." But it wasn't. (*James Cousins's note*).

Note 8, page 98. Dr Bodkin kindly notes: "We had a wonderful weekend there. AE painted in Lord Headford's woods amid thousands of pheasants, till we were all ejected by a keeper. We rowed on the lake where in brilliant sunshine James Stephens composed and recited to us his poem "Washed in silver is the moon". In the evening we capped verses and when our stock of quotations was exhausted I went to the village and bought a pack of cards and a large bag of pink comfits for use as counters and taught the two poets to play Poker. AE proved a master of the game and rooked us both. On the journey back to Dublin he produced the comfits and the cards, made a table with our suitcases had the door of the railway carriage locked, and played with equal efficiency all the way up to town. I don't think he ever played the game again: and he used to get a little disconcerted whenever I alluded to the escapade in the company of his more serious followers."

Note 9. *page* 100. Francis Ledwidge (1891–1917). His poems were first printed in the (Drogheda) *Independent*. To Lord Dunsany's request for a room at Plunkett House, in which Ledwidge could be left alone, to write, whilst he visited Dublin, Russell replied kindly (December 1, 1914); there were no vacant rooms. Incidentally he mentioned this cheque, etc., to Dunsany as "the Mother and Father of Ledwidge's soul", thinking he should know all his protégé's "little ways". Russell says in this extremely kind letter that he thinks of poets as though they were his own children. Lord Dunsany asked the editor not to print AE's letter to himself, about Ledwidge, "who would have relied on me not to give him away". *Songs of the Field* (1915) with an Introduction by Lord Dunsany; *Songs of Peace* (1916), *Last Songs* (1918), *Complete Poems*, with Introductions, ed. Dunsany, 1919.

Note 10. *page* 107. To Thomas Bodkin, Stephen MacKenna expressed his opinion that Russell's friendship was not in Stephens's best interests, Intellectually Russell and Stephens had ranged the same ideas without exploring the European literatures. C. P. Curran wrote to the editor (July 21, 1957): "I don't know the date or context of Stephen MacKenna's remark but I think I understand how he could come to make it. AE, James Stephens and MacKenna were always good friends and the friendship between AE and Stephens, as the years went on, grew to be very close indeed. I suppose that in AE's early theosophic years his intimates thought along more or less identical lines. That was far from being the case in his middle and later years. His mind was hospitable and generous, and it was our differences on even fundamental issues

that gave savour to our discussions. AE was intuitionist and often impatient with the ways of scholars. His friends Stephen MacKenna and Osborn Bergin were pure-blooded scholars dyed in the wool of the European, classical tradition against which–saving some Greeks–AE was most often in revolt. His devotion to eastern ways of thinking blinded him to many of the things his friends valued most. This was very evident in the years when I first met him, which corresponded with the time when I also first met Stephens. James Stephens was then writing the poems which later made up his first book of verse, *Insurrections* published in 1909. These with much of the material which went into *The Crock of Gold* were beginning to appear in Arthur Griffith's *United Irishman* and attracted our attention by reason of the grotesque originality and racy, local vernacular which wrapped up a deep humanity. Stephens's humour and sense of life appeared to us very different from AE's *Earth Breath* or *Homeward;* his work was indigenous as compared with the exoticism of Yeats or AE. His roots were in our own soil, his fancy grounded in occidental realism. Stephens's next book of verse was his *Hill of Vision* (1912) and what I said to you in agreement with Stephen MacKenna stemmed from the difference between the *Hill of Vision* and Stephens's earlier writing. Blake both as poet and painter stood in the first rank of AE's admirations and Blake's influence is evident in *The Hill of Vision*. This book appeared to me in 1912 to be apprentice work and no notable advance on his first work; and since it was AE who introduced Blake to Stephens and introduced at the same time a certain eastern cloudiness alien as I thought to his natural self, I found myself when talking to you last year reviving this early impression. I need hardly say that it does not do justice to any of the poets concerned. Stephens's originality was not impaired nor did AE at any time fail to respect and stimulate the native vistas in any of his friends. . . ."

Note 11. page 112. In another letter–not included here–Russell wrote to Weekes: "You will find a chapter on aristocracy and democracy, and their place in National life, in *National Being*. Don't praise me unless you have read the book. You might find it different from what you thought. The book was written for the younger men in Ireland, fellows at the Universities and the like, to give them an intellectual conception of Irish nationality, on lines entirely different from the old concepts. It is being read here, I believe. There is no news over here. We are all like the characters in a Greek tragedy where Nemesis, an invisible deity, is among us, and what we say or do matters not, for the result is in the hands of the Gods." (To Charles Weekes: "Wednesday"–probably 1916: letter beginning, "Glad to hear from you again".) Easter Monday, 1916 was April 24.

Note 12, page 118. Joanna Fortune (born Chicago, 1876?) daughter of Mary Agatha (Lacey) (died 1886) and Peter Fortune (1835-1912) who had moved to Chicago from Ferns, county Wexford, in 1856. The brewing firm he established with his brother John, in 1866, terminated with prohibition in 1919-1920. Mrs W. Vaughn Moody introduced Miss Fortune to Padraic and Mary Colum when they arrived in America. They seemed forlorn; she befriended them: they told her about AE's paintings and his financial dependence on their sale. Although not interested in pictures she consulted Howard Shaw (1869-1926) and Harry Aldus (who had been interested in the Abbey Theatre), directors of the Chicago Art Institute, and arranged the exhibition there of AE's

paintings, having bought several as gifts for her friends. Miss Fortune first met AE, in Dublin, during her visit there in September 1920. In an unpublished letter dated September 13, 1922, AE thanked Miss Fortune for a gift of $2,500 donated for relief work in Ireland. Miss Fortune met him again in 1924; and sought him out during his visits to America later.

Note 13. page 123. Senator J. G. Douglas writes: "I have a copy of a circular letter signed by Maurice Moore, G. W. Russell and myself dated March 17th 1917 which was sent out to a number of prominent persons with I think a copy of a statement which formed the basis of A.E.'s *Thoughts for a Convention*. I enclose a copy of this letter but I have not a copy of the statement. Unfortunately I have no recollection of the meeting referred to in the letter, nor have I any list of the names of the persons to whom it was adressed.

"AE, Colonel Maurice Moore and I visited London but did not see the Colonial Premiers. I had an interview with General Smuts and explained our views. Smuts was sympathetic but said that Dominion status was, in effect, Independence; and he feared the British people were not ready for it. I think AE also saw Smuts but am not certain." In 1920 A. D. Lindsay (1879-1952), then tutor at Balliol College, Oxford, urged Plunkett to call on Smuts again, for advice on a settlement.

Note 14. page 129. Horace Plunkett wrote in his *Confidential Report to the King, on the Irish Home Rule Convention 1917-1918:* "August 28, 1917 (paras 40-42). . . . For a brief moment religion in its political garb took the floor. Mr E. E. Lysaght had been nominated by the Government as being in close touch and in full sympathy with the Sinn Feiners, although they have refused to be officially represented. His competence to speak for them soon became manifest. We knew that he was a Clare landlord, a business man, and a man of letters, and he told us that he had voted for de Valera. He declared himself to be heart and soul at one with the principles of Sinn Fein. At the same time his presence there was evidence enough that he recognised the ideals of others and hoped for a settlement, believing, as he did, that if no settlement was found the consequences would be appalling. (Plunkett then quotes Lysaght's speech) . . . The effect of this utterance was apparent in many subsequent speeches. Generally speaking, it may be said that the Convention was glad to hear Mr Lysaght declare his attitude so frankly, though to some of his hearers the declaration sounded too much like a threat and too little like a warning, as he obviously intended it to be." Plunkett noted in his personal diary on Saturday, August 25, 1917: "A half day at the Convention Office . . . to lunch with AE, Lysaght, [Shan] Bullock, . . . and [Cruise] O'Brien to discuss with them Sinn Fein difficulty, i.e. how to prevent dangerous drilling and arming without undue repression of political exuberance. . . ." The entry for Tuesday, August 28, 1917 reads: "The first full day of the Convention . . . Lysaght read a badly constructed ten minutes' shocker about Sinn Fein and its wondrous and horrible doings. . . ."

Dr MacLysaght (formerly Lysaght) has kindly supplied the following entry from his own personal diary, without knowing what Plunkett had written either in the *Report to the King* or in his own diary. The entry is dated May 25, 1918: ". . . I am a bad diarist. For example I see on looking back that I omitted all references to one rather interesting episode, which occurred during my political 'career'. It was about the end of August I think. I know that I made my speech in the Con-

vention one morning after having hunted up de Valera at his house in Munster Street and brought him to AE's office where we had a talk about the situation. Previously AE and I had been to lunch at Sir H.P's where we met Duke who laid down the principle that Sinn Feiners might say what they liked in public provided they did not actually incite to rebellion and that they would not be interfered with unless they drilled, wore uniforms or otherwise contravened the terms of the recent Government Proclamation. AE had an idea that a sort of tacit agreement for mutual forbearance might be arrived at but de Valera, with commendable caution perhaps in dealing with a stranger, was not at all inclined to give himself away."

Note 15. *page* 130. In the Convention's afternoon session on September 19, 1917, Russell made what Plunkett's diary note calls "a rather intemperate attack on Pollock". The "Secret Committee" session on October 30 discussed "Fiscal Autonomy versus Fiscal Union" for Ireland. Russell, Dr O'Donnell, John Redmond and W. M. Murphy strongly supported autonomy; Pollock, Barrie, and Londonderry equally strongly supported fiscal union. The session was adjourned in deadlock. On November 3 Professor A. C. Pigou [1877–March 7, 1959] arrived from Cambridge "to help" Plunkett "think out the economics".

Sub-committee meetings followed. On November 11 Plunkett noted in his diary, "AE to lunch and I tried to calm him in his Convention attitude". The Convention's Grand Committee re-assembled on November 22, and was again adjourned on 29th, re-assembing on December 11. On December 31 Russell and MacLysaght visited Plunkett in his office; they were "in a very bad temper and talked as if they were determined to wreck the Convention.

The situation . . . looks a bit cloudy but what are the political sorrows of Ireland to the appalling suffering of the nations?"

Note 16. *page* 130. Lord Midleton (1856-1942) whose *Records and Reactions* (London, 1939: Murray) includes an account of the Home Rule Convention (pp. 237-238 on Plunkett). Earlier he had written *Ireland, Dupe or Heroine* (London, July 1932: Heinemann). See Margaret Digby's *Horace Plunkett* (Oxford, 1949: Blackwell), p. 228, note 1; Midleton's compromise proposal to the Convention, concerned with fiscal relations: "That in the event of the establishment of an Irish Parliament there shall be reserved to the Parliament of the United Kingdom full authority for all imperial services including . . . levying of customs duties, but subject to the above limitations the Irish Parliament shall control all purely Irish services including Judicature and Police with internal taxation and administration." Lord Midleton led the southern Unionists at the Convention.

Note 17. *page* 135. To Plunkett, resigning from the Convention, with effect from January 22, 1918. Plunkett in his *Report to the King* (p. 73, para. 133) wrote: "Mr Lysaght . . . had written to the Prime Minister asking for a definition of the 'substantial agreement', which was thought to be the condition precedent of legislation on the Convention's Report. If Ulster's consent, of which he despaired, was essential, he felt it useless to continue his work as a member of the Convention. Not being satisfied with the Prime Minister's reply, he resigned, and deprived the Convention of its youngest but by no means least capable member." Lysaght's resignation was announced in the Irish press; at Plunkett's request the Censor, Lord Decies, suppressed the reasons, in

an effort to prevent public damage to the Convention discussions. Plunkett defined the Convention at January 23, as "more than ever reacting to outside opinion . . . [it] began to divide itself into three main groups. At one end stood the Ulster Unionists . . . at the other, a new Nationalist party, whom we may call the Progressives, was being formed. Its policy was to detach all but the extreme separatists from the Sinn Fein camp by holding out for the maximum of independence to be found 'within the Empire'–in other words for Dominion self-government with fiscal autonomy. Between these two sections a middle party was being built up out of the more conservative Nationalists, who still followed Mr Redmond, nearly all the Labour representatives, and the southern Unionists who followed Lord Midleton and frankly accepted Home Rule . . . [the Moderates]. . . . The Progressives were led by the powerful combination of Mr W. M. Murphy, with his widely-circulating *Independent*, the Bishop of Raphoe [Dr O'Donnell], and Mr George Russell. On the Customs issue Mr Murphy would hear of no compromise whatsoever . . . [his case] arguing for complete control by the Irish Parliament of all forms of taxation. . . . His amendment [i.e. to the *Home Rule Act*, 1914] in substance demanded full Dominion Home Rule . . . was ultimately moved by Dr O'Donnell . . . the treasurer of the United Irish League, . . . who was also by character and capacity the natural successor to Mr Redmond, who had resigned . . . through ill-health." In the debate (January 22-24) "Mr George Russell contributed a powerful and eloquent speech. . . . He gratefully acknowledged the sacrifice of feeling made by the southern Unionists, and would have accepted their proposals had Ulster come in. Failing that essential of a settlement, which would ensure the immediate setting-up of an all-Ireland Parliament, he could not accept a compromise which meant 'a bow to God and a wink to the devil'." Russell wanted full self-government immediately, before the "socialistic" reforms spread from Russia to western Europe. Lord Midleton had tabled a motion on January 2, 1918: "That, in the event of the establishment of an Irish Parliament, there shall be reserved to the Parliament of the United Kingdom full authority for all Imperial services, including the levying of Customs' duties, but subject to the above limitations the Irish Parliament shall control all purely Irish services, including Judicature and Police with internal taxation and administration."

Note 18. *page* 157. Probably Russell was introduced to Curtis by Sir Horace Plunkett at his home "Kilterah". Curtis and Russell were among his guests there on November 8, 1912. Lionel George Curtis (1872-November 24, 1955) advocated federal government, and powerfully exerted his influence by systematic exposition of his theoretic ideal. *The Commonwealth of Nations* (1916), *Dyarchy* (1920), *Civitas Dei* (3 vols. 1934-1937) (1 vol. 1951); *World War, its Cause and Cure* (1945), *The Open Road to Freedom* (1950), *Evading a Revolution* (1954). Curtis was from 1921-1924 Adviser to the British Colonial Office, on Irish Affairs. Curtis wrote a *Memorandum on Dominion Status* during the autumn of 1921, when he and Thomas Jones (1870-October 15, 1956,) were secretaries of the British delegates to the Conference as to a Treaty, held in London October 11-12, 1921; and was on the Truce sub-committee which met October 12: Erskine Childers being secretary for the Irish delegates.

Note 19. *page* 165. Miss Janie Stewart (died October 24, 1940, aged 87 years) lived with her brother Charles Stewart (died February 9, 1933, aged 84). AE stayed there every summer for at least fifteen years, probably from 1913. He arrived at Breaghy each year by jaunting-car, from Dunfanaghy Road station, some four miles distant. "He occupied a long low bedroom, which could be described as an attic stretching the full width of the house." His tastes were simple; home-baked bread "which old Janie made to perfection in a pot-oven". He drank copiously of buttermilk. "He was a pleasant unassuming man, who in the evenings came to the kitchen to chat . . . he was interesting to listen to and easy to talk to. When he wished to relax he read four-penny Cowboy paper-backs–dozens of them." "It was his custom, near the end of his holiday, for G. Russell to put his holiday paintings on view, and the important local people were invited to Breaghy to see them. He talked a lot about his tour of America–and about the Irish language and the co-operative movement. Fairy-tales or perhaps I should say folk-lore, was of great interest to him. He dressed mostly in dark grey." Janie Stewart "was a very handsome woman, and good at hand-crafts–principally rug-making and poker-work". None of AE's letters to Miss Stewart have been preserved by the family. AE gave her one of the copies of the photograph of himself taken in Washington. Whilst staying at Breaghy (at "Hillcrest") "he made many journeys to the 'Fairy House' in Marble Hill wood–a small play-house for the children of the Law family, who owned Marble Hill House at that time. It was there that he painted. . . ." (Quotations from a letter to the editor written by Charles Stewart's son and his wife.) The editor's accidental reference to Russell during one of his own holiday visits to Dunfanaghy, was immediately taken up by his hosts, who remembered AE as a kind reflective visitor, known to the community when they were children, always called Mr Russell.

Note 20. *page* 165. On September 8, 1922 Horace Plunkett wrote to J. S. Cullinan (1860-1937), an American corporation official, proposing the revival of the *Irish Statesman*, "To advocate a persistent endeavour by the State to improve the conditions of every section of the Irish people. . . ." Edward L. Doheny (1856-1935) invited likely supporters to dine at the Bankers' Club, New York, on October 16, 1922. Subsequently an organising committee [Doheny, Richard Campbell (1872-1935), Morgan J. O'Brien (1852-1937), James Byrne (1857-1942), John Quinn (1870-1924), Lawrence Godkin (1860-1929), George MacDonald, John A. Poynton (18--?-1934), and Culli-nan; with James A. Healy as assistant secretary to Campbell] was formed. They secured 100 persons to underwrite an Agreement in equal amounts to total £30,000. The committee was to act in an advisory capacity to the Controlling Committee [Plunkett, chairman, James G. Douglas, Lionel Smith-Gordon, Dr George O'Brien, Lennox Robinson; with AE as editor, and Percy J. Gillespie as general manager] in Dublin. AE had initially refused to become editor, but when pressed by Plunkett accepted, conditional upon total independence of editorial coercion, and provided the *Irish Homestead* feature articles were retained. Plunkett arrived in New York, January 1, 1923. He telegraphed to Cullinan the opinion expressed by Doheny: fewer than 100 should underwrite the agreement. Doheny agreed to underwrite $75,000 (half the amount required), by three annual instalments. The first instalments were to be paid not later than March 1, 1923, second in December 1923, third in December 1924. James Byrne paid-up the

total amount early, dissatisfied with the small number of contributors to the fund. Each of the American supporters received securities to the extent of his participation, unless such securities were sold for the purpose of expanding circulation: in such circumstances he would be refunded his proportionate amount from sales. The paper's trading loss in the first year was £3,366, second year £2,844. In 1925 further support for the paper was tardily won. Funds were advanced from America and from Plunkett (£1,000), and publication continued. Early 1928 AE earned money for the paper by lecturing in America. President Cosgrave had urged Plunkett, during private discussions preceding revival of the *Irish Statesman*, to avoid presenting editorially any partisan political viewpoint. Plunkett wrote to Campbell (February 25, 1925): "I knew that AE would be a great editor, but I do think he has excelled himself in the guidance he has given to the Government of the Free State and in the way he has protected them from the Republicans."

Note 21. *page* 175. The constants in AE's mind, by which he tested theory and action, had been thought through by him. But instead of fabricating a personal nomenclature he used, among those who were acquainted with them, the precise terms of the Vedantic philosophy and of modern theosophy, which in India is known as Brahmavidya or all-knowledge. Above, *Tamas* is inertia and materiality, *Rajas* is activity as such, and *Satva* is the conscious wisdom that gives all things their proper place in individual and organised life. (J. H. C.)

Note 22. *page* 179. Seumas Clandillon, Director of the Dublin Broadcasting Station, and his wife, Maighread Ni Annagain, Plaintiffs. Dónal Joseph

O'Sullivan, Clerk of the Free State Senate, George W. Russell (AE), editor of the *Irish Statesman*, and the Irish Statesman Publishing Company, defendants. The action was heard in the High Court, Dublin, before Mr Justice Hanna and a Jury. Plaintiffs claimed £2,000 compensation for alleged libel which they had read into O'Sullivan's review of their book *Londubh An Chairn* (London, October 1927: Oxford University Press) which had been printed in the *Irish Statesman*, November 19, 1927. The hearing began on Monday, October 29, and was concluded on Tuesday, November 13, 1928. Plaintiffs were represented by Mr Martin Maguire, KC, Mr J. Geoghegan, KC, and Mr George Moonan, instructed by Mr C. J. Murray, LLD; Mr J. M. Fitzgerald, KC, Mr C. Lavery, KC, and Mr C. A. Maguire represented Mr O'Sullivan; AE and the *Irish Statesman* Publishing Co., were represented by Mr C. Bewley, KC and Mr T. G. Marnan, instructed by Messrs A. Cox and Co. The plaintiffs' case closed on Monday, November 5. Sir Richard Terry (1865-1938) spoke as a defence witness on November 5, O'Sullivan was cross-examined on 6th and 7th, Herbert Hughes (1882-1937) deposed on 7th, Osborn J. Bergin on 7th and 8th, Professor T. F. O'Rahilly was also heard on 8th and AE was cross-examined on November 8 and 12. Mr Justice Hanna summed-up on November 13. The Jury deliberated for 7½ hours without agreeing a verdict. The Judge declined to accede to the plaintiffs' application for judgment on the Jury's findings. They lodged an appeal which was dismissed without the defence being called. Osborn Bergin wrote an account of the hearing for John Eglinton's *Memoir of AE*, pp. 200-201. The defendants' costs were about £2,500. The Appeal Fund signatories included Lord Lansdowne.

Note 23. page 181. Several years before this letter came to his notice the editor was given an account of this meeting, precisely in the terms of this letter, by Mme Téry. Similarly she corroborated an account he had been given independently, without her knowledge, of the trip she made to Ireland in 1935. She had longed to see AE again, and sensing his need, went to London, and straight on to Bournemouth, where she was met by C. P. Curran who had to tell her AE had died the day before. As there has been some mystification and inaccuracy in reports from some among AE's acquaintance, his friends will forgive this intrusion of the editor's evidence for the veracity of this report of these events.

Note 24. page 193. Extract. Text from John Eglinton's *A Memoir of AE*, pp. 231-232. Nicholas Vachel Lindsay (1879-December 5, 1931) the poet. The late Mrs Elizabeth Lindsay returned most of the letters written to her husband, as a courtesy to the writers, after his death. Mrs Lindsay's 90-page catalogue of the remaining papers does not include any letters from AE, although she remembered one illustrated letter from him. The collection is now owned by the Seven Gables Bookshop, New York 36. J. S. Starkey told Dr Gibbon there were no AE letters to Lindsay among the papers AE gave him. Dr Magee did not recall who loaned it to him for use in his Memoir. Lindsay's *Selected Poems* were published in 1931. See also *Vachel Lindsay: A Poet in America* by Edgar Lee Masters (New York, 1935: Scribners).

Note 25. page 201. Among the twenty-nine letters he received from AE is one described by Lord Dunsany as ". . . written at great length because AE had to conceal that there was nothing to say, was trying to explain away Yeats's jealousy in keeping me out of the Irish Academy of Letters for as long as he could. . . . Gogarty once said openly at a dinner of that Academy, 'since the object of the Irish Academy of Letters was to keep Dunsany out of it; now that Dunsany has been elected should it not be dissolved?' Yeats, who was in the chair, sat there very silent." (Letter to the editor, August 23, 1955.)

Note 26. *page* 202. Dr Best advised the editor that AE was asked by George Moore's brother Maurice Moore to deliver a funeral speech. AE did not attend the burial of Moore's ashes on Castle Island, Lough Carra: a mile from Moore Hall, across the lake and opposite the Kiltoome woods. AE asked Dr Best to speak the oration he had written.

There were two manuscripts in Dr Best's possession. The text printed here is the final version, spoken over Moore's ashes. In a letter to E. A. Boyd (dated June 18, 1933) AE wrote: "The oration was, as Yeats said, a masterpiece of double meaning. Moore would have admired it." Quoted in the *Colby Library Quarterly* (Waterville, Maine), May 1955, p. 45. This oration may be contrasted with the characterisation of Moore in AE's fantasy *The Avatars* (1933). Dr Best expressed to the editor his opinion that AE "funked" speaking this "farewell" to Moore.

Note 27. *page* 209. Michael O'Donovan (b. 1903) generally known by his pseudonym "Frank O'Connor", the distinguished Irish short story writer, now resident in America. Mr O'Connor received a large number of letters from AE, which he lost when he left Ireland. They were not found by Mrs Garvey, although she told the editor that she had retained many letters to Mr O'Connor from W. B. Yeats. This text is taken from Mr O'Connor's article in the *Yale Review*, September 1939, "Two Friends: Yeats and AE". Concerning that article, Joseph O'Neill wrote to the editor

(March 5, 1951): ". . . Frank O'Connor, was and is so sensitive in company that as one woman put it–'He never seems to know whether he is standing on his head or his feet.' The Francis Hackett's asked him down to meet Lady Ottilie Morrell and he acted so giddily that Lady Ottilie could not be got to realise that he was full of depths. . . . I wasn't there that day but Lady Ottilie could not be persuaded, when I met her, that O'Connor's mind was most profound and penetrating. She kept on comparing him to Lytton Strachey who in fact hadn't half O'Connor's depth, to judge by letters which she gave me to read. O'Connor never does himself justice except when he sits down alone to write. What he writes is always full of illumination for me, even when I disagree with him, as I most definitely do in his theory that AE was schizophrenic. However, Frank may have penetrated more deeply into AE's mind than the rest of us. . . ." See also Mr O'Connor's "AE–A portrait in *The Bell: a Survey of Irish Life* (Dublin), vol. I, no. 2, pp. 49-57 (November 1940).

Note 28. *page* 211. The late Lord Dunsany wrote to the editor (October 18, 1950): "No, as it turned out I never attempted any portrait of AE. I was painting a good many portraits about that time, but I imagine that when he came we were much more interested in his talk. . . ." And he added (November 9, 1950): "But, you see, I regarded him so much as a prophet and bard, and almost whenever we met he started talking straight off about spiritual things, that I no more connected him with economics or politics than I would have connected the prophet Jonah with agriculture and fisheries, though no doubt he would have known a good deal about both. . . ."

Note 29. *page* 211. "AE's generosity of appreciation and encouragement to other writers became a proverb. The critically minded could not help saying that AE's swans were all geese. I hope there was at least one exception. Anyhow, to find oneself in company with the immortal Indian epic on the north coast of Ireland under AE's eye was enough to make one's hair grow longer. His anticipations as to his own writing, unfortunately for humanity, were oracles of destiny, for he returned to England (not Ireland) from his second American tour early in 1935, and on July 17 of that year became what the Chinese call 'a guest of heaven'. The quotations to which he refers are the lines from his poetry that I used in *A Study in Synthesis*. He refers to 'Keller', and the name of tha yet to be appreciated poet is thus spelt in an obituary by one of AE's closest friends in Dublin, Harry F. Norman in a recent number of Seumas O'Sullivan's *Dublin Magazine*. But a letter and an inscription on a slender sheaf of verse is spelled 'Keohler'." (J. H. C.)

Note 30. *page* 212. Ruth Pitter (born 1897) the English poet. She was introduced to AE by A. R. Orage who had early befriended her by publishing her poems in the *New Age*. Between their introduction, probably in 1933, and AE's death, they met "several times". Miss Pitter kindly wrote for the editor an account of the holiday which she and her mother had with AE, at his invitation, in Donegal, in 1934. "My mother and I spent two or three weeks with him on the coast of Donegal. It was very beautiful. I had never been in Ireland before, and wondered at the pure colours of the scene, the poetical speech of the people, the wonderful wild flowers, and above all that intense feeling of the unseen world *only just* invisible–as though at any moment gorgeous legendary figures might appear out of that gorge, on to that empty shore, or an ancient ship cast anchor in the bay. I

remember thinking it was all very *foreign*, and the way of thinking of the people oblique, as it were, to our own. I am not in the least 'psychic', but I felt as never before the supernatural all about me. AE, of course, was very matter-of-fact about this, as though it were common knowledge. He said he had taken a stock-broker out to the Rosses once, and the man had seen things and fallen on his knees and confessed his sins. I asked him about a sound of music I had heard once or twice in my life, in lonely places when it was frosty moonlight (in spite of not being psychic). 'Ah yes,' he said, 'it's the moon-music; caused by the rays of the moon striking the earth's atmosphere.' Quite simple, you see. We had lodgings in a small farmhouse, and it was really almost annoying to find how *hypnotic* was the effect of poetry chanted by him in an atmosphere of peat-reek. The walls seemed to melt away. I am too English to be comfortable about this, especially as my mother always adored 'the Occult', and, I am afraid, would cheat a little to improve the effects; thus, when he told us to close our eyes, and imagine a gold ring hanging in the air, and then to see it grow bigger and bigger and to behold a scene through it–what did we see? I saw nothing and said so; but my mother produced a wonderful Oriental fantasy to oblige, and well I remember his look of polite suspicion. She did not mean to belittle his mysticism, but she could not bear a negative result.

"It was wonderful weather, and we had many a delightful walk. I can see him now (1950), 'wading on the strand', in the same clothes that he had worn in Bloomsbury– dark suit, broad hat, but his trousers rolled right up and his boots hung round his neck. With stately gesture he talked continually, wading majestic among such droves of prawns and shrimps as I have never beheld since. I once caught a good bagful, but when I started to boil them the lightning struck. Nothing, he said, should be done to death with boiling water in his house. He was beautiful in anger, his whole person expanding and his eyes altering completely. To make up for my loss, he bought some from the lobsterman which had been decently boiled out of sight somewhere. One quiet Sunday morning, when the tide was out, he suggested that we should make some statuary out of the excellent muddy sand of the foreshore, which was a perfect medium. This proved absorbing, and I had just finished a large Boddhisattva, or some such thing when I looked up, and there was half the village silently roosting on the cliff, completely bewitched by the creative spectacle. AE was rather perturbed, grabbed his boots and dodged round a rock to put them on. It was the only time I had seen him self-conscious.

"He had been painting a great deal of the time, and gave me five examples. . . . I later gave one to William Rothenstein. . . . The fifth was very good; some children wading in from the sea, keyed very high, sparkling with light, with lovely aerial perspective. It is one of my most treasured possessions. . . ."

Miss Pitter has written: *First and Second Poems* (London, 1927: Sheed and Ward), *A Mad Lady's Garland* (London, 1934: Cresset Press), *Urania* (selection) (London, 1950: Cresset Press), etc.

Miss Pitter's description of AE reminds the editor of L. A. G. Strong's later description: "On a sudden impulse I asked him if he could give me a word of power. I call it that rather than a maxim or a motto; these, after all, generally concern outer life only, and are practical in the lesser sense of the word. What AE gave me was practical in the deepest sense. It concerned outer life all right: and the longer I live, the wider–and deeper–its ripples spread. AE . . . said: 'Seek on earth what you have found in heaven.'

"That piece of advice, with all its implications, seems to me to sum up the intensely practical mysticism which AE lived; and it is by that, and the smile with which he said it, that I best remember him." (*Listener*, March 10, 1955.)

Biographical Notes

ANDERSON, Robert Andrew, born at Mount Corbet, Buttevant, near Doneraile, county Cork, on June 26, 1861; one of two sons and a daughter of Captain Anderson. He first worked as an agent on Lord Castletown's estate at Doneraile, and then moved to Manchester in 1889, to work for the Co-operative Union. In England he met Plunkett who appointed him secretary of the I.A.O.S. in 1895: a position he retained until he retired through ill-health, September 1921. Plunkett's diary entry for January 9, 1910 notes that AE and Anderson were staying at "Kilteragh", "Anderson having very wisely and properly taken the mystic to my home to convalesce . . .". Anderson was "a swift thinker, a keen dialectician, and witty *raconteur*". His later life was marred by the death in France during the 1914 war of his sons Philip and Alan. His other son, Neville, since deceased, married a Dublin solicitor's daughter and emigrated to South America. There is a photograph of R. A. Anderson in the *Irish Homestead*, vol. 7, p. 373 (June 8, 1901). He died December 25, 1942, his wife having predeceased him. His book, *With Horace Plunkett in Ireland* (London, 1935: Macmillan), gives useful information about the co-operative movement amongst farmers in Ireland.

BALFOUR, Arthur James (1848-1930), statesman and philosopher. He was Chief Secretary for Ireland, 1887-1891; (Conservative) Prime Minister, 1902-1905; First Lord of the Admiralty in 1915 (after W. S. Churchill), and Foreign Secretary from 1916-1919. Whilst Chief Secretary he created the Congested Districts' Board (1890). He wrote *A Defence of Philosophic Doubt* (London, 1879: Macmillan) and many other books. In 1924 he delivered a speech concerning the (Irish) Boundary Commission which caused AE to lose his respect for Balfour. A pamphlet by Balfour *Nationality and Home Rule* was published in December 1913 (London: Longmans).

BAX, Clifford (b. 1886), the English dramatist, brother of the composer Sir Arnold Bax. In early life his thought was probably deeply affected by John Ruskin, and Rudolf Steiner (1861-1925), whose *Erkenntnisse der hohern Welten*, he translated as *Initiation and its Results* (London, 1909: Theosophical Publishing Co). His dramatic writing culminated with: *Socrates* (London, 1930: Gollancz), *The Venetian* (1932), *The Rose Without a Thorn* (1933: both Samuel French, publishers, London), *The Buddha* (1947: Gollancz), and *Circe* (London, 1949: Fredk. Muller). There is a chapter about AE in *Inland Far* (London, 1925: Heinemann). An appreciative *Anthology of the Work of Clifford Bax* (London, 1953: Favil Press), was compiled by Mrs Meum Lindsell Stewart (1892-1957). There is a pencil portrait of Mr Bax by his friend Harry Jonas (1955?), and other portraits.

BERGIN, Osborn Joseph son of Osborn Roberts Bergin and Sarah (*née* Reddin), (born in Cork city, 1873, died in Dublin, October 6, 1950), since 1907 "regarded as

the supreme authority on Irish linguistics"
(D. A. Binchy). Educated, and subse-
quently lecturer in Irish, at Queen's
College, Cork; he later studied in Berlin
and Freiburg (1904-1905). Bergin was
successively, in Dublin, Professor of Irish
in the School of Irish Learning (1906); of
Early Irish, in University College (1909-
1940); and finally for a few months Senior
Professor, and Director of the School of
Celtic Studies in the Institute for Advanced
Studies. His published work includes
*Stories from Geoffrey Keating's History of
Ireland* (1909, 1925, 1930), Irish translation of *Eventyr* by H. C. Andersen (1912),
Miscellany presented to Kuno Meyer (1912),
ed. Bergin and C. Marstrander, *Lebor na
Huidre* (1929), ed. R. I. Best and Bergin,
Stories from the Táin (1944), ed. J.
Strachan, rev. Bergin, Rudolf Thurney-
sen's *A Grammar of old Irish* (1946), trans.
with D. A. Binchy, *The Book of Leinster*
(1954), jointly with R. I. Best. Nonetheless his published work is said to have been
marginal to the immense and beneficent
influence he exerted as a teacher. His
childhood friend, and ex-colleague on
Cork Grammar School staff, H. R.
Chillingworth, wrote out some of his
reminiscences in the *Irish Times*, October
12, 1950. Professor D. A. Binchy wrote an
obituary notice in the *Irish Times*, October
7, 1950. Other notices were printed in
Irish Times, October 7, 12, 14, 1950, *Irish
Press*, October 7, 1950, *Studies* (Dublin),
December 1950; and by Eleanor Knott in
Eriu (Dublin), vol. 16 (1952), with an
excellent photograph. The tribute to
Bergin and Kuno Meyer, by R. I. Best,
originally broadcast by the B.B.C.,
January 8, 1954, is printed in the *Dublin
Magazine* January 1958 (correcting an
imperfect version printed in the preceding
issue without Dr Best's knowledge). In
early life Bergin had keenly appreciated
music; but his appreciation was atrophied

in later life. In a letter to the editor (March
2, 1951), Mr Chillingworth wrote of
Bergin: "He was very reserved; but his
reserve was, I believe, due to shyness. He
was a bachelor, and I shouldn't be surprised to learn that his forlorn condition
had been largely due to his shyness. . . .
There was no grimness in the man. He
was lonely and, I think, longed for human
sympathy." He had had several sisters
who predeceased him. His surviving
brother, William, had lived many years
in China, retiring to the south of England,
with his second wife. William died in
1956. Joseph O'Neill wrote to the editor
(February 7, 1951): "Of all the men I
knew, he had the greatest sense of humour.
He loved epigrams, humourous stories,
everything that makes men laugh . . .",
and in another letter, concerning AE and
Bergin (February 11, 1951): ". . . their
loss has been a deep gash in my life. With
AE I felt that he had in a sense gone home;
but with Bergin I had no such consolation,
for he had no belief, as far as I could discover, in any future life." (Bergin was
reared as a Baptist, or, according to the late
Gerard Murphy, as a Plymouth Brother,
later joining the Church of Ireland.) Dr
Bergin wrote to the editor (March 17,
1950): "You may be shocked to learn that
a good deal of AE's poetry seems to me
rather pallid. I think of the shades in *The
Odyssey*, Bk. XI, who have to drink blood
before they can speak. To misapply Mac-
beth's words, 'It will have blood, they say,
blood will have blood'. I must be a bit of a
Philistine. . . . I loved the man, and always
thought him greater than his writings.
Undoubtedly he had visions where all was
opaque to me. A brilliant talker, but
according to him 'The gay romance of
song, Unto the spirit life doth not belong'.
When challenged to write a *real song* that
would stir men's hearts like the sound of
a trumpet, he replied, 'I'm not interested

in trumpets'. We cannot all have everything." An oil portrait of Bergin, by Sarah Purser (exhibited R.H.A., 1927) is now in University College, Dublin.

BEST, Richard Irvine son of Henry and Margaret Jean (Irvine) Best, born in Londonderry, Northern Ireland 1872. The illustrious Irish scholar. Dr Best wrote to this editor (October 8, 1957): "I owe a good deal to AE. It was he who brought me down to the *United Irishman* office, and persuaded Arthur Griffith to publish a translation by me of M. H. d'Arbois de Jubainville's book on the *Irish Mythological Cycle*. I had met Griffith and Moore at his house a few days ago. Griffith welcomed the suggestion, and I set to work on it. That was in October 1901. I got to know Griffith well during the period it ran through the paper, and I contributed another series of my own afterwards" (Dublin, March 1902: O'Donoghue). In *Eriu* (Dublin) during 1912 Best's "Notes on the Script of *Lebor na Huidre*" exposed conclusive paleographical evidence for the conjecture that the book was the production of more than one scribe. With the late John Strachan and the late Kuno Meyer he founded the School of Irish Learning (Dublin) in 1903 and was its indefatigable honorary secretary until it was discontinued in 1924. He was Assistant Director of the National Library of Ireland from 1904-1923, and Director from 1924-1940. His *Bibliography of Irish Philology and Manuscript Literature* (Dublin, 1942) and the *Bibliography . . . of Printed Irish Literature* (Dublin, 1913) are indispensable to students of Irish. Best contributed articles to many philological journals, including *Ériu* (Dublin) (of which he was joint editor, with Bergin, for several years), *Hermathena* (Dublin) and *Zeitschrift für Celtische Philologie* (Hallé). He was senior professor in the School of Celtic Studies in the (Dublin) Institute

for Advanced Studies, 1940-1947, and chairman of the Irish Manuscripts' Commission, 1948-1956. His editions *The Book of Leinster* (with O. J. Bergin, and Professor Michael O'Brien), with the Very Rev. H. J. Lawlor, *Martyrology of Tallaght* and *Annals of Innishfallen*. Among the honours with which his peers commended him were the Leibniz Medal of the Royal Prussian Academy (1914); the Silver Medal of the Pontifical Academy of Sciences (1937) for his facsimile edition of the Milan *Codex* (1936); President of the Royal Irish Academy; the National University (1920), and Dublin University (June 1923) conferred on him honorary degrees, DLITT, and LITTD. He married in 1906 Miss Edith Oldham (1868-1950) a gifted musican, sister of Professor C. H. Oldham of University College, Dublin. Best helped organise the *Feis Ceoil*, an expression of his life-long love of music, deepened by his marriage. Their fine courtesy and generous hospitality were extended to many generations of students from all over the world. Dr Best died in Dublin, September 25, 1959. There are two oil portraits, "neither of them very good" (Binchy): first by Miss S. Harrison, now in the Irish National Portrait Gallery; and much later by James Sleator, now in the Royal Irish Academy.

BLAVATSKY. *See* HAHN.

BODKIN, Thomas, born in Dublin July 21, 1887, the elder son of the late Judge Mathias Bodkin (M.P. for North Roscommon) and his wife Arabella Norman. He was educated at Clongowes Wood College, and the Royal University of Ireland, from whence he graduated BA in 1908 having distinguished himself by winning the Gold Medal for oratory, and another for legal debate. He was called to the Bar, at King's Inns, 1911 and practised for five years. He was appointed secretary to the Commissioners of Charitable Donations and Bequests in Ireland in 1916 (member from 1925 to 1961); from 1927 combining that office with the Directorship of the National Gallery of Ireland. He resigned those appointments in 1935 to become the first director of the Barber Institute of Fine Arts, and Barber Professor of the Fine Arts in the University of Birmingham. He retired in 1953 (under age), remaining adviser to the Trustees of the Barber Institute on the purchase of works of art, until October 1959. The collection has been formed entirely on Dr Bodkin's advice: it was justly described in *The Times* (October 5, 1959) as "The most remarkable collection formed in Britain in the last quarter century". When young, Stephen MacKenna advised him "Guard your health even more than your virtue": but he always overworked. In Ireland he served the Free State Government on various Committees: to advise the Minister of Finance on Coinage (1926); on National Museum Organisation (1927); Art Education (1927). The popular success of his book *The Approach to Painting* (London, 1927 many editions, 1945, 1954: afterwards published by Collins, Fontana Books) has ensured the initiation of his readers into the techniques for discerning what is good art and what is bad. His style is lucid, bold, and irradiated with wit: achieving through knowledge and grace a balanced survey of the implications of art in life. On November 6, 1959 the governments of Ireland and the United Kingdom signed a *Memorandum of Agreement* by which the thirty-nine pictures cited in the disputed Codicil to Sir Hugh Lane's Will shall be exhibited in equal proportions, and in rotation between the National Galleries in London and in Dublin. That Agreement may well have been devised under Dr

Bodkin's guidance. At Mr W.T. Cosgrave's request Dr Bodkin examined the subject exhaustively in his book *Hugh Lane and his Pictures* (Dublin, 1932, 1956: Stationery Office). Dr Bodkin wrote some "reproductions of modern French poetry", *May it Please your Lordships* (1917). He enshrines his antipathies in scintillating epigrams. He has written articles in *The Burlington Magazine* (London), the *Birmingham Post*, and elsewhere. His many valuable books include *Dismembered Masterpieces* (London, 1945: Collins), *Four Irish Landscape Painters* [George Barret, James O'Connor, Walter F. Osborne, and Nathaniel Hone] (Dublin, 1920: Talbot Press). Dr Bodkin was a Knight of St Gregory, Officier de la Légion d'Honneur, and held doctorates of literature (*Honoris Causa*) from the National University and Dublin University. There are portraits of him by Sir Charles Wheeler, PRA, busts in terracotta and bronze (the latter being the best likeness of him); Séan Keating, PRHA; James Sleator, RHA, Séan O'Sullivan, RHA; Estella Solomons, ARHA; and Bernard Fleetwood-Walker, RA. He died April 24, 1961.

BONN, Moritz Julius, the eminent economist and author, born in Frankfort on the Main, June 28, 1873. He graduated from the Ludwig-Maximilians-Universität, München, July 24, 1895. "I learned the causes of inflation from sixteenth century Spain", he remarked to this editor . *Spaniens Niedergang während der Preisrevolution des 16 Jahrhunderts* (Stuttgart, 1896) was his first book. In 1898 Sir Horace Plunkett addressed the Economic Society of Newcastle-upon-Tyne: ". . . I was talking the other day to Dr Moritz Bonn who has for the last two years been making a close study of Irish economics in every part of Ireland, as to the reasons why English policy had so signally failed to promote the material welfare of Ireland. He tersely replied–'It is an attempt to impose individualism upon the country without educating the individual' " (*Irish Homestead*, vol. 4, p. 929, November 5, 1898). "In Ireland I learned what colonisation can and cannot do. In that sense I am a debtor to Ireland." (To this editor, 1960.) *Die Englische Kolonisation in Irland* (Stuttgart and Berlin, 1906: Cotta, 2 vols.) he dedicated to Plunkett. T. W. H. Rolleston translated into English a smaller book by Dr Bonn, *Modern Ireland and her Agrarian Problem* (Dublin, 1906: Hodges Figgis). "All my life I have been mainly interested in two problems: inflation and colonisation." (Conversation, 1960.) Throughout his life Dr Bonn has won distinction for those academic institutions which awarded him long-term appointments, in Munich, Berlin (Hochschule), the London School of Economics; and as visiting professor in some American universities. "There I was not always popular with my students; they wanted me to give them facts to learn, but I tried to teach them how to *think*." He wrote in his reminiscences: ". . . I did not want to write history; my task was to analyze and interpret it." Dr Bonn's personal modesty and reserve have prevented journalistic abuse of his name. He has wittily described the circumstances of his appearance on "the fringe" of history as economic adviser to the Weimar Republic, at the Versailles (1919), Spa and Genoa conferences. Justly celebrated as a master of German prose composition all his books are to be re-published in Berlin under his supervision by Duncker & Humblot. Dr Bonn has written English with equal mastery of literary nuance; see *The Crisis of European Democracy* (New Haven, 1925: Yale University Press), *The American Experiment* [translated by Mabel Brailsford, revised by Dr Bonn]

(London, 1933: Allen & Unwin), and *Whither Europe–Union or Partnership* (London, 1952: Cohen & West). In English his style is veined with reserves of meaning and knowledge implied by profuse factual illustration of his thesis, for example in *The Crumbling of Empire. The Disintegration of World Economy* (London, 1938: Allen & Unwin) a literary masterpiece in which he forecast accurately (to date) the economic and political developments of world affairs for future decades. Dr Bonn has extended his thesis in a new German book, a revaluation of history, for which he hazards what he called a "catch-word" title (translated as) *The Triumph of Colonialism*, ". . . because it shows how the communities gaining political self-government have taken over western habits and methods from their former Colonial administrators, rather than attempting to revive, develop, or preserve the remnants of their native culture". "If I don't live to finish this book, the world won't lose much", he remarked during revision for the press. None falling under the fascination of that brilliant mind would agree with him there. The extraordinarily happy circumstances of his domestic life may be glimpsed through the rare autobiographical descriptions in his reminiscences *Wandering Scholar* (New York, 1948: John Day; London, 1949: Cohen & West). His alert and vivid presence emerges through that narrative: a personality elusive and lucid, gentle, humorous, undismayed by stupidities, and not deceived by them. Moral courage, imagination and sagacity radiate from him. Adroit exposition, poetic sensibility and vibrant wit illumine his instruction. His logic is incontrovertible; a swift thinker, he speaks plainly. That beautiful book closes characteristically: "I have been a dreamer all my life, and dreams have often been more vivid

K

to me than things real. I have always controlled them, and I have never mixed them up with 'reality. . . . If I could but go on dreaming dreams until they fade insensibly into sleep eternal, I would bless the future as I have blessed the past."

BROOKS, Sydney (1872–December 17, 1937) journalist. He had lived in America 1896-1900, and constantly revisited it. He edited the *Saturday Review*, 1921, and *Sperling's Journal*, 1917-1922. He was at this time writing regularly for *The Times* (London), especially on American affairs. Throughout Theodore Roosevelt's (1858-1919) Presidency (1901-1909) of the U.S.A. Brooks sent him a weekly statement on American affairs. Possibly through Roosevelt's friendship for both men he and Plunkett may have met. Brooks began life as a sculptor, and had later served as an officer in the Cuban army. Brooks wrote "Sir Horace Plunkett and his Work" in *Fortnightly Review*, June 1912; and *Aspects of the Irish Question* (Dublin, 1912: Maunsel), *Theodore Roosevelt* (London, 1910: Hodder & Stoughton), etc.

CAMPBELL, Richard, born in Larne, County Antrim, October 28, 1872, son of Felix and Mary (Connelly). In 1876 he was taken to America. He graduated LLB from Georgetown University, 1899, having worked as a clerk and bookkeeper. For a time he was a newspaper reporter. Assistant in the Attorney-General's office, P1, 1902; appointed District Attorney, Moro Province, 1906, and Member of the Legislative Council. He was a Judge of the First Instance, 1908-1917, when he resigned to take up private practice, as Gilbert, Campbell and McCool, New York. He was sent to Ireland in 1920 or 1921 by subscribers to the million and a quarter dollars' fund for relief, contributed by America and administered through Horace Plunkett's White Cross relief

organisation. The first person he met was AE, with whom he formed a lasting friendship. Campbell broadcast a *Farewell to AE* on the U.S.A. Station W.J.Z., July 23, 1935. He died October 16, 1935.

COLUM, Padraic, the son of Padraic Colum (senior), was born at Longford in 1881. The father, lately the local Workhouse master, hurried to Colorado in a gold-rush, about 1887, having entrusted his two sons and two daughters to his wife, at her Mother's farm in Carlow. Their poet son commented: "I haven't known anyone else able to cross America without being able to find work, except my father". Padraic Colum senior returned to Ireland, his health broken, and was employed for several years as the station master at Sandycove, near Dublin. The poet and his brother worked as clerks in the local railway freight depôt, moving into Dublin about 1900. Padraic Colum's first play "The Children of Lir", written about 1899, was his first publication (in the *Weekly Independent*). In Dublin he met Arthur Griffith and AE, "Seumas O'Sullivan" and other writers. Griffith published his poems in the *United Irishman*, AE in the *Celtic Christmas* issues of the *Irish Homestead*. AE included some of Mr Colum's poems in *New Songs* (1904), and he had enjoyed much success with performances of several plays. See his recollections of "Early Days of the Irish Theatre" in the *Dublin Magazine*, vol. 24, no. 4, pp. 11-17 (October 1949) and vol. 25, no. 1, pp. 18-25 (January 1950). The plays were probably written under the influence of Ibsen, whose plays he read eagerly. For many years the two brothers maintained their family. "This kept us more in touch with people, working in an office, and I think that responsibility was fortunate" [Conversation, March 19, 1959]. *Wild Earth*, Mr Colum's first collection of poems was published in 1907 and dedicated "To AE, who fostered me". In 1912 Mr Colum married the critic Mary Catherine Maguire (1887-October 22, 1957); they emigrated to America in 1915. The English Department of Columbia University were fortunate enough to persuade Mr Colum to lecture there regularly for many years. See *Collected Poems* (New York, 1953: Devin-Adair), *Ten Poems* (Dublin, 1958: Dolmen Press), and his unforgettable *The Poet's Circuits : Collected Poems of Ireland* (London, 1960: O.U.P.); *Arthur Griffith* (a biography) (Dublin, 1959: Browne & Nolan), and in collaboration with his wife *Our Friend James Joyce* (London, 1959: Gollancz). Broadsheet poems by Mr and Mrs Colum were published by the Dolmen Press in 1958. Mrs Colum wrote: *From these Roots* [a volume of incisive literary criticism] (London and New York, 1937: Scribners), and some reminiscences *Life and the Dream* (1947).

There are portraits of Mr Colum by John B. Yeats (several drawings) and an oil portrait (*c.* 1906), a drawing by AE (1905), a bust by Edmond Quinn (Municipal Gallery, Dublin), an oil portrait by Lily Williams (Abbey Theatre, Dublin), a pencil sketch by Raymond Piper (1958). Patrick J. Tuohy's oil portrait was exhibited at the R.H.A., in 1925; T. Spicer-Simson's portrait medallion is dated 1923; a portrait medal by John Mowbray-Clarke was exhibited at the Kevorkian Galleries, New York from May 7 to June 7, 1919. Amongst the correspondence from Mr Colum to "Seumas O'Sullivan" sold by Messrs Elkin Mathews Ltd in 1959 were "a purple ink caricature of Padraic Colum, probably by William Orpen" showing Mr Colum in frock coat and silk hat, striding along the street, observed by Max Beerbohm (on the back of the sheet Abbey Theatre notes dating it 1907): and

a wash-drawing (about 1904) the artist's name illegible. That collection of correspondence was bought by the University of Buffalo Library. Portraits of Mrs Colum by AE (1922) and Lily Williams.

Padraic Colum's play "The Man who met Death" was based on a story told to him by AE.

COUSINS, James Henry Sproull (born in Belfast, July 22, 1873; died at Madanapalle, Madras, February 20, 1956), the eldest of four children borne by Susan (Davey) of Carrickfergus (1843-October 29, 1915) to James Cousins (184-?-December 7, 1920) of Glastry, Ards Peninsula, a deep-sea mariner before the mast. Moving to Dublin in 1897 J. H. Cousins married in 1903 Margaret E. Gillespie (born, Boyle; November 7, 1878; died at Adyar, Madras, March 11, 1954). Their devoted union was life-long. A representative selection from James Cousins's verse was printed in *Collected Poems, 1894-1940* (Adyar, Madras, 1940: Kalakshetra). The later poems, *Reflections before Sunset* (1946) and *Twenty-four Sonnets* (1949, both Kalakshetra), both sustain the attractive fluency, lyricism and noble sentiment of his earlier poems. Dr and Mrs Cousins's collaborative autobiography, *We Two Together* (Madras, 1950: Ganesh) presents an accurately detailed and copious survey of their life-work; first in Ireland, from 1913 in England; from 1915 (left October 6, 1915), at Mrs Besant's invitation, in India. There they settled, with occasional lecturing tours to Japan, America and Europe. James Cousins established a reputation for pre-eminence as a professor and academic administrator. He was art adviser to the Maharajahs of Mysore, and Travancore (where he formed the first public collections of painting and sculpture). Much of his most lucid and stimulating prose is concerned with the aesthetics of the plastic arts. See *The Faith of the Artist* (Adyar, 1941: Kalakshetra) and his essays on Jean Delville (1867-19-?) and Nicholas Roerich (1874-1947), *Two Great Theosophist Painters* (Madras, 1925: Theosophical Publishing House), reprinted from *The Theosophist* (Madras). Among his best literary criticism is the book on Shelley's work *The Work Promethean* (Madras, 1933: Ganesh). His most comprehensive statements of an aesthetic psychology are *Samadarsana* (*Indian Psychology*) (1925: Ganesh) and *A Study in Synthesis* (1934: Ganesh). In Europe and Asia Mrs Cousins was an enthusiastically effervescent and high-spirited feminist, associated in England with F. W. (now Lord) Pethick-Lawrence and his first wife. See *Indian Womanhood Today* (Allahabad, 1941: Kitabistan). Mrs Cousins was an accomplished musician and pianist: see *The Music of Orient and Occident* (Madras, 1935: B. G. Paul). In later years one of their keenest pleasures was listening to Mr Yehudi Menuhin during a tour of India, and afterwards listening to his recordings. Publicly declaring his object to be an affirmation of the spiritual truth inherent, he believed, in all religions, Dr Cousins was formally admitted to the Hindu worship on January 14, 1937. For him this symbolised revoking *exclusive* religious dogmas. His admission to temples demonstrated the move away from attachment to exclusive rights, in India; a graduation towards a belief held by Dr Cousins, that the objective sought by the practice of worship in any faith, is immersion in their common source (cf. *We Two Together*, pp. 641-649). From 1943 their lives were burdened by Mrs Cousins's paralysis. James Cousins was a great teacher and a true poet. His work reveals a mind and character which were heroic in their aspiration and scope of activity. He was humorous and simultaneously

[248]

profoundly sensible to the grave poetic truths implicit in ideas and action. In personal relations he was incorrigibly loyal, and consistently sympathetic to all free and unbiased enquiry.

DE VALÉRA, Éamonn, born in New York, October 14, 1882, oldest child of Vivion de Valéra (a Spaniard) and Catherine (Coll) of Bruree, County Limerick. Taken to Ireland in childhood he was educated by the Christian Brothers, and elsewhere. A foundation member of the Irish Volunteers he evaded execution after the Easter 1916 insurrection only because of the nationality he claimed by birth. President of Sinn Féin, 1917-1926, and President of Fianna Fail from its foundation in 1926. Mr de Valéra won the parliamentary representation of East Clare in 1917, and has held it continuously since then. President of the unrecognised Irish Republic, 1919-1922, M.P. for Down, 1921-1929, and for south Down 1933-1938. Chancellor of the National University of Ireland since 1921, he has tried to direct Irish educational grants for the service of Dublin University. Opposed to the terms of the Anglo-Irish Treaty he led opposition to Griffith, in the Civil War, and subsequently refrained from Parliamentary appearances until 1927. Leader of the Opposition in the Irish Free State Parliament, 1927-1932: President of the Executive Council, I.F.S., 1932-1937, and Taoiseach (Prime Minister) 1937-1948, 1951-1954 and 1957-1959. Third elected President of the Irish Republic from June 25, 1959. As President of the 68th and Special sessions of the League of Nations (September-October 1932), and President of the Assembly of the League (1938), Mr de Valéra deeply impressed his associates with the burning idealism and flair for practical organisation which have characterised his political career. Even his bitterest opponents have been captivated by his personal charm excepting, some say, Collins and Kevin O'Higgins.

Mrs Mary Colum wrote (July 14 [1920]) to Miss Joanna Fortune of Chicago: "*Peterborough, New Hampshire* . . . We went to see de Valéra and he asked us not to leave America for a while as it was important for Ireland to be represented in America by writers. He said the best thing of all would be for AE to come out for a while. I told him about your asking him, although I did not mention your name. . . . A few weeks after, when Padraic saw him again he asked . . . who had asked AE out here and Padraic gave him your name. . . . de Valéra is really a very remarkable man, more interested in having Ireland culturally represented in the U.S.A. than anything else. He has completely broken with the political group who used to run Irish affairs in this country. . . . He thinks AE the greatest living Irishman."

DOUGLAS, James G. (1887-September 16, 1954), eldest son of John Douglas of Dublin. He was by trade a haberdasher, and a Director of several Irish companies. His mother was a native of Lurgan, AE's birthplace. He was a Quaker, active in the Society's work in Ireland. Arthur Griffith was among his friends. He was Hon. Secretary of the Dublin branch of the Union of Democratic Control (formed 1915); and from 1920-1922 was honorary treasure and trustee of the Irish White Cross organisation. On October 11, 1918, AE, J. G. Douglas, and Thomas Johnson (born 1872, the secretary of the Irish Trades' Union Congress, 1914-1929 and Free State Senator from 1928), visited London to address a joint meeting at the Labour Party Executive, and the Parliamentary Committee of the Trades' Union Congress. AE stayed with Sidney Webb (1859-1947) and Beatrice Webb (1858-1943). See *The Diaries 1912-1924, of Beatrice Webb*, edited by Margaret I.

(Postgate) Cole (London, 1952: Longmans), pp. 131-133. Douglas was Vice-Chairman of the Irish Senate from its inception until 1925; and held other public offices throughout his career. (AE was one of his colleagues on the White Cross Committee, which distributed "relief" in Ireland, prior to the Treaty.) There is a photograph of Douglas in the *Irish Times*, September 17, 1954, p. 1.

DUNLOP, Daniel Nicol, born in Ayrshire 1868, the son of Catherine (Stuart) and Alexander Dunlop (a builder–and Quaker). He was educated at South Beach Grammar School, Ardrossan. He moved to Dublin in 1890, trading as a Tea and Wine merchant in Palace Street, whilst living at the Theosophical Society's lodge, 3 Upper Ely Place, until about January 1893, when he married Eleanor FitzPatrick (1867-1932) and they moved to her parents' home, 71 Drumcondra Road. They had two daughters, and a son the painter Ronald O. Dunlop, RA (born 1894) [see his autobiographical *Struggling with Paint* (London, 1956: Phoenix House)]. In autumn 1897 they left Ireland for America, where Dunlop was employed as a private secretary by Katherine Tingley, the head of the Point Loma Theosophists. She soon sacked him, and he moved to Pittsburgh, to work for the Westinghouse Company. In 1899 they returned to England where he was employed in the Publicity Section of the British Westinghouse Company's London offices. Probably in 1908 he was promoted to be manager of the switch-gear department, at Trafford Park, Manchester, and they moved to Hale, Cheshire. Whilst in Manchester he continued to act as head of the Publicity Section, which had been transferred there from London. Soon after the Westinghouse firm became the Metropolitan-Vickers Company, Dunlop was released by them to organise the

British Electrical and Allied Manufacturers' Association. He was the first Director of the Association; an appointment he held until his death, on May 30, 1935. With financial support from BEAMA he planned and organised the World Power Conference, which first met on June 30, 1924. When he died there were forty-nine member countries whose engineers and scientists were represented at the annual conference. For many years D. N. Dunlop went to Dublin during the early summer and returned with pictures painted by AE; his son thinks he bought them. AE dedicated his *Collected Poems* (1913) to Dunlop. He edited *The Irish Theosophist* (Dublin, 1892-1897), *The Path* (Hale, Cheshire: later London: July 1910, June 1912), and with Clifford Bax was co-editor of *The Orpheus Series* booklets, and the *Theosophical Art Circle Transactions* (December 1907-June 1908), later *Orpheus* (October 1908-April 1914). He wrote some books, reprints of Theosophical lectures, *The Path of Attainment* (1916), *Nature-spirits and the Spirits of the Elements* (1920), *British Destiny* (1916), *Duty* (1919), all published in London. There is an obituary notice of him, probably written by his friend and colleague Charles Weekes, in *World Power* (London) vol. 23, no. 138; June 1935, inserted unnumbered before p. 273, with a photograph. His son painted a portrait which was in his possession in 1951. Dunlop was for many years a member of the Anthroposophical Society (Rudolf Steiner) and was its Secretary-General in Great Britain from January 1927 until his death (except in 1929). There are some notes about him in *The Earth as a Basis of World Economy*, by Walter Johannes Stein; published as vol. 2, special number, no. 7 of *The Present Age* (London, June-July, 1937). It includes a photograph of Dunlop which his children think is the most characteristic likeness.

DUNSANY, LORD, *See* PLUNKETT, E. J. M. D.

FIGGIS, Darrell Edmund, born in Rathmines, Dublin, 1882, he was moved early to India. Probably about 1910 he returned to Ireland, and became known as poet and novelist: *The Crucibles of Time* (poems) (London, 1911: Dent), *The Mount of Transfiguration* (Dublin, 1915: Maunsel); *Jacob Elthorne* (novel) (London, 1914: Dent) and *Children of Earth* (Dublin, 1918: Maunsel). He also wrote critical essays, and *Shakespeare: a Study* (1911: Dent). In July 1914 he assisted in the gun-running at Howth, led by Erskine Childers. In 1917 when Sinn Fein was re-organised he was appointed Honorary Secretary. He was arrested and imprisoned February 22, 1917. He actively opposed conscription in Ireland (1918). In February 1922 Arthur Griffith appointed him acting Chairman of the Constitution Committee when the Treaty had been accepted. He was a clever man, whose intellectual versatility caused many people to distrust him; his humourless manner would not encourage easy relations. *The Times'* obituarist described him as "a politician of real but hectic and irregular ability". In 1923 his novel *The Return of the Hero* was published over the pseudonym Michael Ireland (London: Chapman & Dodd). He had become embittered by lack of sympathetic appreciation. His wife committed suicide in November 1924. On October 26-27, 1925 he took his own life. Stephen MacKenna wrote: "Darrell did well; little in his life so became him, poor fellow: great gifts, I liked him well yet foresaw, much, this" (*Journal & Letters*, pp. 225-226). Figgis also wrote *The Irish Constitution* (Dublin, 1922: Melliflont Press), *A Chronicle of Jails* (1917: Talbot Press), *A Second Chronicle of Jails* (1919: Talbot Press), *The Gaelic State in the Past and Future* (1917: Maunsel), *The Paintings of William Blake* (London, 1925: Benn), and posthumously issued his *Recollections of the Irish War* (London, 1927: Benn.) A bibliography by P. S. O'Hegarty was printed in the *Dublin Magazine*, vol. 12, no. 3 (July 1937), pp. 47-54.

FINLAY, Thomas Aloysius (1848-January 8, 1940) was the first editor of the *Irish Homestead;* succeeded by J. K. Montgomery (1897), and H. F. Norman (1899) before AE's appointment in 1905. He was ordained a Jesuit priest in early life; was Vice-President of the I.A.O.S. from 1894-1940. With his brother Father Peter Finlay appointed in 1883 jointly to the Professorship in Mental and Moral Philosophy in University College, Dublin. In 1900 he succeeded W. P. Coyne (died January 3, 1904) as Professor of Political Economy in University College. From 1882-1887 he was Rector of Belvedere College, and was for many years a Commissioner of National Primary Education. With Father Matthew Russell (1834-1912) founded the *Irish Monthly* (Dublin: 1873, in progress), in which he serialised a novel *The Chances of War* over the pseudonym A. Whitelock. The novel was published over the pseudoym (Dublin, 1877 and 1908: M. H. Gill). New edition published in Dublin by Fallon's, 1911). Revised and re-edited it was republished over his own name, with a new title, *With the Army of O'Neill* (Dublin, 1930: Educational Co. of Ireland). In 1887 Finlay founded *The Lyceum* (Dublin, 1887-1894) which was superseded by the *New Ireland Review* (1894-1911) which in turn was superseded by *Studies* (Dublin, 1912: in progress). Finlay translated Albert Stoeckl's *A Handbook of the History of Philosophy* (Dublin, vol. 1, 1887: Gill), reprinted by Fallon's (1903), besides writing various pamphlets, most pseudonymously, including *Foxford and the Providence Mills* (1932). His portrait was painted by Leo Whelan. George Moore introduces him as a character in *Salve*. He had the reputation for being "not always a glad sufferer of fools", and to have had a laconic gift in speech. Obituary notices were printed in the *Irish Monthly* (vol. 68, pp. 142-144) and *Studies* (vol. 29, no. 113, pp. 26-40), both issued in March 1940, written by Dr. George O'Brien. A notice by H. F. Norman was printed in *The Yearbook of Agricultural Co-operation* (London, 1941: P. S. King & Son).

GILL, Thomas Patrick, born at Ballygraigue, Nenagh, County Tipperary, October 25, 1858: died in Dublin January 19, 1931. Educated at Nenagh, Kilkenny and Trinity College, Dublin he emigrated to America and edited the *Catholic World* (New York) and was associate editor of the *North American Review*, 1883-1885. Returning to Great Britain he was Nationalist M.P. for South Louth, 1885-1892. Horace Plunkett appointed him to the staff of the Irish Agricultural Organisation Society, but Plunkett's unpublished *Diaries* record his subsequent distrust of Gill, and their political disagreement during Plunkett's period as Vice-President of the Department of Agriculture and Technical Instruction for Ireland (1899-1907). Gill was appointed editor of the *Daily Express* (Dublin) by Plunkett from July 1898 to December 1899, whilst he held a controlling financial interest in the paper when it was bought out by Lord Ardilaun, "an extreme Unionist". Gill was a foundation member of the International Institute of Agriculture in Rome (now taken over by the Food and Agriculture Organisation of U.N.O.).

GONNE, Maud, daughter of Colonel Gonne who had been on the staff of the Irish Command, born in 1866. She was educated in France, and lived intermittently in Dublin after 1882. Both her parents died before she was 21. She addressed meetings on behalf of the Land League, and other causes, becoming an ardent Nationalist. Her physical splendour attracted attention wherever she went, and W. B. Yeats was inspired by her to write his love poetry, perhaps most powerfully in *On a Bronze Head*. Whilst living in Paris she met and married Major John MacBride, who had recruited and led the Irish Brigade for service with the Boers. Major MacBride was executed after the Easter 1916 insurrection in Dublin. Their son Mr Séan MacBride (b. 1904) was Irish Minister for External Affairs, 1948-1951. Maud Gonne was irreconcilably opposed to acceptance of the 1921 Anglo-Irish Treaty. She lost all her letters from AE during "the Troubles" and wrote to this editor that the volume of Yeats's poems, illustrated by AE, which she had prized, was among the papers which were destroyed. Her fragmentary autobiography *A Servant of the Queen* (London, 1938: Gollancz) is free from any bitterness. She contributed an essay to *Scattering Branches, Tributes to . . . W. B. Yeats* (London, 1940: Macmillan). Laurence Campbell's bust of her in old age is now in the Municipal Gallery of Modern Art, Dublin. She died in Dublin, April 27, 1953.

GORE-BOOTH, Constance (1868-July 15, 1927) sister of Sir Josslyn and Eva Gore-Booth. In 1900 she married the Polish painter Count Casimir Dunin-Markiewicz. During 1913 she actively supported the Larkinist Labour movement. In 1914 her husband returned to Poland, intending to join the Russian army. At Easter 1916 Countess Markiewicz joined the militant nationalists, and commanded the Volunteers whilst they occupied the College of Surgeons, Dublin. She was captured by the British army and sentenced to death. (At that time AE remembered Eva's

anxiety, and sent her a copy of his book *Gods of War;* this copy is in the editor's possession.) The sentence was commuted to penal servitude for life, but she was released in 1917. From December 1918 she was Sinn Fein M.P. for Dublin (St Patrick's), until 1922. From 1923 she was member of Dáil Éireann for Dublin city (south), and Secretary for Labour. Countess Markiewicz was received into the Roman Catholic Church during 1916. Her husband travelled from Warsaw to be with her during her last brief illness. See *The Prison Letters of Constance Gore-Booth*, ed. by Esther Roper (London, May 1934: Longmans). In a cottage at Ballaly, which she loaned to the *United Irishman's* main contributors, AE and Connolly and others often met. See Seumas O'Sullivan's *The Rose and the Bottle* (1946), p. 190. See also Séan O'Faolain's biography of Constance Gore-Booth (1934). C. D. Markiewicz was "a boyish giant" and wrote plays (e.g. *Seymour's Redemption* staged at the Abbey Theatre, March 1908).

GORE-BOOTH, Eva, the second daughter of Sir Henry Gore-Booth, of Lissadell, Sligo (born May 22, 1870, died June 30, 1926). She moved to Manchester to work amongst the poor, in 1897, and remained there until 1913, when ill-health forced her retirement to Ireland. Her *Selected Poems* were edited by her friend Esther Roper, with a Memoir (London, 1933: Longmans). AE's obituary notice was printed in the *Irish Statesman*, vol. 6, pp. 520-522 (July 17, 1926). It was abridged and re-arranged by Monk Gibbon when he reprinted it in *The Living Torch* (1937), pp. 162-166.

GREEN, Mrs A. S. *See* STOPFORD.

GREGAN, Paul (1876-May 7, 1945), with his brother James worked as a banks' organiser for the I.A.O.S., from 1899 or early 1900. A group photograph including him in *Irish Homestead*, vol. 9, p. 339 (April 25, 1903). Some of his poems were printed in the *Irish Monthly* (Dublin), 1894, etc., the *All-Ireland Review* (Kilkenny, later Dublin), *The Internationalist*, and the *Irish Homestead* and *Irish Statesman*. A collection, *Sunset Town* (Kilkenny, 1901) was published by Standish J. O'Grady; it was dedicated "To my dear friend AE". He overworked, and his later years were marred by loss of memory, and the death of his daughter.

GWYNN, Stephen Lucius (1864-June 11, 1950). He married in 1889 and returned to England, where he had been a scholar of Brasenose College, 1882-1886. In 1904 he returned to Ireland and was Nationalist M.P. for Galway city from 1906-1918. He sat on the Irish Home Rule Convention, 1917-1918. He edited *The Anvil of War: letters of F. S. Oliver to his brother W. E. Oliver* (London, 1936: Macmillan), and wrote *The Last Years of John Redmond* (London, 1919: E. Arnold), *Collected Poems* (Edinburgh, 1923: Blackwood), etc. See his *Experiences of a Literary Man* (London, 1926: Thornton Butterworth), pp. 200-204 on AE.

HAHN, Helena Petrovna, born August 12, 1831 (Russian Calendar, July 30) in South Russia. Married the Vice-Governor of the neighbouring province, Erivan, General Nikifor Vasilevitch Blavatsky (aged 40) on July 7, 1848. After three months' honeymoon with him she left him. (He outlived her, but she ignored him. In some reminiscences written in later life she described him vehemently, "a swine", and herself as "virgin".) A brilliant personality, she travelled Asia, Europe and America for several years. With H. S. Olcott (1832-1907) as her co-founder she registered the charter of The Theosophical Society in New York, September 1875. *Isis Unveiled*, her first

large book was published in 1877. In 1878 her plea for a divorce from M. C. Betanelly was advocated in the New York courts by Olcott's brother's clerk, W. Q. Judge (a member of the Theosophical Society). In 1885 she moved to London and she died there, May 8, 1891. Madame Blavatsky was described by AE (in 1934) as "a cosmos in an ailing woman's body". Her writings have been summarised with scrupulous fairness by Richard Ellmann in *Yeats: the Man and the Masks* (London, 1949: Macmillan), pp. 58-72. The best biography is *Priestess of the Occult* by Gertrude M. Williams (New York, 1946: Knopf). Her best-known book was probably *The Secret Doctrine* (2 vols. 1888-1889). The copy owned in old age by AE (Los Angeles, 1925: Theosophical Co.) was heavily scored by him in crayon, throughout. Evidently a nature burdened with emotional unrest, she exerted a powerful influence on many strong-minded people, including Annie Besant (1847-1933). Her native flamboyance and exuberant imagination appear to have misled her into rigging *séances*, for the delectation of wealthy amateur spiritualists in India and England. Richard Hodgson's *Report* to the (London) Society for Psychical Research (June 1885) flawed her reputation except among her devoted personal admirers.

HANNAY, Rev. J. O. (1865-1950) wrote many light novels under the pseudonym George A. Birmingham, beside some Church history. In his *Pleasant Places* (London, November 1934: Heinemann) Birmingham wrote on p. 172 that his novel *General John Regan* (London, August 1913: Hodder) is based on a story told him by AE. The same story AE told to Lady Gregory, and she used it in her play *The Image* (Dublin, June 1910: Maunsel). George Moore received from AE the plot which he used for *The Making of an Immortal* (New York, 1927: Bowling Green Press, E. Rudge), a comedy first performed at the Arts' Theatre, London, April 1, 1928, with incidental music composed by Sir Thomas Beecham, Bt.

HANNON, Patrick Joseph, born in Ireland, 1874. A member of the I.A.O.S. staff and from 1899-1905 joint assistant secretary, with AE. In 1905 he went to South Africa as adviser on agricultural co-operation to the Cape Province. He was Conservative and Unionist M.P. for Moseley (Birmingham), 1921-1950. Knighted in 1936. In 1910 he contested East Bristol as a Tariff Reform and Unionist candidate. In consequence AE broke off the "affectionate friendship" which had obtained with Sir Patrick – because of their divergent political convictions. Sir Patrick's appointment in the I.A.O.S. had combined Chief Banks' Organiser with the job of joint assistant secretary. AE wrote an article in the *Irish Homestead* which, "without quoting names, inflicted a grievous wound upon" him. Sir Patrick remained on terms of close friendship with Sir Horace Plunkett. The late Mr J. Dulanty (then Irish High Commissioner in London) told Sir Patrick of AE's fatal illness in the early summer, 1935, whilst they were cruising. Sir Patrick was for many years secretary of the Navy League. He immediately offered AE, through Mr Dulanty's mediation, whatever help might be needful for AE's family; and offered to do anything in his power to make AE's last months happier in practical affairs. His offer was refused. Sir Patrick wrote in a letter to the editor (October 2, 1957): "Mrs Russell was a charming wife and mother and I entertained for her a deep affection. It was my sad lot to attend the funeral of her first-born, and to help George to soothe her grief. . . ." The infant was Bryan; the same name being given

to the second child. An imperturbable negotiator, Sir Patrick has been a power in business as in politics. He is writing his *Memoirs*. A photograph of him was printed in *Irish Homestead*, vol. 11, p. 615 (1905). The finest portrait is by Dermod O'Brien, P.R.H.A. (oils: December 1904).

HARRIMAN RUMSEY, Mary, was born November 17, 1881, the sister of Mr W. Averill Harriman. She married the sculptor Charles Cary Rumsey (August 29, 1879 – September 21, 1922); they had three children. Formerly the owner of a chain of newspapers in the Southern States she became a well-known patron of the arts. For eighteen months she was an administrator of the "New Deal", as Adviser to the American National Emergency Council. She was Chairman of the Consumers' Advisory Board of the National Relief Association, a developer of the Emergency Exchange Association, and a leading member of the American Farm Foundation and of the Eastern Livestock Co-operative Marketing Association. She suffered from a riding accident on her horse, on November 17, 1934, and died as a result on December 18, 1934. For two years prior to her death she had lived with Miss Frances Perkins [(born 1882) who was F. D. Roosevelt's Secretary of Labour from March 4, 1933 to June 1945. In December 1934 she was Chairman of the President's Committee on Economic Security. Author of *The Roosevelt I Knew* (1946), etc.] Mrs Rumsey owned the Sculptors' Gallery, 152 East 40th St, N.Y. City; she appointed Mrs Jeannette Hare its Director. During his 1931 visit to New York Mrs Rumsey gave AE use of her apartment.

HIGGINS, Frederick Robert, born at Foxford, county Mayo, on April 24, 1896, the eldest of nine children born to Joseph T. Higgins (1862-1930) of Higginsbrook, county Meath, a railway employee and his wife Annie (1873-1957) (*née* ffrench) of Clifton, county Galway. First educated, with his sister Frances Ann (1899?-1944) nearby at a Convent school (although Church of Ireland), and from early 1907 at St Columba's National School, North Strand, Dublin. *Circa* 1910 he began working as a clerk in a builder's merchant's office, and was later an active official in the Irish Labour movement. From 1920 he edited various trade papers, including the *Irish Oil and Colour Trade's Review* (1923-1926) (which at some time he owned), and Thom's *Builders' Review* (later *Builders' Provider*) (*c*. 1933); and literary periodicals including (as a boy) *The Reveille* (Dublin), *Shamrock* (Dublin, 1919), *Welfare* (Dublin, 192-?), and *Tomorrow* (Dublin, 1924), etc. He also contributed verse, in boyhood, to the North Strand *Parish Magazine*, Dublin. A Director of the Abbey Theatre from 1935, he was appointed its managing director, although exhausted after successfully organising the company's American tour 1937-1938. With W. B. Yeats he edited the Cuala Press *Broadsides* second series (1935). In 1921 he married the well-known Dublin harpist Beatrice May Moore. He was a foundation member of the Irish Academy of Letters (1932) and its secretary after AE left Ireland. He died in Dublin, January 8, 1941, and was buried at Laracor, county Meath. A ballet for which he had written the scenario, *Puck Fair* (based on a Kerry goat legend) was first staged at the Gaiety Theatre, February 9, 1941. An oil portrait by the great Irish painter Séan O'Sullivan is in the Abbey Theatre; his drawing of Higgins is in the National Gallery, Dublin. There is a bronze bust by Brenda Gogarty and a drawing by Patrick J. Tuohy (1926). A Bibliography, by M. J. MacManus, was

printed in the *Dublin Magazine*, vol. 21, no. 3, pp. 43-45 (July 1946). His first book *Salt Air* (Dublin, 1924) was awarded the Aonal Tailteann prize. His main books are *Island Blood* (London, 1925: John Lane), *The Dark Breed* (1927: Macmillan), *Arable Holdings* (Dublin, November 1933: Cuala Press), and *The Gap of Brightness* (London, 1940: Macmillan)-title of a painting exhibited in the AE Memorial Exhibition (Dublin, 1936)-which includes his beautiful lament for Padraic O'Conaire. His one play, *The Deuce of Jacks* was performed at the Gaiety Theatre in 1935. He edited *Progress in Irish Printing* (Dublin, 1936: Alex Thom). Obituary notices were printed in the *Irish Times*, January 9, 1941 by "Lynn Doyle" (Leslie Montgomery), and "Brinsley MacNamara", January 10; by Donagh MacDonagh, January 11 and 13. *Irish Press*, January 9, by M. J. MacManus; *Dublin Evening Mail*, January 8, by Lennox Robinson; January 10 and 13. The letters which AE preserved between 1932 and 1935 were those which he received from Lord Dunsany, C. M. Grieve ("Hugh MacDiarmid"), Irene Haugh, F. R. Higgins, Séan O'Faolain, H. E. Palmer, William Rothenstein, G. Santayana, James Stephens, Stephen MacKenna, Simone Téry, Helen Waddell, and W. B. Yeats. The editor has seen all excepting those from James Stephens- which were not returned to the writer, nor retained with AE's other papers. Apart from those printed in this book, the most interesting are the letters from Higgins and Mr O'Faolain. Higgins dedicated *The Dark Breed* "To AE, most generous of givers". AE wrote a Foreword to *Island Blood*.

HONE, Joseph Maunsell (February 8, 1882-March 26, 1959) son of William Hone and Sarah Hone (*née* Cooper of Co. Limerick) of Killiney, Co. Dublin; the eminent Irish literary critic, thinker and biographer. He wrote, with Page L. Dickinson (born 1881) *Persia in Revolution* (London & Dublin, 1910: T. Fisher Unwin; Maunsel), after an expedition to the Caucasus and Persia. With M. M. Rossi he wrote *Swift, or the Egotist* (London, 1934: Gollancz). He translated: Émile Montegat's *John Mitchel* (London, 1915), M. M. Rossi's *Pilgrimage in the West* (Dublin, 1933: Cuala Press), introduced E. A. A. L. Seillière's *The German Doctrine of Conquest* (Dublin, 1914: Maunsel). He also translated Daniel Halévy's exemplary *Life of Nietzsche* (London, 1911: Unwin) concerning which he wrote to this editor: "Old Fisher Unwin got my translation for £25, and T. M. Kettle's Introduction for two guineas. He also exacted that Kettle should revise my translation. May he rest in peace." Mr Hone wrote *W. B. Yeats* (Dublin, 1916: Maunsel), *Ireland Since 1922* (London, 1932: Faber), *Thomas Davis* (London, 1934: Duckworth), and biographies of *George Moore* (London, 1935: Gollancz), *Henry Tonks* (1938: Heinemann), *W.B. Yeats 1865-1939* (1942: Macmillan), and *The Moores of Moore Hall* (1939: Cape); biographical notes to complement Dr F. G. Hall's *The Bank of Ireland, 1738-1946* (1949). Mr Hone married Vera Brewster, a witty American, in 1911. Two sons and a daughter survived. His cousin was Miss Evie Hone (1894-1955) the glass-staining artist. Mr Augustus John's portrait of Mr Hone is in the Tate Gallery, London. Under the pseudonym Nicholas Marlowe he collaborated with Warre Bradley Wells in *A History of the Irish Rebellion of 1916* (Dublin, December 1916: Maunsel), etc.

HUGHES, John, the sculptor, born in Dublin, 1864. He was a fellow student, with Oliver Sheppard and Russell, at the Metropolitan School of Art, Dublin. Later he taught there, retiring in 1902. He lived in Paris, with two sisters, until about 1920, when they moved to Italy for about six years; returning later to Paris. Hughes was nominated an Associate of the Royal Hibernian Academy, October 18, 1895; Academician, April 27, 1900. He exhibited at the Royal Academy, London, in 1897, 1898, and 1900. Over the high altar a bronze relief, and in the Lady Chapel a Madonna and Child (in marble) are in St Brendan's Cathedral, Loughrea, Co. Galway. A statue of Charles Kickham is in Tipperary. A marble mask of Sir F. Burton is in the National Gallery, Dublin; and a statuette of a boy, and the bust of AE, are in the Municipal Gallery. The statue of Provost George Salmon is in Trinity College, Dublin; the Victoria monument is stored, inaccessible, in Kilmainham. There is also the Gladstone memorial at Hawarden. A statuette of a girl is privately owned; a figure "Padraic" was once owned by Lord Aberdeen; "The Finding of Eurydice" (in marble) is in the Municipal Gallery, Dublin. In 1928 he had lost heart, and earned money playing a flute in Paris cinemas. This editor's survey of Hughes's life and work, with letters, is ready for the press.

JOHNSTON, Charles, born February 17, 1867, the son of William Johnston of Ballykilbeg, Co. Down, by his third wife Georgina Barbara (daughter of Sir John Hay, Bt, of Park, Scotland). Charles attended the High School in Harcourt Street, Dublin, where he was the young contemporary of W. B. Yeats. He also received some schooling in Derby (England) before passing to Trinity College, Dublin. He studied the course for admission to the Indian Civil Service (1886), passing the final examination in August 1888. He married Vera Vladimirovna de Zhelikhovskaya (H. P. Blavatsky's niece) on October 14, 1888.

Russell lamented this news to Yeats, swearing he would never again make anybody his ideal (*Letters*, p. 91). Johnston was accepted for the Bengal service, arriving in India, November 1888. He visited Bombay, Madras, Calcutta, and Allahabad. Two years later he was invalided out of the service; returning to Europe *via* Russia, he travelled in Austria, Germany, France, Holland, and Belgium. Evidently a tough invalid. A brief selection from his numerous translations, *From the Upanishads* (Dublin, January 1896: Whaley) bears a dedication to AE. In October 1896 Johnston and his wife went to America, taking out citizenship there in 1903. They lived in New York, where Johnston died, October 16, 1931; his wife died in 1922. Johnston was an editor of the *Encyclopaedia Britannica*, besides contributing articles on Oriental subjects to the *New York Times' Book Review;* and others, between 1904-1921, and 1928-1931, to *The Gael* (New York), *North American Review*, *American Review of Reviews*, *Atlantic Monthly*, *Era*, *Arena*, etc. His copious contributions to theosophical journals included translations later reprinted in volume form: *The Crest Jewel of Wisdom*, etc. He translated books from the Russian, German and Sanskrit, including Tolstoy's *What is Art?*, Merezhkovski's *Julian the Apostate* (in 1898 and 1899 respectively), Paul Deussen's *The System of Vedanta*. He also wrote *The Memory of Past Births* (1900), *Kela Baj* (1900), *The Parables of the Kingdom* (1909), and *Why the World Laughs* (1912). Johnston visited Europe during 1918-1919, whilst serving as a Captain in the Military Intelligence Division, U.S. Army.

KELLOGG, Frank Billings (born Potsdam, New York, 1856, died at St Paul, Mo., December 21, 1937). He was elected U.S. Senator in 1917, and was appointed U.S. Ambassador to Great Britain in 1924. As Secretary of State from 1925-1929 he was joint author of the Kellogg-Briand Pact, which declared war renounced as a means to settlement in international disputes. He was awarded the Nobel Peace Prize, 1929. From 1930-1935 he served on the permanent Court of International Justice.

KEOHLER, Thomas Goodwin, a company secretary, died in Dublin, aged 68, May 26, 1942. With his family, he changed his surname to Keller. Keohler was an early member of the Dublin Theosophical lodge. AE included some of his poems in *New Songs* (1904). H. F. Norman contributed a memorial article, "Unheard Music: in Memory of Thomas Goodwin Keller" to the *Dublin Magazine*, vol. 17, no. 4, pp. 26-30 (October 1942). The article was reprinted as an introduction to *Unheard Music*, a selection from Keller's poems (Dublin, 1945: privately printed, 150 copies). Keohler's other book was *Songs of a Devotee* (Dublin, 1906: Maunsel) in the first series of the Tower Press Booklets.

LANE, Hugh Percy, born in county Cork, the son of the Rev. J. W. Lane (and a nephew of Lady Gregory), 1875; drowned with over 1,200 victims when the *Lusitania* was torpedoed and sank, returning to England, May 7, 1915. Whilst employed by Martin Colnaghi, from the age of about 18, he developed a flair for appreciating paintings, collecting, and then trading as a picture-dealer. He was a Governor of the Irish National Gallery from 1904, and its Director from 1914. At the Royal Hibernian Academy and in Belfast he organised winter exhibitions; in 1908 exhibiting his fine collection of the French impressionists at a temporary gallery in Harcourt Street, Dublin. Lane intended the collection to be his gift to the nation, if the Dublin Corporation would house them in a gallery to be designed by Sir Edwin Lutyens. This was not done and Lane loaned them to the National Gallery, London. In 1909 he was knighted. He formed the collections of seventeenth-century Dutch pictures in the National Gallery, Cape Town, and the modern works for the Johannesburg Municipal Gallery. He was a liberal patron, commissioning many new paintings, including the portraits by Antonio Mancini (1852-1931) of W. B. Yeats and Lady Gregory. He bequeathed his French paintings to the National Gallery, London. Shortly before he sailed to America on his last visit, he added a codicil revoking that bequest, and substituting the Dublin Corporation as the beneficiary (on certain conditions). He signed the codicil, but it was not witnessed, and is legally invalid. The French pictures remained in London, because no special legislation was introduced to cede the pictures to Dublin, from England, until 1959 when arrangements were made to loan the pictures to Dublin. Dr Thomas Bodkin's *Hugh Lane and His Pictures* (Dublin, 1932, revised edn. 1956: Stationery Office) supplies the exhaustive details and legal commentary.

LAW, Hugh Alexander, born in Dublin, July 28, 1872, the second son of the Rt Hon. Hugh Law, PC (Lord Chancellor of Ireland, 1881-1883). Hugh A. Law ("Hugo") was a barrister, and although a Protestant he stood as Nationalist Member of Parliament for West Donegal, 1902-1918. From 1927-1932 he was a member of the Irish Free State Parliament. In later life he became a Catholic. His wife was Charlotte (Stuart, of Bogay, Co. Londonderry). Mrs Law died April 7, 1957, at Marble Hill, Co. Donegal. There is a drawing of Hugh Law by K. Verschoyle. He died April 2, 1943. Hugh Law edited *Speeches and Letters on*

American Affairs by Edmund Burke (London, 1908: Dent), and with the Rev. Robert H. Murray wrote a *History of Ireland* (London, 1924: Hodder & Stoughton). He also wrote *Why is Ireland at War?* (a pamphlet) (Dublin, August 1915: Maunsel), and *Anglo-Irish Literature* (London, 1926: Longmans) to which AE wrote a Foreword. For many years AE spent his summer holiday with Mr and Mrs Law, staying nearby at Breaghy. In the woods below their house they built and furnished a cottage, "the fairy cottage" as it is still called, for his use; originally as a playhouse for their children. (See the photographs in John Eglinton's *Memoir*.) In spring the cottage, now derelict, is still surrounded by bluebells. AE dedicated a section in his *Selected Poems* "To Hugh and Lota" (Law). Their children, Jean, Ruth and Mary, figured frequently in AE's paintings, sometimes with their brother Lt-Col. Francis Law.

LIPPMAN, Friedrich, a Russian. He died by his own hand in America, probably in 1890. Katharine Tynan wrote about him in *Twenty-five Years*. Dr Roger McHugh adds a note on Lippman in *W. B. Yeats' Letters to Katharine Tynan* (1953), p. 167. He may well be related to the Reuben Robert Lipman (b. Kovna, Russia, 1868 or 9) who attended Rathmines School; Russell is listed 1272 (in 1882), and Lipman 1348, in 1883. See T. W. E. Drury and T. F. Figgis's *Rathmines School Roll, 1858-1899* (Dublin, privately printed 1932).

LYSAGHT, Edward E., born during a sea voyage, 1889; the son of Sidney Royse Lysaght (1856-1941). Since 1911 a forester and farmer in county Clare. He was a Government nominee to the Irish Home Rule Convention, 1917-1918; and a foundation member of the Irish Senate, 1922-1925. Lived in South Africa, 1929-1930, and 1936-1938. In 1920 he resumed the use of his full Irish name, MacLysaght. From 1943-1954 he was Chief Herald and Genealogical Officer, Dublin, and Keeper of Manuscripts, National Library of Ireland, 1949-1955. Since 1956 he has been Chairman of the Irish Manuscripts' Commission. AE's most interesting article on Dr MacLysaght was a review of his *Poems* (Dublin, 1928: Hodges Figgis), as "The Contented Man", in the *Irish Statesman*, vol. 11, pp. 298-300 (December 15, 1928). AE also wrote a keenly appreciative review of *Poems* by Sidney Royse Lysaght (London, 1928: Macmillan) in the *Irish Statesman*, vol. 10, p. 275 (June 9, 1928). Dr MacLysaght's most notable historical books are probably *Irish Life in the 17th Century* (Cork University Press and Oxford, Blackwell, 1950) and *The Kenmare Manuscripts* (Dublin, 1942: Irish Manuscripts' Commission). He also compiled the invaluable *Irish Families* (Dublin, 1957: Hodges Figgis); second volume, *More Irish Families* (Galway and Dublin, 1960: O'Gorman Ltd).

MAGEE, William Kirkpatrick (1868-May 9, 1961), essayist. With Frederick Ryan (1874-April 7, 1913) edited *Dana* (Dublin: May-December 1904). Under the pseudonym "John Eglinton", wrote occasional articles and essays. His books include: *Pebbles from a Brook* (1901), *Bards and Saints* (1906), *Anglo-Irish Essays* (1917), *Irish Literary Portraits* (1935), a translation of some *Letters to Édouard Dujardin*, from George Moore (1929), *A Memoir of AE* (1937). He prefaced a selection from Edward Dowden's *Letters* (1914). He edited and had privately printed in Bournemouth a selection from the letters written to him by George Moore (1942). Under the quaint title *Confidential, or Take It or Leave It* (London, 1951: Fortune Press) he issued a selection from his verses, with an autobiographical Preface, and a separate note as to his

relation to the Christian church (his father was a Presbyterian minister in Dublin – a fact not generally known). Dr Magee worked on the National Library of Ireland staff for many years, retiring to Wales, later to England, rather than remain in the Irish Free State. Like his elder and younger brothers, Hamilton Malcolm and James Henry Magee, Dr Magee was born in Dublin. His lifelong sympathy for Emerson and Goethe was manifest in photographs of them on his mantelshelf, as recently as 1950 and 1954. The Rt Hon. Laurence A. Waldron (1862-1923), a prominent Dublin stockbroker, wrote to J. M. Hone (March 27, 1919): "I asked Magee to dinner last night, but he said he was engaged; so I wrote him a line saying how sorry I was he could not come, and that I supposed his friends could only see him in the evenings by attending lectures by Yeats, etc. Bodkin drives him to the verge of madness by asking him what the *Irish Times* thinks on all sorts of questions; a 'wheeze' invented by you but now very well established. . . ." (At that time Mr Hone was resident in France.) H. R. Chillingworth wrote an article about Dr Magee in the *Irish Times*, April 7, 1952.

MARTYN, Edward (1859-December 5, 1923), the author of *The Heather Field*, *Maeve*, and other plays. He was a close friend to George Moore the novelist, and was characterised with keen insight, and rather ruthless candour, in *Hail and Farewell*, Moore's Irish autobiography. See Denis R. Gwynn's *Edward Martyn and the Irish Revival* (London, 1930: Cape).

MILLIGAN, Alice Letitia, born at Omagh, county Tyrone, September 14, 1866, died at Tyrcur, Omagh, April 17, 1953. With her friend Anna Johnston ("Ethna Carberry" the poet wife of Seumas MacManus) edited *The Northern Patriot* (1894-1895) and the nationalist magazine

Shan Van Vocht [Poor Old Woman] in Belfast (January 1896-April 1899), until Arthur Griffith founded his Dublin nationalist weekly *United Irishman* (1899-1906). AE selected the poems for Alice Milligan's book *Hero Lays* (Dublin, May 1908: Maunsel). Dr MacManus selected, edited and introduced his own and poems by Ethna Carberry and Alice Milligan as *We Sang for Ireland* (Dublin, 1950: M. H. Gill). Those fresh and vivacious poems are distinguished for tender energy, unsullied by dismal introspection. Delightfully romantic, the poems express with generous directness healthy emotional states. See Henry Mangan's exemplary edition of Alice Milligan's poems (Dublin, 1954: M. H. Gill).

Alice Milligan described AE in verses "An Agriculturist", in *Sinn Fein*, July 10, 1909. Her prose memorial tribute to him was printed in the *Dublin Magazine*, October 1935.

MITCHELL, Susan Langstaff, the eldest daughter born to Kate Teresa (Cullen) and Michael Mitchell (manager of the local Provincial Bank), in Carrick on Shannon, December 5, 1866. Michael Mitchell died in 1873 and Susan was adopted by her aunts Mrs Susan (Mitchell) Wegg, Miss Margaret Mitchell and Miss Jane Mitchell; living first in Dublin, afterwards at Birr (her father's native town). Later she lived with J. B. Yeats's family in London (Bedford Park), moving to Sligo in 1899. Probably in 1901 she moved to Dublin, working as sub-editor on the *Irish Homestead*, and subsequently the *Irish Statesman*. There is a fine oil portrait by J. B. Yeats the Elder and a drawing of her by AE, in the National Gallery, Dublin. Another pencil drawing, by J. B. Yeats, is in Mr C. P. Curran's collection (1958). Her poems, *The Living Chalice* (Dublin, 1908: Maunsel, enlarged edn, 1913: Maunsel), *Aids to the Im-*

mortality *of Certain Persons in Ireland* (Dublin, 1908: New Nation Press, enlarged edn, 1913: Maunsel) contains her lightly mocking and satirical verse. *George Moore* (Dublin, 1916: Maunsel) is a collection of jokes against Moore, disguised as a biography. Her *Christmas Poems* were collected, with a verse tribute, by M. J. MacManus (Dublin, 1934, privately printed). *Frankincense and Myrrh* (poems), with a frontispiece by J. B. Yeats the Younger, was printed by the Cuala Press (Dublin, n.d.) in December 1912. [See also *The Dun Emer Press and the Cuala Press*, a complete list of books, pamphlets, leaflets, etc., compiled by William Maxwell: privately printed, 1932.] A book on current poetry, by Susan Mitchell, was advertised for inclusion in the series *Cumann Leigheacht an Phobail* (Dublin, 1922-1923: Stationery Office), but it was not published. The editor has not found any evidence that it was written. Susan Mitchell wrote many book reviews, printed in the *Irish Homestead* and the *Irish Statesman*, and poems and facetious verses were printed in *The Lady of the House* (Dublin, 1907, etc., edited by Crawford Hartnell for Findlaters the Grocers: Christmas issues), and to *Studies* (Dublin), etc. She died in Dublin, March 4, 1926. An obituary tribute by AE was printed in the *Irish Statesman*, vol. 6, p. 3 (March 13, 1926). His article *The Poetry of Susan Mitchell* was printed in vol. 6, pp. 71-74 (March 27, 1926). It was reprinted, abridged by Monk Gibbon, in *The Living Torch*, pp. 145-148.

J. B. Yeats the Elder wrote to Susan Mitchell (October 21, 1912): "Every now and then I turn to your few poems and like them better and better–it is because you have such a poignant way of dropping suddenly into some personal 'particular'. It is what I call your *naïveté*–and because of it you have something which I find neither in AE or in W. B. Y. I think it might be called a *Quality of intensity.* If you would write more and *use your own life more*, we should have not only more poetry, but it would be stronger and more intimate" (*Letters*, ed. Hone, p. 150; see also pp. 151-152). The collection contains other characterisations of her including the description of a kitten: "It has such large eyes, such soft paws,—and such claws, *only it is a boy* we would call it Susan, after Susan Mitchell."

Susan Mitchell had a warm contralto voice, and sang enthusiastically.

A manuscript collection of her poems, with water-colour illustrations by AE, was presented to the County Museum, Armagh, by her surviving sister Mrs V. D. Franklin, in 1954. Most of the poems were printed in her two collections of verse. Mrs Franklin also presented to the Armagh Museum a book into which AE had written many of his own poems.

MUNRO, Hector, born May 24, 1869, at Kilmonivaig, near Inverness, one of two sons and a daughter of Hector Munro, an Exciseman. He spent his childhood at Fort William. He qualified MB and CM at the University of Aberdeen, 1894 (registered August 21, 1894), and went to Vienna to continue with post-graduate work. He followed what was then the usual course, spending a year as a ship's doctor, aboard the British East India Company's steamship *Golconda*, before settling in Bradford (Yorks), in partnership (1896-1900) with Peter Macdonald (born Oban, April 16, 1870; MB, CM, Aberdeen 1894, died August 28, 1960). Margaret McMillan (1860-1931) was resident in Bradford 1893-1902, promoting the compulsory medical inspection of elementary school children; she was also a member of the Independant Labour Party there. Munro was influenced by her insistence on statutory instruments for ensuring child-welfare; he became

interested in socialist politics. But when his young wife (*née* Ford) whom he had married before 1898 died, he moved away, to Letchworth (Herts), and in 1903 to London where he remained until 1914. He was in Belgium when war was declared; returned to London and formed an ambulance unit which he controlled until he was blown-up by an exploding shell. Consequently he was totally deaf in one ear, and was psychologically distraught. Courageously he recovered, and persisted in continuing his relief work, in Vienna and Budapest. In the 1918 parliamentary election he contested Ross and Cromarty as a socialist, but was defeated. He then advocated support for the "Save the Children" fund, and went to Ireland to "develop a spa" on the west coast. He probably met AE then. His enthusiasm for dietetics, and his research into vitamins, was followed by similar enthusiasm for unusual methods of diagnosis. His partner in later life, in London, was probably either George Grant MacDonald (born at Ardiquhill, June 13, 1879; died January 21, 1958) or William George MacDonald (born ?1874: MB, CHB, Aberdeen, 1898, died October 1958). He was keenly interested in psychic research. Apart from Medicine his enduring interests were politics, chess and Highland Dancing. His patients at various times included Ernest Bevin (1884-1951), G. K. Chesterton (1874-1936), M. K. Gandhi (1869-1948), James Keir Hardie (1856-1915), George Lansbury (1859-1940), J. Ramsay MacDonald (1866-1937), and Henry W. Nevinson (1856-1941). Munro was well known among his friends for disparate qualities; his character was charming and lovable, but he was un-businesslike and eccentric. His enthusiasms were not sustained by application, to expand specific knowledge, but were supplanted by new interests. He died

December 8, 1949. A brief obituary notice, with a photograph, was printed in *Radiesthesia* (London) vol. iv, pp. 37-42 (issue dated 1952).

NORMAN, Harry Felix, born either January 16 or 23, 1868. He was friendly with AE probably from 1893, and was a member of the Dublin Theosophical lodge from 1894. Early in life he worked under Eleanor Skipworth's father in the Dublin office of the London and North Western Railway Company. He had desired a musical education, which his father was prepared to permit; but he renounced it, preferring not to burden his parents with that expense. Throughout his life he wrote musical notices which were printed in the Dublin papers. From *c.* 1899 to 1905 he edited the *Irish Homestead;* exchanging then, with AE, and thereafter organising rural banks in Ireland. Subsequently he was appointed Assistant Secretary of the I.A.O.S., and from September 1921 until August 1926, he was Secretary; succeeded by Dr Henry Kennedy. From August 1926 H. F. Norman acted as consultant in Dublin for the Horace Plunkett Foundation (London). He died in Dublin, December 31, 1947. In July 1916 he had married Edith White (December 1867-July 1939); they had no children. H. F. Norman's main recreation, besides listening to music, was walking in the Wicklow Mountains. Photographs of Mr and Mrs Norman are owned by the editor. H. F. Norman wrote articles on AE in *The Theosophical Forum* (New York), vol. 8 (February 1936), and in the *Yearbook of Agricultural Co-operation, 1936.* He also broadcast a talk about AE, for *Radio Eireann,* February 12, 1936; a typed copy of his script is owned by the Horace Plunkett Foundation Library, London.

O'BRIEN, William, born at Ballygurteen, Clonakilty, county Cork, 1881. Not to be confused with the well-known Nationalist M.P., William O'Brien (1852-1928). Mr O'Brien was Secretary of the Irish Transport and General Workers' Union for many years; President of the Trades' Union Congress, 1913, 1918, 1925, and 1941. He is now (1957) a Director of the Central Bank, Dublin. From 1897-1916 he was associated with James Connolly in the Socialist movement in Ireland. After the 1916 Rising he was deported and imprisoned at Knutsford; later being moved to other English and Welsh prisons. In 1920 he was interned in Wormwood Scrubs Prison, but was released after he had carried through a hunger-strike. He was a member of the Executive of the Irish National Aid and Volunteers' Dependants' Fund, 1916-1918. Member of the Dublin Mansion House Anti-Conscription Conference, 1918. Member of Dáil Éireann for Dublin city south, 1922-1923; Tipperary, June-September 1927 and 1937-1938. He is justly reputed to be the best informed man living, concerning events in Ireland since 1880.

O'GRADY, Standish James (1846-May 18, 1928) an Irish barrister who turned to provincial journalism and literature. He edited the (Dublin) *Daily Express* for several years, resigning in 1898 to edit *The Kilkenny Moderator.* (The Christmas issue, 1898, is believed to include contributions by W. B. Yeats, AE, T. W. Rolleston, etc.) O'Grady founded and edited the *All-Ireland Review* (Kilkenny, later Dublin: weekly, January 6, 1900-April 21, 1906). His *History of Ireland : Heroic Period* (1878: 2 vols.) was widely read. In his obituary notice, contributed to the *Irish Statesman,* vol. 10, p. 231 (May 26, 1928), AE recorded his first meeting with O'Grady having taken place forty years earlier; and that O'Grady had him in mind when writing *The Flight of the Eagle* (1897). (Reprinted, but abridged by Monk Gibbon, in *The Living Torch,* pp.

143-145.) See *Bibliography of S. J. O'Grady*, by P. S. O'Hegarty, in the *Dublin Magazine*, vol. 5, no. 2 (April 1930), Austin Clarke's interesting essay was printed in the *Dublin Magazine*, vol. 22, no. 1 (January 1947), pp. 36-40. In later life O'Grady became an advocate of Guild Socialism, writing for A. R. Orage in the *New Age*.

O'LEARY, John, born in Tipperary of prosperous shopkeepers, in 1830. He was educated at the Erasmus Smith School, Tipperary (one of the few endowed Grammar schools of Ireland), and entered Queen's College, Galway, aged 20. James Stephens (1825-1901) appointed O'Leary editor of the *Irish People* (November 28, 1863-September 14, 1865). It was the organ of the Irish Republican Brotherhood, familiarly called the Fenians. After a police raid on the office, all the paper's senior staff were arrested. O'Leary was convicted on a charge of "treason felony", and was sentenced to twenty years' penal servitude. After serving five years he was released conditional upon not returning to Ireland. He lived the next fifteen years (1870-1885) in Paris, with his sister the poet Ellen O'Leary (1831-1889). He returned to Ireland in 1885. He was the pivotal figure in the group who published *Poems and Ballads of Young Ireland* (1888). He appears to have been unsympathetic to either the Irish Parliamentary party or the Gaelic League, being not so much an ardent Nationalist as "a hater of established institutions" (*The Times*). His *Recollections* (2 vols.) were published in 1896 and reveal an enthusiasm for the writings of Thomas Carlyle. In his old age he was once offered amiable condolence on his being neglected: "Ah," he replied, "they'll make up for it by giving me a grand funeral." He died in Dublin, Saturday, March 16, 1907. The bust by Oliver Sheppard, RHA, is in the Dublin Municipal Gallery.

O'NEILL, Joseph (born in Arran, December 1884, died in Dublin, May 2, 1953), the son of Mary (*née* Quigley) and Martin O'Neill. He was educated (1898-1902) at Queen's University, Galway. His First employment was lecturing at Owen's College, Manchester; there he first developed attachment to the countryside near the Roman Wall, Northumberland, which was the setting for his book *Land Under England* (1935). Afterwards he continued his education at the University of Freiburg; there he formed a life-long friendship with Osborn Bergin, who characterised O'Neill as "Gallio" in a series of comical poems. Copies of these poems are owned by this editor. O'Neill married the poet Mary Devenport O'Neill in 1912; she survived him. They were close friends of Russell from about 1920; probably they were introduced to AE by Bergin. AE regularly visited them on Saturday evenings, in their home. O'Neill was a Government Inspector of Primary Schools (Ireland) from 1907; of Secondary Schools, 1909; Civil Service Commissioner for the Irish Free State, 1923; Local Appointments' Commissioner for Eire, 1926-1946; and Permanent Secretary to the Department of Education (Ireland) from 1923-1944. He wrote other novels, besides *Land Under England; Wind from the North* (1934), *Day of Wrath* (1936), etc. He was also an occasional contributor to the *Dublin Magazine*. O'Neill and his friend H. R. Chillingworth (died, aged 81, August 1954) wrote to the editor a long series of letters about their friendship with AE and Bergin. An *Appreciation* of O'Neill by Chillingworth, was printed in the *Irish Times*, May 6, 1953. O'Neill was a shy man, he shunned any form of publicity; with his wife, ski-ing was his hobby. Their last years together were saddened by O'Neill's ill-health. There is a fine photograph of O'Neill taken by Lafayette, Dublin, although the monochrome does not show his healthy complexion.

ORAGE, Alfred Richard (born at Dacre, near Bradford, January 22, 1873, died November 5-6, 1934). Exponent of Guild Socialism, and from 1918 associated with Major C. H. Douglas (1879-1952) as the most persuasive advocate of social credit economy. Purchasing power should be issued to correspond with the equivalent value of distributed produce. From 1907-1922 Orage edited the *New Age* (London). Conscious of a rift in his own values, and incapable of resolving his inner discord, he subjected himself to the practice of Gurdjieff's method for self-integration, at Fontainebleau, in 1922. Gurdjieff had divined the biological origin of psychological disorder. This consolidated Orage's view that economic remedies should be applied to elucidate the public's political psychology. From 1923 Orage was Gurdjieff's evangelist in America. There he met and married happily his second wife. In 1931 he returned to London and founded the *New English Weekly*. Implicated in whatever he witnessed, but on a plane remote from self-indulgence, he ventilated his ideas in the editorial columns of that journal: a compensation for his apparent failure to exercise any legislative influence on public affairs. See *A. R. Orage: A Memoir* by Philip Mairet (London, 1936: Dent). AE's "Memories of Orage" was printed in *New English Weekly*, November 15, 1934.

PALMER, Herbert Edward, the eminent English narrative and lyric poet, born in Market Rasen, Lincs., February 10, 1880. Educated in England and Germany, he taught in Germany and France before appointment as senior English master at St Alban's School (relinquished 1921). *Collected Poems* (1933), *Summit and Chasm* (1934), here acknowledged by AE. His earlier books were appreciatively reviewed by AE in the *Irish Statesman*. A prose fishing-book, *The Roving Angler* (1933), and the fragmentary autobiography of childhood, *The Mistletoe Child* (1935) (much admired by the late Walter de la Mare) are probably his most popular books. He has been a sensitive critic of English poetry. See *Post-Victorian Poetry* (1938). The stories in Mr Palmer's narrative poems are generally symbolical. Mr Palmer's *The Old Knight* (London, 1949: Dent) is a poem-sequence confirming his acceptance of experience. *The Ride from Hell* (London, 1958: Hart-Davis) is his least personal and his most consistently religious book, instinct with concern for the spiritual plight of human life. He married Harriet Emily Preston, by whom he had one son.

Mr Palmer has recited his own poems, with inspired animation and skill, for tape recording by this editor.

There are two large etchings of Mr Palmer, by Frederic Carter (*c.* 1934); an oil portrait by Alice M. West (1946), exhibited at the Royal Society of Portrait Painters, 1947, and at the Paris *Salon*, 1949; two pencil sketches by Robert Holding (1955) and an oil portrait by Gordon Stuart (1957). Died May 17, 1961.

PLUNKETT, Edward John Moreton Drax, 18th Baron of Dunsany, was born in 1878; he died in Dublin, October 25, 1957. He succeeded to the barony in 1899, joined the 1st Battalion the Coldstream Guards and served with them as Second Lieutenant during the Boer War, in South Africa. Dunsany's fluent story-telling, dramas and poetry, continued throughout his life. The only thing about which he was methodical was the list of everything he wrote, "however slight", with the date and place of writing: place and date of publication he omitted. Lord Longford's article in the *D.N.B.* will supply the brief biographical particulars. See Edward Hale Bierstadt, *Dunsany the Dramatist* (Boston, 1917, 1920: Little, Brown & Co.) and Hazel G. Littlefield Smith's *Lord Dunsany: King of Dreams* (New York, 1959: Exposition Press Inc.)–a memoir in which many of Dunsany's letters are quoted. Dunsany's first book *The Gods of Pegana* (London, 1905: Elkin Mathews), and *Time and the Gods* (1906: Heinemann), *The Sword of Welleran* (1908: G. Allen) and *The Book of Wonder*(1912: Heinemann) were illustrated by Sidney H. Sime (born Manchester 1867). [Sime had been co-editor, with A. Lawrence, of *The Idler* (1892, vol. 15, etc.). Dunsany's obituary of Sime, deficient in facts, was printed in *The Fortnightly* (London), vol. 158, pp. 129-131 (August 1942). See "Sidney Sime" by Frank L. Emanuel in *Magazine of Art* (London) 1904 issue, pp 214-218.] Other stories were *A Dreamer's Tales* (1910: G. Allen), the various "Jorkens" books (1931, 1934, 1940, 1948, 1954), etc. His autobiography *Patches of Sunlight* (1938: Heinemann) was continued in *While the Sirens Slept* (1944: Jarrolds). *My Ireland* (1937: Jarrolds) included a short chapter about AE. Dunsany's play *The Gods of the Mountain* ran at the Haymarket Theatre, London, during 1911: *If* ran for five months at the Ambassadors' in 1921: *The Tents of the Arabs* (1922) has been presented only by amateurs: *Alexander* at the Malvern festival in 1939. *A Night at the Inn* was a success in New York in 1916. His verse, most of it occasional, was collected into several volumes, *Wandering Songs* (1943: Hutchinson), *War Poems* shockingly proof-read–not by Dunsany– (which Dunsany had named *Songs of a Local Defence Volunteer*) contained some of his best lyrics, *Mirage Water* (1938: Putnam), and *Fifty Poems* (1929: Putnam).

Dunsany was a huntsman, and a crack-shot with the rifle. His was a regal character and he would not reply to facetious criticism of his life or his books. Ignorant wiseacres deplored the encouragement he lavished on Ledwidge. Although Arthur Bourchier, C. B. Cochran and Arthur Hopkins (of Broadway) accepted and paid for his plays there is justice in his having surmised the subsequent opposition to his plays having been the expression of high-pressure advertising policy. "I am told that 300 million pounds a year are wasted in England alone on advertisement. So you can see, and I have reason to know, what power they have; greater than the Press or the Prime Minister." [To the Editor, August 23, 1955.] There is a water-colour portrait of Dunsany in uniform (1918) by Brockhurst, one in oils by A. Jonniaux (*c.* 1919), by E. March (oils, 1934), a good bronze head by S. Strobl (1935), and an oil portrait by Orlando Rowland is located in America. Theodore Spicer-Simson's medallion is dated 1922.

This editor wrote in *The Times* (October 31, 1957): Lord Dunsany's literary prowess was distinguished by a vein of magnificent generosity when appreciating other talent; witnessed by his discovery and propagation of Francis Ledwidge's poems; and of S. H. Sime, whose weird illustrations to Dunsany's tales were a distinctive contribution to the craft of book-illustration. Dunsany's good taste in this may have been derived from another of his gifts: he was a painter, although he chose not to exhibit his work.

In painting he had a singular flair for captivating ranges of colour upon one canvas. His landscapes combine lineal fidelity to actual shapes with an original viewpoint, from which the scene is displayed. His most successful portrait in oils was probably that of his friend the late Oliver St John Gogarty.

Lord Dunsany lectured American university audiences in recent years. There his heroic demeanour and candid denunciations (with verse citations from the most celebrated among contemporary poets) caused some stir. He was incapable of meanness, and his literary criticism, although vehemently expressed, and perhaps ill-judged, was never spiteful. He was a complete man, no whining half-man. Apparently he hated lackeys and loved courage. Paradoxically he did not love even courageous poets unless their poems conformed to his own rather rigid notions about the nature of poetry, and its substance. He was incapable alike of society gabble, provincial smugness, and the elective snobbery of bureaucrats. He was always ready to meet any honest writer as man to man, without exacting deference to his eminence from their insignificance.

Thirty years have passed since any of his plays were professionally staged in London or New York. His outspoken criticism of degraded techniques for advertisement (e.g. *Cheezo*), combined with his wonderfully simple and invincible belief in the present validity of the Greek cardinal virtues in human conduct, may well be responsible for this extraordinary neglect. His lyrical poems are transparently melodious, succinct in thought and feeling. His grandson is a gifted painter. There is a fine bronze bust of Lord Dunsany by Albert Power (exhibited R.H.A., 1921).

PLUNKETT, Horace Curzon (1854-1932). After several years as a rancher in America he returned to Europe and in 1889 began interesting Irish dairy farmers in the co-operative marketing scheme, and founded the Irish Agricultural Organisation Society in 1894. He was Unionist M.P. for south County Dublin, 1892-1900. Vice-President of the Department of Agriculture and Technical Instruction for Ireland, 1899-1907. He was a Commissioner on the Congested Districts' Board for Ireland, 1891-1918. He was elected FRS in 1902. He was a Senator of the newly constituted Irish Free State Senate, 1922-1923, when ill-health enforced his retirement. Apart from numerous pamphlets he wrote *Ireland in the New Century* (London, February 1904: John Murray), *The Unsettlement of the Irish Land Question* (London, August 1909: Simpkin) and *The Rural Life Problem of the United States* (London, July 1910: Macmillan). See *Horace Plunkett: an Anglo-American Irishman* by Margaret Digby (Oxford, 1949: Blackwell). There is a concise brilliant character-study of Plunkett by his friend Moritz J. Bonn, in his reminiscences *Wandering Scholar* (London, 1949: Cohen & West), pp. 82-87. Oliver Sheppard's bronze bust of Plunkett was exhibited by the R.H.A., 1925.

PORTER, Arthur Kingsley born Stamford, Conn., February 6, 1883; archaeologist. He travelled widely in Europe, as a young man, to complete his education. From 1915 he was Lecturer on the History of Art at Yale University. He was appointed assistant-professor, 1917-1919. In 1920 he was appointed Professor of the History of Art at Harvard, until 1924 when he was appointed Professor of Fine Art there, until his death. He was drowned on July 8, 1933, a day when AE was expected to arrive as the guest of the Porters at Glenveagh Castle, Donegal. Lucy Kingsley Porter edited and published the letters she and her husband had received from AE, as *AE's Letters to Mínanlábáin* (New York, February 1937: Macmillan) with a touching tribute to AE in her *Introduction*. Kingsley Porter wrote *Medieval Architecture* (London, 2 vols., 1909: Batsford), etc. Among his scholastic honours he was a Member of the Archaeological Institute of America, and a Fellow of the Medieval Academy of America. There is a portrait of him in *Medieval Studies in Memory of A. Kingsley Porter* (Cambridge, Mass., 2 vols., 1939: Harvard University Press).

PRYSE, James Morgan was the seventh of eight children (three boys, Will, James, John); and was born on August 14 or November 14, 1859, at New London, Cincinatti, Ohio. His father James M. Pryse, MA, was minister to the First Presbyterian Church, Cincinatti. His wife Mary (Morgan) had moved to Ohio, with her parents, from Aberystwyth, aged 12. Weakened by overwork the Rev. Pryse moved to Emporia, Kansas, 1863; and later to a Welsh settlement church near Mankato, Minnesota; and thence to Prescott, Wisconsin, Sound Bend, and Lake City, Minn. Their son James learned Greek and Latin. He left home in 1876 and taught in a school near Red Cloud, Nebraska. Next he prospered as a commercial photographer, before working in a printing office. He bought, edited and published a weekly paper; sold out, to buy another in Blue Springs, Neb., with his brother John as partner. They moved to Montana and on to Prescott, Wis., and ran a paper there. James was admitted to the Bar in Shakopee, Minnesota, January 1886. From there he went to Lacrosse, Wisconsin, where he was Telegraph Editor of the (socialist) *Republican Leader*. He went on, to Jacksonville, Florida (where Frederick Delius resided in 1885) working on a daily newspaper. For a year he helped issuing a magazine in a co-operative colony at Hammonton, New Jersey. Evidence as to dates conflict. He corresponded with Mrs Julia Campbell ver Planck (*née* Wharton) (later Archibald Keightley's wife),

who was known as "Jasper Niemand", a theosophist, after she had written praising some of his magazine articles. They met in Philadelphia. She gave him an introduction to W. Q. Judge, whom she assisted in editing *The Path* (New York). Pryse joined the Theosophical Society in July 1887, at Los Angeles, reunited with his brother John who had also joined the T.S. Whilst in Los Angeles James is said to have learned some Sanskrit, under Roehrig, Professor of Oriental Languages in the University of southern California. The brothers travelled through Peru and Panama, arriving in New York, July 1888, where they founded the Aryan Press. James was head printer of *The Path*. In August 1889, Madame Blavatsky summoned James to London, to run the H.P.B. Press, which used American machinery. He lived "Under the same roof with the wonderful woman and teacher". The H.P.B. Press closed late 1894, or early 1895 when Pryse moved to Dublin, to print the *Irish Theosophist*. He remained perhaps one year before returning to New York. After Judge died (March 21, 1896) he toured the U.S.A. and Canada as a theosophical lecturer. He then continued writing *Re-incarnation in the New Testament* (New York, 1899: E. B. Page & Co.) and *The Magical Message of Ioannes*, a verbatim translation of St John's Gospel (New York, 1909: Preface dated 1910: Theosophical Publishing Co.). His first book, *The Sermon on the Mount*, having been serialised in the *Irish Theosophist* (said to have been published in a new edition 1904). In 1900 Pryse moved to Galesville, Wisconsin and practised law in partnership with Robert Christiansen, until February 1904 when he returned to Los Angeles. He married Miss Jessie Mayer, of San Diego, on December 21, 1901. Abandoning Los Angeles' legal practise Mr and Mrs Pryse farmed a lemon orchard in the San Gabriel Valley, 1905-1910). His book *The Apocalypse Unsealed* (New York, 1910: John M. Pryse) was followed by *Restored New Testament* (New York, 1914: J. M. Pryse, London: J. M. Watkins), Aeschylus' *A New Presentation of the Prometheus Bound* (dedicated to AE) (Los Angeles, February 1925: John M. Pryse) and Euripides' *The Adorers of Dionysus* (*Bacchae*) (London, September 1925: Watkins). From 1910 the Pryses lived in Los Angeles. John moved there, from New York, in January 1925, or earlier. Jessie Pryse suffered a paralytic stroke, August 10, 1928, and died August 27, 1928. James Pryse contributed a brief memoir of AE to *The Canadian Theosophist* (Hamilton, Ontario), vol. 16, no. 6 (August 15, 1935). James M. Pryse died in Los Angeles, April 22, 1942. The best published photograph is in *The Path* (New York), vol. 9, June 1894 (between pp. 90-91).

PURSER, Sarah Henrietta, born March 22, 1848; died August 7, 1943. She studied art in Paris and became a celebrated portrait painter. With her friend Edward Martyn (*q.v.*) she founded (1903) a stained glass industry in Dublin which was run as a co-operative business. Its most distinguished worker was Michael Healy (d. September 1941) of the Art-Workers' Guild. Her oil portrait of Russell (painted *c.* 1902) is now in the National Gallery of Ireland. She was well-known for her wit.

QUINN, John (born Tiffin, Ohio, April 24, 1870; died July 28, 1924). Educated at Michigan, Georgetown, and Washington. A Company lawyer in New York. For many years he generously patronised writers and artists. Probably met AE first in 1902 during a visit to Ireland. Quinn's art collection was sold after a *Memorial Exhibition* (fifty paintings) at the Art Centre, New York, from January 8, 1926.

"The Dove Grey Sands" and "Tug of War" among others by AE; five paintings by Jack B. Yeats, three by Augustus John, etc., were included. List in *Art News* (New York), vol. 24, no. 13, pp. 1 and 3, January 2, 1926. Joseph Brummer managed the sale.

REA, Caroline Clements (August 4, 1865-November 10, 1954), fifth of the eight children of Samuel Rea (born 1823) and Sarah Gordon of Tynan and great-grand-daughter of James Rea (1746-1828) of Ballydugan, Co. Down, she married Robert Emmet Coates (born 1863, died at Point Loma, Calif., August 29, 1928). Coates was musical and interested in poetry. In 1892 he had joined the Dublin lodge of the Theosophical Society; and succeeded F. J. Dick as its secretary. Most of his forty years in the employ of Messrs Easons (news' agency and publishers) of Dublin, he was manager of their book department. In 1922 Mr and Mrs Coates moved to the T.S. Headquarters at Point Loma, where Mr Coates assisted in the publishing department. An obituary notice of Coates was printed in *The Theosophical Path* (Point Loma), vol. 35, no. 5, pp. 491-496 (November 1928); a photograph of him is printed on p. 491. Mrs Coates returned to Ireland when widowed. Extracts from the early letters were printed in the *Dublin Magazine*, January and April 1940. Mrs Coates's account of her friendship with Russell was first delivered as a lecture, in Belfast, during November 1936. It was privately printed (1939: Dublin), as *Some Less-known Chapters in the Life of AE* (*George Russell*). From her reception of Russell's guidance Mrs Coates was a life-long member of the Theosophical Society.

RIDDALL, Charles Coates, born in Belfast, March 22, 1878; son of the late Very Rev. Walter Riddall (Dean of Connor, and

Rector of the Church of St Mary Magdalene, Belfast). He joined the I.A.O.S. in November 1899 and worked as a Banks' Organiser, mainly in Munster (south) but also in the west and north, from 1907. He was appointed (jointly with Sir L. Smith-Gordon, 1917-1919) assistant secretary of the I.A.O.S. in 1917, retiring in 1954. In 1957 he was elected a Member of the I.A.O.S. Committee; the first ex-employee to be so honoured. Mr Riddall wrote *A Handbook for Committees and Managers* (of Creameries) (Dublin, 193?: I.A.O.S.). His articles "Some things I remember" (written at the request of the late Fr E. J. Coyne) were printed in *Agricultural Ireland* (Dublin, 1941-1942). *Agricultural Co-operation in Ireland* which he contributed between January 1945 and April 1947, was reprinted as a pamphlet in 1950 (I.A.O.S.). Mr Riddall wrote the "Dairy Notes" for the *Irish Homestead*. Mr Riddall died December 27, 1958, at Kingswood, Surrey.

ROBERTS, George, born in Castlewellan, county Down, January 8, 1873, the son of Oliver Goldsmith Roberts (died in London, October 21, 1886), manager of Murland's Linen Mill at Castlewellan until about 1883, when he moved to London intending to trade independently. After O. G. Roberts's death the family moved to Belfast. George Roberts moved to Dublin, encouraged by his friend J. H. Cousins, on January 1, 1900. He was a printer, and founded Maunsel's, publishers, with J. M. Hone and S. L. Gwynn as co-directors in 1905. Some of his poems were included by AE in *New Songs* (1904). He was for several years honorary secretary of the Irish National Theatre Society. His first wife, Maire ni Garbhaigh (died in Dublin, ? March, 1946) was a leading actress in the Society. Maunsel's office in Abbey Street was burnt in Easter week 1916. Mr

MacLysaght and Dr Bodkin joined the firm as directors in 1916; Mr Neill-Watson taking Dr Bodkin's place, soon after. All the directors except Roberts resigned in 1923. Maunsel's was liquidated in 1925, its stock and coypright being taken over by the Talbot Press (an adjunct of the Irish Educational Co., managed by a Mr Lyon), Roberts moved to London in 1926, and died there November 9, 1953. He had begun writing his reminiscences. From his manuscript all that was completed (the remainder is worthless) has been printed in the *Irish Times*, July 13, 14, 19 and August 1 and 2, 1955. There is a red crayon drawing of Roberts, by Ivan Opfer, dated 1932, in Mrs E. Roberts's possession. All the interesting old letters (from Miss A. E. F. Horniman, *re* the Irish National Theatre Society, etc.) and Abbey Theatre letters and papers, were sold at auction in Dublin and London, 1956-1957. Excepting only a few minor papers purchased for the National Library of Ireland, the main collections were purchased for the Theatre Collection, The Houghton Library, Harvard University; including Reading Committee notes taken by Roberts between June 29, 1904 and October 29, 1905; and notes for the Annual General Meeting, May 25, 1906. A photograph of Roberts was printed in *James Joyce's World* by Patricia Hutchings (Mrs Robert Greacen) (London, 1956: Methuen), p. 116.

ROBINSON, Esmé Stuart Lennox, seventh and youngest child of Andrew C. Robinson (a stockbroker who took Orders in the Church of Ireland, at 50), born October 4, 1886, died October 14, 1958. The Irish playwright. A friend of Horace Plunkett he was described by another friend (Mr J. M. Hone, in the *Irish Times*, October 17, 1958) as "a compassionate and lovable man". From 1910-1914, and 1919-1923

Letters from AE

he was manager of the Abbey Theatre, and a Director from 1923-1956. From 1915-1925 he was organising librarian of the Carnegie Trust. During 1917-1918 he was a member of the staff of the Irish Home Rule Convention. His best-known plays are *The Clancy Name* (1908) and *The Whiteheaded Boy* (1916). He edited Lady Gregory's *Journals* (1946) and wrote a memoir of her (as yet unpublished). He wrote several novels, edited *Letters* by John Butler Yeats (Cuala Press), Thomas Parnell's poems (1927), and a *Golden Treasury of Irish Poetry*. His autobiography is contained in *Three Homes* (1938) and *Curtain Up!* (1942). In December 1948 an Honorary LITTD was conferred on him by Dublin University.

RUMSEY. *See* HARRIMAN.

SITWELL, Constance Evelyn Mary, younger daughter of the late Susan Frances (Elwes) and Gustavus Chetwynd-Talbot (of Hemel Hempstead) (1848-1920), born in Ceylon, 1888. Her sister Cecil Emily was Lady Hugh Gladstone (died July 6, 1949); her brothers Humphrey, and Gilbert Talbot. The social conditions of her youth, in Hertfordshire, and abroad, are delicately described in her reminiscences *Bright Morning* (London, 1942: Cape); although her books are all essentially coloured by autobiography. AE said of her, "Your *Dharma* will be flowers". Mr E. M. Forster perceived the depth and radiance of her mind and has recorded his appreciation in his Foreword to her first book *Flowers and Elephants* (London, 1927: Cape). See also *Lotus and Pyramids* (1928: Cape), *White Thorn* (a novel; 1932: Cape), *Petals and Places* (1935: Cape), *Seek Paradise* (an anthology) (1948: Cape); and the serene characteristically beautiful *Smile at Time* (London, 1953: privately printed). In 1912 she married Brigadier-General William Henry

[270]

Sitwell (1860-1932) author of *The Border from a Soldier's Point of View*, and *Stones of Northumberland and other Lands* (published 1927, 1931 in Newcastle-upon-Tyne, by Andrew Reid). Brigadier-General Sitwell was a cousin of Dame Edith, Sacheverell and Sir Osbert Sitwell, Bt. Mrs Sitwell's cousin, Constance Lane, painted a water-colour portrait of her in 1913. Other portraits include a bronze bust by Frank Dobson (*c.* 1920), and one pencil drawing each (1957) by Gordon Stuart and Ahmad Kamal. Mr Ben Nicolson in his early jug-painting period, made a dusky oil-portrait of her: Mrs Sitwell, amused, commented to this editor: "You see by my colour it was not a bit like me. He was then rather overpowered by his father, and Sir William's reputation; that was before his first marriage. My friend Miss Helen Sutherland invited him to her home; his first action as guest was to turn all her paintings to the wall. As you have seen she bought several of his paintings, afterwards. When he found his own style his work became lovely. I prefer Ivon Hitchens' myself; you remember the little oil-painting he made of our home, Barmoor Castle? He was such a gentle and unassuming man." Mrs Sitwell has written in *Light* (London: a psychic research journal). Her *Conversations with Six Friends* (London, 1959: privately printed) includes a chapter on "AE".

STARKEY, James Sullivan, born in Dublin 1879, one of two sons born to William Starkey, MD (a native of West Cork: 1836-1918), a chemist in Rathmines, by his wife Annie Starkey (died November 22, 1922). His early poems were published by Arthur Griffith in the *United Irishman* and by Standish O'Grady in *All-Ireland Review* and elsewhere. In 1923 he founded the *Dublin Magazine* (monthly, August 1923-August 1925) which he later revived and issued quarterly (1926-1958). His personal charm and imposing figure attracted company, and he was a popular guest at Dublin's literary parties. Padraic Colum, Oliver Gogarty, James Cousins and James Stephens were early friends, and Susan Mitchell and AE had much affection for him. Among the younger Irish poets F. R. Higgins was probably more attached to him than any others. His poems have been neglected for many years; due perhaps mainly to their dreamy lilt and romantic poignancy; far removed from the astringent power and compelling energy of Yeats's fashionable later verse. His contemporaries could appreciate the delicacy of his ear, the quiet eloquence of his rhythmic poise and clarity. Richard Rowley, for one (the Belfast poet), wrote to Starkey (April 26, 1940) of the relish he had for Starkey's poems and translations. Starkey was associated (1904) with George Roberts in the Dublin publishing business Whaley & Co. Their enterprise was discontinued after protest from Charles Weekes, founder of the earlier firm, Whaley. Roberts (with other partners) founded Maunsel & Co. Starkey was joint-editor with James Connolly (not the labour leader) of their *Tower Press* booklets. Most of Starkey's published verse and prose was signed with the pseudonym "Seumas O'Sullivan". His *Collected Poems* (Dublin: Orwell Press) was published in 1940. *Poems and Translations* (Belfast: 1950). In 1939 an Honorary LITTD was conferred on him by Dublin University. He was a foundation member of the Irish Academy of Letters which awarded him their Gregory Medal in 1957. He married Estella Solomons (born 1882) a gifted artist and Associate of the Royal Hibernian Academy: she survived him. He was an inveterate book-buyer, collecting about 20,000 volumes, including many interesting copies of rare

editions. Part was sold at Christie's (London), December 8, 1958. Part was sold to Messrs Elkin Mathews Ltd in 1959. A bibliography of his published writings was printed in *Dublin Magazine*, vol. 5, no. 3, pp. 47-50 (July 1930). He was a foundation acting member of the Irish National Theatre Society. Outside the theatre he was unworldly. He slept unsheltered on the Wicklow mountains, hoping to locate the haunts of fairies, and to catch them dancing. Whether his vigils were rewarded as he had hoped he would not say. His declining years were characterised by indisposition, physical and temperamental. He did not complete the projected autobiography. Lacking an ampler source, gleanings will be found in *Essays and Recollections* (1944) and the most aptly named sequel *The Rose and Bottle* (1946). Dr Starkey died in Dublin, March 24, 1958.

STEPHENS, James, parentage, birth-place and date were known only by his widow. The date circulated in reference books, given by Stephens is wrong. Oliver Gogarty's guess, in *D.N.B.* is wrong. But he was certainly born before 1882. Stephens may well be an adoptive name. In Dublin rumours are still circulating which may be true, concerning his father, and his early life. He was anxious to be known solely for his own literary achievement. From about 1903-1913 Stephens was employed as a scrivener by Thomas Tighe, McCready & Son, solicitors, 91 Merrion Square, Dublin. (A testimonial to his industrious work "indexing and filing, as well as typing and shorthand, mainly at correspondence" is lodged in Joseph Holloway's *Diary for 1915*, facing p. 66: now in the National Library of Ireland.) Stephens was previously and first employed by Michael Hanmore, solicitor on Ormond Quay, Dublin. He was appointed unestablished Registrar of the National Gallery of Ireland, from August 5, 1918. Established Registrar and Accounting Officer there at £200 p.a. by £10 to £250 p.a. from December 15, 1918. He retired voluntarily on January 18, 1925 pleading "change of Government" to excuse his distaste for that job. Padraic and Molly Colum prompted Mrs W. Murray Crane to invite Stephens to America in 1925, for his first lecture tour. Mr W. T. H. Howe later entertained Stephens during his lecture tours. Despite the kindness of such friends as Mr Howe, Stephens resented their impositions on his time; for example, to sign his own books by the score. He had respected John Quinn (an earlier patron), for his genuine devotion to creative workers, but could not entertain such warm feeling for Mr Howe. His health was undermined by gastric ulcers from 1920. Surgical operations exasperated his tense nervous system, and his later years were marred by occasional unprovoked emotional storms, and physical weakness. His earliest close friend was "Cynthia", the daughter of Thomas Howard Gardiner, a distinguished designer of artistic fabrics and household furniture. With her family she had travelled the world; later marrying a company director, John Brannig Kavanagh (of Dublin). They both tried to help Stephens, and took him into their home. Other early friends were AE, Arthur Griffith, Dr Bethel Solomons, Lady Glenavy, Mrs Betty Bloxham, and Thomas Bodkin. With Dr Bodkin, Stephens felt secure. His friend sympathised with his personality, his literary work, and his domestic uncertainty. Whenever he was in trouble Dr and Mrs Bodkin helped, and Dr Bodkin's parents also became his benefactors. Stephens and his wife resided in Paris from 1913-1915: and again intermittently from 1925 onwards, although maintaining a home in London for their children. The marriage between Stephens and Millicent Josephine ("Cynthia") Kavanagh (a widow) was registered in the St Bride's ward, London, in November 1918. Their son James Naoise Stephens (died, aged about 25 on Dec. 24, 1937) was a gifted writer. The two daughters of Mrs Stephens's first marriage have survived. Stephens died in London, December 26, 1950. See *James Stephens: A Literary and Bibliographical Study* by Birgit Bramsbäck (Dublin, 1959: Hodges Figgis. Also Uppsala, Copenhagen, and Cambridge, Mass.), for a comprehensive list of his published writings and manuscripts. See this writer's AE *Bibliography* for references to Stephens's writings about AE. His books were written early in life: *The Charwoman's Daughter* (1912), *The Crock of Gold* (1912) (title from Martin Tupper), *The Demi-Gods* (1914), *Deirdre* (1923), *In the Land of Youth* (1924), etc., and *Collected Poems* (1926: 1954). Stephens was first televised by the B.B.C. in 1937. His main creative work in later years was the composition of pithy "impressions" of other writers (with other "talks") which he broadcast for the B.B.C. Fortunately the B.B.C. preserved all the recordings of Stephens's broadcasting: some have lately been issued commercially in America. Mr Padraic Colum believes "Stephens will live longer in the legend than in a *Life*", but he hopes to find time to write a memoir, and to persuade other good friends to write theirs. Under the stress of illness Stephens could not be preserved from some lionising whilst on tour. He could be wheedled into excessive boozing, became inflated and quarrelsome with his friends, and was afterwards crushed by remorse instead of a hangover. When he was with steadfast friends, and with his family, he was always companionable.

Mrs Stephens died in London (aged at least 74), on December 18th (or early 19th), 1960. Their dearest lifelong friend Padraic Colum wrote a beautifully precise "Appreciation" of her for *Irish Times*, January 18, 1961. Mr Lloyd Frankenberg's *James Stephens a Selection*, to which Mrs Stephens had looked forward gratefully, will be published by Macmillan (New York) in 1961.

The portraits include three pencil drawings by Sir William Rothenstein (all idealise him) and an oil portrait (*c.* 1940); an oil portrait (*c.* 1910) by AE (owned by Mrs Stephens), a drawing by AE (April 13, 1930); a bust by Albert Power (1883-1945) of which Dr Bodkin owned the plaster and Mr C. P. Curran a bronze cast; a wax portrait-medallion (made in Paris, June 1913) by T. Spicer-Simson (owned by Mrs Stephens) of which Dr Bodkin owned a plaster cast; a lithograph by Mary Duncan (*c.* 1912-1913) presented by the artist to the National Portrait Gallery, London; a drawing by Norman Morrow (of *Punch*), reproduced in *Irish Booklover* (London), vol. 5, no. 7, p. 123 (February 1914); a bust by Edmond Quinn (1925); several caricatures by "Mac" (Miss Isabelle MacNie); an oil portrait by Patrick J. Tuohy, in the National Gallery of Ireland (believed by Mrs Stephens and Mr Colum to preserve a faithful likeness). Sir Max Beerbohm's ink caricature of Stephens (1930) was owned by Mrs Stephens. There are drawings of him by Julietta Huxley (1934?), Ker Eby (1936); and Ivan Opfer's 1922 sketch made in Paris (reproduced in *John O' London's Weekly* (London), February 17, 1923); a drawing by Mervyn Peake (May 1938); a full-length caricature by Wyncia King and a drawing by Edith Hosking.

STOPFORD, Alice Sophia Amelia, born 1847 (a niece of Stopford A. Brooke); she married the historian John Richard Green (1837-1883) in 1877. She was associated with E. D. Morel in his (Belgian) Congo Reform Association (1904-1912), and among her other work she tried to secure Roger Casement's release. She returned to Ireland about 1917, was a foundation member of the Free State Senate, and died in Dublin May 28, 1929. AE wrote a Foreword to her pamphlet *The Government of Ireland* (London, 1921: Labour Publishing Co.). His memorial notice after her death in *Irish Statesman*, vol. 12, p. 266 (June 8, 1929) was reprinted in *The Living Torch*, pp. 172-174, abridged.

TYNAN, Katharine, the poet-daughter of Andrew Tynan, a farmer living at Whitehall, Clondalkin, county Dublin. She was born in 1861, married a barrister, Henry A. Hinkson (died 1919) in 1893. She wrote her reminiscences; best-known being *Twenty-Five Years* (1913), and *The Middle Years* (1916). Russell wrote an appreciative introduction to her *Collected Poems*. She died April 2, 1931. Miss Pamela Hinkson is editing the numerous interesting letters received by her mother.

WEEKES, Charles Alexandre, the second of three sons, was born in Dublin on June 11, 1867, to Francis and Charlotte ("Sarah" Johnston) Weekes. His elder brother, Francis, emigrated to Canada early in life, and died there. The younger brother, William, remained in Ireland longer than Charles, but later settled in England, where he worked as a racing cyclist, and wrote for the cycling papers. He lived for years with their mother, and died after an accident, about 1935. Francis Weekes was much older than his wife, and he died when Charles was only six. Their second son was educated at the Erasmus Smith High School, Harcourt Street, Dublin. There he met W. K. Magee with whom he enjoyed a life-long friendship. Weekes entered Trinity College, Dublin, March 1886, and last attended in Hilary term 1892, without graduating. He twice lost credit in Arts, and was in the Law School for a few terms. Probably in 1890 or 1891 Weekes met Russell, who interested him in Theosophy, without beguiling him into membership of the Theosophical Society. Madame Blavatsky, whom he met, laughingly called him "ever a doubter". Nonetheless, amongst his numerous contributions to magazines there are several to the *Irish Theosophist* and to the (Dublin) *Ethical Echo*. No record of his contributions to magazines has survived, and this editor has traced few. To the *Irish Homestead* and the *Dublin Magazine*, for instance, besides his contributions to trade journals. In 1893 Weekes came first to England, where Fisher Unwin published his first book of poems *Reflections and Refractions* in May 1893. It was dedicated to Russell. He withdrew the book from circulation almost immediately, although it contains some characteristically fresh and subtle poems, including the beautiful "Think, the ragged turf-boy urges". In 1894, having returned to Dublin he used "his full blandishments as a tempter" to persuade Russell to publish a collection of poems. To achieve his purpose he set up as a publisher under the imprint "Whaley". His first publication was AE's *Homeward, Songs by the Way*, which was dedicated "To C. W., truest friend". The business lost money and Weekes abandoned publishing early in 1896. He was called to the Irish Bar in 1902. He was married in London, at the Covent Garden Registry, to Ellen Johanna Nôrregaard, on May 25,

1901. (Mrs Weekes's sister married Richard le Gallienne as his second wife; they had one daughter, the actress Eva.) Mrs Weekes translated from the Danish *Criminal Types in Shakespeare* by Mr Justice B. August Goll (London, April 1909: Methuen). Weekes began work in London as a reader for George Allen, Charing Cross Road (Ruskin's publisher, later amalgamated with Unwin). Later he was literary editor of a paper run by a friend called Lang. He was appointed first editor of a magazine *Everybody's* in 1904. Having quarrelled with its financial backer, a Mr Mandeville, he left in 1905 to become assistant to N. Carleton (later President of the American Western Union Telegraph Company) on the staff of the British Westinghouse Company. In July 1907 his second book of poems, *About Women* was published in Dublin by Maunsel's. It was dedicated to his friend Gordon Lloyd Trevor Kenyon, a solicitor and keen fisherman. A collection of his unpublished poems has been preserved by Mrs Weekes. "John Eglinton" made a selection from them and wrote a Preface. The selection was to have been published by the Cuala Press, but the Press ceased before issuing the Weekes's poems. In 1911 Weekes joined D. N. Dunlop on the staff of the re-formed British Electrical and Allied Manufacturers' Association, as its Legal Adviser and Secretary to the Council. He retired in 1938, and died in London on January 6, 1946. Mrs Weekes died August 12, 1957, aged 90.

Russell was prone to adopt a haughty tone towards Weekes in early and middle life; but in his declining years he relied on Weekes's business efficiency with pathetic trust. As John Eglinton wrote (*Dublin Magazine*, vol. 21, April 1946): "There was really something beautiful and characteristic of Weekes in the self-forgetfulness with which he applied himself to establishing Russell's reputation as a poet." The letters in this collection are witness to the characters of both men: Russell ardent, Weekes no less ardent but more humorous and reciprocally appreciative. Weekes's favourite authors were Horace, Marcus Aurelius, Matthew Arnold, George Meredith, Kipling, and Lord Grey of Falloden. He frequently attended parliamentary sessions, being interested in current affairs. During the first World War he joined the Anti-aircraft Observation Corps, stationed in St James's Park, London, but was invalided from the service after a severe attack of bronchitis. He was a communicant of the Church of England, but was more a Christian than a churchgoer. In personal appearance Weekes was typically Irish, having deep-set eyes, grey with a touch of blue. His hair was fairly dark brown; he went bald early, but grey only late in life. His voice was warm and attractive; he read poetry well. He won many friends through taking care to help young people whenever he had an opportunity. An Indian, Mr Colaco, again sought him after eighteen years, to express gratitude for the encouragement and practical help he had received without stint from Weekes when in youth he had most needed help. Apart from his few published poems his sole visible monument is the current BEAMA *Conditions of Sale and Contract*. A brief obituary notice was printed in the *BEAMA Journal*, vol. 53, no. 104, p. 75 (London, February 1946).

YEATS, Jack Butler, born in London, August 29, 1871, the fifth and youngest child of Susan (Pollexfen) and John Butler Yeats the Irish portrait painter; died in Dublin, March 28, 1957. He grew up in Sligo; moving to Dublin when he was about 15. His father then painted the portrait of him which is now in the National Gallery, Dublin. Mr Yeats told the editor, ruefully, that their father constantly worried about his brother W. B.; seeming never to doubt Jack's ability to develop independently. Practising first as a line-illustrator, in *Comic Cuts*, etc., he worked for a Fleet Street sporting paper when about 26 (moved to Manchester; thence to Strete, near Dartmouth, with his wife, about 1899). He married happily early; his wife's death (in 1947) is commemorated by his marvellously poignant *The Great Tent has Collapsed* (once exhibited in the Municipal Gallery, Dublin). About 1897 he first painted in oil; water-colour remaining his usual medium until 1905; thereafter increasingly displaced by oil. The cogent force of all his work, in whatever medium, derived from his sense of the organic design, essential to accurate book-illustration. Later, in oils, form and movement were merged into compositions unparalleled for rhythmic energy and brightly harmonised colour (e.g. *Men of Destiny*, in the Municipal Gallery and *Two Travellers* in the Tate Gallery). He wrote *Modern Aspects of Irish Art* (Dublin, ?1922: Stationery Office, no. 8 in the series Cumann Leigheacht an Phobail), and short plays (1900-1910, with his own illustrations) and stories, e.g. *Sligo* (London, 1930: Wishart). A bibliography of his writings (signed E. MacC.) was printed in the *Dublin Magazine*, vol. 20, no. 3, pp. 47-52 (July 1945). His writings and speech in old age became increasingly elliptical, riddled with paradox and romantic appreciation for authors now unfashionable, such as Bret Harte. He knew and admired AE from youth, but regretted AE's "urge to drive himself too hard". There is a fine bronze bust by Laurence Campbell and a superb portrait drawing by Séan O'Sullivan, RHA (owned by the late John Burke, solicitor, of

Dublin). See *Jack B. Yeats: an Appreciation* by Thomas McGreevy (Dublin, 1945: Victor Waddington), and *Jack B. Yeats, his Pictorial and Dramatic Art* by Ernest Marriott (London, 1911: Elkin Mathews), which includes reproduction of a John B. Yeats's drawing of Jack in boyhood. Mr Yeats wrote some epitaphs (unpublished); on AE, Dermod O'Brien, Thomas Bodkin, himself, etc.

Notes on Lurgan, Armagh and district in the late Nineteenth Century

T. G. F. PATERSON

As to social conditions in Lurgan in the period from Russell's birth until his departure for Dublin ten years later, I should think he was much too young to have been interested in any of the local societies of those days such as the Mechanics Institute, which in the year following his birth erected a fine new hall with an assembly room capable of seating eight hundred people, and used extensively for lectures, concerts, dramatic performances and similar functions. It was a source of much benefit to the community because of its excellent library and comfortable reading room. It also included a School of Design, with rooms for evening classes, besides accommodation for billiards, chess, and kindred games. Originally founded in 1858, the Institute still functions but in a much more limited sense than in the period 1867-1877. I am not sure whether membership rolls survive but, if so, I should imagine that we ought to find the name of Russell's father therein. He was a lover of music and it seems probable that the Russell boys would have been taken to suitable concerts. At the same time the town boasted a good musical society and flourishing boat, rifle, cricket, and football clubs. We know, of course, that he was a pupil at the Lurgan Model School with his elder [?] brother and sister, but no particulars as to his scholastic abilities are available.

After leaving Lurgan there is no evidence of return visits, though we know from Mrs Coates that besides coming from Dublin to Armagh he also visited at his maternal grandparents' farm at Drumgor, midway between Portadown and Lurgan. Like his parents, they also were Church of Ireland and parishioners of the very ancient parish of Seagoe, whereas his father and mother worshipped in the parish church of Shankill in Lurgan town. As a youth he must have found the visits to Drumgor very pleasant. Indeed, he always looked upon that townland as the place of his birth, but his birth certificate gives Lurgan instead. At any rate Drumgor is pleasantly situated and one wonders whether AE, whilst there on occasional visits, ever traversed the few miles between there and Lough Neagh, the largest freshwater lake in the British Isles, a lake of many legends, its shores inhabited by fisherfolk who from generation to generation have handed down mystic stories and legends.

Russell's friendship with Carrie Rea (*later* Mrs R. E. Coates) came about through one of his aunts taking up residence in the Shiels Almshouses here in Armagh, an institution curiously enough that came into being in the year after Russell's birth. The almshouses in question were founded to help persons of small income who had seen better days. I always understood from Mrs Coates that the Rea children had an aunt living there at the same time (*c.* 1880) and that brought about an intimacy between the two families. She also informed me that Russell when on visits to his aunt had permission to walk in the Palace Demesne, from the higher points of which there are wonderfully extensive views bounded by the Sperrins, a range of mountains more than fifty miles distant, and that it was there in the vicinity of the ruined Franciscan Friary and around St Brigid's

L

Well (both on the same property) that he first felt an urge to try his hand at drawing and writing. Despite those facts, however, I feel that Carrie Rea was an added inducement. There is no doubt but that they were mutually attracted, and we know that they remained friends for life. Indeed their acquaintances in Armagh were positive that they would eventually marry, but the romance did not end that way. It is certain, nevertheless, that they did have a warm affection for each other and retained a kindly interest in each other's welfare to the end of their days.

The only surviving friend of the Armagh days that I know of now is Miss Florence McClelland, who told me that Russell's father often came to stay with his sister at Shiels Almshouses. According to Miss McClelland "he married Miss Mary Ann Armstrong, a cousin of his mother's. He was musically inclined and his sister was a clever well-read woman."

The birthplace of Thomas Elias Russell is somewhat of a mystery. I have been told that he was born in County Tyrone and came from thence to Lurgan as book-keeper to the firm of Bell & Co, Cambric Manufacturers in Lurgan, some years previous to his wedding. That is as may be, but there is a tradition that Drumgor, County Armagh, was his place of origin and the fact that his wife was also of Drumgor and a cousin of his mother's does suggest a link with that townland, which, by the way, still houses several families of Russells, one part, because of that, being known as "Russellstown". Against that, however, I must state that Mr William James Russell of that place, whom I visited in April 1946, had no recollection of ever having heard of a kinship with AE's father.

Miss McClelland told me that AE "was like a skeleton in his youth but that even as a boy he was a beautiful reader and that old people delighted to listen to him." She said that "his mother never appreciated his poems but that his father recognised his gifts—that she always understand her son Tom better." Further "she always worried about George. 'If George would only eat his food' was her constant lament when his accomplishments were mentioned."

"His father and mother both disapproved of his interest in Theosophy. George's brother Tom was as fat as George was thin—he married and left children also. AE had little furniture in his first home, but there was always excellent conversation and people seldom noticed the lack of such amenities. My mother knew the Russell family intimately and visited Miss Russell every Tuesday."

From Miss McClelland I received the photograph of AE's parents of which I gave you a copy (reproduced as Plate 1). I cannot very well date it, though it was taken here in Armagh by Hunter & Co. That firm is long out of existence and his successor discarded the accumulated ledgers of his predecessor many years ago.

The McClellands, Reas and Russells were Church of Ireland, but AE's father was a definite evangelical type and as such inclined to attend services outside his own communion.

When AE first began visiting Armagh, Marcus Gervaise Beresford was Archbishop, and we can be quite sure that he often accompanied the Reas to the Cathedral to listen to that very gifted member of the Waterford family. He may have had closer contact, however, with the famous William Reeves, Dean of Armagh from 1875 to 1886, in which year he was consecrated Bishop of Down, Connor, and Dromore. Reeves was a most accomplished historian and the author of many important works, besides being Keeper of the Public Library, in which he laboured magnificently on the medieval registers of the Archbishops of Armagh. He was also keenly interested in the Armagh

Natural History and Philosophical Society and indeed its President from 1872 to 1879. One of his most delightful characteristics was his interest in the activities of the young people of the town. His successor in the Deanery (1886-1896), George Chadwick, later Bishop of Derry and Raphoe, was also a person of great influence with the younger set. Reeves, however, was an authority on the past and, though mostly concerned with ecclesiastical matters, was very familiar with the Cycle of Irish Folk Tales, known as *The Táin*, most of which are linked up with the heroes of the Red Branch, whose ancient seat lay some miles west of the city at Emain Macha, another of AE's places of pilgrimage. Who knows but it was there that AE first heard stories of the Cattle Raid of Cooley, the fate of the Sons of Usnach, the Children of Lir and of the other great figures in Irish mythology such as Cuchullin, Finn MacCool, Connor MacNessa, Oísin and Deirdre.

The Reas were an active family, interested in many things. We can be certain that they took AE to the Observatory to view the heavens and that he accompanied members of that family to lectures in the Armagh Natural History and Philosophical Society Rooms, of which Society their father was a well-known member. He must also have been a visitor at the Armagh United Protestant Young Men's Mutual Improvement Society and other such societies. Unfortunately we have no information as to his contacts with local families other than the Rea and McClelland families. In his visits to Armagh we may be sure he admired the delightful view from his aunt's abode, of the two hills, each crowned by its cathedral, the roofs of the houses rising steeply around the older cathedral sitting within an enclosure dating back to Pagan times and converted to Christian usage from the mid-fifth century, the church that bestowed upon Armagh primatial dignity and made the city the ecclesiastical capital of Ireland.

I had a feeling that although AE must have been familiar with the Ulster Cycle of Folk Tales as a boy, it seemed probable that he undertook no serious reading of the sagas until later in life.

Undoubtedly on his visits to Armagh he must have heard of the great figures associated with Emain Macha, and absorbed something of the legends and myths of the province of which it was the centre. But he would also have listened to stories linked with the coming of Patrick and the subsequent traditions that grew up around our local saints. After all, Armagh is the ecclesiastical capital of our country, was the most distinguished of all Ireland's schools of learning, the throne of kings and queens in her golden age, and the last resting place of saints and warriors "whose names so long as the sea girdeth our isle shall hang in splendour over it". With AE's sensitiveness to atmosphere it is evident that he must have assimilated the traditional background – the mythology and prehistoric monuments, and the later Patrician mission resulting in the conversion of paganism into Christianity – subjects of everyday discussion still.

He was, I know, interested in our local folklore, and one of his earlier note-books (you will remember seeing it in the Carrie Coates Collection) contains a tale about the ghosts of the dead walking on All Hallows Eve, a story which I have heard many times in almost the same words in parishes around the city of Armagh. From the manuscript it is clear that he intended forming the notes into a play, but I do not think he ever did so.

I am certain that AE, despite the fact that he seldom came to Armagh after his marriage, always retained a warm feeling for it. He never lost the magic of those early days when he wandered over its many hills with "Arkon" and her brothers and sisters, and other friends. He may not have discussed his memories of the town with everybody, but from

Mrs Coates it is very clear that he did fully realise that Armagh's appeal lay not so much in what may be seen as in a mystic feeling of communion with the past. Personally, I have no difficulty in believing her assertion that it was in Armagh that he first experienced those spiritual manifestations that afterwards became the great realities of his life.

1954

T. G. F. Paterson, OBE, MA, MRIA,
Curator,
The County Museum, Armagh

Index to Correspondents

General Index